10-

# The Blues Makers

968

# Also by Samuel Charters

*Poetry*
The Children
The Landscape at Bolinas
Heroes of the Prize Ring
Days
To This Place
From a London Notebook
From a Swedish Notebook
In Lagos
Of Those Who Died

*Fiction*
Mr Jabi and Mr Smythe
Jelly Roll Morton's Last Night at the Jungle Inn
Louisiana Black

*Criticism*
Some Poems/Poets

*Biography, with Ann Charters*
I Love (The Story of Vladimir Mayakovsky and Lili Brik)

*Translations*
Baltics (from the Swedish of Tomas Transtromer)
We Women (from the Swedish of Edith Sodergran)
The Courtyard (from the Swedish of Bo Carpelan)

*Music*
Jazz: New Orleans
The Country Blues
Jazz: A History of the New York Scene
The Poetry of the Blues
Robert Johnson
The Legacy of the Blues
The Swedish Fiddlers
The Roots of the Blues: An African Search

# The Blues Makers

Containing reprints of two titles:

THE BLUESMEN
and
SWEET AS THE SHOWERS OF RAIN
(THE BLUESMEN, Vol. II)

## by Samuel Charters

with the addition of a new preface,
a new chapter on Robert Johnson,
and new illustrations

A DA CAPO PAPERBACK

Library of Congress Cataloging in Publication Data

Charters, Samuel Barclay.
    [Bluesmen]
The blues makers / by Samuel Charters.
        p.    cm. – (A Da Capo paperback)
    Reprint. Originally published as: The bluesmen: New York: Oak Publications, c1967.
    This reprint also includes: Sweet as the showers of rain, c1977.
    ISBN 0-306-80438-7
    1. Blues (Music) – To 1931 – History and criticism. 2. Blues (Music) – 1931 – 1940 –
History and criticism. 3. Blues musicians – United States – Biography. 4. Afro-American
musicians – Biography. I. Charters, Samuel Barclay. Sweet as the showers of rain. II.
Title.                                                                                                          91-6978
ML3521.C49  1991                                                                                        CIP
781.643'0973'09041 – dc20                                                                            MN

This Da Capo Press paperback brings together in one volume *The Bluesmen*,
originally published in New York in 1967, and *Sweet as the Showers of Rain*,
   originally published in New York in 1977, with additional material by
the author.  This edition is published by arrangement with the author.

Published by Da Capo Press, Inc.
A Subsidiary of Plenum Publishing Corporation
233 Spring Street, New York, N.Y. 10013

# Contents

# PART II: SWEET AS THE SHOWERS OF RAIN

# Preface

There is always an inevitable uncertainty about memory. What do we remember—really—from all those years ago? What really did happen to us? If there is something like a book that was part of this past, sometimes just going through the pages can help you remember where you were—and who you were—when you wrote it. In the case of *The Blues Makers*, since it's made up of two different books, I find myself remembering two different cities, two different countries, and two different times in my life. I think what surprises me most is that despite the stylistic differences in presentation the two books, *The Bluesmen* and *Sweet As The Showers of Rain*, fit together reasonably well. They were planned together as a comprehensive study of the rural blues before 1940, but the books had to be separated into two volumes because I was trying to cover all of the areas of the South where there had been a great deal of blues recording, and I found there was just too much music for me to absorb all at once. There were too many recordings to be analyzed and too many people to be interviewed. Both volumes were planned at the same time, however, and I think it's because they were conceived as a single project that it's possible to put them together now.

*The Bluesmen* was begun in a run-down fifth floor walk-up apartment on New York's upper West Side in the early 1960s. It was meant to replace my first book on the blues, *The Country Blues*, which had come out in 1959. As I wrote in an introduction to a later edition of that book,

> " . . . *The Country Blues* was two things. It was a romanticization of certain aspects of black life in an effort to force the white society to reconsider some of its racial attitudes, and on the other hand it was a cry for help. I wanted hundreds of people to go out and interview the surviving blues artists. I wanted people to record them

and document their lives, their environment, and their music—not only so that their story would be preserved but also so they'd get a little money and a little recognition in their last years. So there was another kind of romanticism in the book. I was trying to make the journey to find the artists as glamorous as possible, by describing the roadsides, and the farms, and the shacks, and the musicians themselves. What I was doing wasn't academic, and it wasn't scholarly, but it was effective . . ."

Whatever *The Country Blues* was, the suggestion in the book that there were blues artists still living everywhere in the South helped spur an excited search for anyone still playing the early blues. By 1964, when I introduced many of the singers at an afternoon blues workshop at the Newport Folk Festival, nearly every surviving artist from the 1920s had been found, from Son House and Skip James to Bukka White, Mississippi John Hurt, and Lonnie Johnson. *The Bluesmen* was my response to all this new research. I wanted to write again about the major blues artists, using this wealth of information.

When I look at the book again, I am surprised to see that occasionally the writing was as romantic as anything in *The Country Blues*, but in part that certainly reflects some of what I felt at that moment about the blues. Also, I was consciously using the more descriptive passages and the more vivid imagery of some of the sentences to offset the longer sections of complicated technical analysis. I was trying to develop a series of complex ideas about the blues as a musical idiom, while still writing a book that would read easily.

I thought that I would finish the second volume in the next two or three years. Instead, it was almost ten years before I started to work again. A lot of things had happened to the country, and a lot of things had happened to me. I had thought, naively, that if enough of us pointed to the things that we thought were wrong about the American postwar society—its racism and inequality, its lack of responsibility to many of its social groups and to the environment—by simply pointing we could bring about some change. Instead, with the catastrophe of Vietnam, and the violence of the Civil Rights struggle, the country seemed to lose its direction in a series of corrosive upheavals. I found myself so involved with a series of recording projects with blues artists like Junior Wells and Buddy Guy on Chicago's South Side, and then with the Berkeley rock band Country Joe and the Fish, and finally with the demonstrations to end the war in Vietnam, that I was able to write only when there was an empty moment in an airport or still another hotel room. Most of what I wrote in all the confusion was poetry, and the blues was momentarily pushed aside.

I finally realized that the only way to get away from my own anger at the direction the country had taken in the '60s was to get out of the United States. I first left late in the spring of 1970, following the Kent State killings, returned to complete a recording project with Bill Haley and the Comets in Nashville in the fall, and then moved with my wife and small daughter to Sweden later that year. I sometimes thought about the unfinished blues book, but I was completely involved in the new life we'd found in our new country, and also, after the inner searching all of us had gone through in the '60s, I didn't think I should go on writing about African-American culture. What was a white person like myself doing writing about the popular music of the country's black underclass? I decided that it was work for a black writer to finish, and I looked forward to the books that would come out of all the new research.

The books that did appear, however, didn't concern themselves with a stylistic analysis of the early blues, which was the purpose of *The Bluesmen*. Amiri Baraka's *Blues People,* which was published in 1963, was widely read, but it was concerned with larger issues of sociology and racial identity. Other books that I encountered had the same emphasis on more subjective interpretations of the blues, and were as unconcerned about the new historical material. Finally, in the mid-'70s, I was doing a television program in Helsinki, and as the cameras were being put away one of the technicians came up to me and asked, in careful English, "When are you going to do the second volume of *Bluesmen?*" I realized at that point that I would have to go back to the notes I'd brought with me several years before.

The second volume was begun in a small country house outside of Stockholm, and it was finally finished more than two years later in a large, old frame house we'd bought closer to the center of the city. It was obvious that the mood of the second book would be different from the mood of the first. In part it was because I had been living outside of the United States for several years, but also I had been doing considerable research on the backgrounds of the blues in West Africa, and I was working on the book which became *The Roots Of The Blues*. I had begun to see the blues from a different perspective.

What I am also conscious of, in the first book, was that in the early '60s I still had some optimism that the social situation in the United States could change. What is just as obvious, in the second, was that by the mid-'70s I was no longer so concerned with what was happening in the United States. For the rest of the '70s, in fact, I was involved in researching and writing the first book on Swedish folk fiddling, *Spelmännen,* which was published in Stockholm in 1979. I am pleased, however, as I look at the *Sweet As The Showers Of Rain* again, that the romanticism of both *The Country Blues* and then *The Bluesmen* is finally gone. The only vestige of the old hyperbole was the title, which was chosen to make it clear that this was a different book from the first.

What is most important to emphasize in a new introduction to both volumes, however, is the work of so many other blues researchers that went the chapters. I think the most useful way to credit them for their achievement is to repeat what I said in the introductions to each of the books. In the introduction to *The Bluesmen* I wrote:

> " . . . It was not until I began the actual writing of the book that I realized how much material had been gathered. There were articles

in music magazines, in teen-age fan magazines, in jazz magazines, in local coffee house schedules, in folk festival programs, and there was even more material in the liner notes for the hundreds of blues and folk albums that had been released over the last few years. It has been one of the most extensive, the most fruitful, and most exciting research programs ever done in the field of folk music, and it has come—for once—in time to get answers to some of the most difficult problems in the development and the growth of the blues idiom. It was too late to do more than trace the earliest sources and forms of the blues, but it was possible to learn some of the patterns of change and emphasis as the blues has moved—in less than sixty years—from rough field singing to the contemporary Chicago blues band style."

In the last few years there has been some research on the blues which has been assisted by university grants and there are some classes on Afro-American music which discuss the blues, and among many academics who are consious now of the importance of the blues, William Ferris at the Institute of Southern Culture in Jackson, Mississippi, has helped focus some of the institute's activities on his particular area of study, the Delta blues. At the time of these early books, however, the field research into the lives and backgrounds of the blues artists themselves was being done by people who had become involved only because of their interest in the music. At that time most of them were in their mid-twenties, many of them—like guitarist John Fahey—were musicians themselves, and they did their research with whatever money they could scrape together.

Although in many European countries there were active programs to document and record folk music before and after the first World War, the blues recordings in the United States in the '20s and '30s were made by commercial record companies, and in the '50s and '60s it was a relative handful of independent companies that continued to document the country blues. Folkways Records, which was directed by Moses Asch and Marian Distler during much of this period, had always recorded blues singers, but they were handicapped by working in New York, and they didn't have as much opportunity to work with the blues artists who were living in cities like Memphis and St. Louis.

Robert Weinstock at Prestige Records, who had done the first albums with the Miles Davis Quintet, and also done major recordings with Sonny Rollins, Thelonius Monk, and many other modern jazz artists, hired folklorist Kenneth Goldstein to direct a new line called Bluesville, and Ken gathered tapes from a number of researchers, as well as sending field collectors into the South in the early '60s to record the traditional singers in areas like Memphis, St. Louis, and South Carolina. Much of my own field recording in these years was financed by Folkways and Prestige.

There were also individual blues enthusiasts who started their own small record companies to document the music of the artists they'd found, and they recorded material that might have been overlooked by the larger independents. Among the most successful of these dedicated enthusiasts were Chris Strachwitz of Arhoolie Records, Bob Koester of Delmark, Harry Oster of Folk Lyric, Dick and Louisa Spottswood of Piedmont, Pete Welding of Piedmont, and John Fahey and ED Denson of Takoma. Most of the companies were active for only a few years, but the material they recorded continues to be available through licensing arrangements.

A number of these researchers were particularly useful to me in these two books. For *The Bluesmen* I was able to draw on material collected by Pete Whalen, Bill Givens, George Mitchell, Stefan Grossman, Don Kent, Bernard Klatzko, Bob Koester, Pete Welding, Dick and Louisa Spottswood, Nick Perls, Dick Waterman, Charles O'Brien, and Charlie Musselwhite. A number of other people were able to supply me with invaluable information through their articles or album notes, among them Art Rosenbaum, Gayle Dean Wardlow, Lawrence Cohn, David Mangurian, Julius Lester, John Fahey, and Barry Hansen.

The second volume covered different areas of the South and I was able to make use of new material gathered by still another group of researchers, including Bruce Bastin, who worked in North and South Carolina, and published his findings in the book *Crying For The Carolines*. Bengt Olsson interviewed most of the older artists in the Memphis area, and George Mitchell supplied me with information from Atlanta. As I have said before, all of us are in the debt of blues discographers John Godrich and Robert M. W. Dixon for their *Blues and Gospel Records: 1902-1942* as well as the late Mike Leadbitter and Neil Slaven for their *Blues Records: 1943-1966.* Godrich and Dixon also wrote the book *Recording the Blues*, which includes much valuable information about the early years of the blues recording industry. Also of much use to me was Dan Mahoney's monograph *The Columbia 13/14000-D Series*, which is the source for the material on sales figures, as well as dates of release for recordings made for this important blues series. The interview that Mike Seeger did with Frank Walker, who supervised most of the field recording activities of Columbia Records—and who as recording director for the "race" recordings on the OKeh label discovered artists like Bessie Smith early in the '20s—appeared in the Oak Publications Book *The Anthology of American Folk Music.*

I also want to acknowledge again that *The Bluesmen* was dedicated to the blues collector Pete Whalen, who had played so many of the early recordings for me, and that *Sweet As The Showers Of Rain* was dedicated to singer and friend Dave Van Ronk.

Samuel Charters
October 2, 1990

THE BLUES MAKERS
Part I

# The Bluesmen

Book design by Jean Hammons

Photographs on pages 24, 146 and 164 by Ann Charters

*I*... *was obliged to sit all day without victuals in the shade of a tree; and the night threatened to be very uncomfortable, for the wind rose and there was great appearance of heavy rain, and the wild beasts are so very numerous in the neighborhood, that I should have been under the necessity of climbing up the tree and resting among the branches. About sunset, however, as I was preparing to pass the night in this manner, and had turned my horse loose that he might graze at liberty, a woman, returning from the labours of the field, stopped to observe me; and perceiving that I was weary and dejected, inquired into my situation, which I briefly explained to her; whereupon, with looks of great compassion, she took up my saddle and bridle and told me to follow her. Having conducted me into her hut, she lighted up a lamp, spread a mat on the floor, and told me I might remain there for the night. Finding that I was very hungry she said she would procure me something to eat. She accordingly went out and returned in a short time with a very fine fish; which having caused to be half broiled upon some embers, she gave me for supper. The rites of hospitality being thus performed towards a stranger in distress, my worthy benefactress (pointing to the mat, and telling me I might sleep there without apprehension) called to the female part of her family, who had stood gazing on me all the while in fixed astonishment, to resume their task of spinning cotton; in which they continued to employ themselves a great part of the night. They lightened their labour by songs, one of which was composed extempore; for I was myself the subject of it. It was sung by one of the young women, the rest joining in a sort of chorus. The air was sweet and plaintive, and the words, literally translated, were these: "The winds roared, and the rain fell. The poor white man, faint and weary, came and sat under our tree. He has no mother to bring him milk; no wife to grind his corn. Chorus - Let us pity the white man; no mother has he." Etc. Etc...*

*Mungo Park*
*"Travels In The Interior Districts of Africa" 1799*


*People keep asking me where the blues started and all I can say is that when I was a boy we always was singing in the fields. Not real singing, you know, just hollerin', but we made up our songs about things that was happening to us at that time, and I think that's where the blues started ...*

*Son House, 1965*

# Contents to Part I

The Notes and Index to Part I can be found at the back of the book.

# A Note on the Musical Examples

As the blues is essentially an Afro-American musical idiom it is very difficult to transcribe the music into the standard Euro-American system of scales, rhythms, and note values. These transcriptions have tried to keep as close as possible to the original, although the singer may be singing in a concert pitch that has little relationship to the guitar key that he is playing in; since the guitar is tuned to itself, and not to a fixed pitch instrument. In many of the pieces a tone of the scale is a "neutral tone," neither major nor minor, as in the various European scales. These tones have been marked with an (x) above the staff, and the best way to approximate their sound is to strike both the major and the minor of the note on a piano simultaneously and listen to the resulting mixed tone.

Since the blues is strongly colored with the harmonic patterns of the work songs and the hollers from which it developed, the harmonic structure of the purest country blues can only occasionally be approximated by conventional chord symbols. Usually the guitar is in a local tuning, and often the finger picking syle makes any kind of elaborate harmonic movement extremely difficult. For many of the blues there is no change in the accompaniment harmonies and the only chord change is suggested in the voice. Because of this nearly all of the examples have been left without chord symbols. It would be misleading to suggest that these pieces can be played with conventional guitar harmonies, and the sound would be uncomfortably distant from the complex structure of the original performance. The country blues is a highly individual style, rather than communal folk music. For someone who is interested in the accompaniments, the recordings themselves, along with the descriptions of the tunings and the styles with the individual examples, will be the most helpful.

# THE AFRICAN BACKGROUND

One of the most distinctive song forms that has grown out of the confusion and the violence of the twentieth century is the blues of the American Negro. The blues is not only a musical expression, but as a unique song style it is also a social expression; since the existence of a separate body of Negro song within the larger American culture is an insistent reminder of the separateness of the Negro himself in American society. Since he has been forced to live outside of the majority culture he has developed his own culture, and found within the difficulties and the pain of his experience the materials for a rich and vital music. Of all the forms of contemporary Negro music in the United States it is the blues which is still most closely related to the noisy emotional directness of everyday life, and it is also the musical form most closely related to the African song styles which were its most immediate cultural heritage, despite other influences on its development.

On a Friday afternoon, November 26, 1936, in San Antonio, Texas, a young Negro singer still in his teens, named Robert Johnson, recorded a song that he called "Cross Road Blues." "I went to the crossroads, fell down on my knees ... I asked the Lord above, have mercy, save poor Bob if you please." He was accompanying himself with a guitar, playing it with a metal slide on the little finger of his left hand in the Mississippi "bottleneck" style. His vocal style and the melodic line of the verse were African in the hard, intense tone and the descending pattern of the phrase. The melodic scale, a gapped hexatonic scale pattern, was African. At the beginning of the second line of the third verse, "Uumh, oh dark gone catch me here," he used a nasal falsetto tone that was probably derived from even earlier Islamic influences on African music. The guitar itself was European, but the rhythmic style and the tuning, an open, almost lyre-like tuning, used both African and European elements. The complex interrhythmic relationships in the accompaniment were related to the complex drumming patterns of much African music, but the strong emphasis on the four-beat measure

15

unit and the harmonic structure was European. The use of an open tuning was similar to the tunings of the West African harps and lyres and small metal keyed thumb "pianos," but in his tuning the strings outlined a European harmonic triad. His use of a bottleneck to play a melodic line in unison with the voice could have been influenced by the high, whining one-string Arabic instruments that were used to accompany singing along the slave coast, or by the country fiddle styles of the American South, which also repeated the melody behind the vocal line. The verse form of the blues used the English elements of a loose pentameter rhythm and terminal rhyme, but the pattern of two repeated lines and a final rhyming line was unique to the blues. The language was an American regional dialect, and the emotional situation that produced his song was the law in Mississippi that forced all Negroes off the roads at sundown. Even in its isolation within the Negro community the blues is a vivid example of the many-leveled acculturation that has characterized the growth of American society.

The African presence in the blues can only be distantly glimpsed, like the sun as it drifts through the clouds on a hazy morning. Nearly two centuries have passed since there was extensive movement from Africa to the then new United States, and in this long period of tumult and up-heaval the music of Africa, as well as the music of the African in America, has changed. How much, and in what ways, will always be difficult to tell. There was no careful field documentation of either musical style until well into the Twentieth Century. Between African ritual singing, however, and a blues club like Pepper's Lounge in Chicago's southside Negro slum, there was a long and complex development of music within the slave culture, and elements of this older music still could be found among southern work gangs, often in prisons, when the first efforts at documentary recording were done in the late 'twenties. The pattern of development was clearly from the African communal song to the slave work song, and from the work song to the blues. It is also now becoming evident, as the first extensive work is being done in African music, that there was a widespread solo song style in West Africa that was probably the strongest influence on the solo blues style that emerged from the work song. Often these were "praise songs," that described an important man's fields and houses and cattle, and the singers sometimes had a professional status in the community. "... The Manding people for one, have had praise-singers for centuries. These singers either attach themselves to particular men of influence, such as powerful Moslem marabouts (religious leaders) and wealthy merchants, or travel independently from town to town singing at marriages and other fetes. Those who travel spread news, gossip, and sing the praise of their patron throughout a wide area. Singing with the accompaniment of a twenty-stringed instrument called a kora, they per-form compositions of their own, making up the words as they go along. They extemporize with ease, using a huge wealth of stock phrases and metaphors that are combined and recombined in an infinite number of ways."[1]

Among the Ila and the Tonga people, the solo song forms were even

more closely related to the blues that were to develop on another con-
tinent more than a century later, not only musically, but also as a concept
of an individual song style developing in the midst of a communal music
tradition. Both the men and the women had personal songs that they
performed at the "beer drink" parties. The woman's song form, the
Impango, was high and fast, the men's, the Ziyabilo, was sung very
slowly, usually unaccompanied, but sometimes the man singing would
play a small drum. The women's songs were more directly involved
with the social occasion. A woman would decide that she wanted to have
an Impango to sing about her husband, usually praising him for his
strength and his possessions. When she had decided on the things that
she wanted in the song she and her friends went to someone in the village
who was regarded as skillful in making songs and told the other person -
usually a woman - what she wanted in her piece. The other woman would
accept a gift and tell her to return in two or three weeks. When the
woman came back she brought her friends with her again and the woman
who had made the Impango would begin to teach it to her, line by line.
Usually it took several sessions before the woman had her song mem-
orized, and she brought her friends with her so that they could learn it
as well and prompt her if she forgot some of it. Then, when she'd
learned it, she practiced it to herself until she was ready to perform it.
When a new song was performed at a beer drink there was considerable
excitement and friends and relatives either interrupted her to give
her presents, or-if they were too poor to give anything - to sing their
own Impango as a compliment to her. This wide spread style of singing
was one of the few areas of solo performance within a communal framework in West Africa.

The men's songs, the Ziyabilo, were more diverse in subject than the
women's songs. Often the men made up songs as they spent hours alone
tending cattle or mending fishnets. The songs were "... a meandering
sort of tune in a free rhythm," a phrase which could almost be a description of the American field "holler," a slow, introspective song
form of the slave period that survived in the southern prisons. The men
alone in the fields with the mules, or breaking up the dirt between the
cotton rows, sang to themselves in loosely rhymed verses that had a
"meandering" feel to their drifting, irregular rhythms.

As early as 1915, John Work, in his "Folk Song Of The American
Negro,"[2.] had noticed the relationships between the melodic scales used
in African and Afro-American music. In a chopping song of the Kroo
people, sung by three or four men as they stood around a tree with their
axes, (the same way that the chopping was done on the slave plantations),
he found that the scale used only five notes, omitting the fourth and the
seventh tones of the European seven-note diatonic scale and altering
the third tone to a sound that was somewhere between the European
major and minor modalities. These "gapped pentatonic" scales were
as widely used in the South as they were in Africa. Work even went so

far as to say that the scale used in Afro-American music was only the African scale with a flatted seventh tone used harmonically. The scale patterns in the South, however, were considerably more varied, and reflected the diverse African cultures that had been engulfed by the slavers. A group of work songs collected in the Carolinas in the 1920's showed some of the range of the folk scales. [3.]

**Example 1.**

Lower auxiliary

The blues, as a melodic form, has tended to group around the pentatonic scales, and this same pentatonism has been noted in other areas where there is a strong body of African influenced music. An ethnomusicologist in Venezuela has written of the Negro music of the Venezuelan coastal areas: "... The melodies of these songs, so far as they have been studied, present certain universal characteristics, such as pentatonism and melodic independence." [4.] African music, probably because of its strong outside influences, is no longer as dominated by five and six-note scales as it seems to have been in an earlier period of development. In 1958, however, Hugh Tracey, in an analysis of the scales used by eighty African tribes, found that thirty-three of the tribes still used pentatonic scales for their entire musical expression, and that although the other tribes studied also used six and even seven-note scales, there was still a widespread use of the five-note scales for much of the vocal music. [5.]

The melodic outline of the blues also seems to have a base in the African singing styles. A.M. Jones, in his description of African melody, could also have been describing a general characteristic of the blues.

> *Broadly speaking, the outline of an African tune is like a suc-*
> *cession of the teeth of a rip-saw; a steep rise (not usually*
> *exceeding a fifth) followed by a gentle sloping down of the tune;*
> *then another sudden rise - then a gentle sloping down, and so*
> *on.   The tendency is for the tune to start high and gradually*
> *to work downwards in this saw-like manner.* [6.]

In an analysis of two hundred and fifty-nine blues melodies it was found that nearly two hundred of them had the same pattern of descending from a higher melodic tone that Jones had noticed in Africa. Of the two hundred and fifty-nine melodies studied, one hundred and ninety-one were in this category, twenty used a compound verse that delayed the introduction of the usual descending line with two lines of half-spoken recitative, eight used the same fast country dance melody, and the last twelve used a variety of other melodies. There may be some relationship between this melodic approach and the African method of singing scales from the highest to the lowest notes, rather than in ascending patterns as in the European practice. This descending line was common in African music, in the American work song, in the Venezuelan Negro song, and in the blues.

**Example 2.**

There was also in Africa a strong tradition of guitar-like instruments, and most of the early accompaniment styles in the blues seem to have grown from the rhythmic finger picking styles that had been developed in West Africa. The instrument was introduced into Africa by the Portuguese in the fifteenth or sixteenth century in its earliest European form as the small "machet" or rabequina. Using this as a model the African musicians built crude guitars that were called rabekin, ramakienjo, raamakie, rampi, rabouquin, or ramki. The first traveler's mention of the instrument was in 1733, but it had clearly been played along the coast for many years before this. In 1781 another traveler wrote,

> *The rabouquin is a triangular piece of board with three strings made of intestines, supported by a bridge, which may be stretched at pleasure by means of pegs, like those of our instruments in Europe; it is indeed nothing else than a guitar with three strings.*[7.]

Three stringed instruments were common, but most of them had six, as well as the characteristic guitar finger board, sound box, and moveable pegs. As guitars have become more available the older instrument has almost disappeared in Africa, but it was clearly an influence on the American musical style. It was even common for performers to press a string against the fingerboard with their chin, a guitar technique still found in some of the mountain areas of the South. Many of the instruments that have survived have hand carved capo d'astros to raise the pitch of the strings. Little is known about the tunings of the ramki, but all of the travelers agree that it was finger picked in repetitive rhythmic patterns. Younger performers in Africa now play a little with a flat pick, but this has come into the music only recently. Many of the American blues singers remember making their own guitars and banjos when they were small children, and the instrument they describe usually has some of the characteristics of the ramki, even to the use of metal pans for the sound box, as was often done in Africa. It may have been that they were helped with the building by a grandmother or a grandfather, whose memory went back to the slavery period when there was still open importation of men, women, and children from Africa.

The strongest American influences on the developing blues were in the area of form, while the most important influence from Africa was on the performance style. African music often is characterized by an elaborately developed rhythmic structure that has continually shifting stress points as the individual performers alter their beat patterns. The blues, generally, is much more oriented to the Euro-American concept of the heavily accented downbeat at the bar line, even though with many of the earlier blues men the bar line emphasis seems to be almost a reluctant afterthought superimposed on a more fluid rhythmic structure. Also the concept of a harmonic structure is less highly developed in African music, and in many of the slave areas two hundred years ago may even have been unknown. Even where there is a use of harmony, the technique is usually limited to parallel harmonies in thirds or fifths with the vocal line. In the blues the harmonic structure is so persistent that the form is often defined by its chord pattern of tonic, subdominant, and dominant relationships. Among the blues singers themselves it is felt that if the piece moves too far from the customary progressions it is no longer a blues, even though it still has many of the other melodic and textual characteristics. Country singers who used open guitar tunings often made only the most perfunctory effort to follow the chord changes of the more or less conventional twelve bar blues form, but they usually sang the harmonic changes, even if they didn't alter the accompaniment figures.

Through the failure of the American academic community to take any interest in the growth of new creative art forms in the United States, it will probably never be possible to determine what musical styles were the dominant influences on the young blues styles. At the point when a few moments conversation with a young singer would have answered nearly all the problems of source and concept there was no one who was interested in either the music or the singers. As late as the 1920's, when the first books were being written on Negro music in the United States, it would have been possible to talk with nearly every major figure in the early blues. Instead the writers spent much of their efforts on the already thoroughly discussed spirituals and made half-hearted efforts to deal with some of the least important areas of local work song. Only John Work, who had earlier noticed the similarities between the African and Afro-American scales, went to a singer. In 1935 he interviewed Gertrude Rainey, who as "Ma" Rainey had been one of the most important of the early women blues singers. [8] When he talked with her she was still singing, and was staying at a Nashville hotel while her stage show played in the city. She was not able to give him much information, but what she told him does make it clear that the blues form was not generally known throughout the South much before 1900. Her own first memory of the blues was hearing a girl sing a slow, "minor" song in Missouri in 1903, when Ma was singing with a show there. The girl was not from the area, and she had been singing her new kind of songs for the people in the town where the show had stopped. The few local collections of song that were done in Alabama, Louisiana, and Mississippi, don't include a single blues in the fully formed three line stanzaic form, although the emotional attitudes that dominated the later blues were already present.

The pervasive influence of the commercial record business also has made it difficult to untangle the knotted strands of the blues fabric. The first commercially successful recordings were done by young theatre and cabaret entertainers, nearly all of them women, who were working in the larger cities of the North. Their recordings, mostly of songs written for them by professional Negro song writers, were sold everywhere in the South, and when the companies began working with the male singers four or five years later their interest was in "blues," which they usually considered as a twelve-bar, three-line stanza song, like the songs that the girls had recorded. It is clear, from the strength and the variety of the male singing, that the creative impetus in the early blues had been from the country blues men, but the styles had already begun to change by the time these singers were recorded; so the relationships between the blues and closely related forms like the work song and the holler were blurred. The three line verse form was a distinctive poetic form within itself, and as little is known about its line of development from the simple two line rhymes of the work songs. It could have been developed by the singers who improvised their lyrics and found that repeating the first line gave them an additional moment to think of a rhyming line. Although this form was the most widely used there were many variations of the stanza form, from simple two line couplets to complex five and six line verses with involved repetitions of lines and phrases. There was also a compound verse form that developed in the 1930's, which used two lines of more or less recited text, then went back to the sung lines at a slower tempo. The compound verses became especially useful for songs with narrative material and are now used by a number of younger singers. Like the three line stanza, the early forms of the more complex verses are difficult to trace.

Even with the confusion of sources and influences, however, it does seem clear that it was in the Mississippi delta counties that the first blues were sung, and of all the southern areas where the blues became a deeply rooted folk style, it was in the delta where there was the richest creative growth.

MISSISSIPPI

# 1. MISSISSIPPI

The Mississippi delta is a flat, hot country of straggling lowlands and mounded hills of clay and mud left by the swelling floods of the rivers that meander across its eroded earth. It is an inland delta, the land flooded over by the Yazoo River and the rivers that flow into it from the north, the Tallahatchie and the Sunflower. The rivers wander over the countryside, their banks crude levees of heaped earth and clay, sometimes strengthened near the towns with stones and concrete pilings. The wavering river channels can be followed across the land by the growth of sycamore and poplar left to grow against the levees. Flood control projects have lessened the strength of the spring floods, but the rivers still twist and shift in their beds with the gray rains of late winter and spring.

In the upland pine barrens the soil is streaked with yellow and darkened with the red stain of surface clay. It is poor soil, and its covering is a sparse, meager growth of pine and thin grass. The barrens are lonely and poor, the farm roads only muddy tracks dragging their red clay ruts after them into the stillness of the trees. But on the flat lands near the rivers, the flooding has covered the clay and sand with a heavy layer of topsoil, and the earth is good for cotton. In the long, hot days of late summer the dust from the fields settles over miles of ripening cotton, and the men and mules, even the heavy machines, working the rows are only distant shapes in the haze of the sun. The delta counties, Tunica, Coahoma, Leflore, Sunflower, Yazoo, and Humphreys, are the third largest cotton producing area in the United States, even with a farming system that is still only partially mechanized. The delta counties have a seven month growing season, steady rains in the spring, and the long, hot weeks of July and August, when the clouds drift over the fields with slow indirection and the sun brings the temperature to ninety in the shade as the cotton swells and splits in the gasping air.

Cotton is cruel and demanding in the spring and late summer months; in the spring when the new growth has to be weeded and thinned, and in the fall when it has to be picked. The weeding and thinning goes on for weeks, men working with a hoe, "chopping cotton" up and down the rows, sometimes using a mule or a tractor to drag a cultivator down the soft lines of wavering green stems and leaves. By the end of the summer the plants have dried into a red-brown tangle of spiny stalks, the cotton hanging in its nest of barbs about the level of a man's thigh. For these months the labor in the cotton fields is hard and unending, and for the labor the South, through the century and a half that it has grown cotton, has used Negroes. The delta land was cleared by Negro slave gangs, the fields were leveled and planted, the first cotton picked, ginned, and baled by slaves. When the Civil War ended the system went on almost without change, and the Negro field hand was held to the land with the ruinous "share-crop" system of planting. In 1945 more than sixty percent of Mississippi's farmers were still working as share croppers, and by 1955 the percentage had dropped only to forty-six percent, still the highest in the United States.

Even on the large plantations of the delta, which have become increasingly mechanized, the labor is still done by Negro workers. They live with their families in unpainted shacks along the plantation roads, straggling from plantation to plantation, poorly paid and forced to live under a crude system of paternal semi-slavery. Under the earlier methods of cotton planting so many hands were needed in the fields that for the hundred years between 1840 and 1940 Negroes were in the majority in the state, and in the delta there are still two or three Negroes to every white. Tunica County, a shambling, poor countryside of pine barrens and eroded earth on the Mississippi River below Memphis, has a population that is eighty-one percent Negro, one of the highest percentages of any county in the nation. The only relief for the Negro families caught in the grinding poverty and viciousness of life in rural Mississippi has been flight to the North, and it has been their migration out of the state that has finally given the white population a majority. Between 1950 and 1960 over 325,000 Negroes, out of a Negro population of less than 900,000, fled the state's racism, ignorance, and brutality.

On Saturdays in the small towns of the delta, on a bench near the courthouse or under the trees on one of the side streets, with its old wooden buildings and painted brick store fronts, there is the noise of voices and laughter, shouts as the trucks come in from the plantations and farms and park in front of a store. The courthouse square is crowded with people in to shop, and the trucks and battered farm cars sit along the worn grass of the courthouse park with children waiting impatiently for the adults to get finished and get back to the car. The Negro farmers mingle with the white, their eyes on the ground, looking carefully away when somebody says something to them. They're in faded overalls and work shirts, always with a hat, sometimes in pressed trousers and a white shirt, their wives in shapeless dresses, a handkerchief tied over their hair. Sometimes there are even momentary exchanges between them and a few of the white men, the guarded, uncomfortable effort of the Negro to answer the careless questions of the white man that is sometimes thought of by the white Mississippian as "friendship." But out of the towns, in the rows of farm shacks where the people of the delta live, there is an oppressive isolation. At a rutted cross roads the field workers sit on the ground beside a general store, leaning against the clapboards and the torn advertising posters, wary if a car slows down. If a stranger comes toward a row of shacks at the edge of the stretching fields of new-plowed ground the voices fall silent and a nervous face is pressed against a window in answer to a knock. In the Negro sections of the small towns, the streets unpaved and the side-walks worn and broken, the men standing in front of a barbership will scatter into the stores and houses if someone unfamiliar walks into the neighborhood.

The music of the delta bears the marks of this separation between the people of the delta. Negroes were more heavily concentrated in the delta than they were in many other areas of the South, and because of the violence of the Mississippi caste system they were kept at an even further distance from the influence of southern white music. With the exception of a few small groups - the people of the sea islands of Georgia and the Carolinas and the families living in the Talladega Forest of Alabama who were so isolated that they retained even fragments of African speech - the delta field hands were less a part of southern life than any other large Negro group. The music that developed in the counties of the delta was so little influenced by American popular music that it was still closely related to the distant African background, and in many ways seemed to be an intense distillation of the slave music that had emerged from the diffuse tribal and cultural influences of the slave society. The delta music had the strength of the work song from which it had only half emerged.

The dominant strains of older music in the delta, the gang work song and the field holler, were entangled with the growing cycles of the cotton crop. The land was cleared by work gangs who felled trees to the rhythm of song leaders, their axes swinging in the light as their voices joined his for the simple responses, grunting as the axe bit into the wood. There were gang songs for chopping, hauling timber, pulling stumps, lifting bales, even for cutting weeds with a hoe. This has long been a characteristic of African music, and it took root throughout the Americas. The mahogany cutters of British Honduras moved their logs through the forests with gang songs and the Bahamas fishermen launched their small sloops with improvised pulling songs. Men sweating under the July sun in a work gang still had the gang songs ringing in their ears when they sang in the cabins at night, and the music of the work songs, with its short vocal phrases, limited melodic range, and insistent rhythm, left its mark on the developing blues style. Sometimes the singers even kept the rhythmic emphasis of the axe fall, pausing before beginning the phrase, and the blues had the feel of the work song, even though the rhythm was usually changed so that the song could be used to accompany dancing.

27

Example 3.

The two dominant song forms, the work song and the holler, were distinctly different musical forms, and these differences also found their way into the early delta blues style. A holler is an individual song, and it is very freely structured in its rhythm and its phrasing. It is the song of the man working alone in the fields, musing to himself as he works. Often someone chopping cotton sings a lonely holler, and the plantation mule drivers sing quavering hollers to the animals as they begin work in the first spreading mists of morning. Like the work song, the field holler was closely related to African music, most closely to the praise songs and the individual mens' songs of the West African tribes. The holler left its imprint on the delta blues in the extended vocal phrase, the falsetto voice, the mordent on specific scale tones, and the irregular, embellished cadence.

Example 4.

Tommy Johnson

(falsetto)

The uneasy social line that was drawn between the field hands in their weathered board cabins and the white foremen and townspeople also left the singers to themselves in the development of their vocal scale and the accompaniment rhythm and harmonies. It is difficult to tell how strongly the singers were influenced by the conventional three line blues verse which was used as the first strain to Handy's "St. Louis Blues" in 1914, but the poetic form was widely known. Since Handy found his material in folk sources and spent many of his young years playing with dance orchestras in the delta, the form itself may already have been widespread through the delta, and the conventional blues song of the 1920's may reflect an earlier delta influence - rather than similarities between some delta blues and the conventional popular blues techniques indicating an influence on the Mississippi men. The verse form was generally the three line stanza, but with each singer there was a highly individual approach to the problem of fitting a singing style that was still strongly influenced by its African backgrounds to a harmonic and rhythmic structure that was vaguely derived from standard European harmonic practice. The Mississippi vocal scale was generally a gapped pentatonic, although there were also four and six note groupings. The third of the scale was almost always altered to avoid a clear European major-minor definition. Like most early jazz scales and the folk ragtime scale the modality was mixed, including both major and minor elements, often sounding simultaneously.

**Example 5**

Skip James
( If You Have'nt Any Hay)

(Special Rider Blues)
(altered)( passing)

Robert Johnson
(Walking Blues) (auxiliaries)

(Hellhound On My Trail)

The third was altered toward either a sharp or flat tonality, depending on its place in the phrase. Although the fourth was generally used, and there was in many of the blues a suggestion of the conventional subdominant harmony in the second line of the verse, it was not a strong tone in the scale and was generally used as an auxiliary to color the third or the fifth in more involved melodic phrases. When the second was used it was generally an auxiliary; although as the delta styles developed in complexity the second became more important through an increasing concern with more sophisticated harmonic patterns. The seventh, in the few scales that it was used, generally had little of the strong leading tone tendency that it has in the European scale, and often seemed to be used an approximation of a harmonic progression to the dominant, where it became the third of the dominant triad.

The African-derived scales, with their strong relationship between the first and fifth tones and their ambiguous use of the third to avoid strong major-minor coloration, dominated the delta blues. It was only with difficulty, however, that they could be fitted to the conventional harmonies of the European guitar; so the accompaniment styles fell back on the older techniques of the rampi, the lyre, and the bow. There was little conventional harmonic movement. Sometimes the guitar was even re-tuned to an open chord so that it could be played more easily in a repetitive accompaniment ostinato. With the strings tuned to an open E chord or an open G chord there was considerable flexibility in the rhythmic figures that could be picked with the fingers of the right hand, while the left changed the tones to follow the voice. The open E tuning was usually e-b-e'-g-b-e '', a minor tuning, but it was played with one finger on the third string, raising the g to the major g#. Some singers, however, tuned to the major chord, with the g raised the half step. The singer Skip James uses the minor tuning, playing it in major with strong overtones of the minor modality. He calls it "cross-note" tuning because of the crossing between the major and minor during a piece. The G tuning was generally d-g-d'-g'-b-d'', sometimes called the "Spanish" or "slack key" tuning because of the slackening of the lowest e string down a whole step to d. It is a major tuning, and it was usually played with the strings open, sometimes even with the guitar flat across the singer's lap. It had a darker sound than the E tuning because of the lowering of the bass string to the fifth of the key. The cadential V-I used the lowest strings of the guitar, and descending bass lines could move down the lowest string from the tonic G to the dominant D. Charley Patton often used this tuning, pulling the bass string with a strong slapping sound on the descending line. There was a tuning in open D-d-a-d-g-b-d''. and the standard guitar tuning was used as well, the e-a-d-g-b-e' European tuning, sometimes called "minor" tuning or "the key of minor" in the delta. With all the tunings, however, the guitar was usually as much as a fourth below standard concert pitch. It was difficult to change chords in the open tunings, except by barring across at the fifth fret for the subdominant or the seventh fret for the dominant, but the blues of the delta were dominated by the voice and the rhythmic pattern, and the harmonic style was less intensively developed.

In a few of the blues there was no harmonic change, and there was not even an effort to follow the movement of the vocal line with accompaniment figures in the guitar. Instead the singer picked an ostinato pattern over and over in the guitar and sang against it in an elaborately developed melodic structure that was only loosely tied to the rhythm of the accompaniment. This style was closely related to the African music of the slave coast, in which accompaniment instruments repeated a simple figure over and over while the chanted melody was sung against it. Although the style was musically limited there was considerable variety within the repetitive patterns. Closely tied to these styles were accompaniments which combined the ostinato patterns with an effort to sketch in the more conventional blues harmonies. In these accompaniments the guitar played an insistent note or an open chord under the vocal phrase; then followed the voice with an ostinato figure. These accompaniments became almost a characteristic of the delta style, even though they forced the singers into irregular rhythmic patterns. If the vocal phrase ended in the middle of a measure and then was followed by a four beat accompaniment figure, as many of the patterns were, then the blues line became an uneasy phrase of irregular measure length. Often the singers simply adjusted to the irregularity, rather than trying to alter their accompaniment, and many blues have measures of 5/4 and 6/4 between the standard 4/4 measures. There was also a wide use of a half measure of 2/4 within the vocal line to introduce the sung phrase of four measures of 4/4 rhythm.

One of the dominant characteristics of the delta accompaniment style was the use of the guitar to play a melodic unison, or near unison, with the voice. It was so strongly tied to the early delta style that singers can often be placed by the extent of the melodic doubling between the voice and the guitar. Often these lines were finger picked, as part of the more complex ostinato patterns. Charley Patton, in pieces like "Down The Dirt Road Blues," used this finger picked melody in 8th notes against the reiterated fundamental tone in the lower strings. The guitar, however, was limited by its metal frets to tones that were more or less within the diatonic framework of a European guitar style. The singer could alter the tones to some extent by "choking" the string, (pushing it to one side on the finger board to raise the pitch), but this was difficult to do for a more extended melodic line. In part because of this melodic limitation and in part because of the distinctiveness of the sound, many Mississippi singers used a bottleneck or metal ring on the third or fourth finger of the left hand. With this they were able to play a melodic line that followed the voice very closely, even when the vocal line used tones that were within the pentatonic scale framework. This unison melody played with a slide of some kind and a bass line of alternating root and fifth tones played with the thumb became widespread among the delta singers.

The vocal style of the delta was hard and unrelenting; the voice usually heavy, the tone produced at the back of the throat with rougher growling tones, and the falsetto voice used for contrast or emotional emphasis. Often the melodic range was limited to a few notes within a partial octave, probably from the long hours on the work gangs, where melodies were kept as simple as possible so that they could be sung over and over and still leave enough breath to use an axe or a pick. A few singers, among them Robert Johnson and Skip James, used some vocal embellishment, and scale tones were used with some flexibility within the phrase, but the usual melodic movement was in intervals of a third or a fourth, and the tones were clearly focused. It was generally in the blues with a field holler background that there was more use of the mordent and the embellished cadence.

It is difficult to find traces of the earliest blues styles, but it was in the delta, in Cleveland, Mississippi, that W. C. Handy heard a man singing a blues in 1895. It is the earliest moment at which someone remembers hearing the blues in the South, and it could have been in the delta that the blues finally emerged as a musical style distinct from the field holler and the gang song of the rest of the rural South. There was the heavy concentration of Negro field workers, an almost complete isolation from the white society, and a strongly developed tradition of rhymed work song material; all of these are factors that could have led to the growth of a distinctive musical style. The roots of the delta blues, with their half remembered elements of African song and the work rhythms of the years of slavery, go as deep within the singers as the roots of the cotton in the hot, dusty fields go deep within the delta soil.

Without the phonograph record the blues styles of the Mississippi delta would have been only a vaguely remembered sound, like a bird's whistle across the fields in the sun. Fortunately, however, many of the singers were able to record. With the move out of Mississippi by many younger Negro families in the years after the first World War there was a market in the northern slums for the music from "down home," and the companies found a strong musical tradition when they began looking for local blues singers. Victor Records, with a field unit in Memphis set up by Ralph Peer, recorded a number of important singers in the late 1920's, and Paramount Records, through their talent scout, H. C. Spears in Jackson, brought some of the most creative singers up to the studios in Grafton, Wisconsin. Columbia did little work in the area, but there were delta singers among others on Brunswick, Gennett and OKeh labels. The great delta folk blues artist, John Hurt, recorded for OKeh in Memphis, then again in New York in 1928. In the 1930's there was continued interest in the delta music and the American Recording Corporation, Vocalion Records, and the Bluebird label of R.C.A. Victor used delta singers for considerable material. The amount of Mississippi music recorded before the second World War was very large, and it included some of the most creative blues to be recorded during the late 'twenties and the 'thirties. Some important Mississippi singers were probably missed by the companies, whose interest in the music was only sporadic, but from the reminiscences of some of the older singers it would seem that most of the dominant figures in the development of the delta style were recorded, and some of them extensively. Of the dozens of singers to be recorded a handful have already emerged as among the most significant artists that the blues has produced, among them men like Charley Patton, Son House, Skip James, Robert Johnson, and Booker White, who seem to represent the musical tradition which shaped them, and was in turn shaped by their own creative expression.

# 2. CHARLEY PATTON

The delta blues grew out of the earth of the delta countryside, but the same piece of ground can grow ragweed, mullien, jack pine, field grass, or black-eyed daisies. A developing art form grows like the weeds beside a road, dozens of styles growing together until one crowds aside the others with its strength and vitality. In the early period of growth in the music of the delta it was Charley Patton, from a farm outside of Edwards in Hinds County, who left the deepest impression on its blues. As a younger singer, Booker White, remembered,[1.]

> *I always wanted to be like old Charley Patton, long time ago when I was a kid out here, and play them numbers about "Hitch up my buggy and saddle up my black mare," and I used to pick cotton and come around in Clarksdale there to them cafes and things eating cheese and cracker - none of the other boys, they didn't have any idea what I was thinking about - I'd say I wants to come to be a great man like Charley Patton, but I didn't want to be killed like he did, the way he had to go. I've always realized I knew I had to die, but I didn't want one of them old sandfoot womens coming up and cut my throat or do something to me that's unnecessary. I tell you the truth the first drink of whiskey that I ever drinken, Charley Patton gave me a little in a spoon. He said, "You're too young to drink too much of whiskey, but I'm going to give you enough to know what it's about." And I still think about that. I wish I'd asked him to give me the spoon... I just wish today I could shake Charley Patton's hand...*

Charley was a small man, short and slight with a thin face and soft, wavy hair, but he has left a long shadow in the memories of people in the delta who heard him sing. In August, 1963, two men trying to follow the threads of Charley's life, Gayle Dean Wardlow, a young white Mississippian who was living in Jackson, and Bernard Klatzko, an

34

accountant from Long Island, found that despite the thirty years that had passed since Charley's death he was still remembered by most of the people living in the sections of the countryside where he had played. Gayle had learned a few months before that Patton had died on Dockery's Plantation, outside of Cleveland, Mississippi, in Sunflower County. As Klatzko later described their trip,[2.]

> *... We entered Sunflower County ... three miles from the County line we stopped at a general store -- all there was of the town of Dockery. Out beyond the general store and to its right, there was this big blue sign over an entranceway to a large plantation. Its white lettering read: WILL DOCKERY AND SON JOS. DOCKERY.*

> *We drove in, passed some farm machinery and a cotton gin and came upon a vast, beautifully tended cotton field. However, we turned our attention to a row of Negro houses that stood opposite the field. At the first house a middle age woman answered our knock on the screen.*

> *"Did you ever hear of Charley Patton?" I started off.*

> *"Charley Patton? He's dead."*

> *"Did you know him?"*

> *"No. I only moved here about 10 years ago. Why don't you ask some people who have lived here a long time. You can find them on the other end." She said this pointing to the other group of houses which lay to the left of the entrance road; we had turned right on entering...*

> *The next few inquiries proved very fruitful. At the first house, a young woman directed us to her father-in-law, Johnny Wilder, who ran the gasoline pump in front of the general store and who had known Patton well. In the next house, dwelt Patton's cousin, who directed us to the machine shop where Tom Cannon, Patton's nephew, worked. Sure, he remembered his uncle, but didn't know too much about him. "Why don't you ask my mother, Viola Cannon? That's Charley's sister. She can tell you all about him. She lives in Cleveland." We went back to the general store and bought Johnny Wilder and ourselves bottles of Coke and sat on a bench in the shade. It was another blistering hot day.*

> *Johnny Wilder was brown and lean, of medium height and grey-headed. He was most amiable but I detected an air of uneasiness about him when we started to ply him with questions. "Charley Patton was living here when I came here back in 1917. He traveled all around but always came back to*

*Dockery's. Then a few years later, he left for good. Mr. Jed fired him."*

*"What songs did he sing?" Were there any other blues singers on the plantation?"*

*"He sang 'Hitch up my pony/Saddle up my grey mare' and 'What you want with a rooster...' As for other singers, there was Son House on Dockery's at the same time. He came from Drew, and Nathan Bank, also from Drew, played with them. There was Willie Brown, too. They all played for picnics and jook joints."*

*"Patton sang about Tom Rushen. Did you ever hear of him?" I asked.*

*"Tom Rushen is Iry Rushen's brother," said Johnny. "Iry Rushen was Will Dockery's bookkeeper. He just died recently."*

*With that, we left for Cleveland to find Viola Cannon. After several inquiries we were directed to the "new" houses. We arrived at a street of comparatively new frame, one-story, painted homes, but no larger than the unpainted variety. A man we enlisted for further help pointed to Viola's house and added that if we wanted to know more about Patton we should ask Millie Toy. She had been married to Patton and now lived in Boyle. Viola came to the door. She was about five foot five, very lean, unsmiling, proud and seemed a little disturbed by the intrusion. She had yellow brown skin, and a long lean face with strong, regular features.*

*"Charley was a great blues singer" she said. "He taught them all, Howlin' Wolfe, Willie Brown, Son House. He made up all the songs himself. He followed a guitar player around Dockery's as a boy. I forgot the guitar player's name, but Charley didn't learn any singing from him. Charley made up his own singing."*

*"Where was Charley born?" Gayle asked.*

*"He was born on a farm outside Edwards in 1887. He had two brothers, William and Will C. and two sisters, Katie and myself. All are dead. I'm the last. We moved from Edwards to Dockery's when Charley was still a young boy. He didn't start to play guitar until we were on Dockery's. My father was a very big man and my mother was short and real good-looking with long, straight hair. Charley himself wasn't too big and he was thin."*

*"Was Charley religious?" I asked.*

*Viola chuckled and said, "No, he wasn't religious."*

*"Then how did he learn all those religious songs and why did he sing them?"*

*I felt a little embarrassed asking that question.*

*"My father was the elder of a church on the plantation. Charley knew all those religious songs from boyhood and sang them later 'cause they're good songs, I guess."*

*"Did you ever hear of Minnie Franklin?" asked Gayle.*

*"Well, Charley's first wife was named Gertrude. He met Minnie Franklin in Merigold in 1921 right after he left Dockery's. Then, he followed her on down to Vicksburg after his best gun and money." Viola recalled this incident with fits of laughter.*

*"Where did Charley do most of his playing?" I interjected.*

*"Charley played all over. He traveled with medicine shows and played with Blind Lemon," she replied.*

*"Did Charley drink much?" I wanted to know.*

*"No. He hardly drank at all..."*

A delta singer who had left to live in St. Louis in 1925, J. D. Short, remembered meeting Charley when he was a young man.[3.]

*"He used to play the guitar and he'd make the guitar say, 'Lord have mercy, Lord have mercy, Lord have mercy, pray, brother, pray, save poor me.' Now that's what Charley Patton'd make the guitar say."*

J. D. was quiet, dark man who struggled against the difficulties of St. Louis slum life with a gentle good nature. He was able to fill in a little of the life that Patton had led when he was in his twenties. J. D. met Charley,

*... out on little Mirthy Bow from Hollandale, Mississippi ... he was doing some logging out in there, hauling logs, hauling timber and stuff out in there ... that's mostly what he did. He mostly followed timber camps and levee camps and stuff like that ... he always kept a guitar, but he didn't usually carry it with him. He would come along driving a wagon or something back in them days and somebody had a guitar around playing and he wasn't in a hurry he'd just stop by and play the guitar some and let the people hear him.*

37

As they drove across the Mississippi cotton counties looking for Patton's last wife, Bertha Lee, Wardlow and Klatzko found that the mention of Charley's name usually brought a response like J.D.'s - a memory of Patton as the singer and entertainer.[4.]

To the people who lived with him, and to his friends, Charley was a small, intense, fretful man who blustered his way out of fights, sang with fierce strength, and survived as best he could in a violent country-side. Son House, who met Patton in 1930, remembers going back to Bertha Lee after he and Charley had been out on a two day drunk, and he heard them arguing in the next room; then there was a crash and he heard Charley saying, "I told you not to get me angry." Then he heard more sounds of a fight and a louder crash and Charley called out to Son to come in and help. Bertha Lee was bigger than Charley and she had him down on the floor. "Son," Charley said, "Get this woman away from me before I hurt her." Son told Julius Lester, who talked with him in New York in 1964, of another time he and Willie Brown found Charley getting out of a fight.[5.]

> *I remember one night Willie and I and Charlie were to play at the same place and Willie and I were late, but Charlie had gotten there kind of early. And the guys got off the center kind of early, too. Got to fighting and shooting off those old owl-head pistols. Well, Willie and I got near to the house and we heard such a gruntin' and a rattlin' coming up through the stalks, and I said, "Wait a minute, Willie. Hold it. I hear something coming up through the cotton field. Don't you hear it?" He said, "Yeah. It's something." We were always suspicious, you know, about animals. Out in the country around there, it wouldn't be anything to see a teddy-bear or something. So we got the idea we wanted to hurry up and get to the road where we could see it. Finally, who should pop out to the roadside but Charlie! He looked and saw us and said, "I'll kill 'em all. I'll kill 'em all." Me and Willie started laughing and told him, "How you gon' kill 'em all? We heard you running."*

Patton's music was as much a part of the delta as the mud on the banks of the Sunflower River or the smell of the fields back of Belzoni. He sang in cabins, in ramshackle road houses, in country dance halls, even in gardens and plantation house back yards. He sang for everybody in the delta, white and colored, and he had songs for every kind of audience. Nearly half of the songs that he recorded were play party songs or folk songs, country ballads or gospel songs. He could be thought of almost as a songster, rather than a blues singer, but songsters usually learn their blues from other singers. His blues were among the most compelling and individual of the early blues period. And for once recordings seem to represent a singer at his best. Son House has said that when Charley performed for audiences he was always playing with his guitar behind his head or doing a little dance as he sang, and that his recordings were much better than Charley's singing was in person. A delta singer of Patton's generation, Babe Stovall, who was found in Meridian, Mississippi, by a New Orleans art dealer named Larry Borenstein, still ends his performances playing the guitar behind his head or behind his back, and the effect is a little confused musically, although the sight of Babe standing in a New Orleans patio with his Virginia Military Institute overcoat hanging down to his ankles, and his steel-bodied National guitar sitting on top of his head while he plays a guitar solo, is difficult to forget. Patton, with his rough voice and his heavy guitar accompaniments, must have had the same effect when he stood up in a dimly lit road house to do one of this songs.

Many of Charley's blues had deep roots in the delta. He was one of the most ''local'' singers even of the early period, when there was considerable mention of local towns and counties in the blues. He seems to have known every small town and plantation and sheriff and bootlegger within fifty miles of his cabin - and to have been unconcerned with much that was happening anywhere else. Some of the most difficult passages to understand in his blues often turn out to be the names of people in the area, or of the small towns of the country side. In ''Tom Rushen Blues'' it was Mr. Holloway, Mr. Day, sheriff of Bolivar County, and the sheriff who followed him into office, Tom Rushen.

> I lay down last night, thought that I would have my peace, (sleep?)
> umhuh,
> I lay down last night, thought that I would have my peace, (sleep?)
> umhuh,
> But when I woke up Tom Rushen was shaking me.
>
> When you get in trouble there's no use to screamin'
>     and cryin', umhuh,
> When you get in trouble there's no use to screamin'
>     and cryin', umhuh,
> Tom Rushen will take you back to prison now flyin'.
>
> It was late one night, Holloway was gone to bed, umhuh.
> It was late one night, Holloway was gone to bed, umhuh.
> Mr. Day brought whiskey ('til he dropped under) Holloway's head.
>
> Well, boozie booze, lord, to carry me through.
> It take booly booze lord, to carry me through.
> Well, the days seem like years in the jailhouse where there is
>     no booze.
>
> Got up this morning Tom Day was standin' 'round, umhuh.
> Got up this morning Tom Day was standin' 'round, umhuh.
> If he lose his office now he runnin' from town to town.
>
> Let me tell you folkses just how he treated me, umhuh,
> I'm gon' tell you folkses just how he treated me, umhuh.
> Lord, he caught me an' I was drunk as I could be.

In "High Sheriff Blues" he sang about Belzoni, in Humphreys County, its sheriff, Mr. Ware, and Mr. Purvis, who seems to have been a local landowner.

> When the trial's in Belzoni, ain't no use screamin' and cryin',
> > umhuh,
> When the trial's in Belzoni, ain't no use to scream and cry,
> > umhuh,
> Mr. Ware will take you back to Belzoni jail house umhuh,
> > (for life?)
>
> Let me tell you folkses, how he treated me, umhuh,
> Let me tell you folkses, how he treated me, umhuh,
> And he put me in a cellar just as dark as it could be.
>
> It was late one evening Mr. Purvis was standin' 'round,
> > umhuh,
> It was late one evening Mr. Purvis was standin' 'round,
> > umhuh,
> Mr. Purvis told Mr. Webb, sir, to let poor Charley down.
>
> It takes boozey booze, lord, to carry me through, umhuh,
> It takes booley boo, lord, to carry me through, umhuh,
> (Mr. Purvis...)   jailhouse where there is no booze.
>
> I got up one morning feeling awful mm, umhuh,
> I got up one morning feeling mighty bad, umhuh,
> It must not a been the Belzoni jail I had - blues I had, boy.
>
> While I was in trouble you know no use to scream and cry,
> > umhuh,
> When I was in prison ain't no use to scream and cry.
> Mr. Purvis on his mansion, he just don't pay no mind.

Charley's longest blues about the delta was his song about the floods of 1927, "High Water Everywhere, Part 1 and 2." The verses conveyed a strong impression of the flood waters that streamed over the bottom land during the worst days of flooding. (This piece is also one of Patton's most difficult to understand, but Don Kent, a Patton enthusiast living in Chicago, after several months work has succeeded in transcribing all of the verses, and it is his transcription which follows.) The spoken comments were probably by Willie Brown.

> Part 1.  The back water done rose, sir, an' tumbled down,
> > drove me down the line.
> > Back water done rolled and tumbled, drove poor Charley
> > > down the line.
> >
> > An' I tell the world the water done struck through this town.

Lord, the whole roun' country, Lord, river is overflowin'.
Lord, the whole roun' country, man, it's overflowed.
  Spoken: You know I can't stay here; I'm boun' to go where
        it's high, boy.
I would go to the hill country, but they got me barred.

Now, look a here now, Lelah, river risin' high.
Look here, boys (   ) leave it to me, river is ragin' high.
  Spoken: Boy, it's risin' over there, yeah.
I'm gonna move over to Greensboro, 'fore I take (a good) bye.


Look a here, water now, Lordy, 'sup rol-rolled
   'most everywhere.
The water at Greenville, Lord, it done rose everywhere.
  Spoken: Boy, you can't never stay here.
I would go down to Rosedale, but they tell me
   there's water there.

Now, the water now, mama, done struck Charley's town.
Well, they tell me the water done struck Charley's town.
  Spoken: Boy, I'm going to Vicksburg.
Well, I'm goin' to Vicksburg on that high o' mine.


I am goin' on dry water where land don't never flow.
Well, I'm goin' on a hill where water, water don't never flow.
  Spoken: Boy, (hit Sharkey County and everything slid
     down in Stover.)
But I'll count the water isn't over in Tallahassie, sho'.
  Spoken: Boy, go way for Tallahassie, find it over there.

Lord, the water done rushed all...that 'ol Jackson road.
Lord, the water done reached over the Jackson road.
  Spoken: Boy, it got my car.
I'm goin' back to the hilly country, won't be worried no mo'.


Part 2. Back water at Blytheville, backed up all around.
Back water at Blytheville, done took Joiner town.
It was fifty families and children, some left dead and drowned.

The water was risin', up in my friend's door.
The water was risin', up in my friend's door.
The man said to his women folk, "Lord, we'd better go."

The water was risin', got up in my bed.
Lord, the water is rollin', up in my friend's door.
I thought I would take a trip, Lord, out on the big ice sled.

> Awwwuhhnn I hear the water, Lord, roll above my door.
>
> Spoken: Low water...look a here.
> I hear (it risin', Lord, Loring) sinkin' down.
> I couldn't get no boat ride, left me sink on down.
>
> Ooooh-ahh the water risin', families sinkin' down.
> Say, now, the water was risin', airplanes is all aroun'.
> Spoken: The water is all aroun'.
> It was fifty men and children, come to sink an' drown.
>
> Ooooh - uuhhnn Lordy, women and grown men down.
> Oooh-uhhh, women and children sinkin' down.
> Spoken: Lord have mercy, uh.
> I couldn't see nobody home an' was no one to be found.

He usually used the conventional three line verse in his blues compositions. The folk and country dance songs that he recorded he generally
left in their original form. He sometimes varied the verse form within
a blues, repeating the last few words of the first line except for the
final word, with which he ended the last repetition. In "Moon Going
Down" he began,

> Oh the moon goin' down, babe, sun's about to shine.
> Oh the moon goin' down, babe, sun's about to shine.
> (Henrietta) told me, lord, don't want you hangin' 'round.

and by the fifth verse he had extended the first line to,

> 'Cause the smoke stack's black an' the bell it shine like -
> bell it shine like -
> bell it shine like gold,
> 'Cause the smoke stack's black an' the bell it shine like gold.
> Lord I ain't gonna walk there, can't get 'round no mo'.

It was not an original device with Patton, but he used it with considerable
skill to heighten the tension of his best performances. He also knew a
number of songs which came from the older country traditions. His
version of the boll weevil ballad, "Mississippi Boll Weevil Blues," was
an archaic dance song with only a single musical phrase which repeated
over and over.

**Example 6**

The sketchy "ballad" used verses of a few words each, some of the phrases not even complete as he used the guitar to end the line.

> He's a little Bo Weevil keeps movin'a in the ... lordy ...
> You can plant your cotton and you won't get half a cent, lordy ...
> Boweevil, Boweevil, where's your little home? Lordy ...

It could have been a song like "Boll Weevil" that W. C. Handy heard in Cleveland, Mississippi, around the turn of the century and described as "... one of those over-and-over strains that seemed to have no very clear beginning and certainly no ending at all. The strumming attained a disturbing monotony, but on and on it went...." At a cabin buck dance a song like "Mississippi Boll Weevil" usually goes on until the dancers are too tired to keep up or the singer has run out of words. The singer Handy heard could even have been Patton, who was then a young man living and beginning to play in Cleveland.

Another of the blues that had the feel of the older field traditions was "When Your Way Gets Dark," a brooding composition that used lines from prison work songs almost as a single line verse. The vocal phrase was followed by a set melodic pattern in the guitar; then there was a cadential line that drew on Charley's usual final verse rhymes. His other blues often used conventional verses in haphazard arrangements, but in all of them there were moments, lines, phrases, entire verses, that were tied to Charley Patton's life in the Mississippi delta before the 1930's.

The delta haze hangs over some of Charley's years of wandering and singing, but it is possible to sketch in a few of the details for a rough portrait. He was born, as his sister said, on a farm outside of Edwards in 1887, and his family moved to Dockery's when he was still a boy. He grew up there, learned to play the guitar a little and began singing. His first wife was a girl named Gertrude; in 1908 he married Minnie Toy. He stayed on at Dockery's as a field hand and wagon driver until the early 1920's when he was fired. He went to Merigold and met Minnie Franklin and lived with her, probably in Vicksburg, for a year or so. About 1924 or 1925 he came back to Merigold with a woman named Sudy and lived with her "...near Pimbles Ferry on the other side of the Sunflower River," as Sam Manifield remembered. Charley drifted in and out of most of the delta towns as well, although he doesn't seem to have gone out of the state for any length of time. In 1929 he was in Jackson for a few months, and during these months Charley Patton, the delta blues man and songster, brushed against the outside world of American popular music.

In the late 1920's Paramount Records, a Chicago company which had been very successful in selling blues to the new urban Negro market, was making an effort to find singers who were still living in southern rural areas. The company had made an arrangement with a man named H. C. Spears, who had a music store on North Farrow Street in Jackson, to do tests of anyone he thought might sell some records in the area. Thanks to Spears, Paramount left behind what is probably the most important collection of blues material ever to be recorded in the United States. Spears sent Patton on to Arthur Laibley, who was one of the recording directors for Paramount, and Charley did his first recordings at Richmond, Indiana, in the old Gennett Record Studios, on Friday, June 14, 1929. He was in Indiana only long enough for the sessions and went back to Jackson when he had finished recording. Six weeks later, on July 27, 1929, his first release was advertised in the Chicago *Defender*.

## PONY BLUES
### by Charley Patton

*Here is a hot record by the one and only Charley Patton - a new Paramount artist - one of the best known singers and guitar players in the South. What he can't do with a guitar ain't worth mentioning. He starts off for Paramount with a bang - with Record No. 12792, "Pony Blues"...*

At almost the same time Paramount issued one of Charley's religious songs, "Prayer of Death" - actually one side was "Prayer of Death" and the other side was an alternate take of "I'm Going Home" - on Paramount 12799, under the name Elder J. J. Hadley. Charley's religious singing was almost as exciting as his blues singing, but Paramount was probably trying to circumvent the usual reluctance country people felt at buying religious records performed by a blues artist. The blues release, "Pony Blues," was a song that Charley had been singing around the delta for years, and there must have been some response to the record. Paramount brought him up for three more sessions during the next thirteen months and even made an effort to advertise his new releases. Booker White remembered that he couldn't "fit into a room" in Clarksdale when Charley's newest record was being played. For the second advertisement Paramount made an effort to sell Charley as a "Masked Marvel," and on September 14, 1929, the Chicago *Defender* had a drawing of a sophisticated looking man in evening clothes wearing a mask, with the words, "Who sings this great new Paramount Record? Who is the Masked Marvel?..." The record was Paramount 12805, "Screamin' And Hollerin' The Blues" and "Mississippi Bo Weevil Blues." The picture must have surprised the "Masked Marvel," if he ever saw it.

Early in 1930 Charley was living in Lula, a small town off Highway 61 in Coahoma County, north of Clarksdale, and in Lula he met both Son House and Bertha Lee, the woman who lived with him until he died four years later. As Son remembers,[6.]

44

# "PONY BLUES"

## by *Charley Patton*

**H**ERE is a hot record by the one and only Charley Patton — a new Paramount artist — one of the best known singers and guitar players in the South. What he can't do with a guitar ain't worth mentioning. He starts off for Paramount with a Bang — with Record No. 12792, "Pony Blues". Be sure and get it from your dealer, or send us the coupon.

{ **12792—Pony Blues** and **Banty Rooster Blues,**
Charley Patton and His Guitar. }

**12791—Sing Song Blues** and **Smiling Blues,** Jack O'Diamonds; Guitar acc. by Bob Coleman.

**12790—Fetch Your Water** and **Soon This Morning Blues,** Charlie Spand and Guitar; piano acc.

**12788—Gutter Man Blues** and **Wobblin' in the Mud,** Geo. Hannah; instrumental acc.

**12773—Bucket Of Blood** and **Playing The Dozen**—Piano Solos by Will Ezell.

**12714—Selling That Stuff** and **Beedle Um Bum,** The Hokum Boys; Piano-Guitar acc.

**12771—Oil Well Blues** and **Saturday Night Spender Blues,** Blind Lemon Jefferson and His Guitar.

**12796—Wasn't That Doggin' Me** and **Rockin' On The Hill Blues,** Beale Street Sheiks and Guitars.

### Sacred Numbers

**12798—How It Is With Me** and **I Want To Know Will He Welcome Me There,** Norfolk Jubilee Quartette.

**12880—His Eye Is On The Sparrow** and **I Wouldn't Mind Dying If Dying Was All,** Norfolk Jubilee Quartette.

**SEND NO MONEY!** If your dealer is out of the records you want, send us the coupon below. Pay postman 75 cents for each record, plus small C. O. D. fee when he delivers records. We pay postage on shipments of two or more records.

# Paramount
## The Popular Race Record
### ELECTRICALLY RECORDED

The New York Recording Laboratories
12 Paramount Bldg.
Port Washington, Wis.

Send me the records checked (✓) below 75 cents each.

( ) 12792  ( ) 12791  ( ) 12790
( ) 12798  ( ) 12773  ( ) 12714
( ) 12771  ( ) 12796  ( ) 12788  ( ) 12880

Name.......................................
Address...................................
City .................... State...........

CHARLEY PATTON ADVERTISEMENT

Forrest City · R. · Whitehaven · MEM. · Moscow · & · Middleto

Palestine · Linden · Norfolk · Poplar · Corner · Plum Point · Slaydens Crossing · Early · Grove · Michigan City
etley · Due West · De Soto · Front · Day's · Nesbitt · Pleasant Hill · Olive Branch · Lamar · Canaa
Brinkley · Bledsoe · DESOTO · McKays · Hernando · Byhalia · Hudsonville · Spring Hill · Black Jack · BENTON
Clifton · Alexis · Rosa · Bower · Eudora · Cockrum · Watson · Holly Springs · Red Banks · Colbert · Salem · Yellow R.
Marianna · Bordeaux Isl. · Commerce · Prattsville · Love's Sta. · Palestine · Wall Hill · Independence · Waco · Coleman · Pott's Camp · Ashland · Shelby · Ripley
La Grange · Tunica · Donnell · Arkabutla · Thyatira · Waterford · Chulahoma · Lebanon · Tuscaleeche · Hickory Flat · Cotton Plant
Duncan · Lee · Austin · Hudson · Strayhorn · Senatobia · Tyro · aw's · Hill · Nicksville · Cornersville · Darden · Myrtle · New Alba
Marvell · Planters ville · Flower Lake · Dubbs · Poplar · Looxahoma · Glenville · Como Depot · Harmontown · Abbeville · Maple Springs · Walton · Fredonia
Palmer · Barton · Eagle Lake · Glendale · Longtown · Strattons · Melrose · Peach Creek · Sledgeville · College Hill · Caswell · Beulah
Helena · Mastodon · Pleasant Grove · Star Place · Sardis · PANOLA · OXFORD · Liberty Hill · Esparanza · Poplar · PONTOTOC
Old Town · Delta · Pleasant Grove · The Gums · Tallahatchie · Cora · Denmark · Cherry Creek · PONTO
Halsteadville · Friar's · Jonestown · Batesville · Springport · Yocona · LaFayette Springs · DeLay · Dixie · Toccopola
Point · Prairieville · Belen · Clarksdale · COAHOMA · Central Academy · Reynolds · Taylor · Orwood · Paris · Dallas · Mud Cr. · Randolph · Algo
Hulberton · QUITMAN · Eureka Springs · Courtland · Elliott's Mill · Spring Dale · Red
Pushmataha · Sunflower Landing · Baxter · County Line · Pope's Depot · Water · Sarepta · Matthews · River
kansas · Malone's Landing · Dublin · Crevi · Harrison Sta. · Dickson · Valley · Banner · Money · Houlka
Post · Australia · Teasdale · Oakland · Pine Valley · Yota
Lake Concordia · Concordia · Centre Point · Charleston · Tillatoba · Air Mount · YALOBUSHA · CALHOUN · Reid · Cherry R. · CH
poleon · Victoria · Terrene · Hood · TALLAHATCHIE · Garner · Coffeeville · Cotton Valley · Elzy · Houston
Rosedale · Barlow's Lake · Sharkey · Liveretts · Hardy Sta. · Torrance · ann's Mill · PITTSBOROUGH · Sonora · Spar
Riverton · Goose Lake · Swan Lake · Graball · Junction · Cole's Creek · Benela · Erh · Atlanta
Talledora · Black Bayou · Cascilla · Grenada · Williamsville · Big Creek · Sabougla · Hopewell · Dixie · Spring
Beulah · Sporine · SUN · Minter City · Graysport · Slate Spring · Bently · Hohenlinden · Ander- · Cumberland
Neblett's Landing · Emmaville · GRENADA · Felix · Providence · Cadaretta · Monte Vista · son · Line Cr. · Tom
BOLIVAR · Stormville · Lehrton · McNutt · Elliott · Redding · Embry · Spring · Bluff
Cath's Point · Bolivar · Shell Mound · Smith's Mills · Eskridge · Sweatman · Duck · Bellefontaine · WEBSTER
Gladstone · Porter's Bayou · Jone's Bayou · Valley Hill · Sawyers · Hill · Alva · WALTHALL · Greensborough · Spring Valley · Ste
Mound Landing · FLOWER · LEFLORE · Winona · Lodi · Double Springs
Offutt · Moss Bend · Saint's Rest · Greenwood · MONT · Greensborough
Spanish · Longview · Eatonia · GEORGIA · Itta Bena · Carrollton · Mayfield · PAC. · La Grange
Stoneville · Indian Bayou · Johnsonville · Roebuck · Hemingway · Kilmichael · Bywy · Dido · Agricul
eenwood · Woodburn · Sidon · CARROLL · Poplar Creek · Bankston · CHOCTAW · OK
ding · Refuge · Arcola · Kinloch · Sky Lake · Sheppardtown · Vaiden · GOMERY · Huntsville · Chester · Wilcox · Snowville · Wb
Glenora · Estill · Gumwood · Markysville · 52 Mile Siding · Liddell · French Camps · New Prospect · Spay · Webster
Isl. · WASHINGTON · Deevolante · Idlewild · Acona · Black Hawk · Irvingville · Conkerville · Barks- · dale · Thompsonville · Sim
Lake Washington · Westburgh · Belzona · Tchula · Emory · Brock · West · Beatty · Mitchell's Mills · Hesterville · Wells · Louisville · Perk
Leota Landing · Sharkey · Palmetto · Marcella · HOLMES · McGee's · Durant · ATTALA · Newtonville · WINS
Carolina · Nittayuma · Gum Grove · Roseneath · Lexington · Gray's Mill · Kosciusko · Rome · Randall's Mill · Noxapater
Augusta · Hollands · Home · Rokeby · Kosciusko Jc. · Goodman · Wamba · Coopwo
Duncanspy · McKinneyville · Parkers · Chew's Landing · Sallis · Centre · Plattsburg
Rolling Fork · Lake City · Green Hill · Belle Prairie · Pickens Sta. · Cuba · Vowell · Yorka · North Bog
Triune · Free Run · New Port · Oak Ridge · Palona · Hemus · Lake Burnside
Mayersville · Campbellsville · Home Park · Couparle · Thomastown · Conway · Coosa · M
SHARKEY · Watsonia · Yazoo City · Vaughans · City · Deason- · ville · Camden · Kirkwood · Carthage · Edinburgh · Philadelphia
Hay's Landing · Evana · Benton · Ofahoma · LEAKE · HINESHOB
Arcadia · Smedes · Halpin · YAZOO · Way's Bluff · Sulphur Springs · Lamenta · Colah · Laurel · Milldale · Watkinsville · Cush
Ingomar · Dick · Santartia · Millville · Sharon · Standing Pine · Madden · Tuscola · Dixon · Tucker · M
QUENA · Phoenix · Dover · Woodbine · Good Hope · Lena · Estesmill · Walnut Gr. · Beech Springs
Russellville · Vernon · Cash · New · Ireland · Lacerne · Union
Brunswick · Flower · Livingston · Calhoun · Ludlow · Horaceville · Damascus · County · Mount
Haynes Bluff · Fox Landing · Prattville · Goshen Spring · Beach · Harpersville · Line · Batt
Forest · Redwood · Oak Ridge · MADISON · Canton · Fannin · Leesburgh · SCOTT · NEWTO
allulah · Home · Bolton's Depot · Madison Sta. · Lucknow · Pelahatchee Depot · Morton · Hillsborough · Conehatta · Decatur · M
WARREN · VICKSBURG · Clinton · Touga · Spears · Tank · FOREST · Newton · Hickory
Mound · Bovina · Edward's Depot · VICK · Rowells · Brandon · Homewood · MERIDIAN · Lake · Lawrence · Tarlow R.
JACKSON · Bolers · HIS · DS

*"I went up to Lula to see my aunt, and being up there, I heard that that was where Charlie Patton lived. I'd heard of him, heard a lot of his records, so I made myself acquainted with him. I knew a little more about him than he did me. Now Willie Brown, he was living up on Robinsonville, and he and Charlie Patton had known one another for years. They'd gotten together out on a white man's place they call the Dockery Plantation. It's way down and out from Ruleville -- somewhere down in there."*

Charley had already brought another friend, a fiddler and singer named Henry Sims, from Farrell, Mississippi, as well as a second guitarist and "commentor," who was probably Willie Brown, for sessions late in 1929. For his session in July, 1930, he brought up Willie and Son, as well as a girl, Louise Johnson, who was from Willie's town of Robinsonville. The music from these sessions is one of the most significant group of delta blues to be recorded, and it is possible to hear in each of the other singers as well an influence from the voice and personality of Charley Patton.

The delta soil that produced Charley, Willie and Son left its dust on all of them, but each of them was strongly individual. They all spoke with a delta accent, but each of them spoke in his own manner. Charley's was a heavier voice than the others, heavier and stronger despite his small size. His accompaniment style was as intense as his singing. In his blues he used a number of scales, with the pentatonic forms predominating, although in his folk songs and gospel pieces the scale was often the European diatonic. For his most personal blues he used melodies which became distinctive with him, although they may be older songs that he altered for his own use. Without earlier recordings or field transcriptions it will always be impossible to tell with any certainty the sources of the delta blues that were recorded in the late twenties. The melody he used most frequently was a repetitive pattern of only four notes, and may have been derived from an older field song.

Example 7

(High Water Everywhere)
♩ = 132

Lord the whole 'round country the river is overflowed

Lord the whole 'round country, man it's over-

flowed                                    I would

go to the hill country, but they got me barred.

His accompaniments for the melody varied considerably, but there was usually an ostinato in an 8/8 rhythm for the first line, which resolved with more or less confusion to one of his less difficult accompaniment patterns in 4/4 for the rest of the verse. He used this melody for several blues, among them "High Water Everywhere," "Moon Going Down," "Bird Nest Bound," "Revenue Man Blues," "Jersey Bull Blues," "Screamin' And Hollerin' The Blues," "Love Is My Stuff," "Rattlesnake Blues," and "Heart Like Railroad Steel." The other melody which was distinctive with Patton was the ballad-like melody that he used for the two narrative blues about his prison experiences, "Tom Rushen Blues" and "High Sheriff Blues." The scale was close to a European diatonic in its use of the second, not only as an upper auxiliary in measure 2, but as a passing tone in measure 8. Usually Patton moved his melodic line by disjunct intervals of at least a third, but in both these blues the angularity of his line was softened by the use of the second and sixth of the scale. The vocal line ended on the fifth of the scale- e in the key of A - in both of the opening two lines; so Patton reinforced the tonic A by humming a c# - a to end the phrase.

Example 8

(High Sheriff Blues)

♩ = 110

When trial's in Bel_zon_i ai_n't no use scream_in' an'

cry — in', Um — m, When the trial's in Bel_zon_i

ain't no use to scream an' cry, Um — m. Mis_ter

(X)          (guitar)

Ware will take you back to Bel_zon_i jail_house for life.          When

50

For other blues he often used melodies that were widely known throughout the Mississippi and Tennessee area. The Memphis medicine show singers were in the delta every summer, and they left as many melodies behind them as they picked up for their own use. The melody which Patton used for "It Won't Be Long" and "Banty Rooster Blues" was the melody known in Memphis as "Brownsville Blues," and used by a number of singers in that area. "Banty Rooster Blues" may have been derived from a 1927 recording made in Texas by Walter Rhodes, "The Crowing Rooster," but it seems more probable that both of them learned the song from an earlier source which is still untraced. Patton's "Going To Move To Alabama," - derived from Jim Jackson's "Kansas City Blues" - is one of the few songs which can be tied to a direct source. "Elder Green Blues" also used one of the widely known melodies, the "Don't You Leave Me Here" melody, which early became part of the developing musical vocabulary of instrumental jazz. Although many of his other songs came from either work gang chants or religious hymns, he used little vocal embellishment, centering the tone directly on the note and limiting himself to occasional portmenti, descending sliding tones on notes ending his verses. The voice itself was very dark and forced, with an almost harsh tone.

The blues is a loose form which is thought of by most blues singers as an expression of words or emotion rather than musical complexity, and the melodic rhythms have almost always been dictated by the text of the verse. Patton kept in many of his blues, like the vestigial tail of a spring tadpole in the mud of the Sunflower River, the irregular rhythmic pattern of a spontaneous work song. In these blues the accompaniment phrase between the lines was shortened and the first words of the vocal phrase became a half measure, almost always in 2/4. The usual rhythmic pattern for the verse was 2/4 - 4/4 - 4/4 - 4/4 - 4/4 - 2/4 - 4/4 - 4/4 4/4 - 4/4 - 2/4 - 4/4 - 4/4 - 4/4 - 4/4. It was an awkward form, but it was an effective variant on the more conventional blues forms.

Example 9

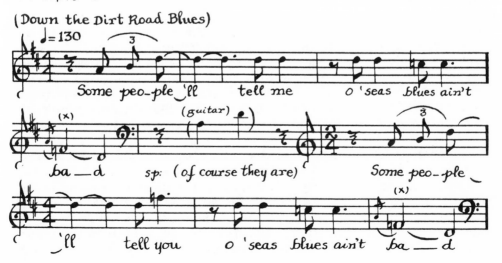

(Down the Dirt Road Blues)

51

It must not have been them

O' seas blues I had.　　　　(pick up)

In his accompaniments he used E and G tunings, as well as the conventional "minor" tuning. For some of his songs, among them "Pony Blues" and the "Moon Going Down" group, the accompaniment was built on tonic harmony in ostinato patterns, but for most of his blues and for many of the hymns and folk songs, he played a melodic line in near unison with the voice and picked a bass line with his thumb. The bass line usually alternated between the lowest tonic and the octave or the fifth above it.

Several of the blues were finger picked, among them "Down The Dirt Road Blues" and "Elder Green Blues." He still used a melodic line which closely followed his voice, and to sustain the guitar note he usually played in doubled 8th note patterns. Often the interplay between the vocal rhythm and the guitar rhythm in this style was highly complex, and he also used hesitations - following a note in the guitar with a short figure in the voice - in several of the pieces. Most often, however, he used a knife or a bottleneck to play a melodic line that was closer to the altered scale of the voice. "Banty Rooster Blues," "Tom Rushen Blues," "Hammer Blues," and most of the religious songs were played in this style, with the thumb reiterating an insistent bass line in the lower strings of the guitar. In the open E tuning he limited himself to a suggestion of harmonic change in his blues, but in religious songs like "I'm Going Home", he barred at the fifth fret for the subdominant chord. In the G tuning he was able to outline the I - IV - V blues harmonic patterns, and in the conventional tuning he had some skill in more elaborate chord progressions. In his performance of "A Spoonful," an old country song that Paramount labeled "Spoonful Blues," he even developed an accompaniment in an embryonic VI - II - V - I progression. There was, however, an earlier recording of the song by Papa Charlie Jackson, "All I Want Is A Spoonful," and this harmonic progression was a characteristic of Jackson's style; so Patton's recording may have been influenced by Jackson's performance five years earlier.

The largest group of songs other than blues that Charley left on record were religious. As his sister remembered he learned them from his father when he was still a boy. Many of the performances, especially the "Prayer of Death" and the duet with Bertha Lee, "Oh Death," were as harsh and searing as his blues. The accompaniments were played with a knife or bottleneck, and there was the forceful rhythm of the lower strings and the thin whine on the upper strings to reinforce the rough vocal shout. Although he was an exciting religious singer, he will be always thought of as a blues singer because he sang the gospel material in generally conventional texts, but in his blues he was intensely individualistic.

Charley's life didn't change much when the Paramount sessions ended. He had to sing almost every night to make a living, and he moved from small town to small town in the delta. He went back to Lula after the July, 1930, session, and began living a tempestuous life in a plantation cabin with Bertha Lee. He was in his forties and she was sixteen when they began living together. He even mentioned her in one of his songs, "Poor Me."

"Don't the moon look pretty shining down through the trees,
I can see Bertha Lee, Lord, but she can't see me ...

They lived in Lula for a year or so, then moved to Holly Springs, in northern Mississippi, about forty miles south-east of Memphis. The store keepers near the cabin where Charley and Bertha Lee lived remembered - talking to Wardlow and Klatzko - that she was "young and wild," that Charley was drinking a lot, and that he and Bertha Lee "... did their share of fighting with each other." Bertha also sang the blues, although she learned nearly all of her songs from Charley. "I couldn't compose things the way he could." Sometimes they sang in the back of the store and one of the owners, a white man named John Allen, played the fiddle with them. It was a rough life. As Bertha Lee remembered, "We broke down many a plantation house having parties every night." For Charley, who did most of the singing, the life was hard and demanding. Bertha Lee was young and strong, but Charley's early years of field work and the constant playing had begun to wear on him. He was already suffering from a heart leakage, so he wasn't able to do any work in the fields and he had to keep singing. They traveled together on most of his trips, and in Cleveland, Mississippi, she remembers sitting and listening while Charley tried to teach his style to a young singer named Chester Burnett, who was to become known in Chicago as "Howling Wolf." "Charley worried with him all day before that man would leave him alone." The limits of Charley's world had again become the vague, violet gray line of the horizon, the meandering dirt tracks across the fields, and the straggling pine woods of the delta. His recordings for Paramount, however, were a tenuous cord that still tied him to the commercial music world. Late in the fall of 1933 he was contacted by Mr. Callaway, the recording director for Vocalion Records, and he and Bertha Lee went together to New York to record in January of 1934.

> *Mr. Callaway sent for us to come up on the train and we were
> there about three weeks making records. We didn't work all
> the time, because it took the morning before Charley had his
> voice ready. The company picked us up at two in the evening
> and we always did our singing then. There were great big
> bottles of whiskey sitting on the floor, but I just drank a little
> to keep my nerve up. I'm not an extreme drinker. Then after
> we'd finish we had dances for Mr. Callaway and them every
> evening in the studio...*

They were in the studio three afternoons, Tuesday, Wednesday, and
Thursday, January 30, 31, and February 1, 1934, and they went back to
Holly Springs a few days later.

It had been four years since Patton had recorded, but there was very
little stylistic difference between the later sessions for Vocalion, and
the earlier sessions for Paramount. There were differences, but they
were more of a technical nature than musical. Vocalion used a much
better microphone and positioned it closer to him, so the sound was a
little lighter and clearer. Also, he was using a different guitar, and it
had a slightly wirier sound. He did two of his earlier songs in different
versions. "Pony Blues" on Paramount, became "Stone Pony Blues" on
Vocalion, and "Tom Rushen Blues" became "High Sheriff Blues." The
singing had changed so little that the difference between the two versions
was probably no greater than the difference in the sound of Charley's
voice when he'd just started singing at a dance and when he finally
finished five or six hours later. The improved recording technique made
it obvious that he was having some trouble with hoarseness, but this had
always been a problem. He forced his voice, and the strain was evident
in all of his sessions. If there was the beginning of a change in his style
it was in the guitar accompaniments. In 1934 there was a rhythmic
diffuseness, and less of the finger picking that had characterized the
accompaniments of 1929 and 1930.

Less than half of the songs that he and Bertha Lee did for Vocalion
were issued in the bleak years of the Depression, but even without
them he was still a prolific singer by the standards of the early blues
period. Nearly sixty titles were released, more than thirty of them blues
and the rest gospel and folk songs. In his recordings, more than in the
recordings of any other delta singer of the period, it was possible to
sense some of the variety of delta music. There were strains from older
work songs in pieces like "When Your Way Gets Dark" and there were
vivid sketches of delta life in blues like "High Water Everywhere."
There were dance pieces, country ballads, even bits of white sentimental
country music in pieces like "Some These Days I'll Be Gone." In all
of the songs his style was the same, a harsh, heavy voice used without
embellishment, the melodies emphasizing a few notes within an octave
range, the guitar accompaniment roughly following the voice in the upper
strings and reiterating the rhythm in the lower strings. In all of them
there was, as well, a fierce, almost raging power, and an insistent
strength and rhythm.

Perhaps because his music was so much part of the delta soil the young men like Robert Johnson who hung around the dances where he was playing didn't learn much of his style. Patton in many ways came at the end of a period of musical development, and even though he extended and developed the music of the plantations and the cabin rows he still kept its entanglement with the life of the delta counties. The younger men were more restless, they traveled further, and their blues, through the influence of phonograph records, had more than a delta accent. The singing of Charley's close friends, Henry Sims and Willie Brown, and Bertha Lee, was strongly influenced by him, but when Booker White said that he "... wanted to be like old Charley Patton", he meant that he wanted to be like the man Charley Patton more than that he wanted to sing like him. In all of Booker's recorded blues the only suggestion of Patton's style is in the dark voice, and perhaps in the melodic line of "Fixin' To Die," which seems to have some relationship to Charley's beginning vocal phrases in "Frankie And Albert." Son House was already singing when he met Patton, and the only suggestion, again, is in the voice and perhaps in some of his guitar style. Robert Johnson hung around Charley and Son at dances, but it was Son that drew him more than Charley. The only element of Charley's style that he took seems to have been the haunting knife passages on the upper strings in Charley's "When Your Way Gets Dark." They became part of Johnson's later "Come On In My Kitchen." Howling Wolf, perhaps, learned the most from Patton, and despite the changes in his music as the blues moved from the country cabins to the city slums, some of Charley's voice and inflections still color Wolf's style. But if Charley was not to be a strong influence on the development of the blues in the 1930's, he was one of the greatest singers the blues had yet produced, and it is difficult to find another Mississippi singer whose achievement, in breath, range, and consistency, can be measured against his.

Charley and Bertha Lee went back to their cabin when the sessions in New York ended. It was a small, run-down shack at a place called Longswitch, just outside of Holly Grove. It was one of a row of shacks owned by a man named Tom Robinson. Willie and Son had gone up to Lake Cormorant, a small town in De Soto County about twenty five miles south of Memphis, and they heard from Charley a few days after he'd gotten back. Son remembers that it was for some more recordings. [7.]

> *... He got in touch with another record company -- one in Jackson, Mississippi -- called Spear's Phonograph Company, 111 North Farrow Street. This man wanted Charlie to get Willie and I to come down to Jackson to make some church songs. So Charlie sent his wife, Bertha, up after us in a car. We hung around Holly Ridge two or three days before we lit out for Jackson, and we made the songs. This guy wanted us to make like we were "sanctified" people and make some "sanctified" songs and not use our names. So we made a song for him,*

> *"I Had A Dream Last Night Troubled Me," concerning King Nebuchadnezzar. After that, we went on back to Charlie's and we stayed about three more weeks. We went all around through the country playing, all three of us together. So Willie and I went on back to Lake Commorant, where we were living then, and about two weeks after we got back, we got a telegram from Bertha, that was the girl said to be his wife. The telegram said that Charlie was dead...*

Bertha Lee lives in Chicago now, a large, good-natured woman who spends her days working in a shabby used clothing store on Chicago's west side. There is a bare bulb hanging from the ceiling, an oil stove in the middle of the floor. Bertha Lee sits at a small table near the door, the radio turned on to a local music station, helping the people who lean against the heaped piles of old clothes trying to decide if something will fit. "That's too small for you, dear, there's another skirt down in the pile somewhere that's more your size." She has glasses now, and usually wears a dark dress and a sweater as she sits at her table. She remarried after Charley died, and she was widowed again when her second husband died a few years ago, but she has lived in Chicago since 1949 and she has friends and family to keep the evenings from getting too lonely. More than thirty years have passed since she was the "young and wild" girl who lived with Charley Patton in a shack in the Mississippi delta, but she still smiles when she thinks back to the singing and the dances, and even to the fights that she and Charley had while they lived together. He died only a few weeks after they got back from New York. Like most men who become local heroes there were stories that he had been poisoned, or that he had died of a tetanus infection from a knife wound, or that he had been killed in a fight, but his heart, already damaged, had been weakened by chronic bronchitis, and the life he was leading was too chaotic for him to rest. Bertha Lee looked out through the window, across the street to a crowd of children playing on the sidewalk, their scarves wrapped around their necks against the winter cold and their ears covered with bright cloth ear muffs.

> *Charley was playing for a white dance - you have to work so much harder at a white dance in the South, they don't want to stop dancing. When he come home he was so hoarse he couldn't talk and he couldn't get his breath. He had to get up out of bed at night and open the windows so he could get some air. He lived three weeks after that but he was too weak to do anything. He was laying across my lap when he died.*

# 3. SON HOUSE

A tall, gangling man, moving a little stiffly from his long years as a field hand and a laborer. At the edge of a crowd his white Stetson hat turning like a leaf in the spring wind as he answers questions in a low voice. His face - still thin and handsome despite the lines etched by the worries and the disappointments of his sixty-three years - looks from one to another of the young white faces pressed around him, unsure of their attitudes toward him, unsure of their response to his music. A delta blues man, the only singer left of the group around Charley Patton, Eddie James House Jr., ''Son'' House, at a folk festival in New York City in the late spring of 1965.

Until the summer of 1964 the delta blues was still only a few names on phonograph records. The field song elements in the music, the glimpsed presence of endless work, drinking, prison, the sexuality of the words, the raw strength of the singing - from these sources it wasn't difficult to relate the delta style to the life of the sharecroppers and field hands living in the steaming swelter of the Yazoo cotton country. But art is only in part sociology. Each of the delta singers came from the same backgrounds, from the same rows of plantation shacks, the same weathered clusters of buildings around a crossroads country store, but each of them sang in his own style. Until the 1963 trip by Wardlow and Klatzko there were only a few scattered reminiscences of the delta singers. ''Robert Johnson played one night with us at a dance hall in West Memphis.'' ''Charley Patton was a large, fat man who come 'round the cabin when my daddy was living.'' ''Son House was playing in a road house with Charley Patton when I seen him. He got drunk and climbed up on a table to give a sermon.'' Not enough to fill in the human quality of the individual singers. Without the background of their lives it was impossible to tell why their voices were different, their emotional concerns were different, and their music - even though it came from the same sources and backgrounds - was different. It has only been since the early weeks of July, 1964, that it has been possible to discuss the delta blues as personal art instead of impersonal sociology. Working separately, but within a few days of each other, John Fahey, Bill Barth, and Henry Vestine, driving from California, found Skip James in the Tunica County Hospital; and Dick Waterman, Phil Spiro, and Nick Perls, driving down from Cambridge and New York, found Son House. When they located him it was another long drive - Son had left Mississippi and moved to Rochester, New York, twenty years before - but their long drive has meant not only priceless information about the great Mississippi singers, but also the return to music of one of the greatest of these blues men, still singing in the purest delta blues strain. Through Son, and through Bertha Lee Patton, who had finally been traced to Chicago by Bernard Klatzko a few months before Son was located, the story of the Mississippi blues has become a living, human story.

In the winter of 1965 Son talked about his life to Julius Lester, a young writer living in New York, and his reminiscences not only filled in the backgrounds of his own musical style, but also of the music of the other singers he encountered in his wanderings. He was born on March 21, 1902, on a farm in Coahoma County, just outside of Lyon, a small town a few miles from Clarksdale. As he told Lester,[1]

> *... They called it Riverton, and right down the road a little past Riverton -- about two miles -- is where I was born. After I got up around seven or eight years old, my mother took me to Louisiana, and that's mostly where I grew up to call myself a man. We moved to a place called Tallulah, Louisiana. That's up in the north part of Louisiana, across the river from Vicksburg.*

> *My mother and my father they separated, and when I got up to be some size, I started working. One while, I was gathering moss down in Algiers, Louisiana. That was in 1917, '17, and on up to about '20. I wasn't big enough to occupy a heavy job. I was gathering that grey moss out of trees. Did it near about like they do cotton. Bale it up and ship it away and they would make mattresses and things out of it. I was quite young then -- twenty, twenty-one -- along in that category.*

> *I wasn't playing guitar then. I was mostly a church man. Brought up in church and didn't believe in anything else but church, and it always made me mad to see a man with a guitar and singing these blues and things. Just wasn't brought up to it. Brought up to sing in choirs. That's all I believed in, then.*

> *My father, though, was kind of ratty along then. He had seven brothers and they had a little band that played music all the time for the Saturday night balls. He played a bass horn. He had been a church man, but he had gotten out. Finally, he*

*went back to church and laid it all down, quit drinking, and became a deacon. He went pretty straight from then on.*

*After my mother died, I left and came back up in Mississippi where the rest of my people was. So I was just to and fro then. I wouldn't stay anywhere too long after I got to be called myself a man, you know. I just wanted to ramble. I wouldn't get too far away from home, though. I'd get up around Memphis, over in Arkansas, back through Louisiana, and on back to Mississippi. And I'd make a living by working in the cotton fields. I could plow, pick, and chop cotton. One while, I worked for a man who was in the cattle business. That was down in Louisiana and that was when I started wearing a cowboy hat. I got that style from the other guys. The hat I wore was a big brown with a white band around the crown, and when I went to playing guitar, I was still wearing it. I liked it. But something happened and I got rid of it. It got too old or something, so by the time I was making records, I wasn't wearing it.*

*At that time, there was mostly farm work, and sometimes it got pretty critical. Low wages and -- well, people kind of suffered a little during some of those years. Suffered right smart. In some places, they got along a little better than they did in others. But they stayed up against it mostly. Bad housing and all that kind of stuff. Of course, they'd get plenty of just old common food, but they didn't make enough money to do any good. Some of those that grew crops -- if they paid their debts for the food they ate during the year, why, if they came out and cleared as much as forty or fifty dollars for a year, they were satisfied. Out of a whole year's work! Of course, along then, they didn't see into it too much because they'd been used to it for so long. They didn't worry over it because they always knew if they didn't have the money, they was still going to eat and have a place to stay, such as it was. So they didn't complain and worry too much about it.*

*After they commenced waking up, some started going different places and came back with the news that they were doing so much better. "Up in such-and-such-a-place, they pay so-much-and-so-much. That's what I make." Well, that wakes the other guys up. He sees his old buddy all dressed up and looking so nice, and so they comment from one to another and commence to easing out to these different places. If they get far as St. Louis, oh, Jesus! They thought they was way somewhere.*

*I did it myself! I had a friend who was up there working in the Commonwealth Steel Plant in St. Louis. He came back and was telling me about it, and the first thing you know, I'd sneaked out and gone to St. Louis. We were getting a dollar an hour along then. That was big money, you know. That was way back yonder. A dollar an hour! Whooo! That was along in 1922 or '23. The Commonwealth Steel Plant. We lived in St. Louis, and the plant was in East St. Louis, just across the river. Making that dollar an hour. I was a big shot then. I stayed up there about six or eight months and got the hot-foot again and came on back down in Mississippi. I wasn't contented anywhere long. I was young and just loved to ramble.*

*I was just ramblified, you know. Especially after I started playing music. That was the one thing gave it to me. People wanting us to come over in Arkansas to play for picnics, and we just didn't want to be stationary, to be obligated to anybody. We figured we could make it better without plowing so much.*

*I started playing guitar in 1928, but I got the idea around about 1927. I saw a guy named Willie Wilson and another one named Reuben Lacy. All before then, I just hated to see a guy with a guitar. I was so churchy! I came along to a little place they call Matson, a little below Clarksdale. It was on a Saturday and these guys were sitting out front of a place and they were playing. Well, I stopped, because the people were all crowded around. This boy, Willie Wilson, had a thing on his finger like a small medicine bottle, and he was zinging it, you know. I said, "Jesus! Wonder what's that he's playing?" I knew that guitars hadn't usually been sounding like that. So I eases up close enough to look and I see what he has on his finger. "Sounds good!" I said. "Jesus! I like that!" And from there, I got the idea and said, "I believe I want to play one of them things." So I bought an old piece of guitar from a fella named Frank Hopkins. I gave him a dollar-and-a-half for it. It was nearly all to pieces, but I didn't know the difference. The back was all broken in, but I got it from him and began to try to play. It didn't have but five strings on it, though. So I showed it to Willie Wilson and explained to him what I wanted to do. I wanted to learn to play. He said, "Well, you'll never learn this way. You need another string. Takes six strings. It's all busted in the back, too. Tell you what I'll do. I'll see if I can fix it up for you." So he got some tape and stuff and taped it all up and got a string and put that on and then he tuned it. He tuned it in Spanish to make it easier for me to start. Then he showed me a couple of chords. I got me an old bottle. Cut my finger a couple of times trying to fix the thing like his, but finally I started to zinging, too. Finally, I got the idea about how to tune it myself. I used to be a leader in the choir and they were singing the old vocal music at that time, you know, like the "do-re-mi's", so I got the idea to make the guitar go like that, and in a couple of weeks time, I was able to play a little tune. It was a little tune I'd heard Willie Wilson play called, "Hold Up, Sally, Take Your Big Legs Offa Mine." So the next time he came by, I showed him I could play it. He said, "Come on and play with me tonight." It was Saturday night. I said, "I ain't good enough for that." He said, "Oh, yes, you is. You just play that. I'll back you up." So I started with him just like that. Finally, he left from around there, but I kept on playing and got better and better, you know. I'd set up and concentrate on songs, and then went to concentrating on me rhyming words, rhyming my own words. "I can make my own songs," I said. And that's the way I started.*

Many of the delta men went into recording studios during this period, but Willie Wilson does not seem to have done any recording. Lacy recorded for Paramount a year after Son heard him play. It was only two years before Son himself recorded for Paramount. He went to Lula to see his aunt, met Charley Patton while he was there, and through Charley he did a test for H.C. Spears in Jackson. In his conversation with Lester he remembered, [2].

*There was this man, A. C. Laibley, who was Charlie's manager at that time. He was in Grafton, Wisconsin. That's where the Paramount Record laboratory was. He came down on a little tour hunting talent,, and he stopped by and told Charlie they wanted him to come up for recordings again. Well, Charlie had been recording for them and he told them about me. So they said, "Bring him along with you and bring Willie Brown." So he left a hundred dollars for expenses. He got another fella that had a car. This other fella had a group, a gospel group, and they called themselves the Delta Big Four. They made themselves famous with a song called "Four and Twenty Elders On Their Knees". His name was Will Ford and he had a good car, so A. C. Laibley left the money for him to drive us up there. There was a girl named Louise Johnson who came along with us. She and Willie were both from Robinsonville. So we went up there and made our recordings separately, except for about two songs Willie and I played together. I recorded "Preachin' Blues", "Black Mama", "Mississippi County Farm", and "Clarksdale Moan". Willie Brown and I played that last one together. I think that's about all. Close as I can get to it. It's been so long.*

*The girl playing the piano, Louise, well, we'd spike in and help her a little bit. She was a good piano player, but being up there and being among a lot of people, well, you know, some people get nervous. So we'd cheer her up by yelling to her and saying funny things and we'd hit a lick or two with the guitars. Just to give her more spirit.*

*I got paid forty dollars for making those records. At that
time, I just had the big eyes. Forty dollars! Making it that
easy and that quick! It'd take me near about a whole year to
make forty dollars in the cotton patch. I was perfectly satisfied. I showed off a whole lot with that when I got back to
Lula, Mississippi.*

The sessions were held in Grafton, Wisconsin, sometime in the summer
of 1930, and Son did three long blues and three shorter ones. Copies
have not yet been located of all of the songs, but the three long pieces
have been found: "My Black Mama, Parts 1 and 2" on Paramount 13042,
"Preachin' The Blues, Parts 1 and 2" on Paramount 13013, and "Dry
Spell Blues, Parts 1 and 2" on Paramount 12990. Each of the three
was among the greatest blues performances recorded in the 'twenties.
"Dry Spell Blues" was the most socially directed of the three, and it had
some of the largeness of concept of Patton's "High Water Everywhere."

Them dry spell blues are fallin', drivin' people from door to door.
Dry spell blues are fallin', drivin' people from door to door.
Them dry spell blues has put everybody on the kindlin' floor.

Now the people down South soon won't have no homes.
Lord, the people down South soon won't have no homes.
Lord, this dry spell have parched all the cotton and corn ....

Pork chops forty-five cents a pound, cotton is only ten.
Pork chops forty-five cents a pound, cotton is only ten.
I can't keep no women, no no now or then.

So dry old boweevil turn up its nose and die.
So dry old boweevil turn up its nose and die.
Now ain't nothing to do to make moonshine and rye ....

It's a dry old spell everywhere I been.
Oh it's a dry old spell everywhere I been.
I believe to my soul this old world is bound to end.

Lord, I stood in my back yard, wrung my hands and grieved.
I stood in my back yard, I wrung my hands and grieved.
Oh I couldn't see nothing, couldn't see nothing green.

Oh Lord, have mercy if you please.
Oh Lord, have mercy if you please.
Make your rain come down and give our poor hearts ease ....

In the other blues there was less of Patton's concern with place, and
the pieces had a highly individualistic textual and musical orientation.
There was little use of the unison melody in his accompaniments;

62

usually the guitar played a bare, drumming rhythm in the lower strings and Son sang against it with considerable melodic freedom. His voice was strident and tense, and the rhythms had little of Patton's regularity. There was also much more vocal embellishment, and the guitar, played with a bottleneck, developed its own set figures at the end of each vocal phrase. There was no harmonic change in the accompaniment of "Preachin' The Blues," and the harmonic progression in "My Black Mama" was limited to the bass note played with the thumb. "My Black Mama" was a loosely grouped set of verses more or less well known through the delta, but in "Preachin' The Blues," even though many of the verses were also conventional, it was possible to sense some of the confusion in Son that gave his music its decisiveness. He had been unable to decide completely between the irreligious life of the blues man and the Christian life of the preacher. It is an indecision that still disturbs him more than thirty years later. As he sang in the blues, "I have religion on this very day ... But the womens and whiskey, well, they would not let me pray." He feels that "Preachin' The Blues" itself is a reflection of his confusion. "I can't hold God in one hand and the Devil in the other one ..."

Oh, I'm gonna get me a religion, I'm gonna join the Baptist church.
Oh, I'm gonna get me a religion, I'm gonna join the Baptist church.
I'm gonna be a Baptist preacher, and I sure won't have to work.

Oh, I'm preach these blues and I want everybody to shout.
Umh, I want everybody to shout.
I'm gonna do like a prisoner, I'm gonna roll my time on out.

Oh, 'way in my room I bow down to pray.
Oh, in my room I bow down to pray.
Well, the blues came 'long and they blown my (babe) away.

Oh, I wish I had me a heaven of my own.
  Sp. (Great God Almighty!)
Umh, heaven of my own.
Well, I'd give all my women a long, long happy home.

Well, I love my baby just like I love myself.
Umh, just like I love myself.
Well, if she don't have me she won't have nobody else.

Well, I'm a poor man, I'm gonna kneel down in prayer.
Oh, I'm a poor man, gonna kneel down in prayer.
Well, I guess I'm gonna do my preachin' (          )

Now, I met the blues this morning walking just like a man.
Umh, walking just like a man.
I said "Good morning, blues, now gimme your right hand."

Now, there's nothing now baby, lord, that's gonna worry my mind.
Umh, now that's gonna worry my mind.
Oh, to satisfy, I got the longest line.

Oh, I got to stay on the job, I ain't got no time to lose.
Umh, I ain't got no time to lose.
I swear to God, I got to preach these gospel blues.
   sp. (Great God Almighty!)

Oh, I'm gonna preach these blues until my feet have set down.
Oh, I'm gonna preach these blues now, until my feet have set down.
Well, it's very (constructive) I want you to jump straight up and
    down.

In the straining impatience of the melody there was still some of the
exhortation from his years as a rural preacher, and he was forced into
considerable rhythmic irregularity by the emotionalism of his singing.
The accompaniment was an insistent 8/8 pattern that continued without
change through the piece.

His "My Black Mama" was almost as irregular in the singing, but the lines were built around the hesitation in the opening phrase that was characteristic of the axe songs. In these songs the singer usually hesitates on the first beat of the measure as the blade of the axe bites into the log, and Son kept this hesitation in most of the verses; even though it meant breaking the line into two separate rhythmic units to give himself room for the hesitation. The accompaniment was in a mixed rhythm that had strong ties to the African background rhythms. The harmony was the root chord of I, V, I, IV, I, and the rhythmic pattern was,

4/4, 4/4, 4/4, 4/4, 6/4, 4/4, 4/4, 6/4, 4/4, 4/4

In an unguarded moment Son reiterated his feeling that he should never have left the church in an introduction to "Preachin' The Blues" at a concert at the University of Indiana in November, 1964. [3]

*This is one on me. Just (as) well admit it. This is the truth. 'Cause, some of it is a little addition, but the biggest of it is the truth. I used to be a preacher. I was brought up in church and I started preaching before I started this junk. Well, I got in a little bad company one time and they said, "Aw, c'mon, take a little nip with us. "I says, "Naw." "Aw, c'mon!" So I took a little nip. None of the members were around, so I took the little nip. And that one little nip called for another big nip. So there got to be a rumor around among my members, you know. And I began to wonder, now how can I stand up in the pulpit and preach to them, tell them how to live, and quick as I dismiss the congregation and I see ain't nobody looking and I'm doing the same thing. I says, that's not right. But I kept nipping around there and it got to be a public thing. I says, well, I got to do something, 'cause I can't hold God in one hand and the Devil in the other one. Them two guys don't get along together too well. I got to turn one of 'em loose. So I got out of the pulpit. So I said the next time I make a record, I'm gon' to name it "Preachin Blues." I'm preaching on this side and the blues on that side. I says, well, I'll just put 'em together and name it "Preachin Blues."*

It is this indecision which seems to give his blues some of their intensity of emotion, some of their pain and anguish. Often the most moving piece that he sings in a set is a religious song like "Motherless Children Have A Hard Time," the guitar playing a unison line with the bottleneck behind the voice. For Son singing the blues means a choice, and he still seems unable to reconcile himself to the choice he has made. Sometimes in a club he introduces each song with the same mumbled introduction, saying again and again,

> When they found me they got the news that I was a part-time
> preacher. Well, I was a preacher for a while, but I got to
> slipping around and doing ... other things. Then I went back
> to being a preacher; so you could say I was just a part-time
> preacher.

In the early 'forties Son left Mississippi and moved to Rochester. [4.]

> ... A friend of mine had moved up there and was working for
> a firm they call Simelton and Gold. They were making some
> kind of war equipment and he wrote and told me about them
> and what good wages they were paying. So I went on up. I
> worked on that job for a payday and then I quit. I didn't like it
> too well. So then I got a job with the New York Central out to
> East Rochester in the dispatch shop where they make boxcars
> and things like that. I got a job as a rivet-heater and kept that
> about two or three years. I got a promotion from the railroad
> company and they sent me over to Buffalo to get signed up for
> a job as a porter. There was a big fat colored guy over there
> doing the hiring at that time, so I got right on and stayed with
> that job ten, eleven years.

He kept playing mostly because he was still close to Willie Brown, and
they saw each other on occasional trips. Son went back to Mississippi
for a vacation, and Willie even came to Rochester for a brief period.
With Willie's death about 1948 Son finally put his music aside. "I said,
'Well, sir. All my boys are gone.' That was when I stopped playing."

"After he died, I just decided I wouldn't fool with playing any more. I
don't even know what I did with the guitar."

Son looks back over the years without much bitterness, but he feels
that all of them should have continued to record through the 'thirties,
despite the depression that hung over Mississippi. "We did our best
things then, after we'd got a little used to recording and knew what we
wanted to do."

Son was able to record again in 1942, when he was still playing regularly, and his individual style had reached a high point of development.
He went back to Mississippi for a visit and he was in Robinsonville
visiting relatives when Alan Lomax came to a local crossroads store
and set up portable recording equipment to collect material for the
Library of Congress archives. Son sang for him all day, even showing
him tunings and discussing his techniques; then he found that all he was
to be paid was a Coca Cola. He still smiles about it. "All I got was a
bottle of coke, but it was good and cold." It was ironic for everyone who
had been looking for Son for nearly a dozen years to learn that Alan had
known of his whereabouts all during this time.

In 1942 Son had lost some of the tense emotionalism of the first sessions, but his style was unchanged. There was still the hesitation before the beginning of the vocal phrase, the barren drumming on the bass strings of the guitar, and the whine of the bottleneck on the upper strings. He had developed the interplay between the voice and guitar to a high level of complexity. The guitar used melodic material that was often closely related to the vocal line, but still free from it, instead of the repetitive patterns in his older recordings. The integration in tone and rhythm between the two voices, the guitar's and his own, was perhaps the most sensitive that any blues singer has ever achieved. In the "Depot Blues," or as it was inadvertently titled for a later release, "I Ain't Gonna Cry No More," the guitar's melodic line moves for some measures in unison with the voice; then it ends the phrase with its own melodic materials, keeping the same hesitation in the first beat of the measure. He played it in the standard guitar tuning, which he calls the "Key of Minor."

Example 11.

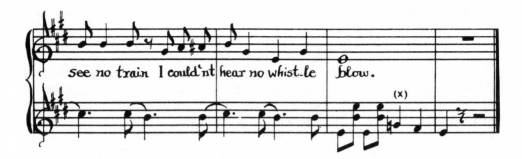

see no train I could'nt hear no whist-le blow.

(x)

Some of his finest blues were recorded on that hot summer afternoon in Robinsonville. He had honed down his old "My Black Mama," giving the verses a greater tension and cohesiveness. The new version, "My Black Woman," was moving and effective blues poetry. The text has been extensively analyzed in the book "The Poetry Of The Blues."

> Well, did you get that letter I mailed in your back yard.
> Uumm - that I mailed in your back yard.
> It's mighty sad to say that your best friend, we have got to part.

> Well, I got a letter this morning, how do you reckon it read?
> Got a letter this morning, how do you reckon it read?
> "Better hurry, hurry, 'cause the gal you love is dead."

> You know I got my suitcase and I took on down the road,
> Uumm, took on down the road,
> But when I got there she was laying on the cooling bo'd.

> You know I walked up close and I looked down in her face,
> Uumm, I looked down in her face.
> You a good old gal, but you got to lay down to judgement day.

> You know, I fold my arms and I slowly walk away.
> Uumh, I slowly walk away.
> You a good old gal, I just can't take your place.

Also in the session he emerged as a songster. Unlike Patton, however, his songs were as much individual compositions as his blues. One of them, a song concerning his feelings at the beginning of the Second World War, was unlike anything recorded by any other blues singer. It was in waltz tempo, but he sang it with the heavy voice and strongly rhythmic guitar of the delta blues style.

No use to shedding no tears, no use to having no fears.
This war may last you for years.


Well, the red white and blues (?) at you,
You ought to do everything that you can.
Buy war saving stamps, young men go to the camps,
Be brave and take this stand.
    No use to shedding no tears, no use to having no fears,
    This war may last you for years.


Oh the struggle sometime will upset your mind;
So you won't know just what to do.
Just keep pushing keep shoving, don't be angry be loving,
Be faithful and honest and true.
    No use to shedding no tears, no use to having no fears,
    This war may last you for years.


You can say yes or no, but we got to win this war;
Because General McArthur's one friend.
There won't be enough japs to shoot a little game of craps;
Because the biggest of the all will be dead.
    No use to shedding no tears, no use to having no fears.
    This war may last you for years.


This war sure do bother our mother and father,
Our sisters and brothers, too.
Dear friends and relations, the war's end creation,
Don't let this worry you.
    No use to shedding no tears, no use to having no fears,
    This war may last you for years.

(This War Will Last You for Years)


This was also accompanied in standard tuning. Most of his bottleneck blues, however, still are done in the "cross Spanish" tuning, e-b-e'-#g-b-e'', and he chords the tonic E on the seventh fret of the first string and the eighth fret of the second string, as in standard tuning. He wears a piece of metal tubing on his third finger, using it on the middle strings as well as the top string for the unison melody. Often he stops the sound of the strings with his second finger to keep the sound from becoming muddied. Nearly all of the right hand picking is done with the first finger plucking the string upward, after a strong down stroke with the thumb on a bass string. There is as much embellishment of tone and pitch in the bottleneck playing as there is in his voice. The interplay between his hands has almost the grace and fluidity of a dance as they move in their endless patterns over the neck of his metal National guitar.

It has been difficult for Son to adjust to playing again, despite the careful attention of Dick Waterman, one of the men who found him and who now travels with him. There is often a sense of isolation about him, as though he still half expects to find Willie Brown or Charley Patton sitting beside him with their guitars. As he has grown older, too, his confusions about his own relationship to the blues have increased; so he is sometimes indecisive as a performer. To hear Son at his best, however, is one of the most moving experiences that the blues can offer. He seems to look uncomfortably out at his audience; then his head goes back and his eyes close, the eyeballs uncomfortably rolling up under his eyelids. He clutches the guitar, and with a nervous gesture hits the string with the metal slide. In the whining, trembling sound of the guitar and the almost painful outcry of his voice is the smell of weeds along the Sunflower River, and the sound of the wind in the trees along a red clay road, the stifling heat of the July sun in the endless rows of the cotton fields. Afterwards, outside of the club where he was playing, he tries to answer questions, standing with his guitar propped up on the sidewalk, his jacket carefully buttoned and his tie straightened under his collar. But after a moment the questions usually die away, and he is able to get to the bus that takes him back to Rochester. Son is so completely the embodiment of the delta blues style that it often seems difficult for him to reach across the differences between himself and the people that want to talk to him. His music, however, stretches across the differences, and in a room as he sings, the whole world of the Mississippi delta seems to crowd within the walls.

# 4. SKIP JAMES

Each of the delta blues men has had to find his own resolution between the fiery Christianity of southern Baptist or Methodist churches and the amorality of his music. Some, like Patton, were able to move from one kind of song to the other, almost unconcerned with the conflict between the two attitudes. Others, like Son House, hesitate, irresolute and uneasy. One of the most consciously creative singers of the delta, Skip James, has given most of his life to the church, but his blues still reflect some of the introspective brooding that went into his decision.

Like Patton, Skip was born into a religious family, but his father was more active in the church than Patton's. When Skip was born - June 9, 1902 on the Whitehead Plantation a mile and a half from Bentonia, in Yazoo County north of Jackson - his father was preaching to a Baptist congregation on the plantation. His parents, Reverend Nehemiah James and Phyllis James, named him after his father. His given name was Nehemiah - but Skip has said, "In my young days I used to like dancing and I'd skip around at the parties people used to have in their houses so they give me the name of Skippy." The Skippy became Skip when he was a young man. He was an only child, and he grew up wandering alone on the banks of the Big Black River, just behind the plantation. He began to learn the piano and organ as a boy, and he played for services in his father's church. He was able to get to school, unlike most of the other delta singers, and he finished high school in Yazoo City. He began playing the guitar about the same time, learning some chords and changes from two musicians at Bentonia, Rich Griffin and Henry Stuckee. Stuckee played with a simple two-finger picking and Griffin "wrapped behind a fiddle," straight rhythm with an accented second and fourth beat of the measure. They played country "frolics," and from them Skip "...got an idea about music." He learned some of the tunes they did together and recorded one of them, "Drunken Spree," years later on a recording, Paramount 13111, that was listed in a Paramount release sheet but has still not been found. Skip's guitar style is a complex and distinctly original three-finger picking technique, but he learned the roots of his music on the plantation where he lived as a boy.

Because of his close relationship with his mother and father Skip never left the South, but he was restless as a young man, and he spent most of his life moving from one part of the South to another. With his high school education he could have gone into teaching, but instead he spent years drifting as laborer, as though he wasn't entirely at ease either singing in road houses and dance halls or following in his father's foot-steps into the church. When he finished school he left Mississippi and went across the river into Arkansas. He worked in a saw mill in Weona and met a pianist named Will Crabtree, who was working in a saloon on Market Street in Marked Tree, Arkansas, a town a few miles from Weona on U. S. 63 north of Memphis. From Will he learned enough of the blues to begin developing his own style as a blues pianist, and when he went back to Mississippi he worked as a musician for fifty cents or a dollar a night, playing either piano or guitar. He was in Memphis in 1926 or 1927 and heard Bessie Smith and Clarence Williams, who were touring with a stage show. He played some country dances around the delta, but he was afraid to play on the rougher plantations. "I'd take a chance some time, but in those plantations they had those rusty old pistols..." He met another pianist, Little Brother Montgomery, in Yazoo City, and they went into Vicksburg together. He learned his "Special Rider Blues" from Little Brother, and Montgomery learned his famous "Vicksburg Blues" from Skip.

Skip remembers learning his first blues, "Alabama Blues," on the Bentonia plantation when he was about twelve years old; so he had been playing for nearly fifteen years when Paramount Records began to take an interest in the delta singers. He learned the song with the old "straight wrap" accompaniment, "frailing," as he calls it, and he still plays it that way fifty years later. During one of his stays in Jackson the Paramount scout H. C. Spears got in touch with him. "I'd like you to come down tomorrow and play a piece or two." Skip remembers that there were forty or fifty singers at Spears' music store when he got there the next day, but he was the only one that "passed." He sang two verses of "Devil Got My Woman" for Spears and Spears told him that was enough. Spears signed him to a two year contract with Paramount, and in the early spring of 1931 sent him on the bus to Arthur Laiblee at the Paramount studios in Grafton, Wisconsin. He remembers doing twenty-six titles over three days of recording. Most of them were delta pieces, but others were composed during the sessions. As he says, "I could compose a song in three minutes." On the last afternoon Laiblee mentioned the popularity of the "Forty-Four Blues" and asked Skip, "Could you make a record comparing to that?" They talked about the caliber of the revolver and Skip decided on something smaller, a 22-20. "Do you think you could make a record on that? You only have three minutes." Skip had his song within the three minutes and recorded it with piano accompaniment. The words were undistinguished, but his piano solo in the middle of the record was a hard-rubbed gem of country blues playing.

Example 12.

(hand pulled up keys)

(hand pulled up keys)

He went back to Mississippi when the sessions were finished and moved in with a young singer named Johnny Temple, who was living in Jackson. He waited for months for his records to bring him some kind of recognition, but he still angrily remembers that he was never fully paid for the recording and that the company went out of business before his records were even distributed. Disappointed, and unable to find much work in the depression panic that had seized Mississippi, he suddenly decided to join his father in Dallas. He began working in the church in Texas in 1932, and it was thirty-two years before he sang the blues again.

In his brief working sessions in Grafton Skip had already left a major group of blues on record, and he has added to this body of work since he again became part of the blues world in 1964. His style was one of the most distinctive to come out of the delta, and it was dominated by an intense lyricism that shaped every element of the music. His singing was closely related to the field holler, and he was freer in his vocal rhythms than men like Patton or Son House. In his accompaniment there was often a complex picking style in the upper strings, with a bass pattern that had the sombre inevitability of the movement of the sun across the Mississippi sky.

The rhythmic subtlety was one of his most distinctive characteristics, but he was also one of the few singers to use a falsetto voice, instead of the heavier Mississippi vocal tone, and he used melodies and harmonies that were more definitely minor than those in the blues of other singers. He used two tunings for most of the songs with guitar accompaniment, the standard e-a-d-g-b-e', and what he called ''cross note,'' e-b-e-g-b-e''. He thinks of it as ''cross note'' because ''... the major and minor cross during the music.'' Played open the strings would be an E minor chord, but for the tonic position he generally holds his first finger on the first fret of the g string, raising it to the major third, g#. One of the sounds that typifies his accompaniment style is his tonic grouping over the low e fundamental. He plays the open e string with his thumb; then descends on the upper first and third strings, the e'' and g, from the seventh to the fifth to the third fret; then to the open top strings, holding the g# in the third string. The fingering inverts the usual descending thirds of this harmonic pattern, and they become the more interesting interval of the major sixth. He usually played a melodic line in unison with the voice, like most of the other Mississippi singers, but he filled the openings between the vocal phrases with rhythmic figures in the guitar that had a distinct complexity.

In their melodic and rhythmic outlines his blues were deceptively simple. The beat had an almost monotonous regularity and the melodies moved in easy intervalic relationships. But by limiting himself in these areas he could move with less restraint in others. There were display pieces like the hymn ''I'm So Glad,'' with its mixing of falsetto and natural voice and its brilliantly difficult accompaniment; but even in a less obvious piece, like ''Special Rider Blues,'' he made considerable use of complex details like triplets, half measures, and suspensions in the accompaniment, and mordents, the falsetto, and cadential embellishment in his voice.

Example 13

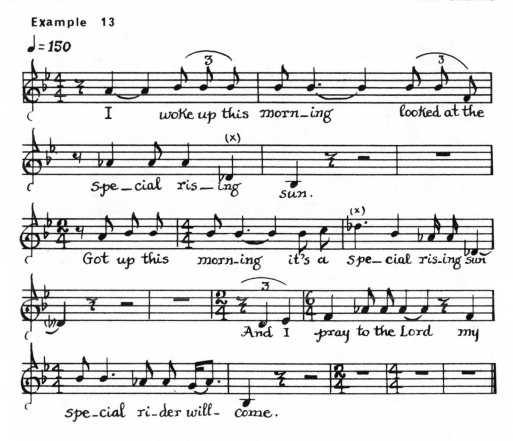

The triplets in the opening measures were probably derived from his piano style. This was a standard early blues piano technique, and he made extensive use of it in his own playing. The mordent came each time on the third of the scale, the turn ending on a definite minor modality. With the mordent on the third he had considerable ambiguity in the major-minor elements of the piece. The scale was a gapped pentatonic, with the second and fourth present only as passing tones. He generally used the pentatonic or hexatonic blues scales, even in the pieces with piano accompaniment. In the piano pieces the fourth became a scale tone, and the harmonic movement from I to IV was more clearly defined than in his guitar pieces.

Example 14

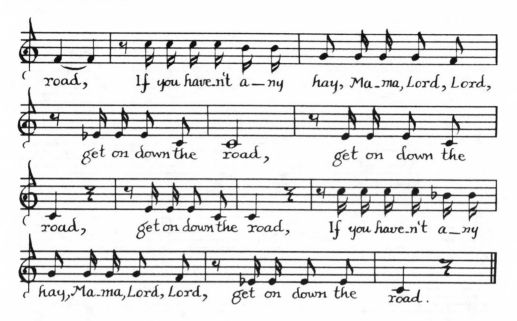

road, If you have_n't a—ny hay, Ma_ma, Lord, Lord, get on down the road, get on down the road, get on down the road, If you have_n't a_ny hay, Ma_ma, Lord, Lord, get on down the road.

The e is an altered mordent in the voice, but in the accompaniment it is played as the minor e flat. His use of the mordent on the third was consistent in his blues pieces and had the subtlety - in the equivocation between major and minor - of the less restricted field holler. The piano style itself is as complex in its irregularity as his guitar style is subtle in its restraint. He bends over the keys, his left hand tentatively drumming on an open chord as he finishes a vocal phrase; then the right hand suddenly moves into a hurried run or a crashing chord rhythm. There has never been anything in music that even vaguely resembles Skip's piano style. At moments in the first recordings there was an almost frenzied incoherence as his fingers groped to find a rhythmic figure that was beyond the limits of the blues idiom. His foot could be heard urgently tapping an irregular rhythm, against which his voice and the piano surged in swirls of sound. His playing, now, has lost some of its fire, but the four pieces he did with piano accompaniment in February, 1931, "Little Cow And Calf Is Gonna Die Blues," "How Long 'Buck'", "22-20 Blues," "If You Haven't Any Hay Get On Down The Road," will always stand uniquely alone in the history of the blues.

Although Skip was a skilled blues poet his verse material never had the vividness and the individuality of his music. Sometimes the blues was begun with a strong emotional motivation, but he usually drew on conventional material for the rest of the verses. One afternoon he was cutting timber at Cypress Grove, about nine miles from Bentonia on the road to Flora, and it was "...hot and contrary" working in the swamp; so he decided to write a song about it, using the same idea as the religious song, "I don't care where they bury my body; just so my soul's in heaven." But his "CypressGrove Blues" became only an erotic complaint, and even in the opening verse there was no effort to describe his afternoon in the swamp.

I would rather be buried in some Cypress Grove,
I would rather be buried in some Cypress Grove,
I'm going away now, I'm going away to stay.


Lord, I'm going away now, I'm going away to stay.
Lord, I'm going away now, I'm going away to stay.
Be all right, pretty mama, might need my help some day...

Except for his religious pieces, the verses were usually erotic, and
they were almost always derivative. He was able to suggest a larger
social context in some of his verses, however, most obviously in his
''Hard Time Killin' Floor Blues,'' one of the few open social statements to come out of the delta.

Hard times here 'no; everywhere you go.
Times is harder than ever been before.

And the people are drifting from door to door,
Can't find no heaven I don't care where they go.
Umum ...

Let me tell you people just before I go,
These hard times 'll kill you (just try long so)
Umum ...

When you hear me singing my old lonesome song
These hard times can last us so very long.
Umum ...

If I ever get off this chittlin' floor
I'll never get down this road no more.
Lord, lord, lord, lord,
    I never get down this road no more.

If you said you had money you better be sure,
'Cause these hard times'll drive you from door to door.
Umum...

Sing this song and I ain't gonna sing no more.
Sing this song and I ain't gonna sing no more.
Umum...
    Hard times'll drive you from door to door.

When he was most individual the pieces were still shaped by the lonely
field hollers that dominated his vocal style. In ''Devil Got My Woman,''
one of his most moving blues, there was even the ruminative quality
of the holler in the text, as the verse form grew from a simple rhymed
couplet to a complex six line verse that ended the song. It had the
looseness and the lonely introspection of a man singing softly to his
mule, as he plodded behind it in the mud furrow of a spring field.

I'd rather be the devil than be that woman's man.
I'd rather be the devil than be that woman's man.

Oh, nothing but the devil changed my baby's mind.
Oh, nothing but the devil changed my baby's mind.

Oh, laid down last night,
Laid down last night,
Laid down last night,
Start to take my rest.
Oh, my mind got to rambling like the wild geese from the west.

Oh, woman I love,
    Woman that I love,
    Woman I love,
Stoled her from my best friend.
But he got lucky, stoled her back again.
And he got lucky, stoled her back again.

A musician like Skip, considering himself part of the commercial music business, probably would have changed his style considerably if he had continued playing during the 1930's and the 1940's, just as most of the other young singers of the 1920's did. He was competitive as well as musically sophisticated enough to have moved into a number of musical areas, perhaps even into jazz piano. But his decision to join the church meant, instead, that he stopped playing secular music, and when he was found in Mississippi in the summer of 1964, his old style was still in his fingers and his voice.

Skip's restless wandering went on for more than twenty years, despite his decision to work in the church. He had been to Texas with his father when he was still in his teens, and in 1932 he moved to Dallas to help his father organize a gospel quartet. After a year of traveling to churches in Texas, Oklahoma, and Arkansas his father was offered a position as head of a Baptist seminary in Birmington. Skip returned with him and studied for the ministry; then he went back to his traveling, this time as a minister with a gospel group that did the singing. He gave services as a visiting preacher, a widespread practice in southern Baptist churches. He gave a twenty to thirty minute "sermonette," with music to introduce and close the service. He toured through Mississippi, Alabama, Oklahoma, even parts of Kansas. He was still unsure of his calling, and for two years gave up his Missionary Baptist affiliations and worked in his mother's church, the African Methodist. At the end at this period, however, he returned to his father's Baptist faith, and until about 1950 he was in the Birmingham area preaching and working days in an iron strip mine. His father had been head of schools in Selma and Tuscaloosa during these years and Skip spent much of his time with his parents. He was also alone for long stretches. As he has said, he was an only child so he "...always likes to be alone."

In 1951 he returned to Mississippi, going to work as a sharecropper. His mother had died and his father had remarried and was living again in Birmingham. A few years later Skip had become a field hand and was living with his wife Mable in a cabin outside of Dundee, in Tunica County. He was no longer working in the church, and he had given up music. His father died in April, 1963, and he was in Birmingham for the funeral, staying with his step-mother in the house on 15th Way, S.W., for a few days; then he went back to his life as a field laborer.

During this period, however, the interest in the delta blues had grown, and intensive efforts were being made to find the singers who were still living. Gayle Dean Wardlow, the young Mississippian who had traveled with Bernard Klatzko on the trip tracing Patton's backgrounds in the summer of 1963, learned, in the late spring of 1964, that Skip had been raised in Bentonia. Wardlow was still in classes; so he was unable to get to Bentonia for a few weeks, but he had already found another blues man from the early period, Ishman Bracey, living in Jackson, and he told Bracey that he had found a lead to James. While Wardlow was finishing his classes John Fahey, Bill Barth, and Henry Vestine drove to Jackson from California and found Bracey's name in the Jackson telephone directory. Bracey told them that he'd heard Skip was from Bentonia, and they began driving the same afternoon, without even taking time to stop and see Bracey. It took only three inquiries in Bentonia before they'd located a cousin, Martha Polk, who had seen Skip at the funeral in Birmingham the year before. The next day they found Skip in the Tunica County Hospital convalescing from a stomach operation.

Within a few days of his release from the hospital Skip was brought from the South to live in the empty house in Newport, Rhode Ireland, that had been turned over to the blues singers for the 1964 Newport Folk Festival. He was quiet, withdrawn from the others, a slight, thoughtful man, his hair graying, his face guarded. He was still weak from the operation, and he had done only a little playing; but he seemed ready to perform, even though he had only three of his old numbers ready and a new piece that he'd written while he was in the hospital. It was at a blues workshop on a cold and damp Saturday afternoon that he finally sang, along with most of the other blues men who had come up from the South for the Festival. He sat expressionless as he waited to be introduced, but as he stepped slowly onto the small wooden platform to sit down he was trembling and nervous. From behind him on the platform, after introducing him to the three thousand people sitting under gray skies on the wet grass in front of the stage, it seemed as though he might not even be able to sing. His first notes as he began his guitar introduction were fumbled and incoherent; then his left foot suddenly began tapping, the guitar introduction emerged as the old cross-note picking of "Devil Got My Woman," and his voice rose in the same clear falsetto he had used on his recording thirty-four years before. When he finished there was a long, excited roar of applause.

79

Later in the afternoon Skip sat on a cot in one of the shadowy rooms of the house where he was staying, leaning against a window, playing the guitar for a handful of people who had come back with him from the concert. The sun had fallen below the clouds and there was a lingering, pale sunset behind him as he bent over to show something to one of the boys sitting near him. "See, there's nothing hard to it. You can do it if you try a little." It was clear, from his smile, that he had come back to the blues for good. Despite a recent operation for cancer and the difficulties any of the older blues men has in making a living, he has been playing steadily, and like the Skip James of 1930, he has continued to develop his art into an even more unique expression of the complex patterns of his life.

SKIP JAMES                                    Photo by Ann Charters

CHARLEY PATTON

JAYBIRD COLEMAN
Courtesy of Pat Cather

TOMMY JOHNSON

ISHMAN BRACEY

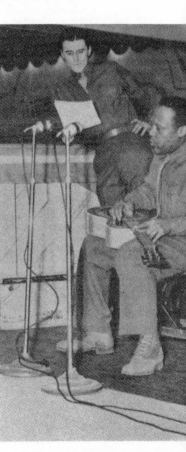

B.K. TURNER, "BLACK ACE"

BOOKER WHITE                                    Courtesy of John Fahey

BERTHA LEE PATTON

Photo by Ann Charters

MISSISSIPPI JOHN HURT                                    Photo by Ann Charters

# 5. ROBERT JOHNSON

*... I was living on, I believe it was 2320 Carr Street during that time and I was playing at Ernest Walker's "House Party" on Jefferson. Robert Johnson had ome over to find me, and he was a stranger in the town so he told me, "Look, I've heard about you." He was just traveling through and he says, "Where you working at tonight?" so I told him and he says, "Can I come over?" and I said "Yeah," so he come over to Walkers'...*

*Well, we sat in the back yard and that fellow, he went over some guitar and I thought, well, this guy's got it. I mean he was amazing. I was a little bit older than him, but I didn't think anybody had any seniority over me on the guitar, but this guy made me look little. During the time I was fixing to leave town, really, and he played for Ernest Walker for about three weeks and I came back and he stayed with me another week over there, for a very small scale, of course. He held the job until I came back and the truth is it was Robert's job when I came back. Robert continued until he was ready to leave; then the boss put me back to work. Robert was very decent about it, I mean we worked together, but as far as the job was concerned it belonged to Robert ... I don't really know where he was going when he left. He said he was going to Chicago...*[1]

Henry Townsend, a blues musician from St. Louis, sitting in his front room on a hot summer night in 1962, thinking back to the first time he'd met Robert Johnson in 1935. In towns up and down the Mississippi River, through the delta, and west into Texas many local singers must have had this same glimpse of Robert Johnson. The thin, guarded teenager who stood in their doorway telling them that he'd heard of them. Then in a club or at a neighborhood party he sat down with a guitar and played them into the floor. Townsend called Robert - as a musician "aggressive." Johnson was more than aggressive, he was on fire with

87

See also *ROBERT JOHNSON—A NEW CONSIDERATION* on page 211.

his music. Even Son House, who knew him when he was still a boy, and taught him some of the pieces that he recorded, remembers him with some uneasiness.[2]

> *... we'd all play for the Saturday night balls and there'd be this little boy standing around. That was Robert Johnson. He was just a little boy then. He blew a harmonica and he was pretty good with that, but he wanted to play a guitar. When we'd leave at night to go play for the balls, he'd slip off and come over to where we were. His mother and step-father didn't like for him to go out to those Saturday night balls because the guys were so rough. But he'd slip away anyway. Sometimes he'd even wait until his mother went to bed and then he'd get out the window and make it to where we were. He'd get where Willie and I were and sit right down on the floor and watch from one to the other. And when we'd get a break and want to rest some, we'd set the guitars up in the corner and go out in the cool. Robert would watch and see which way we'd gone and he would pick one of them up. And such another racket you never heard! It'd make the people mad, you know. They'd come out and say, "Why don't y'all go in there and get that guitar away from that boy! He's running people crazy with it." I'd come back in and I'd scold him about it. "Don't do that, Robert. You drive the people nuts. You can't play nothing. Why don't you blow the harmonica for 'em?" But he didn't want to blow that. Still, he didn't care how I'd get after him about it. He'd do it anyway.*
>
> *Well, he didn't care anything about working in the fields and his father was so tight on him about slipping out and coming where we were, so he just got the idea he'd run away from home. He was living on a plantation out from Robinsonville. On a man's place called Mr. Richard Lellman. And he ran away. Didn't want to work on any farms.*
>
> *He stayed, looked like to me, about six months. Willie and I were playing again out at a little place east of Robinsonville called Banks, Mississippi. We were playing there one Saturday night and, all of a sudden, somebody came in through the door. Who but him! He had a guitar swinging on his back. I said, "Bill!" He said, "Huh?" I said, "Look who's coming in the door." He looked and said, "Yeah. Little Robert." I said, "And he's got a guitar." And Willie and I laughed about it. Robert finally wiggled through the crowd and got to where we were. He spoke, and I said, "Well, boy, you still got a guitar, huh? What do you do with that thing? You can't do nothing with it." He said, "Well, I'll tell you what." I said, "What?" He said, "Let me have your seat a minute." So I said, "All right, and you better do something with it, too," and I winked my eye at Willie. So he sat down there and finally*

*got started. And man! He was so good! When he finished,
all our mouths were standing open. I said, "Well, ain't that
fast! He's gone now!"*

*So he hung around about a week or more, and I gave him a little
instruction. Said, "Now, Robert. You going around playing
for these Saturday night balls. You have to be careful 'cause
you mighty crazy about the girls. When you playing for these
balls and these girls get full of that corn whiskey and snuff
mixed together, and you be playing a good piece and they like
it and come up and call you 'Daddy, play it again, Daddy' --
well, don't let it run you crazy. You liable to get killed." He
must not have paid it much attention. He laughed it off, you
know. I said, "You gotta be careful about that 'cause a lot of
times, they do that; and they got a husband or a boy friend
standing right over in the corner. You getting all excited over
'em and you don't know what you doing. You get hurt." I gave
him the best instruction. So he said, "Okay." Finally, he left
and went somewhere else again with his guitar. We heard a
couple of his pieces come out on records. Believe the first
one I heard was "Terraplane Blues." Jesus, it was good. We
all admired it. Said, "That boy is really going places." So he
left and went out there from Greenwood, Mississippi. Somewhere out in there...*

The name of the plantation was Letterman's plantation, the small town
nearby, Robinsonville in Tunica County, a few miles east of the Mississippi River. An older brother died a few years ago in Robinsonville,
and efforts to trace the rest of the family have been unsuccessful.

Few of the older delta singers realized that the music they had been
singing all their lives could get them out of their weatherbeaten cabins
and away from the squalor and indignity of their lives. But the younger
musicians - Johnson was eleven or twelve years old when the forty-two
year old Charley Patton did his first recording - grew up conscious of
the large audience which was developing for blues both in the South
and in the larger cities of the North. It is difficult even to talk about the
"Robert Johnson style." He was one of the first delta musicians who
listened seriously to recordings. Verses, accompaniment patterns,
melodies, even vocal inflections from recordings by Leroy Carr,
Scrapper Blackwell, Joe McCoy, Willie Newburn, Kokomo Arnold,
and Lonnie Johnson found their way into his own compositions. Even
some of his delta pieces had elements that he'd taken from recordings.

The "32-20" that Robert recorded was taken almost directly from
Skip James' Paramount recording of "22-20," with a guitar accompaniment instead of the piano. He used most of Skip's verses even though
the first verse didn't make a great deal of sense at the time he recorded
it. Skip, recording in a studio in Grafton, Wisconsin, had sung,

> If I sent for my baby, and she don't come,
> If I sent for my baby, and she don't come,
> All the doctors in Wisconsin, he won't help her none.

In his first verse Robert, recording in a hotel room in San Antonio, Texas, remembered to change Skip's line to a more local setting.

> I sent for my baby, and she don't come.
> I sent for my baby, man, and she don't come.
> All the doctors in Hot Springs sure can't help her none.

But in repeating the verse later in the song he forgot and used Skip's line,

> ...All the doctors in Wisconsin sure can't help her none.

With his facile guitar technique Robert was able to pick almost any style that he'd heard, and he was also a fair vocal imitator. On two of his recordings, "Malted Milk" and "Drunken Hearted Man," the singing was very close to Lonnie Johnson's, and on his recordings of delta songs he often sounded like Son House. In many of his finest performances his use of the growl seems to have been an effort to imitate the tone of Son's darker voice. On other pieces there was a falsetto sound that was very reminiscent of Kokomo Arnold, who had begun recording two years earlier. Few artists as young as Robert - he was probably eighteen or nineteen when he began to record - have found a distinctive artistic voice, and he had still not assimilated many of his young enthusiasms when he began to record. But it wasn't the finger work on the guitar neck or his ability to use a little of everyone else's style that has given Robert his place in the development of the delta blues. He also left a small group of recordings that were not only intensely personal, but were also fully realized musical performances. They were also to be, through Muddy Waters and Elmore James, the pivot on which the delta blues turned from a local style, with deep entanglements in the land and its people, to the rhythm and blues style that developed in the northern cities after the Second World War. Of all the voices that he sang in, his own was the strongest.

Even in the songs that he took from his delta background Johnson had an immediacy that was distinctively his own. Every performer with a personal style sings almost as though he watched himself in a mirror. The incidents, the emotions of his life become part of his songs, just as the movement of a hand is reflected in the mirror. Most of the singers, however, stood a few feet away and looked at themselves within their social setting. Johnson was younger, and with the intent concentration of an adolescent, leaned forward until all he could see was the reflection of his own face. The usual pattern for a blues is a group of verses loosely held together by an underlying emotional concern. Most of the verses are standard textual material, usually general comments tied to the particular situation that the singer has described. Patton composed longer blues that were more closely knit, but these were narrative blues, with the figure of the singer grouped with the other figures of the song. For Johnson, there often seemed to be only himself. In Son House's "Preaching Blues," which he taught to Robert, most of the eleven verses, even though they reflected Son's inability to keep the secular and the religious sides of his life separated, were derived from other recordings, they were confused in their imagery, and there was little continuity in their development. But one of the verses reflected a more direct meeting with the emotional realities.

> Now, I met the blues this morning walking just like a man.
> Umh - walking just like a man.
> I said, "Good morning, blues, now give me your right hand."

It was this verse, the most immediate, that Robert chose to use first in his later recording, and he followed it with his own second verse that expressed even more vividly the painful intensity of the moment.

> And the blues grabbed mama child, tore it all upside down.
> Blues grabbed mama child, and they tore me all upside down.
> Travel on, poor Bob, just can't turn you around...

It was only after he had come so close to his own emotions that he could reach out his hand and touch the reflection of his own face that he went on to the generalized verses that took him a step back from the intensity of the experience, and his "Preachin' Blues" went on with,

> The blues am a low down, stickin' gyp.
>      sp. (Preach 'em now.)
> Umh - am a low down, stickin' gyp.
> You ain't never had 'em, hope you never will.

> Well the blues am a achin' old heart disease,
>      sp. (do it now, you goin' do it?)
> But the blues am a low down achin' heart disease.
> Like consumption, killin' me by degrees...

Sometimes as he turned away the break in mood was disappointing. One of the most personal and expressive moments in blues poetry is the opening of his "Hellhound On My Trail." All of the images, the blues falling down like rain on him, the leaves on the trees over his head shaking with the wind, intensified the desperation he felt at the thought of the hellhound trailing him through the day.

> I got to keep moving, I got to keep moving, blues falling
>      down like hail, blues falling down like hail.
> Umh - , blues falling down like hail, blues falling down like hail.
> And the day keeps on 'minding me there's a hellhound
>                          on my trail,
>                          hellhound on my trail,
>                          hellhound on my trail.

When he fell back on ordinary verse material for the second verse it
left the sense of a missed poetic opportunity.


> If today was Christmas Eve, if today was Christmas Eve,
>     and tomorrow was Christmas day,
> If today was Christmas Eve, and tomorrow was Christmas day.
>     sp. (Oh, wouldn't we have a time, baby.)
> All I would need my little sweet rider, just to pass the
>                               time away,
>                 umh, to pass the time away.


The feeling of the immediate in the first verse, however, still hung
over the song like a low line of clouds over the levees along the Yazoo
River, and it was one of his most effective performances.

It is not surprising that several of his blues began with a line, "Early
this morning...," "I'm goin' get up this morning...," "Early this
morning when you knocked upon my door," "Well, the blues this
morning..." there is no more personal time for someone young and
alone than the first gray light of morning, and in these lines there was
some of the painful awareness of life of the adolescent Robert Johnson.

"...At the time I met him he was fresh out of Memphis, he'd been
playing out there...he was a dark skinned fellow, kind of round shouldered,
very small and very young. I thought he must have been teenage. Of
course I didn't know whether he was eighteen or seventeen or fifteen,
but he was a teenager at that time. But he didn't like the title of being
kid. He was a man as far as he was concerned..." Henry Townsend
spent only a few weeks around Robert, but he still had a clear memory
of him after nearly thirty years. Two Memphis musicians living in
Chicago now, Johnny Shines and Walter Horton, wandered with Johnson
for nearly two years, and they remember him with rueful affection.
Johnny met him in West Helena, Arkansas, about 1933, Shines was
seventeen and he thought Robert was a year or so older than he was
when they met. Sitting in Johnny's living room on Chicago's south side
Walter laughed and said, "You couldn't run with Robert for long; he
wouldn't stay in one place." They came up to Chicago together, but
Robert drifted out of town just after they'd gotten there. "We were
staying someplace -" Shines shook his head as he thought about it, "I
don't remember where it was - and he got up in the middle of the night
and left. Just like that! I didn't see him for five months." Walter
laughed again. "He was that kind of fellow. If anybody said to him
'let's go,' it didn't matter to him where it was they were going, he'd just
take off and go. It didn't matter either what time of day or night it was..."
Townsend remembered that Robert was guarded. "If he wanted something he would just bring it to you, but the feeling he had deep inside
was hard to tell about..." He was also shy. Don Law, the man who
recorded Robert for Vocalion Records in San Antonio, asked him to

play for a group of Mexican musicians, and he finally played for them facing a wall looking the other way. But there was little shyness in his singing. He sang with the raw openness of a seventeen year old, and many of the songs had an almost tormented cry. Many blues men spent a lot of time thinking about women, but Son House remembers that Robert was driven by sexuality. The relationships at least left Robert with names to use in his songs. His "girl friends" - the term he used in "When You Got A Good Friend" - included Beatrice in "Phonograph Blues," Bernice in "Walking Blues," "Thelma in "I Believe I'll Dust My Broom," Ida Bell in "Last Fair Deal Gone Down," Betty Mae in "Honeymoon Blues," and Willie Mae in "Love In Vain." There is no way of knowing who they were, or if they were anything more to him than someone to spend a few nights with in a new town. The names were usually included in a conventional verse.

> I'm goin' write a letter, telephone every town I know.
> I'm goin' write a letter, telephone every town I know.
> I can't find my Thelma, she must be in East Monroe, I know.

> (I Believe I'll Dust My Broom)

At his last session, in a Dallas office building in June, 1937, he even suggested that he was going to marry one of them, Betty Mae.

> Betty Mae, Betty Mae, you shall be my wife some day.
> Betty Mae, Betty Mae, you shall be my wife some day.
> I wants a little sweet girl that will do anything that I say....

> Someday I will return with the marriage license in my hand.
> Someday I will return with the marriage license in my hand.
> I'm going to take you for a honeymoon in some long, long
> distant land.

> (Honeymoon Blues)

But the next song of the session was one of the most touching of all the blues love songs, "Love In Vain," and the girl that he mentioned in the song was someone else.

> I followed her to the station, with her suitcase in my hand.
> And I followed her to the station, with her suitcase in my hand.
> Well, it's hard to tell, it's hard to tell, when all your
> love's in vain,
> All my love's in vain.

> When the train rolled up to the station, I looked her in the eye.
> When the train rolled up to the station I looked her in the eye.
> Well I was lonesome, I felt so lonesome, and I could not
> help but cry.
> All my love's in vain.

When the train left the station, with two lights on behind,
When the train left the station, with two lights on behind,
Well the blue light was my blues, and the red light was my mind.
    All my love's in vain.

Umh, Willie Mae,
Umh, Willie Mae,
Umh, let me be your -
    All my love's in vain.

After sexuality the most persistent force in Johnson's blues was a brooding presence that he called the "hellhound" or the devil. It seemed to press against him like the heat from the sun in the fields that he hated. Without Johnson to explain the hellhound, it will always be difficult to say what he meant by the image, but it was only in the strong opening verse of "Hellhound On My Trail," that it had a tormenting aspect for him. He was able to sing of the devil with an almost ironic shrug in other blues, even though the insistence with which the image returns suggests that he was troubled by it.

Early this morning, when you knocked upon my door,
Early this morning, when you knocked upon my door,
I said, "Hello, Satan, I believe it's time to go."

...You may bury my body down by the highway side;
    sp. (Babe, I don't care where you bury my body when I'm
        dead and gone)
You may bury my body down by the highway side;
So my old evil spirit can get a Greyhound bus and ride.

                (Me And The Devil Blues)

In a later verse of "Hellhound" he also mentioned a voodoo powder; so the concern with Satan could be a reference to a belief in the local black magic practices, which still had some hold in the rural areas.

You sprinkled hot foot powder all around my door, all
    around my door.
You sprinkled hot foot powder all around your daddy's door.
It keeps me with a rambling mind, rider, every old place I go,
    every old place I go.

                (Hellhound On My Trail)

Robert's endless traveling, from Mississippi to St. Louis, Memphis, Arkansas, Louisiana, and Texas, may have been part of the fear and the torment that he described in "Hellhound."

He was not involved in the delta landscape as Charley Patton was, but he mentioned a number of delta towns in his blues. Some of them were river towns - Vicksburg, Friar's Point, Jonesboro, and Rosedale - and when Willie Borum, a Memphis singer, heard Robert, he was working in the juke joints along the river, playing in rundown roadhouses for the work gangs building levees along the banks of the Mississippi.

The strongest musical influence on Robert was Son House, despite the other singers and the recordings that he heard. There don't seem to have been the long sessions like Patton had with the young Howling Wolf, but Henry Townsend also said that "...if you just went over something once Robert would get it and play it just as well as you did the next time, he was that kind of fellow." Some of Robert's songs, like "Crossroads Blues," sound very much like something Son would have sung, even to a mention of "my friend poor Willie Brown," but Son doesn't sing - or even remember - a song like it. The young boy sitting in front of the little stage in one of the country dance halls near Robinsonville might have picked up bits of song from Son and changed them to a more immediate and more carefully shaped blues, without Son remembering what he had used for a verse the night before. Despite Patton's strong presence he doesn't seem to have had any influence on Robert's style except for the evocative guitar figures - played with a knife - in Patton's "When Your Way Gets Dark." Johnson used them to suggest the sound of the wind blowing against a shadowed cabin window in "Come On In My Kitchen."

Willie Brown was also playing with Patton and House, and he was considered the best guitar player of the three of them; so it may have been Willie who influenced Robert's more complex guitar style. From House, however, he learned "Preaching Blues," "Walking Blues," "Milkcow's Calf Blues," and "If I Had Possession Over Judgment Day." Despite his changes in melodic material and accompaniment they still had unmistakable elements of Son's style, and sometimes were very similar to the earlier recorded performances that Son did for Paramount in 1930.

Many of these elements of Robert's style were picked up by younger singers; so it was from Son House, through Robert, that the oldest strains of the delta blues became part of the contemporary blues scene. One of the first pieces that Muddy Waters learned when he was beginning to sing was Robert's "Walking Blues," and one of Johnson's melodies - he used it for "When You Got A Good Friend," "Ramblin' On My Mind," "Me And The Devil," and "I Believe I'll Dust My Broom" - was used a number of times by one of the most important of the post war Chicago singers, Elmore James. James was so successful with a new recording of "I Believe I'll Dust My Broom," that it became his theme song, and he named his group the "Broomdusters." Other singers in Chicago, among them John Shines, who did a recording of "Ramblin' " which had a great deal of Robert's sound, were also influenced by the strained, tense music of Robert's blues, and the delta style took root in the new soil like a seed blown in a heavy September wind.

From the older delta singers Robert picked up most of the elements of the classic Mississippi style. He used the open tunings and played with a bottleneck on a number of pieces, as well as finger picking in the lower strings of the guitar. He even used work song sources for blues like ''Last Fair Deal Gone Down.'' He sang with considerable freedom, his voice light and often in falsetto, embellishing the melodic structure with a great deal of variation in both rhythmic phrasing and vocal attack. His blues were often more song-like than the simple melodies of Patton or House, and he used the European diatonic scale for some of his most intense performances. ''Hellhound On My Trail'' avoids only the sixth in its scale.

Example 15

The harmonies for "Hellhound," however, were less touched by the song-like melody than the scale. There was an outline of the conventional I -IV - V blues verse in his singing, but in the accompaniment the guitar was in unison with the voice through most of the verse, only suggesting a leading tone or seventh in the treble strings. The harmony in the lower strings was an insistent open chord. For the delta pieces that he learned from Son he kept the older pentatonic scales.

Probably Robert was so influential among younger singers because of his guitar style. Son had already developed the accompaniments into an open, freely expressive voice. Robert took from him the openness of the sound, the reiterated bass tone, and the treble melodic figure following the vocal phrase; then he tightened the elements into a more rhythmically insistent accompaniment. For "Walking Blues" his accompaniment had the movement and the tension of a three or four piece blues group.

Example 16

97

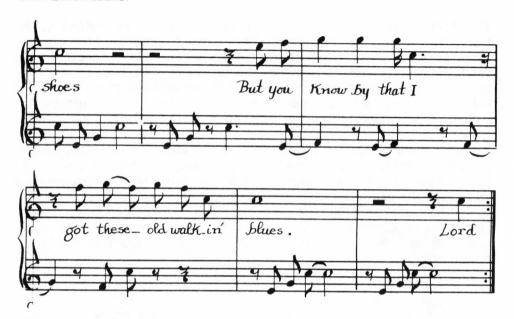

shoes / But you / know by that I / got these old walk-in' / blues. / Lord

Much of the post war Chicago blues was to have this same rhythmic pulse and emotionally vivid singing style.

A salesman for the American Recording Corporation, Ernie Oertle, heard of Johnson, and he brought him to Don Law for the San Antonio sessions. Frank Driggs of Columbia Records, who produced the excellent reissue album of Robert's blues, talked with Law, and much of what Law remembered about Johnson filled in the picture of the young, intensely personal singer that emerged from the recordings themselves. As Driggs wrote,

> " ... *Don Law considered himself responsible for Johnson, found him a room in a boarding house and told him to get some sleep so he would be ready to begin recording at ten the following morning. Law then joined his wife and some friends for dinner at the Gunter Hotel. He had scarcely begun dinner when he was summoned to the phone. A policeman was calling from the city jail. Johnson had been picked up on a vagrancy charge. Law rushed down to the jail, found Johnson beaten up, his guitar smashed; the cops had not only picked him up but had worked him over. With some difficulty, Law managed to get Johnson freed in his custody, whisked him back to the boarding house, gave him forty-five cents for breakfast, and told him to stay in the house and not to go out for the rest of the evening. Law returned to the hotel, only to be called to the phone again. This time it was Johnson. Fearing the worst, Law asked, "What's the matter now?' Johnson replied, 'I'm lonesome.'' Puzzled, Law said, 'You're lonesome? What do you mean, you're lonesome?' Johnson replied, 'I'm lonesome and there's a lady here. She wants fifty cents and I lacks a nickel...''*

There was a note of desperation in many of Robert's recordings. Usually
if the first take was not acceptable on the second take he often became
even more emotionally uncontrolled and the first take had to be used
despite the unsteadiness. The desperate emtionalism, the torment of the
hellhound, the sexual insistence all seemed to be an expression of an
unvoiced fear that he had only a short time to live. He was dead six
months after he recorded in Dallas in 1937, but Son House was surprised
that he lived as long as he did, rather than that he died so young.
" ... he'd go up to a girl he saw at one of those dances and try to take her
off, no matter who was around, her husband or boyfriend or anybody ... "
There were many accounts of his death, all of them different. Dick
Waterman, one of the group that found Son, was told that at a dance at
Greenwood, Mississippi, Robert spent most of the night with one girl;
then left with somebody else. The girl he left at the dance followed them
outside and stabbed him to death in the road. Some of the older singers
think he was poisoned by an older woman after he was unfaithful to her.
As Son said, it's hard to know.[3] " ... The next word we heard was from
his mother, who told us he was dead. We never did get the straight of it.
We first heard that he got stabbed to death. Next, a woman poisoned him,
and then we heard something else. I can't remember what it was now,
but it was three different things. Never did just get the straight of it.
Close as I can get to it, he was about twenty-three or -four. Very young."

# 6. BOOKER T. WASHINGTON "BUKKA" WHITE

In the small towns of the delta the jail is usually in the courthouse in the
middle of the town square, down in the cellar, or upstairs in part of the
second floor. A prisoner there is town property, where anyone can get
at him. For any offense, from drunkenness to using the wrong drinking
fountain, a Negro could find himself locked up in the run down, foul
smelling cells, trying to sleep on a filthy mattress while he waited for
someone to come get him out. For worse offenses he could be sent from
there to the state farm at Parchman, on Highway 49W south of Clarksdale.
The threat of prison hung heavy over the head of any Negro in the delta.

The singers were even more effected by the threat. As they drifted from
place to place playing for country frolics on the plantations or for dances
in the lonely roadhouses, they were always coming up against the local
sheriffs. Mississippi was a "dry" state; so even drinking could get them
into trouble. As they traveled along the dusty roads they were without
any means of support except their battered guitars, and a county judge
could put them on a road gang for six weeks vagracy. If someone's
woman came up and began to get friendly at a dance they could find
themselves in a sullen, drunken fight. Most of them got by like Patton
did, trying to get along with everybody in the area where they did most
of their singing, playing for white dances as well as colored, and staying
out of the way when any trouble started. But the threat was always
there, and all of them sang about it in blues after blues. Charley Patton,

> When the trial's in Belzoni ain't no use screamin' and cryin',
> > umhuh.
> When the trial's in Belzoni ain't no use to scream and cry,
> > umhuh.
> Mr. Ware will take you back to Belzoni jail house alive.

> (High Sheriff Blues)

Son House,

Down South, when you do anything that's wrong,
Down South, when you do anything that's wrong,
Down South, when you do anything that's wrong,
They'll sure put you down on the county farm.

(County Farm Blues)

Reubin Lacy,

Layin' in jail, my back turned to the wall.
And I'm layin' in jail, my back turned to the wall.
And I'm layin' in jail, my back turned to the wall.

(Mississippi Jail House Groan)

Sam Collins,

Lord, she brought me coffee, and she brought me tea.
Lord, she brought me coffee, and she brought me tea.
Fell dead at the door with the jailhouse key.

(The Jailhouse Blues)

For Booker White, the young singer who grew up wanting "... to come to be a great man like Charley Patton," prison was an oppressive reality that drew from him some of his greatest blues.

Booker was born in hill country to the west of the delta. His father, John White, was a fireman on the M & O, and in the late 1880's he left Texas and settled in Houston, Mississippi, the county seat of Chickasaw County, about ninety miles east of Clarksdale. He married a woman named Lula Davis in Houston and Booker, he was named Booker T. Washington, was born on November 12, 1909. He was one of five children. His father took the children to Baptist services, and he was a musician as well, playing both the violin and the guitar. Booker learned to sing in church, and while he was still young his father showed Booker and his sister Etta how to tune the guitar and play a few chords. When he was ten years old - in 1919 - Booker went to live with his uncle, Alec Johnson, on a farm in Grenada, Mississippi. Grenada is the county seat of Grenada County, and is only a few miles from the Yalobusha Rivers, one of the streams that flows into the Yazoo River. In Grenada Booker was in the delta blues country. His uncle had a piano for both his son Buster and for Booker, but Booker was still interested in the guitar, and he managed to get hold of a patched-up instrument. He played it late at night when he thought everybody was sleeping, but his uncle got tired of being wakened by the sound of the music and smashed the guitar. Booker was determined to play though, and he got another instrument. He spent his teens working on his uncle's farm or carrying water for local construction gangs.

Except for his interest in the guitar there was little to set Booker apart from other adolescents growing up in the delta. They worked in the fields from sun up to sun down, already hardened men when they were sixteen, able to work for hours in the summer heat or bend over a chopping hoe through a trickling spring rain. But, as Booker said, he was different. "... none of the other boys, they didn't have any idea what I was thinking about." Charley Patton was playing around the plantations when Booker was growing up, and he felt that he wanted to be just like Patton, even though he absorbed little of Charley's blues style. It was Patton as a man, rather than a singer, that drew him. Booker never had much success as a performer, but he never stopped playing, and he was sure enough of himself as an artist that in more than thirty years his style changed as little as the stones scattered along the banks of the Yazoo River.

Booker matured as a singer during the period when the record companies were beginning to use delta artists. Paramount, through H. C. Spears in Jackson, was able to get most of them, but Ralph Peer was also looking for artists for the Victor field studio in Memphis. He worked through local agents whenever possible, and it was a white Mississippian, Ralph Limbo, who finally talked to Booker about recording in the spring of 1930, when Booker was just twenty years old. He still remembers his excitement at the possibility of recording. Limbo told him to meet him at the railroad tracks by Swann Lake on a Monday morning late in May, and Booker was there every morning for a week before. When Limbo drove up he had two white guitar players with him in a new Studebaker, a colored preacher, and a blues singer named Napoleon Hairiston. Limbo had a contract with Peer for sixteen sides by the colored artists, and Booker did fourteen of them, some of them with Hairiston singing or playing second guitar. Booker also did some religious songs, and they managed to find two church women to sing with him. By the time the records were to be released, however, it was clear that the depression was going to get worse, and only four of the sides were issued. There was an advertisement for two of the religious titles, "The Promise True And Grand" and "I Am In The Heavenly Way," Victor V38615, in the Chicago *Defender* on October 11, 1930. "This Sermon Sung for You by Washington White 'The Singing Preacher' with Guitars and Women Singers." The other release, Victor 23295, used one of the titles that Hairiston sang, "The New 'Frisco Train," and a long narrative train piece that Booker half sang, half recited with guitar accompaniment, "The Panama Limited."

He tried to stay in Memphis after his recordings, but there weren't enough jobs for him to support himself. He learned a little on the piano, played some jobs on guitar and harmonica; then after a few months he drifted back to the delta. These were hard years for everyone in the United States, and they were even harder for a young field hand trying to get out of Mississippi. In 1933 he married Nancy Buchauney and went back to farming in West Point, Mississippi, a small crossroads town in Clay County, about thirty miles to the southeast of his old home in

Houston. He was still singing, working with his wife's uncle, a rough singer and harmonica player from Alabama named George "Bullet" Williams, who had recorded for Paramount in 1928. They had a job at a roadhouse outside of West Point in 1934, and the next year he moved to Aberdeen, in Monroe County about twenty miles north of West Point. It was a rough, hard life, and he had to become hardened to survive. The story is confused, but he shot a man in the summer of 1937. He was arrested, but according to Big Joe Williams he was set free "on bond" until his trial. He broke bond and fled to Chicago and managed to get a session with Lester Melrose, who was recording for the American Recording Corporation there. Williams says that the Mississippi sheriff found Booker in the studio and arrested him in the middle of the session. There were only two sides recorded on Thursday, September 2, "Pinebluff, Arkansas" and "Shake 'Em On Down." They were released during the winter on the A.R.C.'s Vocalion label.

His music hadn't done much else to help Booker's harsh life in Mississippi, but it did get him out of Parchman Farm. The Vocalion release sold well enough that the company was interested in recording him again, and Lester Melrose made an effort to get him released after he'd been in Parchman six months. But their first appeal was turned down and Booker spent two years in prison. Now, as he looks back on his years in Parchman, he feels that in some ways he was better off then than he has been for much of his life since. He was a camp musician so he did little work in the fields. As he told Ed Denson, one of the men who found him living in Memphis in 1963 and who interviewed him extensively, "... he received better treatment there than he has often received since." But the songs that he wrote while he was in Parchman and recorded within a few weeks of his release in 1940 reflect the unhappiness he felt at the deprivations of prison life. He recorded for the Folk Song Archive of the Library of Congress while he was still a prisoner. Alan Lomax was in the prison with recording equipment in May, 1939, and he recorded a great deal of material. Booker, however, did only two songs, "Po' Boy" and "Sic 'em Dogs On Down." It may have been that he was consciously keeping his songs to himself, waiting until he could get out of the prison farm and into a recording studio. A.R.C. was finally able to get him released after he'd served two years of his sentence. On Thursday March 7, and Friday March 8, 1940, he went into the Chicago studio with a washboard player - probably the studio musician George Washington, who used the names Oh Red or Bull City Red - and recorded twelve titles, released under the name "Bukka" White on the Vocalion and OKeh labels. It was these blues that were shaped in the desperation of his months in Parchman Farm.

Booker has always been a literal blues artist. He uses few of the poetic symbols of a Robert Johnson or a Son House. He had some of Charley Patton's feeling for the local and the direct, although his language was often more halting and prosaic. The two years in Parchman didn't change his blues style, but they intensified the emotional expression of his music. His literalness could have been a limiting factor in his development as a singer, but because he had the experience of Parchman to describe, his direct and barren style took on a richer coloration. In a song like "When Can I Change My Clothes," the repetitiveness of the simple idea would have limited the effectiveness of a blues concerned with conventional eroticism. But "When Can I Change My Clothes" was about his first days in Parchman, and the simplicity of the text and the return again and again to the same idea, intensified his description of the emotions he felt at looking down and finding himself in prison clothes.

> I never will forget that day when they had me in Parchman Jail.
> Wasn't nobody would come and go my bail.
> I wonder how long before I can change my clothes,
> I wonder how long 'fore I can change my clothes.
>
> So many days I would be standing down,
> I would be standing down looking down at my clothes.
> I wonder how long before I can change my clothes.
> I wonder how long 'fore I can change my clothes.
>
> So many days when the day would be cold
> They would carry me out into rain and cold.
> I wonder how long before I can change my clothes.
> I wonder how long 'fore I can change my clothes.
>
> So many days I would be walking down the road,
> I could hardly walk with looking down on my clothes.
> I wonder how long before I can change my clothes.
> I wonder how long 'fore I can change my clothes.
>
> Never will forget that day when they taken my clothes,
> Taken my (civilian clothes?) and throwed them away.
> I wonder how long before I can change my clothes.
> I wonder how long 'fore I can change my clothes.

"High Fever Blues" had the same simplicity of idea as he sang about a prison illness, but it also had the sense of deprivation as he sang "They don't allow my lover come and take my hand." Even the use of the word "lover" had a poignancy. Booker was one of the few blues singers to use this term of endearment when he spoke of his wife.

> I'm sinkin' down with the fever, and it won't let me sleep.
> I'm sinking down with the fever, and it won't let me sleep.
> It was about three o'clock before he would let me be.
>
> I wish somebody would come and drive my fever away.
> I wish somebody come and drive my fever away.
> This fever I'm having sure is in my way.
>
> This fever I'm having sure is hard on a man.
> This fever I'm having sure is hard on a man.
> They don't allow my lover come and take my hand.

I wonder what's the matter with the fever sure is hard on a man.
I want to know what's the matter, how come this fever is hard
   on a man.
Lord, they say it ain't the fever, just your lover has another man.

Doctor, get your (fever guage?) and put it under my tongue.
Doctor, get your (fever guage?) and put it under my tongue.
The doctor says all you need your lover in your arms.

I wants my lover come and drive my fever away.
I wants my lover come and drive my fever away.
Doctor says you do me more good than he would in all his days.

Even when the blues was not directly concerned with his prison experience it reflected the obsessions of the men, like him, locked behind the lines of barbed wire in the Parchman enclosure. They worried about their families, about their women, they built eleaborate fantasies about their lives outside of prison, they even dreamed of their own deaths. Booker sang about an effort to find his mother's grave in "Strange Place Blues," about his imagined death in "Fixin' To Die," and in one song, "Sleepy Man Blues," suggested some of the emotional defenses he was able to erect in himself to keep the prison experience from destroying him.

When a man gets troubled in mind he want to sleep all the time.
When a man gets troubled in mind he want to sleep all the time.
He know if he can sleep all the time his trouble won't worry his
   mind,
                              Won't worry his mind.

I'm feeling worried in mind and I'm trying to keep from crying.
I'm feeling worried in mind and I'm trying to keep from crying.
I am standing in the sunshine to keep from weakening down,
                              Keep from weakening down.

I want somewhere to go, but I hate to go to town,
I want somewhere to go to satisfy my mind.
I would go to town, but I hate to stand around.
                              Hate to stand around.

I wonder what's the matter with my right mind, my mind keepin'
   sleeping all the time.
I wonder what's the matter with my right mind, my mind keepin'
   sleeping all the time.
But when I had plenty money my friends would come around,
                              Would come around.

If I had my right mind I would write my woman a few lines.
If I had my right mind I would write my woman a few lines.
I will do most any old thing to keep from weakening down,
                              Keep from weakening down.

The blues from these sessions have a disturbing effect. The melodies he used were bare in their outline, like the stripped limbs of an autumn tree, and the verses, with their insistent repetitions, drummed into the ear. The conventional pattern for the development of a blues is from a verse describing the particular situation - what has happened to the singer - to generalized verses commenting on the vagaries of life and love, or loneliness and the blues. Usually for the final verse there is a return to the particular emotions that began the set of verses. Booker, however, with his concern for the literal statement, tended to avoid abstractions and generalized verses. He usually left his occasional narrative material for songs like "Special Streamliner," a spoken description with guitar accompaniment of a train trip. This left him only a limited area of poetic movement, and he usually went from verse to verse with slow, hesitant steps. Other singers were able to turn from side to side as they moved through a blues, using verses that were only tenuously related, and often by this juxtaposition of material they were able to suggest a larger emotional dimension than the five or six verses of the song could have described with a more literal context. But Booker chose to remain within the limits of his opening verses, sometimes restricting even his choice of words and rhymes to two or three sounds repeated over and over again through the song. The blues that he created were often strikingly original, but for someone used to the larger abstractions of the more conventional blues his literalness was disconcerting. Sometimes he began with a conventional statement of his emotional attitude and its cause, as in "Black Train Blues."

> My heart is filled with pain, I believe I'll catch the train.
> My heart is filled with pain, I believe I'll catch the train.
> The one I love, she love another man.

But his second verse moved only a step in developing this idea,

> Yonder come the train, and I got no change.
> Yonder come the train, and I got no change.
> All I can do, just stand and wring my hands.

and in the next verse he moved so slowly in developing his idea that he even repeated the last phrase of the preceding verse.

> I don't feel 'shamed standing and wringing my hands at the train.
> I don't feel 'shamed standing and wringing my hands at the train.
> I ain't the first man the train left cold in hand.

The rhyme patterns have also been tightly controlled "train, man" "change, hands" "train, hand" and the rhyme sounds themselves have an uncomfortable dissonance.

In "Good Gin Blues" the rhymes were even more limited, rhyming gin with again, in, gin, and men.

Good morning friend, I wants a drink of gin.
Good morning friend, I wants me a drink of gin.
'Cause they told me this morning revenue men would be back again.

Oh, listen you men, don't you let 'em in.
Listen you men, don't you let 'em in.
Well, they might catch me with a pint of gin.

Oh, come in friends and have a drink of gin,
Come in friends and have a drink of gin.
I know it is a sin, but I love my good old gin.

Oh, come back friends when I have my gin.
Come back friends when I have my gin.
'Cause I don't care nothing about for them old revenue men.

If the individual songs were limited, the twelve blues - "Black Train Blues," "Strange Place Blues," "When Can I Change My Clothes?" "Sleepy Man Blues," "Parchman Farm Blues," "Good Gin Blues," "High Fever Blues," "District Attorney Blues," "Fixin' To Die Blues," "Aberdeen Mississippi Blues," "Bukka's Jitterbug Swing," and "Special Stream Line" - in their interrelationships were a major statement of blues themes and attitudes. It was almost as though Booker had chosen to limit each song so that its sparseness and uniqueness would give it a stronger emotional tie to the other songs he had grouped together for the session. Rather than using the generalizations within each song he outlined a larger reality in the entire group of songs, and the twelve blues have a vivid effectiveness.

The singing style for these sessions was more barren and austere than the singing on the single release he had done for A.R.C. two and a half years before. The recordings had the taste of a raw March wind across the Parchman fields. They were mentioned only briefly in one of the Negro newspapers, the *Amsterdam News* in New York in July, 1940. By the time they were released, the last of the classic delta recordings to be released on a commercial market, the big swing bands had taken over most of the popular music world, Charlie Parker and Dizzy Gillespie were slowly building the vocabulary of progressive jazz, and the blues groups in Chicago were beginning to sound more and more like small swing bands. The reviewer didn't even think the releases were blues. Instead he gave them a sentence describing them as "folk music."

Chicago, St. Louis, Memphis, Baltimore. Booker tried to stay out of the delta. He stayed in Chicago for six or seven months after the sessions, then moved to Memphis. During the war years he traveled to jobs around the country. In 1944 his first daughter, Irene, was born; then in 1946 his wife died of ptomaine poisoning on a trip back home to Mississippi. For a time he tried Chicago again, even recording there with a rhythm and blues band as a guitarist in 1952 or 1953, but he was more or less tied to Memphis. His cousin B. B. King had come to town

WASHINGTON WHITE ADVERTISEMENT

TATE — Arkabutla — Independence — Orion — Tuckers — 8 — Booneville — PRENTISS — Burn

Strayhorn — Thyatira — Senatobia — Coleman — Pott's Camp — Hickory Flat — Blue Mountain — Orizaba — 11 — MOBILE

Poplar — Looxahoma — Tyro — Waterford — Chulahoma — Lebanon — Tacaleeche — Guyton — Dumas — Brown's Creek — Geeville

Strattons — Glenville — Law's Hill — Nicksville — 6 — Bethlehem — Beulah — Baker — Molino — Graham — Keown V. — Hickory Plains

Melrose — Como Depot — Harmontown — Abbeville — 5 — Cornersville — Darden — Myrtle — Baldwyn — Buncombe — Corona — Hazel D.

Peach Creek — Sledgeville — Maple Springs — 4 — New Albany — Fredonia — Wallerville — Ellistown — Guntown

Grove — Star Place — Sardis — College Hill — Caswell — Walton — Fairview — Birmingham — Saltillo — Raper

PANOLA — TENN. — Oxford — Liberty Hill — 6 — Poplar Springs — Macedonia — Pine Spri — Manta

Tallahatchie — Cora — Denmark — Esperanza — Cherry Creek — Cedar Grove — Chesterville — LEE — ITA

Batesville — Springport — Yocona — LaFayette Springs — Bruce — Pontotoc — Tupelo — Mooreville — Fult

Central Academy — Eureka — Reynolds — Taylor — Dixie — DeLay — Toccopola — PONTOTOC — Verona — Boland's

Courtland — Pope's — Springs — Orwood — Paris — Dallas — Mud Cr. — Coonewar — Shannon — Eureka

Depot — Elliott's Mill — Spring Dale — Randolph — Algoma — Troy — Bigb

Harrison Sta. — Water Valley — Sarepta — Matthews — River — Red Land — Smithvi

Centre Point — Dickson — Pine Valley — Banner — Money — Yota — Houlka — Central Grove — Cotton G

YALOBUSHA — Oakland — Tillatoba — Air Mount — CALHOUN — Reid — Okolona — Quin

ATCHIE — Garner — Coffeeville — Cotton Valley — Cherry Hill — CHICKASAW — MON

Hardy Sta. — Torrance — Pittsborough — Elzy — Buena — Egypt — Aberd

Cascilla — Junction — Vann's Mill — Cole's Creek — Houston — Vista — McCondy — Prairie Sta.

Grenada — Williamsville — Big Creek — Benela — Sonora — Sparta — Barrs — Temper

GRENADA — Graysport — Sabougla — Hopewell — Erin — Robertson — Muldon — Hamil

Felix — Slate Spring — Bently — Atlanta — Dixie — Montpelier — Palo Alto — Rees S

Providence — Hohenlinden — Pine — Big — Abbott — Border

Elliott — Redding — Cadaretta — Monte Vista — Bluff — Springs — CLAY — Vinto

Sweatman — Embry — Spring Cr. — Cairo — Siloam — West Poin

Smith's Mills — Eskridge — Duck Hill — Bellefontaine — Ander-son — Cumberland — Henryville — Cedar Bluff — Wav

Valley Hill — Sawyers — Alva — Walthall — Line Cr. — Tampico — Rex — Ash Creek — Tilbee Sta.

Winona — Lodi — WEBSTER — Starkville — Mayhew's Sta. — West

Carrollton — MONT- — Greensborough — Spring Valley — Steele's Mills — Hickory Gr. — Artesia — Cobb Sw

Hemingway — Mayfield — PAC. — La Grange — Double Springs — Agricultural College — Sessumsville — LOWND

Kilmichael — Bywy — Dido — OKTIBBEHA — Crawford

CARROLL — Bankston — CHOCTAW — Bradley — Whitefield — Choctaw Agency

Blackmonton — Poplar Creek — GOMERY — Chester — Wilcox — Ennis — Oktoc — Deerbrook

62 Mile Siding — Vaiden — Huntsville — French Camps — Snowville — Pugh — Allgood's Mill — Cliftonvi

Black Hawk — Liddell — Irvingville — New Prospect — Loakfoma — Brookville — Braz

Emory — Brock — Beatty — Conie-ville — Spay — Webster — Prairie Poi

West — Mitchell's Mills — Wells — Barks-dale — Singleton — NOXUBE

McGee's — Hesterville — Thompsonville — Perkinsville — Hamby — Macon

MES — Durant — ATTALA — Louisville — Mashulaville

Gray's Mill — Kosciusko — Newtonville — WINSTON

Kosciusko Jc. — Rome — Randall's Bluff — Cooksvi

Goodman — Wamba — Noxapater — Fearn's Springs — Shuqua

New Port — Sallis — Centre — Coopwood — Handle — Gholson

Couparle City — Thomastown — Cuba — Vowell — Plattsburgh — Wahalak — Binns

Kirkwood — Oak Ridge — Yorka — North Bogue — Chitto — Prince — Kellis' Store

Camden — Conway — Palona — Hemus — North Bend — Kemperton — Peden — Scooba

Carthage — Edinburgh — Coosa — Lake Burnside — Coffadeliah — De Kalb

Ofahoma — Philadelphia — Pea Ridge — Mount Nebo — Moscow

Sulphur Springs — LEAKE — Laurel Hill — NESHOBA — Cushtusa — Herbert — Spinks — Oak Grove

Millville — Lamenta — Colah — Milldale — Watkinsville — Java — Texas — Chickasahay

Sharon — Standing Pine — Madden — Dixon — Tucker — Herbert

DISON — Canton — Good Hope — Tuscola — Walnut Gr. — Beech Springs — Ft. Stephens — Jacksonville — KEMPER

Lens — Estesmill — New — Union — Tamo

and Booker helped him get started as a singer. He was working days at a tank factory, living in a boarding house in Orleans Street, and working occasional jobs with another older singer, Frank Stokes.

Despite his wanderings, however, he had thought of Aberdeen, Mississippi, as his home during the years that he was in prison, and in his "Aberdeen, Mississippi Blues" he had sung "Aberdeen is my home, but the mens don't want me around ..." After a letter to Avalon, Mississippi, in 1963 had led to the rediscovery of Mississippi John Hurt, John Fahey, a young guitarist who was studying at the University of California in Berkeley, wrote to "Booker T. Washington White (Old Blues Singer), c/o General Delivery, Aberdeen." Relatives sent the letter on to Booker a month later, and he wrote to Fahey. Two hours after his letter reached Berkeley, Fahey and another blues enthusiast who was a graduate student at the University, Ed Denson, left for Memphis. They found him in his rooming house, found that he still played, recorded him that first afternoon, and a few weeks later released a long playing record of the session.

There had always been a feeling of strength in Booker's recordings, and the new material made it clear that the strength had grown from his belief in his music. There had been almost no change in style in the thirty-five years that had passed since he began recording. There had been a slight easing of the harshness of his singing for the 1937 A.R.C. session, a suggestion of the popular style of Big Bill Broonzey in the phrasing, and there was a second guitar to soften the sound of his delta open tuning. But in 1964 he was just as he had been in 1930, 1939, and 1940. He even did the song "Po' Boy" that he had recorded for Alan Lomax while he was still in Parchman, a sentimental country song played at a fast tempo with a difficult and complex guitar accompaniment. In 1964, as "Poor Boy Long Ways From Home," the song and the accompaniment were almost unchanged from the earlier version, and there was the same excitement in the strong voice and the guitar picking. He still accompanied it in an open G tuning, D, G, D', G', B, D'', using a knife on the strings with the guitar flat across his lap. There was no longer the tension and the emotional force in the verses, but the songs he recorded for Denson and Fahey were a strong and individual musical statement.

Booker's music is almost an archetypal delta blues style. He sings in the middle of his voice with the tone dark and harsh, and like Patton he tends to move melodically in intervals of a third or fourth, with the interval clearly defined and little vocal embellishment. The accompaniments are very strong, impatient and hard. They are unvarying in their emphasis, usually repetitive patterns of notes played with his thumb on the lower strings and a melody played on the upper strings, generally with a metal ring on the little finger of his left hand. He uses the open E tuning as well as the standard tuning, and as with most delta singers, in the open tunings the harmonies in the bass strings, usually played with an alternate thumb picking, are unchanging. To lighten the heaviness of the accompaniment he tends to sing with considerable rhythmic freedom against it, and his literal concerns within the verse often lead him into lines of very irregular lengths. He often seems to be almost speaking the verses instead of singing them. Few singers have made so little change in the rhythmic patterns of their speech and singing. Because of this even the relentless drive of his accompaniment has to yield to the irregularities of the line, and his phrase patterns vary considerably within a song, sometimes using measures of 5/4 and 2/4 in a generally 4/4 context.

Example 17

(Sleepy Man Blues)

Often he is as restricted with melody as he is with rhyme, but the loose construction of the verbal rhythms makes it possible for him to work within his small limits and still be effective. In his first recording of "Aberdeen, Mississippi Blues" he used only four notes in the vocal line, but the verse was rhythmically very free, as though he were compensating for the melodic barrenness.

**Example 18**

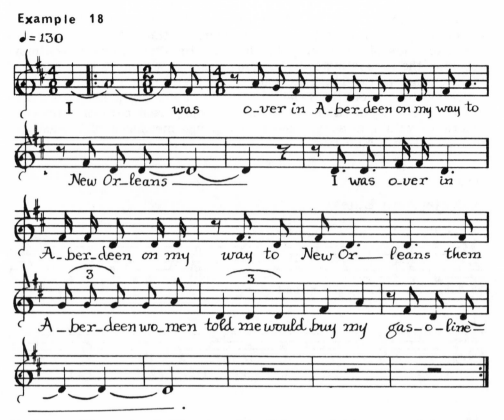

Booker went on to California with Fahey and Denson, and for a few months tried to make a living as a singer. There was further recording, and sessions with Chris Strachwitz for his Arhoolie Record Company in Berkeley. Strachwitz has always used a great deal of imagination in his recording projects and he let Booker extend his songs into lengthy blues stories. On the albums, called "Bukka White, Sky Songs", Booker generally returned to older melodies - "Aberdeen, Mississippi Blues" was used as the melody for "Alabama Blues," "Special Streamliner" for "Bald Eagle Train," "Po' Boy" for "Jesus Died On The Cross To Save The World" - but he improvised new sets of verses. A number of other singers do this, among them Lightning Hopkins and George Montgomery in St. Louis, but they use more generalized material. Lightning often is able to extend his improvisations into effective emotional statements, with considerable use of elaborate poetic imagery. Booker was as literal in the "sky songs" - as he said, "I just reach up and pull them out of the sky - call them sky songs - they just come to me." - as he had been in the 1940 sessions after he'd left Parchman, but without the intensity of the Parchman experience to limit and direct his material, he became diffuse and vague, the verses often contradictory and their narrative movement chaotic. But Strachwitz also recorded a rambling folk tale which he called "Mixed Water," Booker's reminiscences of his early experiences playing the blues against his grandmother's wishes. It was often fresh and engaging and in it Booker was able to talk more freely than he was in the more confining song forms.

There were some jobs for Booker in the first few weeks, mostly at a coffee house called the Cabale on San Pablo Avenue in Berkeley, but it was difficult for him to find an audience for his music. Booker was too strong for his audiences, too strong and too intense, and his songs were too unrelenting. Finally he was left alone in Los Angeles to finish an engagement at a local coffee house. On one of his last nights a young folk singer who had befriended him came to his room to say goodbye. Aware that when the boy left he would have to face the emptiness of the Los Angeles night he suddenly began telling a story, using his hands and his voice to imitate the people he was describing. The story began a little after two in the morning, and when he'd finished it was four hours later and the dawn was breaking. Then, just as he'd done after his sessions, he began to pack to make his way back to Memphis. There have been a few jobs on the East Coast in recent years and some festival appearances, but his music has still not gotten him out of his hard life of rooming houses and laboring jobs.

# 7. MISSISSIPPI - THE COUNTRY SINGERS

Most of the roads through the delta have been paved in the last twenty years, and the black asphalt surface winds across the flat landscape soft and heavy with tar smells in the summer heat; but the mud roads still lead off toward the sluggish creeks and the back waters along the Mississippi. Through the thin trees there is the drifting haze of a wood fire in a cabin stove and paths worn into the dirt by children's bare feet. Beside the cabins the ground has been cleared and in the ragged furrows there is usually a stand of half-grown cotton or rows of summer corn, against a rusting wire fence some hills of beans, peas, squash, the vines straggling over the burned earth. Through the 1920's and the 1930's the blues grew and spread through the Mississippi countryside, and there was a crowded growth of local styles and singers. More and more of the bluesmen left Mississippi for the slums of West Chicago and Detroit as the 'thirties lengthened, but in the 'twenties nearly every cluster of cabins strung out along a plantation road had someone who played the guitar and sang for dances and parties on Saturday night.

Until the commercialization of the blues in the 'thirties there was no weeding or thinning of the local styles, and there was so much recording of the delta music that it is possible to make rough groupings of many of the singers into stylistic areas or influences. Before the period of recording began the styles grew like the weeds along the road, a few men on a plantation, two or three singers in one of the small towns sitting in a crowded room with a bottle of corn whiskey, their shirts soaked with perspiration, following each others' fingers on the neck of the guitar. Even in the delta counties, with their scattering of farms on the back roads, the styles were often highly individual, but there was a tendency for a few men to cluster around a strong creative personality.

Sometimes on the land behind one of the weathered cabins corn and beans were planted together and the vines grew up around the young cornstalks. From a distance, on one of the paths through the fields, the leaves looked like a green tangled mass. It is just as difficult now, after thirty-five years, to untangle Willie Brown from Charley Patton and Son House. Bertha Lee Patton couldn't even describe him without relating him to the other two. "He was shorter than they were, but thicker ..." It was the same for his guitar playing. "Willie was a better guitar player than Charley was, Son House, too. At least he thought so, and they thought so too." When Son House, Willie's closest friend, tried to talk about his playing, like Bertha Lee he had to describe his playing in comparison with Charley's. "Oh, he could beat Charley. Now, you want to hear that 'Pony,' you think Charley can do it good, he's (Willie) the one. They used to fall out about the 'Pony'..."[1.]

Both Charley and Son liked to use Willie as a "commentor" - someone who "kept their spirits up..." when they were recording. Willie's voice was on some of Charley's records, and he played second guitar for Charley on the last two sessions for Paramount late in 1929 and in the summer of 1930, but he did only four pieces of his own, "M and O Blues," "Future Blues," "Kicking In My Sleep Blues," and "Window Blues." Of these only "M and O Blues" and "Future Blues" have been found. In both of the songs there was some of Charley's presence in the voice and the phrasing. Willie's voice was stronger, with a darker quality, but "Future Blues" was another version of Charley's distinctive "Moon Going Down" melody, and "M and O Blues" was closely related to elements in the style of Son House, as well as other Mississippi singers like Kid Bailey and Tommy Johnson. There was assertiveness, the insistence of someone singing to be heard, in Willie's style, but that also was characteristic of Patton. It was in his guitar accompaniments that he emerged most distinctly as a creative performer, even though there were similarities between their instrumental techniques. The accompaniment of "Future Blues" was a brilliantly realized concept, complex, musical, and expressive, similar to the accompaniments that Patton used for the same melody - "Moon Going Down," "High Water Everywhere," "Screamin' And Hollerin' The Blues" - but more carefully developed. It was the "second" part that he had used for his accompaniments with Charley, and that Charley had used, with a number of variations, for his solo versions of the melody. For the accompaniment the guitar was tuned to an open G chord, d-g-d'-g'-b-b", and the style used both finger picking - in the opening descending pattern - and a strum on the open strings - at the end of the second line. The accompaniment for "M and O Blues" was conceived within a different rhythmic framework and used a different tuning - an open E chord - so it is likely that the two still undiscovered pieces, "Kicking In My Sleep Blues" and "Window Blues," will also be in different accompaniment styles. It will be difficult to evaluate Brown's musical contribution to the delta blues until they have finally been found, but although he seems to have been in Patton's shadow for much of his musical career, he had developed his own style from the strongly rooted delta music.

Because of Willie's close relationship with Son House, his life is less obscure than the lives of men like Kid Bailey or Blind Joe Reynolds.

He was born in Robinsonville about 1900, and met Charley when they were both young men working on Dockery's Plantation. Son met them about 1928, and he and Willie traveled together until Son decided to try living in the North during the Second World War. He was able to get Willie to stay with him for a short time, but Willie returned to Mississippi and he died there about 1942. [2.]

*It was while I was in Rochester that Willie died. After I started working for the New York Central, I was writing and telling Willie about it and eventually I got him to decide that he wanted to come up. So I sent him a ticket and a little money to ride on and he came to Rochester and I got him a job. After a little bit, he sent for his girlfirend, and she came. So one night, we were sitting up talking and she told some things that he didn't think she would. He got mad then and wanted to send her back. He told her to get packed and he told me, "Son, I'm going to leave you the money and I want you to buy her ticket. Not going to trust her. You buy her ticket at the Greyhound and see that she gets on with her suitcase. I don't want to see her when I get off from work and come home." He was living with me. So I got the ticket and she left. Well, soon after that, he wanted to go. Back to a little place about twenty miles outside Memphis. That's where he'd been living before he came to Rochester. I said, "Well, Bill, you going to try and find Rosetta now. Ain't you?" "Aw, naw," he said. I said, "Cut it out. That's what you're thinking about." So he left and went on down.*

*Well, the first part of the next year, I had a two-week vacation so I went down to see him. He had just had an operation for ulcers, and everytime he'd eat a meal, he'd have to lay down flat on his back for thirty minutes. Well, after the different guys heard I was there, they all wanted me to come and play for them. "Son House's here!" And they gave extra parties and everything, and Willie would go and play with me. The doctors had told him not to drink any more, but he'd be with me and the fellas would come around offering me whiskey, you know. I'd turn it up and Willie would look at me drink it. He knew how we used to do and he'd want a drink so bad. He'd say, "Let me taste a little of that." I'd say, "Bill, you know what the doctors said," He said, "I'm going to try it anyhow. It looks so good." So he'd take little nips, you know.*

*Well, a couple of weeks after I got back to Rochester, I got a telegram from his girl that Willie was dead. I said, "Well, sir. All my boys are gone." That was when I stopped playing. After he died, I just decided I wouldn't fool with playing any more. I don't even know what I did with the guitar.*

Patton had an even stronger influence on the music of his accompaniest, the rough country fiddler Henry Sims. For at least two of the four songs he recorded, "Farrell Blues" and "Tell Me Man Blues," he used Charley's "Green River Blues" melody, and on all of his recordings Charley played the guitar accompaniment. The only other influence on his singing seemed to be his own violin style, and his vocal melody closely followed his usual blues solo pattern, despite its angularity and rhythmic stiffness. As Klatzko and Wardlow learned on their trip through the delta, he was also personally closer to Patton than either Willie or Son. [3.]

> *Early Tuesday morning, we left for Farrell. Farrell lies just a few miles west of Clarksdale, near the levees of the Mississippi River. There's a general store just off the main road. Another road divides the cotton fields and the inevitable Negro houses whose occupants care for them. The houses were recessed about 150 yards off the paved road with a dirt road leading to the main group, as well as to a few scattered houses.*
>
> *We had come to Farrell looking for Henry Sims, the primitive country fiddler and singer who recorded four obscure sides under his own name and accompanied Patton on many others during Patton's second session. Pete Whelan had first suggested that Sims might be from Farrell.*
>
> *We approached the first house in a row of houses that made up most of Farrell. A large dark woman in her late middle years came to the porch.*
>
> *After our usual opening with a general discussion of old time blues singers, I asked, "Does Henry Sims live around here?"*
>
> *"Henry Sims lives down in the last house."*
>
> *"Does he play fiddle and sing?"*
>
> *"HUH? Oh, you mean Son Sims. He died about three years ago."*
>
> *"How old was he when he died?"*
>
> *"He was about 67 years old. You know, Son Sims was in the army in World War I."*
>
> *"Did you ever hear of Charley Patton?"*
>
> *"Sure, I seen Patton and Sims playing together around here. Charley died some time ago. Son didn't want to play anymore after that. He took it real bad..."*

The record companies who were recording delta singers in the late 1920's and early 1930's were not making an effort to document the local blues styles, but they recorded some of the most individual and creative of the country blues men. The music was developing in such a rich profusion during these years that often the performances went beyond a personal reworking of one of the dominant Mississippi styles, and the singer moved toward a melodic or rhythmic concept that could have been the basis for a whole stylistic development within the blues itself. The blues in this period was a young, still growing song form, and it could sprawl in any direction the singer wanted to try. Often these isolated singers recorded only a handful of sides, but their music still had a tough muscularity. One of these obscure delta men was Garfield Akers, who had begun to move toward a more complex rhythm in his accompaniments. Little is known about his life. He may have been born in Hernando, a small town in De Soto County, just below the Tennessee line about thirty miles south of Memphis on Highway 51. He recorded in Memphis in 1929 and 1930, and finally settled in Memphis where he died about 1962 at the age of sixty. It is possible that he had a son who is still living in Memphis and plays a little in his father's style. The amount of recording that Akers did was almost as slight as the amount of information known about his life. There were four sides, "Cottonfield Blues - Part 1 and 2" recorded in September, 1929, and "Dough Roller Blues" and "Jumpin' And Shoutin' Blues" recorded three or four months later. The melody and the accompaniment style was the same for all of them, except that there was a heavier second guitar on "Cottonfield Blues." The melodic line moved in a series of descending movements from an opening tone a tenth above the fundamental in the accompaniment, and was organized in the conventional three line verse form.

A number of Mississippi men used an accompaniment style for two or three of their pieces that had some similarities to the Texas technique of alternating simple chords under the vocal line with more complex finger picked patterns between the lines. There was a suggestion of this style in the accompaniments of Blind Joe Reynolds, Sam Collins, and Booker White; although in most of their pieces there was a unison melody in the guitar with the vocal phrase. In his accompaniments Akers used a rhythmic variation of this concept, alternating contrasting rhythmic units while still keeping the steady beat beneath the voice. The shifting stresses gave a new impetus to the sung melody. In "Dough Roller Blues" the rhythms alternated in groups of four or six measures; in the other pieces the shift was in smaller groups of two or three measures. One of the rhythms, accompanying the voice, was a simple syncopation,

and the other a more complex unit that was usually,

The complete pattern for the four measure line was,

Within this rhythm the harmonic changes were almost in the standard pattern, I-I-I-I-IV-IV-I-I-V-V-I-I, but the sound of the accompaniment was changed considerably, and the chord movements had less of their rhythmic function. The sound was almost a tonal drumming, and in its repetitive insistence it would have had almost an African sound except for the emphasis on the first and third beats of the measure. The pattern was varied with a beginning phrase in the bass strings of the guitar that he used for at least a verse in each of the pieces. The figure was a series of 8ths through the opening two measures of the accompaniment.

There was also some irregularity in the length of the measures. His singing emphasized the held tones of the line and often he extended the measure to six beats, still keeping the rhythm of the guitar. The guitar measure could be divided into half measure note groups and he used these to fill in the lengthened phrase. His voice was higher in pitch than the heavy tone of Patton or Son House, but it was richer in sound than a voice like Robert Johnson's. Against the rush of the accompaniment it had a strong presence and, despite the use of conventional verse material, his pieces were very effective. Akers had so little opportunity to record that there was only a suggestion in the three blues of the rhythmic concept that he had begun to develop. Only one singer seems to have picked up the style from him, Robert Wilkins, a Memphis singer who grew up in the delta and learned his "Get Away Blues" from Akers. It was unfortunate that so few other bluesmen were able to hear his use of the contrasting beat patterns, since the concept could have helped the later singers to avoid some of the rhythmic monotony that has limited the development of the modern blues. It was, as well, a concept that could give a new dimension to the blues that will emerge from the years of growth and consolidation ahead.

119

The emphasis on strongly marked rhythms was one of the dominant characteristics of the delta style, and one of the first delta men to record, Williams Harris, based his work on a strongly defined 4/4 rhythm, even though other elements of the Mississippi accompaniment were not fully developed. He had left Mississippi with a medicine show and was in Birmingham in the summer of 1927, when the Gennett Electrobeam studio was working in the city. He did two titles for the company in Birmingham and then went to the Richmond, Indiana studios for three days of recording in October of the next year. On pieces like his ''Bullfrog Blues'' he used a verse form with a delayed completion of the first line, similar to Patton's fifth verse in ''Moon Going Down.''

> Have you ever woke up with them bullfrogs on your,
> > bullfrogs on your,
> > bullfrogs on you,
> > I mean mind?
> Have you ever woke up, mama, bullfrogs on your mind?
> Have you ever woke up with them bullfrogs on your mind?

Although the rhythm was in a heavy 4/4 he lightened it with softer after-beats, using a thumb and finger strum on the guitar, rather than finger picking. As a medicine show singer he did a number of the more conventional blues — his ''Hot Time Blues'' was an eight bar song with the same chord progression as Papa Charlie Jackson's ''Salty Dog,' VI-VI-II-II-V-V-I-I-, but his voice had the delta insistence, and the bare, unadorned melodic outline.

Blind Joe Reynolds, who did four titles for Paramount in 1930, was one of the many delta men who, like Harris and Akers, made only a few recordings, but whose style developed another aspect of the delta music. He was a more impassioned singer than Harris and his half shouted, half sung melodic phrase was nearly arhythmical in its irregularity. The guitar was almost silenced during some of the lines, entering after the voice with heavy figures in the middle strings played with a bottleneck. He used an open tuning, strumming the guitar for some of the accompaniment. Reubin Lacy, who was one of the first singers who influenced Son House, also played with an open tuning, but the rhythm was more regular than Reynold's. He played with the strings very slack, tuning the guitar down to his dark and low voice. On his ''Ham Hound Crave,'' a 1928 Paramount release, there was some Barbecue Bob influence in the repeated lines in the later verses, but his ''Mississippi Jail House Groan'' was in an almost pure delta style. In the accompaniment he played a dotted eighth note rhythm on the top string and used a descending bass pattern against it. The note on the top string continued almost unchanged through the piece, functioning as a harmonic pedal tone something like the top string of the mountain five-string banjo, which is unfretted. His beat was very slow and deliberate, the only harmonic change in the accompaniment a tonic seventh anticipating the subdominant of the second line, which he sang as though the harmony had changed even though he went back to the tonic after the momentary change to the I7. He made the chord change by dropping the tone on the top string a whole step to the seventh of the scale, then sliding the note back to the tonic. The text was confused, going from a sombre prison mood,

> Layin' in jail, my back turned to the wall.
> And I'm layin' in jail, my back turned to the wall.
> And I'm layin' in jail, my back turned to the wall.

to a half serious sexual boast,

> And my mama told me, my papa told me too,
> And my mama told me, my papa stood and cried,
> You got too many women now for any boy your size,

still with the brooding presence of the slow rhythm and the droning note on the high guitar string.


Although Son House remembers a number of other Mississippi singers like Lacy, he has no recollection of a blues man who was closely related in style to Patton and to Willie Brown. The singer, Mississippi Kid Bailey, did only two sides for Brunswick in 1929, "Mississippi Bottom Blues" and "Rowdy Blues," the "Mississippi Bottom Blues" using Patton's "Moon Going Down Melody" and "Rowdy Blues" Willie Brown's "M And O Blues." The accompaniments were so close to the guitar techniques of the other two men that Son, after listening to the record, feels that it must be Willie on the guitar, even though he's never heard of Bailey. The accompaniment for "Mississippi Bottom Blues" was the higher eighth note pattern that Patton used in his duets with Willie, letting Willie play the descending bass line. Bailey's performance was considerably more relaxed than Patton's, with the steady, lightly swinging beat that was characteristic of the Jackson singer Tommy Johnson. The vocal line was conceived in terms of the entire piece, almost as an adjunct to the accompaniment; so there was considerable displacement of stress in the verse. There was some of this feeling in "Rowdy Blues," the vocal line, as in "M And O Blues," beginning on a subdominant harmony. The accompaniment was in open E tuning. One of the verses that Bailey used even turned up later in Son's 1942 Library of Congress recordings, although Son could have gotten it from a number of other delta singers.

> Did you get that letter I mailed in your back yard?
> Did you get that letter I mailed in your back yard?
> It's sad, it's sad but true, best of friends have to part.


Bailey's voice was strong and rich, and he seems to have been a sensitive and skillful blues man. Just as with Akers and with Rube Lacy and Blind Joe Reynolds it was unfortunate that he had no opportunity to record more than a handful of songs for release as part of the commercial record output of the late 'twenties.

The blues grew in every part of the Mississippi soil, and often the music from the eastern hill country or the southern pine country had moments with the intensity and the drama of the greatest delta music. In the flat sandy country just above the Louisiana line the music was mingled with influences from recordings and from local white singing, but there was still a deep blues presence. It was an elusive mood, like the shadows under the ground pines, but it dominated the singing of one of the few southern Mississippi singers to record extensively, Sam Collins. Little is known about his life, but Dean Wardlow has learned that he was raised in McComb, Mississippi, about fifteen miles above Louisiana in Pike County, and that he died in Chicago in the 1950's. He did his first recording for Mayo Williams in 1927, when Williams had left Vocalion and was trying to set up his own Black Patti label. Collins was one of his first artists, and there was even an advertisement in the Chicago *Defender* for the first release, with a rough drawing of Collins playing the guitar, on July 2, 1927.

> Here he is, Crying Sam Collins and his Git-Fiddle.
> Blues Oh Lawd, "I Mean." Sam cries and weeps out loud,
> does he make his old Git-fiddle weep and moan "And How!"
> Go to your dealer and ask him for -
>     Black Patti Record No. 8025
> Jail House Blues, Sam Collins and his Guitar.

He continued to record for more than five years, and he did almost fifty titles, nearly as much recording as Patton did, but only nineteen of his sides were released. The issues were on several labels, most of them cheaper labels for the five and ten cent store record counters. They included Black Patti, Champion, Herwin, Silvertone, Bell, Gennett, Supertone, Banner, Perfect, Conqueror, Melotone, Oriole, and Romeo. The companies used a number of pseudonyms for Collins since each of them was selling the same record at the same time. He was "Big Boy Woods" on Bell, "Jim Foster" on Champion and Silvertone, "Bunny Carter" on Conqueror, and "Salty Dog Sam" on the Banner, Oriole, Perfect, and Romeo releases.

Collins wasn't a creative singer on the level of Son House or Willie Brown, despite the number of titles that he recorded, but there was an intensity in his best work, a brooding sense that fused the awkwardnesses of his style into a whole expression that was often moving. However, much of what he recorded was derivative material, often from country white sources as well as other recordings. Songs like "Hesitation Blues" had the sound of one of the Carolina hillbilly bands like Charlie Poole's, and the prison folk song "Midnight Special," sung in a very high falsetto, had the rhythmic quality of white gospel groups like Ernest Phipps and his Holiness Singers. On "It Won't Be Long" he had some of the hesitations and harmonic uncertainty of the Texas singer Henry Thomas in the same kind of white sentimental songs. His gospel pieces were generally sung with a frailed accompaniment and little change in the verses from the standard song book versions.

122

Ben Lomond  SHARKEY  YAZOO  ville  Camden
Providence  Chipland  Evans  Way's Bluff  Sulphur Springs
Tallulah  Watsonia  Dover  Millville
Hay's Landing  Swedes  Enola  Woodbine  Sharon
Arcadia  Halpin's  Santartia  MADISON  Good
Ingemar  QUENA  Dick  Vernon  Canton  Lud
Illawara  Phoenix  Livingston  Calhoun
Russellville  Prattville  Goshen Spring
Omega  Brunswick  Flower ree  Madison Sta.  Fannin  Leesburgh
Waverly  Haynes Bluff  Black  Lucknow  Armiste
Forest  Redwood  Oak Ridge  Pelahatchee Depot
Tallulah  Home  Cardiff  Bolton's Depot  Clinton  Tougaloo  Spears
PAC.  WARREN  Jackson  Brandon
Delta  VICKSBURG  Midway Sta. VICK.  Rowell's  RANKIN
Mound  Smith's  Edward's Depot
New Carthage  Bovina  HINDS  Mississippi Spr.  Monterey  Lynwood
Warrenton  Raymond  Steen's  Steep Bank
Palmyra  Diamond  Oakley  Byram  Creek  Cato
Hurricane  Goodrum  Auburn  Midway  River
New Town  Cayuga  Adams Dry Grove  Braxton
d Bayou  Ursino  Landing  Rocky  Sta.  Chapel Hill
St Joseph  Leo  Springs  Utica  Bear Creek  Terry  King
Nanachehaw  White Oak Creek  Harrisville  Dlo
Grand Gulf  Brook's Landing  Burtonton  Gatesville  SIMPSO
B. Pierre  Crystal Springs  Georgetown  Ria
Joseph  Morehead's  Myles  Gallman  WESTVILLE  Mou
Saint Elmo  McCaleb  Linden  COPIAH
Port Gibson  Hermanville  Hazlehurst  Bridgeport  Rockport
CLAIBORNE  Mount Hope  Tryus  Hebron
Martin  Jefferiesville  Martinsville  Grange  Jay
Rodney  Tillman's Sta.  Beauregard  West Fork  White Sand
Rabbit Harbor  Red Lick  Big Bahala Cr.  Hooker  Silver Creek
Gum Ridge  JEFFERSON  Caseyville  Wesson  Montgomery
Church Hill  Fayette  Perth  Erwinsville  LAWRENCE  Blou
Lowenburgh's  Fowler's  Union Church  Udora  Brookhaven  Monticello  San
Sta.  Cannonsburgh  Veto  Friendship  Fair
NATCHEZ  Stanton  McCall's Cr.  LINCOLN  River
Washington  Hamburgh  Chamberlain  Wilkesburgh
Foster's  Morman's Fork  Bogue Chitto  Oak Vale
ADAMS  Turner's  Meadville  Greens Cr.
Hutchin's  FRANKLIN  Johnson's Sta.  Sartinville
Kibbeville  Little Springs  Topisaw
Knoxville  Bunckley  CHICAGO  Light
Yeagers  O'Neal's  Zion  Smithdale  McComb
Cold Springs  Hill  Summit  China Grove
astra's Store  Merwin  Dickey  PIKE
Wilkinson  Kahnville  Bates  Quins  Holmesville
alo  Mill  Magnolia  Tyler Town  MA
WILKINSON  Centreville  Liberty  Chataw  Hardee's  Walker's Bridge
dryville  Woodville  Carter's  Dillon  Fordsville
Adams  Holly  Gillsburgh  Hill  Live Oak
side  Retreat  Rose  Osyka
Ashwood Sta.  Hill  Palestine
Woodland  Shady Grove
Burlington  Tangina  Franklinton
Greensburgh  Arcola  Welch's Bridge  Gordontown
Pine Grove  Amite City  Yan
Independence

Of all the Mississippi singer   Collins was probably the most limited guitarist. He used an open tuning for nearly all of the blues, an e-b-e'-g#-b'-e"- tuning, and his harmonic change was limited to the barred subdominant at the fifth fret. He may have done some of his playing with the guitar across his lap, but for the blues it sounds as though he were playing in the standard position. Usually he used a bottleneck, or some kind of a knife or slide, and played a unison melody with the voice. He had a consistent sound to the guitar tuning, almost a sour, bitter sound, like a half ripe persimmon, and by the standards of most guitarists he was out of tune, although it may have been the sound he was trying to get. The accompaniment style was only half formed, and may reflect the different streams of music that he grew up with in McComb. The unison melody played with the slide was distinctively Mississippian, but there was no rhythm in the lower strings, either a steady thumb pattern in 4/4, as in Texas, or an alternate thumb picking like many of the delta men used. He used an open tuning, but instead of the cross fingerings or alternate chord patterns that singers like Skip James or Son House developed, he fell back on the barred subdominant. On some of the pieces derived from white sources he even tried to find fingerings for the conventional V and VI chords. On blues like ''Yellow Dog Blues'' and ''Slow Mama Slow,'' however, the guitar style was more effective, and there was an excitement even in the rhythmic irregularity. He moved freely over the guitar fingerboard between the vocal lines, sometimes with a melodic figure played with the knife on the upper, middle, and bass strings. His irregularity in rhythmic structure was still closely related to the basic Mississippi style, and he used the half measure anacrusis for the vocal phrase and the extended guitar bridge between the lines. There was almost an ornate quality to his vocal melodies with their elaborately developed inner rhythms. There was some of the green twisting and bending of levee trees in the wind in the shifting accents of his voice in a piece like ''Signifying Blues.''

Example 19

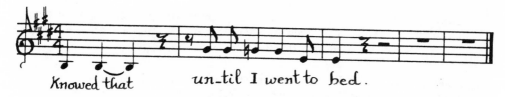

Knowed that        un-til I went to bed.

Most of his pieces were in the gapped pentatonic scale of the Mississippi blues, but the scale in "Signifying Blues" had an interesting use of the seventh tone of the scale, the d in measure 12. It seems to have functioned as the third of the chord on the dominant b, rather than a distinct scale tone, but it was one of the few songs from the early Mississippi music that used the seventh as a melodic tone. The guitar accompaniment for "Signifying" was also unusual for Collins. The pattern was an almost unvarying ostinato, similar in some ways to the kind of finger patterns that were used by the Alabama singer Ed Bell. The accompaniment was in open E tuning, with the harmonic changes only suggested in the bass strings. The text of the blues was vague, but the first verse included the unusual sexual reference to impotence, and the other verses were concerned with the "signifying" man.

> My mama signify that my black snake was dead,
> My mama signify my black snake was dead,
> But she never knowed that until I went to bed.

> I'm goin' tell everybody what a signifying man will do.
> I'm goin' tell everybody what a signifying man will do.
> He will come to my house and he'll talk about you,
>     Go to your house and he'll talk about me,
> But he better mind he ain't goin' signify no more.

> Lord, he's a signifying man, I'll tell you what it's all about.
> He's a signifying man, I'll tell you what it's all about.
> She looked down the street and seen me coming,
>     she put that low down (rascal) out.

> I'm going to tell you what you ought to do.
> I'm going to tell you what you ought to do.
> If you don't believe me you can ask everybody in my neighborhood.

One of his finest blues, "Slow Mama Slow," juxtaposed two blues themes in its four verses, an unashamed sexual enjoyment in the first and third verses, and the "leaving" theme in the second and fourth. They would have been more clearly related if Collins had altered the order to begin with the third, then described the sexual enjoyment of the first and left with the second and fourth; but he chose to leave them with their inter-relationship not immediately clear, so the verses gave to each other a stronger emotional tension by their only half sensed involvement.

125

> Take your time, kind mama, I'm gonna do just as slow as I can.
> Take your time, kind mama, I'm gonna go just as slow as I can.
> I might start shimmyin', don't let nobody hear.
>
> Make your bed up higher, and turn your lamp way low.
> Make your bed up higher, turn your lamp way low.
> I'm gonna hug and kiss you, ain't coming here no more.
>
> Pull down your window, lock up on your door.
> Lock up on your window, lock up on your door.
> I got ways like the devil, I'm slipping on the floor.
>
> Make your bed up higher, and turn your lamp around.
> Make your bed up higher, turn your lamp around.
> Look out your back door, see me leave this town.

By asking the woman to "make your bed up higher," to make it more difficult for someone else to join her in bed, he extended the sexual theme through the song, and the blues had a vivid immediacy even though its levels of meaning were unclear. Although Collins was not one of the stylistic innovators within the Mississippi blues idiom he was enough part of it that in blues like "Signifying Blues" and "Slow Mama Slow," he had some of the intensity of the Mississippi music at its most creative level.

In the winter of 1932 King Solomon Hill, a singer with strong similarities to Collins' singing style, recorded six titles for Paramount in Grafton, Wisconsin. The songs done by Hill were "Whoopee Blues," "Down On My Bended Knee," "The Dead Gone Train," "Tell Me Baby," "My Buddy Blind Papa Lemon," and "Times Has Done Got Out Of Hand." For several years Big Joe Williams, who grew up in Crawford, Mississippi, a few miles from the Alabama state line in the center of the state, claimed that he had done them using a different name and singing in a falsetto to disguise his voice. There were so many differences between these recordings and Williams' pieces done in the same period that it has been difficult to accept them as his, even with a high falsetto. They were, however, so strongly similar to Collins that there have been suggestions that Hill was Collins using a pseudonym to avoid trouble with the American Recording Corporation. Collins had recorded twenty titles for A.R.C. in October, 1931, and if he were to do any work for Paramount he would have to use a pseudonym. Despite the closeness of the vocal style, however, they seem to be separate singers. Dean Wardlow has been told that Hill was also from McComb, and may still be living there. One of Hill's pieces was about Lemon Jefferson, who was from Texas, even though he'd traveled through Mississippi before his death in 1930. So it could be that Hill was from Texas, and the similarities between his style and Collins' were only coincidental. Both of them sang in a high falsetto, with a loosely felt melodic line, but there were many differences in their musical approach, especially in the guitar accompaniments. Unlike Collins, Hill followed the voice with a drumming line in triplets in the guitar. The accompaniment, in an open D tuning, was almost entirely in single note patterns, the strings slackened so that he could get a heavy bass sound something like the lower strings of the Japanese koto.

Hill, like Garfield Akers, was a singer who had brought an individual concept to a high state of development, and his linear accompaniment style could have been a useful enlargement of the blues form. His own playing was even more effective because of his intensely dramatic approach to the music. The biting notes of the guitar were closely tied to the vocal line. He played with a slide on the upper strings and fretted the bass strings, giving him a mixture of tones something like those of Son House, who uses the metal slide as well as fretting. Also unlike Collins, Hill's falsetto was not a clear vocal sound. He sang with a mixed tone, using some head voice in the higher, forced falsetto, and he was able to sing with either a harder rasping tone or with a pure open sound. With this technical approach his voice became as effective a dramatic instrument as the guitar.

Although he used an involved compound verse for "Tell Me Baby," in "Whoopee Blues," "Down On My Bended Knee," and "The Dead Gone Train" the verse form was the usual three line stanza. His verses were not exceptional, but he persisted in an emotional attitude until it yielded some verbal richness. He had moments of self-pity in a blues like "Down On My Bended Knee,"

> At last, at last, down on my bended knee.
> At last, at last, down on my bended knee.
> I am worried about my baby, bring her back to me.
>
> You know I love my baby, that's why we can't get along.
> You know I love my baby, that's why we can't get along.
> Look like everything I do turns out going on wrong...

but they were in the same vein of blues poetry that has persisted from Patton's "Poor Me" to Lightning Hopkins' "A Sinner's Prayer." He was more striking in the developing imagery of a piece like "Whoopee Blues."

> Um, you been gone all day that you may make whoopee all night.
> Baby, you been gone all day that you may make whoopee all night.
> I'm going to take my razor and cut your leg off, you wouldn't
>     think I been servin' you right.
>
> Undertaker been here and gone, I give him your height and size.
> I said undertaker been here and gone, I give him your height and size.
> You'll be making whoopee with the devil in an hour tomorrow night.

You done made me love you, now got me for your slave.
Baby you done made me love you, now got you for your slave.
From now on you'll be making whoopee, baby, in your lonesome
    grave.

Baby, next time you go out carry your black suit along.
Mama, next time you go out carry your black suit along.
Coffin gonna be your present, hell gonna be your brand new home.

I see the devil got 90,000 women,
    he's got me one more ....

If, like many other Mississippi singers who were once only a vague name,
Hill should be found in McComb it would be an important contribution
to the knowledge of the blues style in the area. If Collins and Hill were
both raised in the same town, then the similarities in their vocal approach would be more easily understood. Also, if Hill should be found
then he could trace some of the influences that helped shape his guitar
style and its complex and dramatic involvement with the sung blues
phrase.

# 8. CENTRAL MISSISSIPPI AND JACKSON INTO THE 'THIRTIES

The southern cities like Jackson were less isolated than the country farms and crossroads of the delta country, and there was a steady movement of professional entertainers in and out of the small night clubs and variety theatres. Most of the blues acts didn't get much below Memphis and its Lyric Theatre on Beale Street, but there were enough musicians and singers in and out of Jackson to give the town's music a self-consciousness that most of the delta singing lacked, and often the local blues men were subject to the influence of outside performers and commercial recordings. In the late years of the 'twenties, however, there was a small Jackson group centered around Ishman Bracey and Tommy Johnson that had some of the rough vigor of the freer delta music. Most of the young men in from the country hung around Johnson's house on River Front Street, but Bracey seemed to have a better business sense, and he was usually able to keep some kind of job going in Jackson.

In the early 1960's Bracey was located in Jackson by Dean Wardlow, and since that time he has been interviewed by three or four other blues enthusiasts. He is still playing, but since the late 1940's, when he joined the church, he has played only gospel songs and sacred music. He was born on January 1, 1900 near Forest Hill, not far from Jackson, and began playing when he was in his teens. His style, when he began recording in 1928, was only tentatively formed, and there was considerable variation in his performances, although some of the changes probably represented Bracey's efforts to become commercially more successful. He was perhaps most effective as a singer when he was associated with Johnson, even if Johnson's influence was only indirect. His first sessions in Memphis were probably done with Johnson as an accompaniest and they certainly reflect some of the other man's ideas. At his sessions two years later in Grafton, Wisconsin, there was almost a stylistic uncertainty to his music. Most of Bracey's compositions are still protected by copyright and permission could not be obtained to quote either melodies or texts. His earliest blues "Saturday Blues" and

129

"Left Alone Blues," recorded in February, 1928, were not copywritten, and of his early recordings they were perhaps the most important, especially "Saturday Blues," which used an interesting variation on the usual three line verse form.

There is still some question as to whether Johnson was one of the accompaniests on the record. Bracey had told Wardlow that the second guitarist was Charlie McCoy, another young Jackson musician who usually played mandolin. Johnson, however, was recording at the same time, and all three of them were in Memphis for the sessions. Ralph Peer was recording them for Victor Records. Johnson recorded on February 3 and 4, with Bracey probably playing second guitar, and Ishman did his two pieces when Johnson had finished singing. The accompaniment sound was very full on Bracey's recordings, and it could even have been all three of them. In the background one guitar was being played with a mandolin technique, a flat picked trill on a single string, and there was still a complex accompaniment pattern being played closer to the microphone.

Of all the Mississippi men Bracey was one of the few who sang with a strongly nasal tone. The sound was thin and pinched, and he sang without embellishment; even the common portmenti at the verse endings were left out. He had to depend on skillful accompaniment patterns and strong verse material to be distinctive. His verses, however, were usually derivative, and without the guitarists like Johnson, to at least shape the accompaniment, he was not a distinctive instrumentalist. In the recordings that he did for Paramount two years later, in March, 1930, he even tried using a small instrumental group for some of the pieces. It was an advertising team called the "New Orleans Nehi Boys," with clarinetist Kid Ernest Mitchell and pianist Charley Taylor. He also did two blues with his own accompaniment, "Woman Woman Blues" and "Suitcase Full Of Holes." His voice had darkened since his first recordings, and he tried to use a falsetto voice in "Woman Woman Blues," with an octave leap in the middle of the second line, but the sound was almost clumsy and the accompaniment was unsteady.

In the earlier "Saturday Blues" he used one of the conventional infidelity themes, but the form of the verses had been changed to fit a fresh melodic concept, and in one verse he loosened up enough to sing about skin powders and creams that were advertised as being able to lighten skin color.

> Now you tell me, mama, do you think that's right,
> You with your kid all day and run to me at night.
> With your kid all day and run to me at night.
> With your kid all day and run to me at night.
>
> Now my regular woman took my pocket change,
> And my sometime woman wants to do the same,
> And you better not let my people catch you here.
> Don't never let my people catch you here.

'Cause it 'tain't no tellin' she might do,
She might cut you, she might shoot you too.
Now she might cut you, she might shoot you too.
Lord she might cut you, she might shoot you too.

Now she's the meanest woman that I've ever seen,
And when I asked for water gimme gasoline.
Now ask her for water, gimme gasoline.
Lord asked for water, gimme gasoline.

Now if you want your woman to look like the race,
You buy her high brown powder, Palmer's Skin Success.
You buy her high brown powder, Palmer's Skin Success.
Buy her high brown powder, Palmer's Skin Success.

Now I got four-five puppies, got one shaggy hound,
It takes all them dogs to run my women down.
It takes all them dogs to run my women down.
Takes all them dogs to run my women down.

The harmonic structure was the usual I-IV-I-V-I, but the first line was
a loosely swinging phrase that went on to include the second line of the
verse with only a pause to take a breath. The doubled line was built
on a suspended down beat and running eighth note groups; it had some of
the feeling of a chopping song. Then there was a sudden change in the
third line to an ascending melodic figure at a tempo that seemed to slow
the opening rhythm to quarter note groups. The rising figure, repeated
in the line, almost seemed to be a structural resolution to the easy
movement of the opening phrase, bringing it up with the same motion
as a man reining in a jogging horse on a back road through the hill
country. The last line began with a half measure to open the phrase,
then resolved with an almost standard last line melody and the V-V-I-I
harmonic resolution. It was casually done, but it was a fresh working of
old blues material, and it was musically successful.

Example 20

with your kid all day and run to me at night.

Bracey, at this time, has no plans to play outside of Jackson, and he is still giving much of his time to the church. For him it has been many years since the blues were a deep influence on his life.

Most of the delta singers drifted in and out of Jackson during the 'twenties - certainly Charley Patton, Son House, Willie Brown, and Skip James, at one time or another - but the strongest influence on the music in the town's Negro neighborhoods, as well as on most of the young singers who hung around the town for more than a few weeks, was Tommy Johnson, who was living ".. in a big house on River Front Street,'' as one of his younger pupils, Shirley Griffith, remembers. Bracey has told Dean Wardlow that Johnson was born in Crystal Springs, in Copiah County, about 25 miles to the south of Jackson. Griffith, who was found by Art Rosenbaum in Indianapolis, said that Johnson was nearly fifty when he met him in Jackson in the late 'twenties, so Johnson would have been born about 1880. In the picture that was taken of him at the time of his recording sessions for Victor in 1928, however, he looks younger; so Griffith may have thought he was older than he was. He moved into Jackson about 1926 and lived there for a number of years, occasionally traveling to other Mississippi towns to sing. All of the men who encountered him during these years remember him as a near alcoholic who drank anything he could get his hands on. He finally went back to Crystal Springs and was living there at the time of his death in the mid-1950's.

It is difficult to reconcile Johnson's drunkenness and his difficult emotional life with his wife, Maggie Campbell, with the artistic poise of his singing. He was one of the most consciously artistic of all the Mississippi singers, and each one of his pieces had been worked into his fingers and his voice until it was a carefully distinct musical statement. His blues were like a piece of swamp cedar rubbed against a sleeve until it glistened. Griffith told Rosenbaum that ''Tom was practically a genius on the guitar,'' and in discussing ''Big Road Blues'' as Griffith had learned it from Johnson, Rosenbaum concluded, ''Unlike most blues guitarists who have a characteristic style which they freely apply to the various blues they sing, Johnson seems to have worked out a set accompaniment which fit the special character of each blues he did, and which he played pretty much the same each time. Here, the idea of walking down a road is suggested in the guitar bass line. Shirley says that Tom could stop the strings of the guitar from above when playing this blues, as one would play a piano, rather than bring his left hand around the neck from the bottom in the usual way..."[1.] The bass figure in "Big Road" was one of Johnson's most widely imitated guitar patterns.

Example 21

It was strongly pianistic in style, with its close relationship to the boogie "walking bass," and it may have been because of this that Johnson would sometimes play it pressing down on the strings with his left hand, as a pianist would press down on the piano keys. Nearly every one of the young Jackson singers learned this figure of Johnson's, and even in recent years it has been recorded almost as he played it by Griffith, by K. C. Douglas, who also learned some of his style from Johnson, and by the older Meridian singer Babe Stovall, who was in and out of Jackson when he was a young man. Even the Memphis medicine show performers picked it up, and Furry Lewis still uses it for several of his pieces.

All of the compositions that he recorded for Victor at his Memphis sessions in February and August of 1928 - "Cool Drink Of Water Blues," "Big Road Blues," "Bye-Bye Blues," "Maggie Campbell Blues," "Canned Heat Blues," "Lonesome Home Blues," "Louisiana Blues," and "Big Fat Mama Blues" - are still protected by copyright, and the copyright holder has denied permission to quote either the verses or the melodies. In the winter of 1929-1930 he went north with Bracey and recorded for Paramount, but none of the records have been found. Often, however, he used widely known folk verses in the pieces, and it is possible to consider his style in his reworking of these traditional materials. His voice was carefully controlled, and he was very skilled in his use of falsetto. In one of his effective uses of a local verse he gave the conventional melody a new color and dimension with falsetto leaps of a major sixth or an octave, the pitch consistently true, despite the difficulty of the voice change.

Example 22

line
I asked — for wa_ter and she
give me gas_o_line, Lord, Lord_y Lord

As in most of his songs the scale was derived from the older slave scales. For this verse he used a gapped pentatonic with an altered third used as both major and minor. The second and the seventh were not included. The rhythmic movement was slow, the guitar returning to pianistic figures in the bass strings, as in "Big Road Blues." He separated the vocal phrases with the irregular half measure that was characteristic of Patton and the northern delta singers, in the two beats leading to the new phrase suggesting a subtle rhythmic impetus with the accompaniment. One of his blues, "Big Fat Mama," even used the "Moon Going Down" melody, although he played it with a different accompaniment style. One of the most moving of his pieces was the slow, brooding "Canned Heat Blues," perhaps the most lyric of his blues. The text, which was concerned with drinking Sterno, had a lingering sadness in his insistence that his alcoholism was killing him.

He was often able to rework effectively an older song with only rhythmic shifts and a subtle displacement of emphasis. The melodic changes, against a complex two-guitar accompaniment, stayed in the ear, even when the text was overly familiar.

Example 23

Now — sun gon_na shine, in my back door some day,
my back door some day — Um_m_m sun gon_na shine in
my back door some day — And it
bring those change and throw_ my blues a_way.

He was even able to set the "See See Rider" verse to the same melody, and the younger singers who learned it from him often slip into his melodic patterns after they've sung the traditional version. The piece was developed within the twelve bar, three line verse framework, but his changes gave it unexpected vividness. It was as though he had consciously taken the blues form apart in his mind, and then slowly put it together again. Often he seemed to be using older verses to make his melodic and rhythmic concept more immediately obvious, but it may have been that his use of the traditional verses reflected a creative impulse that was more concerned with the musical than the textual. He seemed to have few of the torments of Son House or Robert Johnson, and he didn't concern himself with the local scene in the way that Patton did. But in his use of the voice and in his accompaniments, he was as personally creative as they were, and in the blues style that was developing in central Mississippi he was deeply influential.

There was an emotional loneliness in the music of the delta singers, the feeling of the long dusty roads through the fields, and the winter sundowns around the thin board cabins when the sun turns the water blood red as it drops below the low line of the horizon. But life in the delta towns was crowded and noisy, and the music for the road houses and the dances had some of this easy gregariousness. It wasn't intense, it wasn't individual, but it was good for the long hours when people just wanted to dance and drink some illegal whiskey. It was the kind of music that went into the juke boxes when the first roadside clubs began putting in brightly lit music machines instead of hiring a local band. The bands could play almost anything, for both white and colored audiences, and the ramshackle buildings would shake with the feet stamping on the board floors as the fiddle and guitar picked up the old country dance pieces. Outside there would be a few dogs lying in the light waiting for somebody to come out and get them back across the fields with a lantern. Over the door were clouds of insects whirling around the bright light bulb that glared on the hand painted sign advertising the building. There were little breakdown bands everywhere in the South, some of them in Memphis using a jug for a comedy effect, but most of them just a fiddle and a guitar, sometimes two guitars or a mandolin, or a washboard and a kazoo. Everybody sang in the band and they usually had to know a lot of numbers to get through the dances. There was none of the creative excitement of the great delta blues in the breakdown music; the bands were like the weeds left to grow in the shade of summer corn, but just as in the fields there were sometimes more weeds than anything else.

The bands, and the men involved with them, had considerable popularity even in Mississippi, with its strong blues orientation. They didn't present the emotional challenge of someone like Willie Brown or Sam Collins, and the music was often old-fashioned, so that everybody could dance to it. A small group of central Mississippi musicians, Charlie McCoy, his brother Joe, the Chatmon brothers, and two Jackson musicians, James Cole and Tommie Bradley, did more recording than all of the delta blues men together, and they continued to work through the 1930's, when the delta style had been momentarily eclipsed by newer sounds in the blues. There was considerable overlapping of musicians between the Chatmons and the McCoys, so that the records often have a similarity of sound. Also, Cole and Bradley both sang or used outside vocalists, so their recordings lacked a strong individuality. But all of them seem to have had some sales since there were many sessions for all of them. The Mississippi Sheiks, usually Bo Chatmon and a violinist, had some releases that were very successful within their market, and occasionally there was some interest in one of the records in one of the northern Negro slums.

The groups all had a similar musical approach, not greatly different from the style of one of the Memphis jug groups, Jack Kelly's South Memphis Jug Band. The rhythm was a heavy 4/4, steady, even monotonous, but clearly defined so that there would be no difficulty dancing to it. At times the rhythms - especially when Bo Chatmon was the guitarist - were so dull that the bands were almost as bad as the white music that was being played in the area. The violinists, Lonnie Chatmon and Walter Vincon with Charlie McCoy's Mississippi Hot Footers and the Sheiks, James Cole with the Cole and Bradley groups, usually played in unison with the voice, and on instrumental breaks played the melody without variation. The accompaniment guitar style was often a flat picked alternate bass note - chord pattern similar to the standard white country style. On the Cole and Bradley recordings there was often some excitement in Eddie Dimmit's mandolin playing and in the still unidentified washboard player's busy style. Since the rhythm was already so steady they were left to buzz around it like bees around a jam pot left outside on a table. With the Sheiks there were usually only Chatmon and the violinist Walter Vincon, and the sound was less colorful; but one of their first recordings, "Sitting On Top Of The World" and "Lonely One In This Town," sold very well and many other country musicians, white and Negro, learned to play it.

Although Charlie McCoy usually played the mandolin there was a heavier sound on the Mud Steppers' recordings, as though he were playing a banjo-mandolin, with the mandolin finger board and a skin banjo head. On their version of "It Is So Good," he played rhythm chords behind some of the singing and the sound was very much like that of a banjo.

The blues that all of them did had a derivative quality, but sometimes there were moments of brilliance. For his "That Lonesome Train Took My Baby Away" McCoy had developed a fast, raggy mandolin accompaniment, and the blues was an effective elaboration of one of the standard "leaving" themes, even though his singing had an amateurish quality. The piece would have gotten everybody out on a dance floor for a noisy minute of loose-legged movement. The song had some of the feeling of a delta blues in the text, even though the music was closer to country ragtime.

Woke up this morning, found something wrong,
My loving babe had caught that train and gone.
Now won't you starch my jumper, iron my overalls.
I'm going to ride that train that they call the Cannonball.

Depot agent, close your depot down.
The woman I'm loving she's fixin' to blow this town.
Now that mean old fireman, the cruel old engineer.
Gonna take my baby and leave me lonesome here.

It ain't no telling what that train won't do.
It'll take your baby and run right over you.
Now that engineer man ought to be 'shamed of hisself,
Take women from their husbands, babies from their
          mothers' breasts.

I walked down the track and the stars refuse to shine.
Looked every minute I was going to lose my mind.
Now my knees was weak, my footsteps was all awry,
Looked like every minute I was stumbling (under the way.)

Although the melody had been slightly changed by the hurried tempo, it was essentially the same as the "Saturday Blues" melody that Ishman Bracey had recorded three years earlier; so it must have been widespread in the central Mississippi area. Tommie Bradley used the same leaving theme for the opening verses of the "Window Pane Blues," with Cole's violin and Dimmitt's busy mandolin.

Lord, when I got up this morning snow was on my window pane.
I got up this morning, snow was on my window pane.
I couldn't even see my baby, couldn't even hear her name.

Lord and my baby is leaving, crying won't make her stay.
My baby's leaving, crying won't make her stay.
Lord if crying would help now, cry myself away....

One of the wildest and most exciting of the Mississippi "juking" bands was a three piece group with piano, guitar, tambourine, and sometimes a doubling on kazoo - probably by the tambourine player - that was recorded in Hattiesburg by A.R.C. in the summer of 1936. The group was called the Mississippi Jook Band, and probably included the blues singer Blind Roosevelt Graves, his brother Uaroy, and a piano player named Cooney Vaughn. Graves and his brother had recorded both blues and gospel songs for Paramount in the late 1920's, but the four sides that were released by A.R.C, "Hittin' The Bottle Stomp," "Skippy Whippy," "Dangerous Woman," and "Barbecue Bust," were closer to the rougher country barrelhouse tradition than they were to the blues. Vaughn had an uninhibited country rag time style, and the little band moved with an exuberant, strutting sound.

137

GARFIELD AKERS ADVERTISEMENT

BO CARTER ADVERTISEMENT

SAM COLLINS ADVERTISEMENT

All of the bands could do Mississippi blues pieces. The Sheiks did a version of Tommy Johnson's "Big Road Blues" called "Stop And Listen Blues," and on other recordings there were local blues verses and melodies. Often they were recording for the white hillbilly market, rather than the blues market. Bo and his brother Sam were able to get almost a country and western purity in their singing, and pieces like "Jail Bird Love Song," sung as a duet, were very effective in their imitation of the white rural singing and accompaniment style. Bo, under the name Bo Carter, also had considerable success as a soloist, and recorded more than a hundred titles between 1928 and 1940. He had developed a musical idiom with some of the immediacy of blues artists like Lonnie Johnson and Tampa Red, and, like the Sheiks, was able to reach both a white and Negro audience. For some of his recordings he used the erotic symbolism that had become popular in the "party record" business, and he seems to have been sold to the white market on this basis. He had other pieces - "Be My Salty Dog," with its momentary similarities to John Hurt's "Candy Man," and his first songs for OKeh, "I'm An Old Bumble Bee," taken from Memphis Minnie's Columbia recording, which had been released a few months earlier, and "I've Got The Whole World In My Hand" - which, although they were not strongly individual were sung with some feeling and taste. He is still living in Memphis, blind and unable to play, his wife asking people to leave him alone so that he can think about the life to come instead of the blues. Their house is a shabby wooden building on the same rutted alleyway behind Beale Street where Will Shade of the Memphis Jug Band lives in helpless squalor.

By the middle of the 'thirties, as the Depression deepened, the delta music began to change, the concept of the blues as song shifting to a more assertive, a more obvious expression. In the new stylistic emphasis there was less concern with the complex musicianship that had led to guitar accompaniments like Willie Brown's "Future Blues" or the beautifully ordered melodies like Tommy Johnson's "Cool Drink of Water Blues." Instead there was a heightened emotionalism, a new intentness. It was the same urgency that dominated Patton's music, but the rhythms had been subtly altered to suit new dancing styles and a new city audience. One of the first Mississippi men to record extensively in the developing style was Joe Williams, who was in his thirties and living in St. Louis when he began recording in 1935. He was born in Crawford, Mississippi, in Lowndes County, about seventy miles north of Meridian. Like Sam Collins, he grew up out of the delta counties, and this was a shaping factor in his musical development. He was one of sixteen children, and he decided when he was still young that he didn't want to stay in the fields as a laborer. He made his own guitar when he was four and a half, and by the time he was in his teens he was already writing blues. For most of the 'twenties he was drifitng around the South, working in levee camps or in the line camps in the back country, playing music for dances and parties. For two or three years he lived in Tuscaloosa, Alabama, working at parties for a local pimp named Totsie King. Finally, in the worst of the Depression, he made his way to St. Louis and settled down. His cousin J. D. Short, who had recorded for Paramount and Vocalion, had been living in St. Louis since 1925, and he and Joe worked around St. Louis together until J. D. began playing saxophone and clarinet with Douglas Williams' dance band. When Joe went to Chicago to record for Bluebird in February, 1935, his second guitarist was Henry Townsend.

With Williams, and with other singers who developed in the late 'thirties and in the war years, the manner of singing became, in itself, the style of the song. He used every kind of blues from Mississippi, as well as pieces he learned from the recordings of men like Sleepy John Estes, and he performed everything with the same shouted ferocity. His "Someday Baby," from Estes' older recording of "Someday Baby Blues," had some of the feeling of Estes loose, jangling rhythm, but Williams sang it with the rough intensity of his own "Baby Please Don't Go," or his "Highway 49." His accompaniment style was a strummed rhythm using dotted note values in an almost loping beat, and insistent, knotted passages of running triplets. Musically the accompaniments were tangled and often confused, but like his voice, it was the expressiveness of the performance that shaped the blues, rather than the musical concept of the piece shaping the performance, as with singers like Tommy Johnson or King Solomon Hill. For his second session in 1935, he began using a larger instrumental group, and on many of his later Bluebird recordings between 1937 and 1941, the sound was closer to the small bands working in the Jackson area than it was to the spare delta accompaniments. The harmonica player Sonny Boy Williamson worked with him for a number of recordings, and Sonny Boy's playing was as emotionally driven as Williams' singing.

Although it was his style of performance rather than his compositions that gave him his distinctiveness, he had considerable variety in his recordings. One of the most interesting of the early Bluebird releases was a fine "My Grey Pony," with some similarities to Patton's style in "Pony Blues," but with a distinctive accompaniment and phrase pattern. "I'm Getting Wild About Her" even used an easy, rolling version of the "Tight Like That" melody. When he began recording as a "folk" blues artist in the 1950's he reworked his old material over and over again, often using phrases and patterns of the guitar accompaniments with a new urgency, and sometimes singing with an even more intense drama. His voice had deepened in the years that he had been away from recording, and his style had become even more knotted in its use of forms and techniques, both from his own background and from other recordings. Some of the individuality of the sound was from his use of altered nine-string guitars. He used old instruments and mounted an additional set of three tuning pegs at the end of the neck. The strings were tuned in unison with the two high strings of the guitar and with the third string of the bass, leaving the two low bass strings and the third string from the top of the instrument as single melody strings. Most of the pieces used the "Spanish" open G tuning, which on Joe's instrument was d-g-d'-d'-g'-b-b-d''-d'', and he alternated a finger stroke on the open strings with heavy melodic passages on the middle strings, usually with a knife or metal slide. For most of his pieces the guitar was played in unison with the voice, although as he became excited the guitar often was left silent while he sang. On the faster pieces, using either a compound verse form or a version of the old "Tight Like That" melody, he stayed with a mixed dotted rhythm and triplet beat pattern, usually accelerating considerably during the song. For most of his blues he used one of his older melodies, accompanying all of them with the same impetuous strength. The phrase length varied considerably in all of his performances, although he sometime was held to a more regular twelve bar pattern by his accompanists. He is still, after nearly forty years of singing, a complex and often effective performer, and his style still is moving toward an even deeper maturity.

The same emotionalism marked the singing of younger men like Robert Johnson, and of less well known delta men who were momentarily drawn into the stream of Mississippi recording in the 'thirties, like Isaiah Nettles - "The Mississippi Moaner," George Torey, and Willie Lofton. Nettles, who recorded in Jackson in 1935, used the falsetto voice and the clearly outlined melody of the older delta blues; but in his "It's Cold In China Blues," the emotionalism of the voice was forced, and the guitar rhythm was close to Big Joe's doubled strumming, almost like a "shake dance" rhythm in its noisy enthusiasm. Torey was one of the singers recorded in Birmingham by the American Recording Corporation in the summer of 1937, but his style had many of the delta characteristics. Older Mississippi singers have vaguely remembered him as being from one of the northern delta counties. Of the three sides by Torey listed in the Dixon and Godrich compilation, one - unissued - was titled "Delta Blues," which strengthens the impression that he was probably a Mississippi man who was either living in Birmingham or who had been brought into town for the session. His other two pieces, "Married Woman Blues" and "Lonesome Man Blues," also recorded on April 2, were released on ARC 7-08-57. His voice had some of Williams' assertive strength, with a consistent vibrato on the held tones and even a dramatic use of dynamic shading. The guitar accompaniment for "Lonesome Man Blues" was in a more controlled bottleneck style, with a steady rhythm in the lower strings - alternating thumb on the chord fundamental and the chord in the middle strings - and a near unison melody with the voice. The rhythm was held even through the fairly elaborate guitar interpolations played with the bottleneck between the vocal phrases. "Married Woman Blues" was more derivative in melody and accompaniment style, with some of the elements of the "raggy" guitar music that the Carolina men like Blind Boy Fuller were recording. The melody was the eight bar blues phrase probably best known in its "Keys To The Highway" version. The harmonic pattern is I - V - IV - IV - I - V - I - I, and it is usually played at a medium tempo. Torey finger picked the accompaniment, without the bottleneck, and some of his finger patterns were very reminiscent of Fuller. The verses, as with "Lonesome Man Blues," were derivative, but he used some of the most effective verses with this theme,

If you love a married woman you gonna always have the blues.
Everytime you want to see her her husband want to see her too...

and he ended with the poignant blues image,

Well, I went to the window and I looked down on that ground,
And my heart struck sorrow and the tears come easing down.

The strident emotionalism was even more evident in a blues like Willie
Lofton's "Dark Road Blues." It was Tommy Johnson's old "Big Road
Blues," but by 1935, when Lofton recorded for Bluebird in Chicago, it had
become the more expressive "dark road" that the singer was going down.
The new version had most of the elements of Johnson's accompaniment in
the ascending bass line and the displaced rhythmic accent, but Lofton
sang it almost twice as fast as Johnson, and the guitar playing had a
hardness and an aggressiveness that Johnson would not have recognized.

By the late 'thirties the rough, shouted blues had become almost a
mannerism, and some Mississippi singers developed a style that was
even more intense than Williams'. One of the most successful was Tommy
McClennan, who was born in April, 1908 on a farm owned by J. F. Sligh,
about nine miles outside of Yazoo City. Yazoo City is in Yazoo County,
about forty-five miles north of Jackson on the Clarksdale Road. He was
already playing when he was in his teens and people in Yazoo City still
remember his version of the juking song "Bottle It Up And Go." He
was living on Charles Street in Jackson during much of the period when
he was recording, a small thin, nervous man who drank heavily. He did
a "Whiskey Head Woman" on his first Bluebird session in 1939, and it
was successful enough for him to follow it with a "Whiskey Head Man"
the next year. Not only had the blues become consciously rough and
assertive, but in McClennan there was a self-conscious glorification of
his own roughness. He introduced it with,

> This is *Tommy McClennan*, the one who put the "Whiskey
> Headed Woman Blues." Instead of putting out the "Whiskey
> Headed Woman Blues" I'm going to put out "He's A Whiskey
> Headed Man Blues," just like myself and all the rest of you
> Whiskey Headed Men.

There had always been a consciousness of the drunkenness and the
amorality of the life that many of the bluesmen lived, but McClennan
used it as the shaping force in his blues style. His singing was often
a toneless shout, a harsh, almost formless vocal line with sudden
moments of excitement or laughter. His guitar playing was limited to
heavy frailing in an open tuning, the intervals between the sung phrases
filled with repeated single notes high on the guitar neck, or abrupt,
hurried open chords. He probably used one of the metal bodied guitars
that had become popular in the delta for its louder sound. McClennan's
style would probably have been less effective without his rich exuberance and noisy vanity. The shouted boast in one of his blues, "I'm a
guitar king, playin' the blues everywhere I go..." was somehow appeal-

ing when it was made by someone who played the guitar as badly as McClennan did.

With McClennan the assertiveness was more than a mannerism. He was noisy and vain and difficult to control. Bill Broonzy remembered that when McClennan first came to Chicago he was singing a piece that used the word "nigger," and he refused to change the word despite Bill's pleas. They went to a party together, Tommy insisting, "The hell with them. I'll sing my song..." and he went ahead and sang it. His guitar was smashed in the fight that broke out and he and Bill had to run to get away from the crowd. When he died in the late 1950's he was a hopeless alcoholic drifting on the streets of Chicago's south side.

McClennan's records sold fairly well, and another singer, Robert Petway, whose style was very similar to his, also had some of his success recording for Bluebird in 1941 and 1942. His beat was heavier and more regular, but the rest of the style - the coarse shout of the vocal line and the fierce assertiveness - was very close to McClennan's. The blues that he did at his two sessions were mostly conventional pieces of the late '30's early '40's, but occasional verses were marked with the stronger emotionalism of the delta music.

# ALABAMA

# 9. ALABAMA

Along U. S. 43, from Mobile on the coast, through Tuscaloosa in the middle of the state, to Florence, not far from the Tennessee line, Alabama is like three different pieces of earth, the edges only loosely joined together as the road moves north through the state. Along the coast, and for almost a hundred miles inland, the land is a sandy plain covered with an endless growth of longleaf pine, rising into small ridges as the land from the rocky coastal shelf breaks through the low plain. It is empty, barren country, the cabins in scattered clearings, the nights dark and unfriendly, the days hot and oppressive. The people of Mobile still have some of the casualness of Louisiana French-Italian country, but in the pine barrens the stillness is a presence hanging in the wind, and the life in the lonely cabins is meager and thin. The pine barrens open out to the north and the land turns darker, to the rich, flat soils of the central Alabama "black belt," its name partly from the color of the dirt and partly from the thousands of Negroes who found themselves living there as "freedmen" at the end of the Civil War. The black belt, almost a hundred miles of it, reaches north of Tuscaloosa, and because of the soil was for many years one of the world's richest cotton areas, despite the debilitating methods of agriculture that were used on the land in the first years of planting. The cash value of the cotton crop was so high that during the slavery period the cotton planters didn't even grow food. They used every acre of the land for cotton and brought their food in from the coastal lands, where the small farmers could get in two or three plantings of corn and beans a year. North of Tuscaloosa the land begins to rise, and the north of the state is hill country, the roads streaked with sticky red clay and the board cabins off the highway in the new growth of loblolly and shortleaf pine, oak and sweetgum.

Culturally the state is divided like its land. Along the coast there is a French creole flavor to the language and customs. South of Mobile, in the bayous, there is as much French spoken as there is in the Louisiana bayous to the west. In Julian Lee Rayford's colorful study of the

Alabama bayou folk culture, "Whistling Woman and Crowing Hen," he found that the people, the speech, and the bayous have mingled into a cultural entity that is no longer French, not yet American, but with an insistent vitality in its moods and tempers. In the black belt African and American elements mingle in the Negro country areas, with the American popular culture strongest in the towns. North of the cotton country, in the hills, the culture becomes Anglo-American. Many of the early settlers were Tories who moved into the new Alabama territory rather than join the revolution, and English ballads and dance songs can still be found on the small farms back in the valleys around Huntsville and Athens. The people who came into Alabama brought their language and song with them, like the cotton seed and the fruit tree cuttings that they had packed into their wagons and saddle bags.

There were as many factors that could have led to a vital blues growth in Alabama as there were in Mississippi. The cotton lands were cleared with slave labor in the 1820's, and at the outbreak of the Civil War the population of the state was nearly half Negro. By 1880 it was still more than forty-seven percent colored, and even in 1950, after three generations of Negro families had begun to move away from the state's vicious social system, there were still more than thirty-two percent colored in Alabama. Most of the people were on farms or in isolated cabins. In 1960 only forty-five percent of the state's people had moved into the urban areas around Mobile, Gadsden, Montgomery, Huntsville, and Birmingham. It is poor country, the rate of growth much below that of the rest of the United States, and the colored men and women in Alabama live outside of the state's white social structure in almost as much isolation as the Negroes of the delta. There is a strong voodoo cult centered in the south of the state and extending up the Tombigbee River, and in the Taladega National Forest there are small groups still using African words and phrases in their speech. One of the few early song collections that included blues verses was done in Alabama, outside of Auburn in Lee County in 1904. But if there was a strong early blues tradition it has been blown into the wind, like cotton lint along the roadsides. There was little recording of Alabama artists away from the state, and there was almost no recording done in Alabama until the Gennett Record Company set up a studio in Birmingham in the summer of 1927. They left after getting some local jazz bands, a few religious groups, and a handful of blues releases. A few recordings done in Atlanta by Columbia Records and a session in Chicago for Paramount by one of the Alabama singers, with a few scattered songs by local artists, are the only pieces left of what might have been a strong indigenous blues style.

Birmingham itself may have discouraged the record companies. It's a dreary, shabby city with rows of ramshackle Negro shacks just south of the main business section. Even along the one or two streets where there are a few Negro businesses the colored men and women have a guarded nervousness if they have to talk to someone who is white. The local men working as talent scouts in other large southern cities brought most of the blues singers to the companies, but there doesn't seem to have been anyone working in Birmingham. The music that was recorded, however, doesn't have the urgency or the emotional excitement of the Mississippi blues, and extensive field recording in the state in the late 1930's, the 1940's, and the early 1950's, did not yield either important blues singers or the remnants of a major strain of blues expression. A social background can only shape artistic expression if the expression is already part of the social environment. Whatever the reason there does not seem to have been the eddying stream of the blues that flooded over the flat lands of the Mississippi delta. Even the Alabama work song was less developed in its forms than the work song of Mississippi. There is only a handful of early examples, but in almost all of them the form is a one line phrase, musically complete, without the rhymed second line that was probably at the root of the blues growth in Mississippi. Without a formed verse pattern, however rudimentary, the development of the blues is severely restricted, and it could have been this lack of a verse form in the work song that inhibited the development of a local blues tradition.

Although the blues strains in Alabama seem to have been thin, the state has a rich musical culture. After a long session of blues and play party songs with a singer from the Selma area, west of Montgomery, his wife asked if she could sing. For an hour she and her sister improvised two voice religious songs with a depth and urgency that her husband's blues had never reached. The strongest song styles in Alabama are religious, and the surge song and the slow two-voice antiphonal hymn have perhaps reached their highest development in the field cabins along the Tombigbee River, or in the older settlements in the red clay country of Fayette or Marion counties.

The Alabama singers who did record, however, were distinctive. Their music was as much an expression of the black belt counties as the Mississippi singing was of the delta. Only two singers seem to have recorded extensively, Ed Bell, and a singer known only as "Barefoot Bill From Alabama," but their style was fully formed, and it is possible to see its outlines in their recordings. Barefoot Bill also worked with another singer, Pillie Bolling, on his 1930 Atlanta sessions, but Bolling had a vocal sound closer to the Georgia singers than to the Alabama, and he may have been an Atlanta man. The singing of Bell and Barefoot Bill was less intense than the Mississippi style, but it was freer rhythmically than most of the delta singing. There was the same use of the half measure for the opening phrase of a line, but the irregular shouted tone of the field song was kept, often forcing the singers into measures of 6/4 in a basic 4/4 pattern. As in Mississippi the scales were generally pentatonic. The relative restraint of the early Alabama men may have been a characteristic of the local blues styles, and the later field recordings in the state are marked with a controlled emotionalism. There also seems to have been less use of the falsetto voice that was common in Mississippi. One of the most distinctive sounds of early Alabama music was the voice of Jaybird Coleman, a harmonica

ALABAMA

MONTGOMERY

player player and singer from Bessemer, in Jefferson County, about thirteen miles southwest of Birmingham. He followed the melodic phrase of the harmonica with his voice, and he strained his voice with a tight, quivering sound to get up into the harmonica's higher range, instead of using the less difficult falsetto.

The guitar accompaniments also differed considerably from the Mississippi styles. There was almost no use of the guitar to follow the vocal melody, either with a unison melody picked with the fingers on the upper strings or with a bottle neck or metal slide. Instead there was a lighter doubled rhythm in 8th notes, the thumb hitting the fundamental of the chord and the first finger brushing back on the strings. The lines of the vocal melody were usually followed by a repeated short phrase in the guitar, generally a measure in length. The guitar style was closer to the African music of the stringed lyres or the sansa, sometimes even repeating a simple syncopated rhythmic unit throughout the piece. There was in some of it the sound of the West Indian meringue style, which was also closely involved with earlier African music, especially in its syncopated rhythm, which was less prevalent in the more isolated delta area. It was a style that could have come into Alabama through the port of Mobile, with its ships going to and from the ports of the Caribbean.

The verse forms were generally the conventional three line stanza, sometimes with the beginning line on a subdominant harmony. Barefoot Bill used a more involved verse form for two or three of his pieces.

> My baby quit me, talk's all over,
>    I said, town,
> My baby done quit me, talk's all over town.
> And I'm too good a man for to let that talk go 'round

(Squabblin' Blues)

Many of the verses were obviously derived from city recordings, but others more directly reflected the squalor of share cropper life in Alabama. In 1963 a field collector for the Newport Folk Foundation, Ralph Rinzler, found an elderly singer named Willie Doss living in Ashford, Alabama, in the southeast corner of the state. Willie was born in Cleveland, Mississippi, and spent his boyhood there, but his singing has the characteristic Alabama softness, and he uses the Alabama 8th note rhythms, without melodic doubling, in his simple guitar accompaniments. He learned many of his songs from recent commercial recordings, but in one of his pieces he used verses that could be a survival of a disguised "escape" song from the slavery period.

> Well, I got a coal black mare, oh lord how that horse can run.
> Yes, she run out on the track at midnight, and she runs
>    all on the road.

151

ED BELL ADVERTISEMENT

Yes, she on the race track at midnight,
'Til she runs both night and day.
Say when day began to break, boys,
She don't never break her gait.

She got pretty gold teeth, earrings in her ears.
She got pretty gold teeth, earrings in her ears.
Yes when you win the race boys, you don't know how it's done.

Well she runs every night
'Til she runs to the break of day.
'Til she runs 'til she runs both night and day.
Yeh when day began to break, boys, she don't never break her
    gait.

The sensed violence was more open in the blues of Barefoot Bill.

Now Mister, Mister, please to spare my,
    I say, life,
Now Mister, Mister, please to spare my life.
I got three little children, I got one little bald headed wife.

(Squabblin' Blues)

My crime, my crime I really can't under -
    I said, stand.
My crime, my crime I really can't understand.
They got me 'cused of murder and I never harmed a man.

Baby, please come down there for my trial.
I said, babe, will you please come down on the trial day.
When my grief comes down you can wipe my tears away.

I'm going to be condemned early tomorrow,
    I said, morn,
Buddy, he condemned early on tomorrow morn.
But I'm not guilty 'cause I done nobody wrong...

(My Crime Blues)

In Bell there was the restlessness and the gnawing loneliness of the
southern itinerant.

Two trains running, never one my way.
Two trains running, never one my way.
I'm going to leave here walkin' on the Santa Fe.

Well, there's one thing I don't like 'bout that railroad man.
One thing I don't like 'bout that railroad man.
They will take your rider never bring her back.

(Frisco Whistle Blues)

That same train, that same engineer,
That same train, that same engineer,
Took my woman, lord, left me standing here...

Hey Mr. Conductor, can a broke man ride your blinds?
Hey Mr. Conductor, can a broke man ride your blinds?
Said "Better buy your ticket, know this train ain't mine."

I stood here looked at the risin' sun.
I was standin' lookin' at the risin' sun.
Train don't run by be some walkin' done.

(Mean Conductor Blues)

Of the two Bell's blues sound closer to the earlier work song style, but his blues include references to railroads like the Frisco or the Santa Fe, which may indicate that he learned them from other singers, since these railroads didn't go through Alabama. Despite lengthy trips through the state, nothing is known either of Ed Bell or Barefoot Bill. Jaybird Coleman has died, but everyone in Bessemer remembered him and said to talk to his brother, Joe Coleman, who shines shoes in a barber shop on Bessemer's main street. Joe keeps shining shoes as he talks, to avoid trouble with the owner of the shop, but he talks about Jaybird as he works, shaking his head from time to time saying, "I sure would like to get one of Jaybird's old records so I could hear him again. He could make that harp talk."

A last factor inhibiting the growth of the blues in the state may have been Alabama's poverty. With the coming of the boll weevil in 1910 the state's already uncertain economic growth was slowed, and despite the recent development of a large missile and electronics complex around Huntsville, the rural areas are still fast in the grip of poverty and prejudice. More than 200,000 Negroes fled the state between 1950 and 1960, and as they found rooms and apartments in the slums of Chicago and Los Angeles, they were followed by thousands of white Alabamians who had also fled the poverty and the sense of economic helplessness. With them has gone much of the elusive sound of the Alabama blues, and only an occasional note or guitar pattern, drifting in a half-open hotel room window near Schuster's Alley in Montgomery, or across a wooden porch on one of the dirt streets behind Davis Avenue in Mobile, still hangs in the air in the slow Alabama twilight.

# 10. ALABAMA INTO THE 'THIRTIES

There was relatively so much less recording in the Alabama area than there was in areas like the delta or north Texas that each of the sessions was an important one. Even Birmingham sessions, like the sides that were done by William Harris and George Torey, used Mississippi men. Except for the two blues men, Ed Bell and Barefoot Bill, most of the Alabama recording in the late 'twenties was done by groups like the Birmingham Jug Band, which did nine titles for OKeh in Atlanta in 1930. The jug band, which may have had Jaybird Coleman on harmonica, had a strong, loosely swinging beat, and their pieces had the tonal richness and the coloration of the best country jug band music. Joe Evans and Arthur McClain also recorded in Birmingham and New York as "The Two Poor Boys," doing minstrel songs and country dance pieces with some of the feeling of white country music of the area. One Alabama religious group, however, the Birmingham Jubilee Singers, between 1926 and 1930 did more recording than all of Alabama's blues men together. Of the handful of other men to record, the two harmonica players, Jaybird Coleman and Bullet Williams, emerged as among the most distinctive musicians within the loose framework of the Alabama style.

The handful of recordings that Coleman did in the late 1920's are still little known, but Jaybird himself is remembered in Birmingham and in Bessemer, a shambling town of low shacks about ten miles south of Birmingham, where he lived for a number of years. His brother was even able to find an old snapshot of him. Jaybird's real name was Burl C. Coleman and he was born in Gainesville in 1891. Joe remembered that his brother learned to play the harmonica "...on the banks of the Tombigbee River," and that there wasn't anyone like him anywhere around Gainesville, even though a lot of people were beginning to play the harmonica. Jaybird was drafted in the First World War, and got his nickname at Camp McClennan. He kept running off the post so much that they began calling him "jaybird," and the name stuck with him. During the 'twenties he became so well known that for a time he was managed by a local Klu Klux Klan group, who got him jobs at neighboring dances and parties. Joe remembers one time when he and Jaybird decided to walk the forty-two miles to Tuscaloosa, Alabama and Jaybird earned them more than ninety dollars stopping by the country cabins and asking if there were any songs that anyone wanted played. During most of this period he was living in Birmingham, and he was one of the small group of artists to record for the Electrobeam Gennett series when the company set up a portable unit in the city. Nothing that he recorded seems to have sold very well, but Gennett was related to a number of other companies and his masters were used for releases on Gennett, Black Patti, Champion, Conqueror, and Silvertone. At his first session, in July, 1927, he tried to work with a guitarist, R. D. Norwood, but their pieces were not used. Instead Jaybird returned to the studio a month later and redid his pieces, including the piece that he had sung with Norwood accompanying him. The musical style - voice, with accompanying harmonica used to follow the vocal phrase - was wide spread in the rural counties, but there were only a few recordings of these harmonica blues. Jaybird's songs were searing, impassioned statements, with the voice and the harmonica straining to answer each other in a series of freely sung work song phrases. Everything that he recorded was exciting, but perhaps the best known of his releases was ''Mean Trouble Blues'' and ''Trunk Busted - Suitcase Full Of Holes,'' on Gennett 6245. ''Trunk Busted'' was the piece that his brother was most anxious to hear. ''Mean Trouble Blues'' used the single line verse form of much Alabama work song and reflected some of the formlessness and the rough phrasing of the music.

Example 24

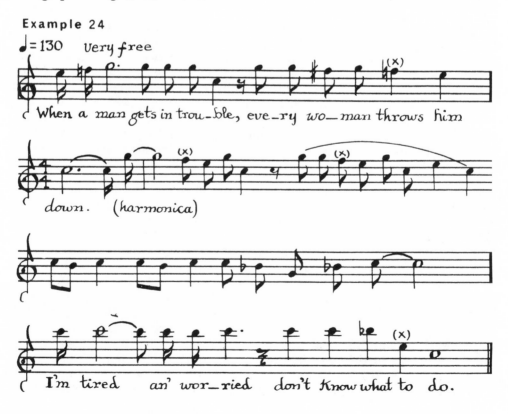

156

When  a  man  gets  in  trouble  every  woman  throws him down.
    (instrumental line)
I'm so worried, don't know what to do.
    (inst.)
I woke up this morning, mama, feeling sad and blue.
    (inst.)
But  the  woman  had  done  quit  me,  didn't  have nowhere to go.
    (inst.)
Hey, hi, hi, hi, hi.
    (inst.)
When  I'm  in  my  good  whiskey  this  the  way I sing my blues.
    (instrumental chorus to end)

Although there was some feeling of rhyme in the end words of the lines, blue- go - do, the other lines, down - hi, were unrelated, and the harmonica line tended to separate the piece into distinctive phrase units, rather than tying it into a related whole.

There  was  a  last  recording  for  Columbia  in  April, 1930, and Jaybird may  have  recorded  with  the  Birmingham  Jug  Band  later in the year, although it is difficult to determine the personnel of the group. Through the  thirties  he  "toughed  it  out,"  moving  to  a small house on West 19th Street in Bessemer. He was almost a lone blues voice in the town, and he finally became the local "clown," with only the crying sound of his  music  to  give  away  whatever  he  was  feeling. He played a lot with the  neighborhood  children,  and  he  made  a  living of sorts carrying a sign board for a local feed store. He stood on the crowded corners on Saturday playing his harmonica and singing, with the advertising signs hanging down his chest and back and a black derby on his head. When he became  sick  early  in  1950  he  was  eligible  for care in a Veteran's hospital, and it was in the Tuskeegee VA Hospital that he died on June 16, 1950.

Coleman  was  an  intense,  earthy  performer,  his  music  still a half-formed blues  style. He used the blues harmonica's pentatonic scale, but his rhythmic sense extended over the long chant line, rather than a clearly  measured  metrical  framework.  He  was  a  transitional blues figure  as  well  as  one  of  the  most  brilliant harmonica players of the 'twenties. Despite the strong elements of the past - the involved rhythm and  the  almost  archaic  scale  pattern  -  the  recordings  were rich and moving as contemporary blues statements.

Like Coleman, George "Bullet" Williams played the harmonica, and there was  some  of  the  same  Alabama  single  line  verse in the recordings he did  with  a  singer  in  Chicago  in  1928.  He  could also play in a more conventional style, however, and he was the harmonica accompanist for Big Joe Williams' first recording for Vocalion in 1929. Like Jaybird, he  was  in  some  ways  unable  to  find  a  way  to  live in the South, so he drank heavily, usually straining the cooking fuel "Sterno" through pieces of cloth for its alchoholic content. In 1934 he was working with his  cousin  Booker  White  at  a  roadhouse  outside  of West Point, Mis-

# COFFEE GRINDER BLUES

Hear **JAYBIRD COLEMAN**
Brag—"*No man in this town
can grind coffee like* mine!"

Record No. 14534-D, 10 inch, 75c

**COFFEE GRINDER BLUES**
Man Trouble Blues } *Vocals . . .* Jaybird Coleman

*Ask your dealer for the latest Race Record Catalog*
Columbia Phonograph Company, 1819 Broadway, New York City

"Magic Notes"

**Columbia** "NEW PROCESS" **Records**
*Viva-tonal Recording – The Records without Scratch*

JAYBIRD COLEMAN ADVERTISEMENT

sissippi, and the next year went with Booker to Aberdeen, Mississippi. Booker remembers that Williams was from a farm not far from Selma, Alabama, and that he had begun playing while he was still living there. He would play until he passed out; then after he'd had some time to sleep it off he'd get back on the bandstand and finish the job. By the end of his life he was drinking almost anything that he could get alcohol out of, like shoe polish, as well as commercial rubbing alchohol. He seems to have lived through the 'thirties, but he is said to have died in Alabama in the 'forties. Like Coleman he was a transitional figure, but the blues that he did with an unidentified singer on Paramount 12680, "Touch Me Light Mama" and "Middlin' Blues," were more formed than Coleman's, and there was, in some of the verses, a use of almost conventional blues material.

Touch me light, pretty mama, this may be your last.
Hey, hey, this may be your last.
Touch me light, pretty mama, this may be your last.
    (spoken) Touch 'em, kid, touch 'em.

I went to the nation, then to the territore.
Couldn't find my good girl, honey, nowhere I go.
    (spoken) Touch 'em again.

Woke up this morning, woke up day before,
Woke up this morning with the same thing on my mind.
    (spoken) Touch 'em now.

I believe to my soul, mama, got to leave your town.
I ain't got no pretty mama, talk baby talk to me.
    (spoken) Touch 'em, boy, touch 'em.

Aw, talk baby talk to me.
Ain't got no pretty mama, talk baby talk to me.

I went to the nation, went back to the territore.
I couldn't find my good girl, honey, no where I go.
    (spoken) Touch 'em, touch 'em.

Honey, I believe to my soul got to leave your town,
-, got to leave your town.
    (spoken) Touch 'em, touch 'em now.

Goin' uptown, mama, talk with the chief of police.
Tell him my good girl done quit me, sure can't see no peace.

The "Touch 'em" (or "Catch 'em - the voice is difficult to understand ) seems to be an exhortation to Williams to play the harmonica. There was a rude verse form developing from the field cry's melodic style, although in some of the verses the rhymes were irregular and forced, territore - go, and in others, town - me, not even considered.

The excitement of the performance was in the dissonant clash between the voice and the harmonica. Williams had developed a style of humming into the harmonica with a high, almost screaming sound, and the insistent instrumental line was an effective contrast with the heavy voice of the singer. The other two sides recorded by Williams for Paramount were harmonica solos, a train piece, "Frisco Leaving Birmingham," and "The Escaped Convict," both released on Paramount 12651.

It is possible that the vocalist on Williams' recordings was a young Birmingham singer named Wiley Barner, who recorded for Gennett in the summer of 1927 with piano and guitar accompaniment by Jimmy Allen and Will Jennings. There were some similarities in the sound of the voice. The vocal tone was strong and heavy, and both men sang almost without vibrato, in a flattened sound that tended to be unsteady in pitch. The singing with Williams, recorded in 1928, was closely related to the Alabama field music, however, and the Barner recordings were more conventional in their melodic structure. Despite the amateurish quality of Barner's 1927 recordings the pieces themselves were of some interest in their verse structure. In "My Gal Treats Me Mean" - released with "If You Want A Good Woman - Get One Long And Tall" on Gennett 6261 - the verse form was one of the less common blues forms that repeats the second line of the stanza rather than the first.

> Take your picture, hang it in a frame,
> When you're gone I'll see you just the same.
> When you're gone I'll see you just the same.
> When you're gone I'll see you just the same.
>
> Believe my soul my gal's got a black cat bone,
> Treat me mean and now won't let me 'lone.
> Treat me mean and I won't let her 'lone.
>
> See that spider climbin' up the wall,
> Huntin' some place to get his ashes hauled.
> Huntin' some place to get his ashes hauled.
> Well, he hunt some place to get his ashes hauled.
>
> Bring my slippers, (    ) my yard.
> Hear me tippin' toward my good gal's yard.
> Hear me tippin' toward my good gal's yard.
> You can't hear me tippin' toward my good gal's yard.

The American Recording Corporation worked in Birmingham again in 1937, and recorded a number of local artists, among them James Sherrill, who used the pianist Robert McCoy as accompaniest. Sherrill's blues, released under the pseudonym "Peanut The Kidnapper," were strongly influenced by the recordings of the popular Peetie Wheatstraw. Mack Rhineheart and Brownie Stubblefield also recorded a number of blues duets during this period, in Chicago and in Birmingham. The music, with piano and guitar accompaniment, was, like Sherrill's, derivative, and was not strongly rooted in any of the southern blues areas. The Alabama music, as it streamed into the main current of southern Negro music, merged its distinctive style with the heavier eddies of music from Mississippi, Texas, Chicago and the Atlantic seaboard.

# TEXAS

# 11. TEXAS

There is a flatness to the Gulf Coastal Plain of Texas, a flatness and emptiness. In the oil country around Beaumont and Houston the lights on the drilling rigs light up the countryside for miles around, their lights on moonless nights like stars hanging above the dark line of the horizon. The coastline itself is a ragged marsh of drowned trees and shifting sandbars, with yellow lines of silt marking the mouths of the creeks and rivers that empty into the Gulf of Mexico. There are few roads along the edge of the water. The highways are further inland, with small dirt roads going down to the creek mouths. The blackened trees are hung with swamp moss and the air is heavy with the noise of birds and insects. In eastern Texas, from the west bank of the Sabine River that marks the boundary with Louisiana, there is a belt of southern yellow pine, still only partly cleared. The trees thin toward the west as they mingle with the scrub oak forest that covers the broad flat lands of the eastern part of the state. The earth becomes dry and sandy, the trees clustered in meandering stream beds or in the lower ground between the low, eroded hills. As the land slowly rises to the west the trees become thinner and the ground is covered with dry, bunched grass. In the cotton country, mostly within the triangle formed by Austin, Houston, and Dallas, the land rises in choppy clay hills, the back roads impassable in the spring rains and hung with choking dust in the summer heat. The land is still empty, stretching in low eddies below the drifting cover of thin clouds, rising only a few hundred feet in the long miles between the coastal swamp and the sharecropper cabins outside of Waco, more than one hundred fifty miles inland.

Driving along the roads of Texas, even in the eastern half of the state, is tiresome and monotonous through the low hills and the empty countryside. Across the grasslands and the stretches of plowed cotton fields the water towers of the small towns gleam like squat moons, and the towns themselves have a shabby similarity. Rosenburg, with its block of one story red-brick buildings and its small, sun bleached houses. Brenham, with its courthouse square and its farm supply stores with their corrugated iron roofs over the sidewalks on the back streets. Everywhere in the United States there has been a persistent drift from the countryside into the cities, and it has been even more pronounced in Texas. In 1930 forty-two percent of the state's population still lived on farms, but, after the Depression and the years of the war, in 1960 less than ten percent were still living outside of the growing cities. Along the roadsides are empty farm cabins with their crumbling walls and broken shutters swinging in the wind. In the smaller towns the older buildings are empty, the warehouses and feed stores doing a slow and intermittent business during the long days of summer. The Texas oil boom, beginning with the Spindletop Well in 1901, has brought wealth to the state, but most of the money has stayed in the cities.

There was little of the oppressive plantation life of the Mississippi delta to shape the Texas blues. It is even difficult to find a fully developed early blues style that is distinctly Texan, although there was a strong tradition of work and play songs. In some Mississippi counties the Negro population is more than eighty percent of the people living in the county, and it is only in recent years that the number of Negroes in the state has slipped to less than half of the population. At its highest point, just after the Civil War, the colored population of Texas was less than thirty percent of the state's still sparse growth. In 1880, as people moved in from other states, the state grew to a million and a half people, and only twenty-five percent were Negroes. By 1950 the percentage of Negro to white in the state had dropped to about twelve percent. Even the farm system which had kept most southern Negroes in economic servitude after the Civil War, share cropping, was not widespread. Less than 10,000 families were still living as share croppers in 1959. This has not meant that life has been easier for colored men and women in Texas, although the larger cities have made efforts to bring about a small degree of integration in recent years. But it has meant a less isolated, less confined life than the brutal closed society of Mississippi. There were fewer people scattered across the countryside of Texas, so they went back and forth more. Since they were scattered so thinly over the dry countryside the rural folk culture didn't develop in the rich depth that it did in the heavy soil of the delta.

The early Texas blues style, like the thin stand of oak to the west of the pine country, was a sparse growth, but it had a rich strain within it, the songs of the slaves that came into the state from the 1850's to the end of the Civil War. It was one of the few areas where the slave songs were still part of the blues, perhaps because there was no strong local growth to crowd out the older verses and styles. In the teeming cabins of the Mississippi delta the older song elements were worked and reworked until the slave music became only a phase in the continuing interaction between the African and the Anglo-American aspects of the musical environment. In Texas, since the population was thinner and more scattered, the songs seemed to retain a more specific nature, almost functioning as a memory of a past that was being handed around from singer to singer, even after the meaning of some of the verses had become lost. In Texas, also, the experience was more recent. When the blues began to take a musical shape there were still men and women who remembered the first years in Texas, and the songs they had sung about it. The most immediate early influence seems to have come from the slave music of northern Alabama, and these song styles have continued to be a presence in the development of the Texas blues.

There was considerable movement within the slave areas during the 1850's, and the drift from Alabama to Texas was a strong one, blowing the Alabama music across the Texas landscape. In the early period of cotton cultivation in Alabama most of the planting was done in the broad valley of the Tennessee River in the north of the state. With increased cultivation, however, prices were driven down - from 30 cents a pound in 1816 to 9 cents a pound in 1829 - and the smaller farmers were forced to sell out and leave. Many of them went south and began clearing land in the more fertile areas in the center of the state, the counties that were to become the "black belt." By the 1850's these men dominated the state's economy. The men who had done the early planting along the Tennessee River had depleted their own soil with continued cotton planting, and poor farming practices had already led to the beginnings of the erosion that was to leave its widening gouge in the red earth. For many of these planters the new state of Texas, which had come into the Union in 1845 as a slave state, was their last hope. They left with their possessions in wagons, their slaves and animals walking along the dusty roads, traveling the hundreds of miles to the open lands of west central Texas. The papers in towns like Huntsville, in northern Alabama, carried hundreds of advertisements like this 1853 notice in the Huntsville *Democrat*.

> "Valuable property for sale - having determined to move to Texas - 1440 acres, 900 cleared..."

As the Civil War turned against the South there was a last effort to get out of the path of the Federal armies, and these forced migrations strengthened the patterns of growth in Texas.

Between 1934 and 1939 the Federal Emergency Relief Administration and the Works Progress Administration made an effort to find and interview the last elderly men and women who had begun their lives as slaves, and among the people who were interviewed there were some who had made the long, difficult trip to Texas. A slave from Georgia remembered,

> "I's born in Georgia, in Norcross, and I's ninety years old. My father's name was Roger Stielszen, and my mother's name was Betty. Massa Earl Stielszen captures them in Africa and brung them to Georgia. He got kilt, and my sister and me went to his son. His son was a killer. He got in trouble there in Georgia and got him two good-stepping horses and the covered wagon. Then he

ATLAS MAP, OF
TEXAS.

chains all he slaves round the necks and fastens the chains to the hosses and makes them walk all the way to Texas. My mother and my sister had to walk. Emma was my sister. Somewhere on the road it went to snowing, and Massa wouldn't let us wrap anything round our feet. We had to sleep on the ground, too, in all that snow....

"He come plumb to Austin through that snow. He taken up farming and changes he name to Alex Simpson and changes our names, too. He cut logs and builded he home on the side of them mountains. We never had no quarters. When nighttime come he locks the chain round our necks and then locks it round a tree. Boss, our bed were the ground. All he feed us was raw meat and green corn. Boss, I et many a green weed. I was hungry. He never let us eat at noon, he worked us all day without stopping. We went naked, that the way he worked us. We never had any clothes..."

A slave who was owned by a Baptist minister,

"...The next spring Old Master loaded up again, and we struck out for Texas when the Yankees got too close again. But Master Bill didn't go to Texas, because the Confederates done come that winter and made him go to the army. I think they took him to New Orleans, and Old Master was hopping mad, but he couldn't do anything or they would make him go too, even if he was a preacher...

"...About that time it look like everybody in the world was going to Texas. When we would be going down the road we would have to walk along the side all the time to let the wagons go past, all loaded with folks going to Texas.

"Pretty soon Old Master say, 'Git the wagons loaded again,' and this time we start out with some other people, going north. We go north for awhile and then turn west, and cross the Sabine River and go to Nacogdoches, Texas. Me and my brother Joe and my sister Adeline walked nearly all the way, but my little sister Harriet and my mammy rid in a wagon. Mammy was mighty poorly, and just when we got to the Sabine bottoms she had another baby. Old Master didn't like it 'cause it was a girl, but he named her Texana on account of where she was born and told us children to wait on Mammy good and maybe we would git a little brother next time...

"Old Master's place was right at the corner where Coryell and McLennan and Bosque counties come together, and we raised mostly cotton and just a little corn for feed...

"...if anybody ask me why the Texas Negroes been kept down so much I can tell them. If they set like I did on the bank at that ferry across the Sabine, and see all that long line of covered wagons, miles and miles of them, crossing that river and going west with all they got left out of the war, it ain't hard to understand."

169

THE BLUESMEN

Some of the slaves were brought by ship from the Mississippi plantations through New Orleans and Galveston and the journey became part of the song background of the Texas blues. A slave from Georgia remembered,

"...Then he...sends us to the port, for to catch the boat. Us gits on that boat and leaves that evening. Coming down the Mississippi 'cross the Gulf, us seed no land for days and days, and us go through the Gulf of Mexico and lands at the port, Galveston, and us comes to Waco on the stagecoach..."

Sixty years later a singer from Dallas named Willard Thomas, "Ramblin'" Thomas, recorded a group of blues for Paramount Records, most of them strongly influenced by commercial recordings. Among his other songs, however, was an older melody using a Mississippi accompaniment style. The guitar was played with a bottleneck or a knife in unison with the voice. The song seems to be a Mississippi field song that was brought into Texas on the boats into Galveston.

Poor boy, poor boy, poor boy long ways from home.

I was down in Louisiana doin' as I please,
Now I'm in Texas I got to work or leave.
Poor boy, poor boy, poor boy long ways from home.

If your home's in Louisiana what you doin' over here?
Said my home ain't in Texas and I sure don't care.
Poor boy, poor boy, poor boy long ways from home.

I don't care if the boat don't never land.
I can stay on the water as long as any man.
Poor boy, poor boy, poor boy long ways from home.

Hey my boat come a rockin' just like a drunken man.
And my home's on the water and I sure don't like land.
Poor boy, poor boy, poor boy long ways from home.

Other slaves were brought by boat up the Red River, and the well known Texas blues, "Red River Blues," may have been first sung during this period. The words are still sung unchanged, though most of the modern singers don't understand their meaning. Country people tell direction by the sun, and someone coming into Texas on the river would orient himself by the change of the sun's direction. From the river's entrance on the Mississippi below Natchez, the boats, with their passengers huddled on the deck, moved first northwest then almost due north. For a slave North was Freedom. Then at Fulton, Arkansas, the river turned due west.

Look where the sun done gone.
Look where the sun done gone.
Look where the sun done gone, poor girl,
Look where the sun done gone.

Yes it's gone God knows where.
Yes it's gone God knows where.
Look where the sun done gone, darling,
Look where the sun done gone.

Now baby, I'm all out and down.
Oh baby, I'm all out and down.
I'm all out and down, I'm (layin' in) this town,
Look where the sun done gone.

I'm a poor boy a long way from home.
Poor boy and a long ways from home.
I'm a poor boy a long way from home, darling,
Look where the sun done gone.

Which way do the Red River run?
Which way do the Red River run?
Which way do the Red River run, poor boy,
Which way do the Red River run?

Yes it runs north and south.
It runs north and south.
Which way do the Red River run, poor boy,
Well it runs north and south.

The swamp land along the Texas coast is rich enough for sugar, and both sides of the Brazos River, west of Houston, are planted with fields of cane. For years the state has maintained prison farms along the Brazos bottoms, and the music in these camps - Ramsey and Retrieve, Central State Farm at Sugarland, Clemens State Farm at Brazoria, Darrington State Farm at Sandy Point - retained many of the characteristics of the African derived slave song that had come into the state in the 1860's. John and Alan Lomax, recording in the camps in the 1930's, found that the prisoners still sang the slow rhythmed choral songs that had almost disappeared everywhere else in the South. The singing was so close to its African derivations that it might even represent an earlier stage of African music than could have been found on the Gold Coast thirty years ago. These camps were less than fifty miles from Houston, and their music was inextricably woven into the texture of the developing blues style. Often similar vocal embellishments were used by both work song leaders and the blues singers, especially slow mordent-like figures based on the equivocal third of the scale. The forms of the work song also made their way into the blues. Often the prison songs alternated a verse by the song leader with a hummed response by the group, and this was often used by Texas country singers, usually as alternate sung and hummed verses. There was even a use of the slow choral song as a blues itself.

The Texas blues of the late 1920's seem to have been influenced by three main streams of music. The first was the body of reels and play party songs of the slavery and post Civil War period, the second the prison work songs, and the third commercial blues recordings. In some of the accompaniment styles there was even a flavor of the white "cowboy" music, and the preference for a high, relatively clear voice might also reflect a white influence. A scattered Negro population was much more susceptible to influence than the more densely populated delta. Before the 1930's the elements of the Texas style were still scattered. Each of the three major areas of Negro song had distinctive melodic and rhythmic characteristics, and many of the best singers could be considered songsters, performers who use a wide range of material without changing its essential elements, instead of the more intensely creative blues singers. The scale patterns also reflected this diversity of influence. The play party songs often used nearly pure diatonic scales, while the prison songs were oriented toward the more African pentatonic and hexatonic groupings. Many of the blues, perhaps because of the influence of commercial recordings, used the conventional city blues scale. It was similar to the delta scales in the ambivalence of the third and the limited use of the second, but there was much more emphasis on the flatted seventh, one of the distinctive characteristics of the city scale patterns.

The rhythms and the accompaniment styles also developed within the framework of the three dominant musical influences. For the "sukey jump" songs the rhythms were in simple binary patterns, the melodic line usually sung without embellishment and the tones clearly defined in pitch. The accompaniments were often "frailed" or "wrapped," that is, in simple chords without finger picking. The rhythms of the work song derived blues, however, were almost completely free. They seemed to be closely related to both the field holler and to the old riverboat "lead line" chants, and the rhythm was an internally stressed chant line. Often the vocal rhythm was almost at complete variance with the accompaniment rhythm; the guitar was silent during the vocal phrase and entered at the end of the sung line. Sometimes the guitar style had a quality of the western white guitar accompaniments and there was considerable stylistic incongruity between the free chant rhythms of the voice and the dance rhythm of the guitar.

The singers using more standard blues material varied considerably in their accompaniments, usually taking elements from the style of the singer from whom they'd learned the song. The knife and bottleneck styles were not widely used, although nearly every singer was able to play at least one knife piece. The style was known, however, and one of

172

the greatest knife players was a Texan, the religious singer Blind Willie Johnson. When the Texas singers began using the flat necked Hawaiian guitar in the 1930's their style seemed to be more influenced by the steel guitar style of the white western orchestras than by the older blues techniques. There was less use of open tunings by the Texas singers and the guitar was usually tuned nearer to concert pitch, rather than the fourth or fifth below it of the Mississippi style.

The Texas guitar style that developed in the 1930's used elements from the older techniques, as well as materials from other blues areas. The form was already roughly shaped by the mid-twenties, and there were recordings using this accompaniment as early as 1926. It was a busy, almost nervous style, more busy than complex. The voice was accompanied with a light, high series of repeated patterns that were distinct from the vocal melody. The harmonic changes were usually regular within the key and the patterns continued through the chord movement. Rhythmically the accompaniment was in three parts, a 4/4 played with the thumb, a brush back by the fingers in a series of 8ths following the thumb note, and - between the vocal phrases - short melodic figures played on the upper strings of the guitar. The steady 4/4 of the bass was rhythmically similar to the Mississippi style. The thumb, however, instead of alternating from the lowest string to a tone a fifth or an octave above it, as in the delta, stayed on the fundamental of the chord, almost invariably on a fretted string at least a fifth above the lowest open string tone. In its earliest recorded forms the accompaniment was still close to the frailed guitar of the country dance songs. As the style developed, however, the voice and the guitar became more closely interrelated. Despite its feeling of nervous busyness the style has emerged as an important accompaniment technique and is widely used by the younger Texas singers.

Pprobably because of the influence of Galveston's sprawling redlight district the piano has also been an important accompaniment instrument in the Texas blues. There was a widespread barrelhouse style related to the ragtime of the years before World War I, and there was also a distinctive blues style that was sometimes known as "fast western." There were strong similarities between the Texas piano and guitar forms, although the keyboard music was essentially pianistic and was more elaborate than the guitar music. There was some use of the walking bass, and the older barrelhouse players used a rudimentary chorded bass similar to the eastern stride pianists, but much of the Texas music used a reiterated open chord in the left hand, usually an open fifth based on the fundamental, alternating with an open sixth. Sometimes the rhythm was doubled, each chord played twice - in eighths - but in slower tempos it had a similarity to the repeated bass note of the guitar accompaniments. The right hand figures were considerably more florid than in the guitar style, and often there was a great deal of rhythmic freedom in the right hand. The voice was usually high, as in the guitar blues, and the accompaniment had the same light, busy quality. During the 'thirties some of the piano patterns were picked up by the guitarists, and in the playing of men like T-Bone Walker there was considerable dexterity on the upper finger board as well as a suggestion of the alternating fifth-sixth chords of the piano bass played on the inner strings of the guitar.

The Texas blues style that emerged from the mingling of its earlier forms of play song, work song, and derivative city blues has some of the thin dryness of the Texas countryside, but it also has a coloring and a shading that is distinctively Texan. The songs themselves are filled with the endless concerns of the blues, eroticism and emotional disappointment, complaint at isolation and poverty, while the singing has some of the high, emotionally veiled mood of the state's western song traditions. The blues meanders across the music of Texas like the rivers across the flat earth of the coastal plain, the water only half covering the gravel of the stream bed, dry and still in the summer heat, but the line of thin trees and cracking mud banks a dusty presence in the Texas landscape.

# 12. BLIND LEMON JEFFERSON

One of the most difficult of the early Texas singers to place within the Texas musical environment is one of the area's most important blues men and one of the most commercially successful Negro country singers of the 1920's, Blind Lemon Jefferson. Of the more than eighty recordings that he did between 1925 and 1929 only a few use elements of the Texas blues style that emerged in the 1930's. He sometimes used prison songs and chants, but even in these songs his style was more personal than it was characteristic of the area. Perhaps even more significantly, despite his commercial success there was little effort by other singers to imitate him. The young blues men growing up in Dallas and Houston tried to sound like Lonnie Johnson more than they tried to sound like Lemon Jefferson. Sometimes he influenced a particular piece, like Ramblin' Thomas's "No Baby Blues," but there wasn't the pervasive influence on a younger man's style, like Son House's on Robert Johnson. There were similarities in phrasing and in the sound of the voice, but all of the men were from Texas, and they spoke with Texas accents. In his accompaniment styles and his rhythmic concepts, even in some of his themes, Lemon was one of the strongly individual figures of the early blues.

Lemon was born on a small farm outside of Couchman, Texas, a few miles from Wortham in Freestone County. The country is barren and almost flat, with low rolling hills above the grass land. In a description from an earlier sketch of Lemon's life,[1] "...From a small hill near Alec Jefferson's farmhouse at Couchman you can see across the fields to the buildings of Mexia, Texas, twelve miles to the southwest. The scattered buildings of Wortham, Texas, stretch along the railroad tracks five or six miles to the west. There are fields of old oil rigs between the two towns, with gasoline engines still working some of the old wells. The spindly scaffoldings are rusted and weathered. The ground is black with oil waste, but the only signs of oil money in Wortham are three or four ugly church buildings, built out of brick and designed to

175

resemble funeral parlors. Wortham's main street runs three blocks
from the Mexia road to the railroad tracks. Most of the buildings are
one story brick, with low, overhanging eaves of corrugated iron sheet-
ing. There is one gaudy metal front building from the 1880's, with low
relief designs and scrollwork stamped into the thin iron sheets. Wortham
is a small market town, a crossroad in lonely country.''

Lemon was born in the summer of 1897, the youngest of the seven
children born to Alec Jefferson and his wife, a girl from a neighboring
farm named Classie Banks. He began singing when he was a young
adolescent. He had been born blind, and there were no other ways he could
earn money. Before the First World War, in 1911 or 1912, he was already
coming into Wortham to sing, and by the time he was twenty he was
singing for parties and country dances throughout the county. He went
into Dallas about 1917, and lived there for nearly ten years, though he
spent months out singing in the cotton country south of the city. His
cousin, Alec Jefferson, rememberd him coming to Waxahatchie to sing
for ''country suppers.''

> Of course, my mother didn't let me go to them country suppers
> often. They was rough. Men was hustling women and selling
> bootleg and Lemon was singing for them all night. They didn't
> even do any proper kind of dancing, just stompin'.
>
> They'd go down to the station and get him in the afternoon.
> He'd start singing about eight and go on until four in the
> morning. Sometime he'd have another fellow with him, play-
> ing a mandolin or a guitar and singing along, but mostly it
> would be just him, sitting there playing and singing all night.[2]

One of the singers who worked with him a few times was the folk singer
Huddie Ledbetter, who was in prison most of the time that Lemon was
in Dallas, but remembered singing with him in the Dallas brothels.
Lemon was widely known for his music, and he finally did well enough
to get a car and a driver. He married a girl named Roberta in 1922 or
1923 and a son was born two or three years later. He sometimes went
back to the farm with his wife, letting his driver give rides to the girls
in town. He seemed to have traveled as far east as Mississippi and
Alabama, and many older blues men remember hearing him when they
were in towns like Jackson and Memphis. In 1925, when the rush to girl
blues singers had begun to slow down, the companies turned to the men
singers, and it was only a few months before Paramount found Lemon
Jefferson.

Dallas was already a growing and active city in the mid-twenties, and
there was sporadic recording activity there for several years, mostly
through the efforts of a local music store owner who, like Jesse
Johnson in St. Louis and H. C. Spears in Jackson, worked as a talent
scout for the Chicago and New York companies. He did a test recording

of Lemon's singing with a portable machine that had been set up in the rug department of a local furniture store sometime in the spring of 1925, and sent it up to Mayo Williams at Paramount. Mayo brought him up to Chicago sometime late in 1925 or early in 1926 for the first of the many sessions Lemon was to do for the company in the next three and a half years.

"Here's a real old-fashioned blues by a real old-fashioned blues singer - Blind Lemon Jefferson from Dallas. This 'Booster Blues' and 'Dry Southern Blues' on the reverse side are two of Blind Lemon's old-time tunes. With his singing he plays the guitar in real southern style."

The ad ran in the *Chicago Defender* on April 3, 1926. There had been a few earlier recordings by country blues men, Ed Andrews, Daddy Stovepipe, Papa Charlie Jackson, but Lemon was considerably more successful than they had been. Two or three of his recordings were among the most widely sold country blues releases of the 1920's, even though the style of the first recordings was so raw and uncompromising that it is difficult to think of them as commercial releases by a commercial company. It was as rough and as individual as any of the music that field collectors were to find in the South in the next forty years of recording. His style was, in some ways, so distinctive because it was a hybrid of the influences on him. Some of the style, the vocal phrasing and the few regular rhythms, was in part from the Alabama styles still sung in Freestone County, but some of the melodies and characteristic patterns were from the commercial recordings by the women blues singers of the early 1920's. His harmonic structure was the usual I-IV-V of the city blues, he generally used the conventional three line verse form, and often his texts were concerned with the usual "leaving trains" and "mistreating women" of the commercial blues song.

But if his blues sometimes were tangled with the conventional melodies and texts his singing style and his accompaniment rhythms were considerably different from the city recordings. The high, clear sound of his voice, despite the inadequate acoustical recording techniques, had a startling intensity, and he kept the freely structured rhythms of the field holler and the Texas gang chant in his guitar. The accompaniments, especially on "Dry Southern Blues," were very complex, and the relationship between the guitar and the voice was very loose. Often he sounded as though he were singing to himself while somebody else played a few tentative phrases on the guitar. His vocal line was very irregular and the guitar only occasionally tried to hold it within the 4/4 rhythm of the usual blues measure. The guitar style had some of the elements of country white "frailing," but because of the tension of the vocal line the patterns were often wildly unpredictable. He was one of the few country musicians who seemed to rely on improvisation in his accompaniments. It was a desolate, lost sound, the voice tinged with loneliness, the restless guitar moving below it as though it were looking for a phrase or a run to end its incessant movement. Although the change from acoustical to electrical recording in 1927 gave his voice more presence, there was little change in his style in the Paramount recordings. His voice darkened, and his accompaniments became less hurried, but his last session, in the fall of 1929, was as direct and as compelling as his first had been more than three years before.

In his recordings he drew on a number of sources for his songs. There were even enough folk and gospel performances to suggest that, like Charley Patton, he was almost as much of a songster as he was a blues singer. He sang for every kind of social function in the Texas back country, and he must have had a wide repertoire of hymns and play songs, as well as his blues. When the younger Texas singer, Lightning Hopkins, first heard Lemon he was singing for a Baptist picnic at Buffalo, Texas, and he would not have sung "Oil Well Blues" or "Black Snake Moan" for a church gathering. Lightning's description catches some of the feeling of what it must have been like to hear Lemon out in the country where he had been born and raised.

> *... I went to the Buffalo Association with my guitar and I run up on Blind Lemon Jefferson. He had a crowd of people around him and I was standing there looking at him play and I just went to playing my guitar just what he was playing. So he say, "Who's that playing that guitar?" So they say, "Oh, that's just a little boy here knocking on the guitar." He says, "No, he's playing that guitar," says, "Where he at? Come here, boy." And I went on over there where he was and he's feeling for me and I was so low he reached down and says, "This here is what was picking that guitar?" They say, "Yeah." So he said, "Do that again." So I did, the little note again, the same one he done. He said, "Well, that's my note," says, "that's the same thing. Boy, you keep that up you gonna be a good guitar player." So he went on and he commenced to playing; so I went to playing right on with him. So I was so little and low the peoples couldn't see me and we was standing by a truck. They put me up on top of the truck, and Blind Lemon was standing down by the truck. And me and him, man, we carried it on...* [3.]

Lemon was restricted by his market, since he began recording when the commercial interest was in the conventional city blues, but he was still able to sing Texas folk songs and minstrel show pieces, as well as country hymns and gospel songs. It seems probable that the Paramount gospel releases by "Deacon L. J. Bates" were recordings that Lemon had done, and Paramount used a pseudonym for him as they had for Patton. Two of the songs are very similar to Lemon's usual style, "He Arose From The Dead" and "Where Shall I Be?", although there is almost a self-consciousness in the rhythm and the voice. He recorded one of the earliest versions of the folk gambling song "Jack O' Diamonds," and many Texas blues men remember his version of the well known "Two White Horses In A Line." It was renamed "See That My Grave Is Kept Clean" for the recording, a 1927 release on Paramount 12585, but it was the same folk melody and most of the verses that were sung not only in Texas but in many other areas of the South. The melody was used by most of the Mississippi singers and was found east of the Appalachians in the Carolinas and Georgia.

Probably because he had learned it as a folk melody Lemon's performance of it was much less irregular than most of his blues, but he wasn't consistent in his use of folk song materials. His third release included "Corinna Blues," his reworking of the song "See See Rider," and it was as free as his most irregular blues pieces. The "Black Horse Blues" on the other side of the record, Paramount 12367, included a variation on the verse that was usually associated in Mississippi with Charley Patton.

> Well, get my black horse and saddle up my black mare,
> Well, get my black horse and saddle up my black mare.
> I'm going over to my good girl, she's in the world somewhere.

Following the success of his "Black Snake Moan" in the winter of 1926 he spent a few weeks working as an OKeh record artist, and did a session for them on March 14, 1927. The only release from the session was a new version of "Black Snake Moan" and "Match Box Blues" on OKeh 8455, but he also did other folk material, and one of the songs was a version of the "Elder Green - Alabama Bound - Don't You Leave Me Here" melody, with the title "Elder Green's In Town." It was close to Patton's version of the piece in both melody and verses, and the similarity strengthens the impression that there were close ties between his music and the field blues of the Alabama and north Mississippi area.

Example 25

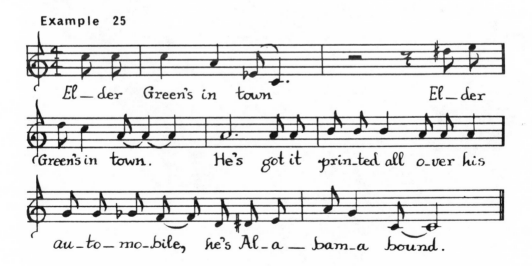

The first verse was the most interesting, with its bridge from the Elder Green song, which has the feeling of an older minstrel tune, to the Alabama Bound phrase. He returned to Elder Green in the last verse, ending with rough country irreverence.

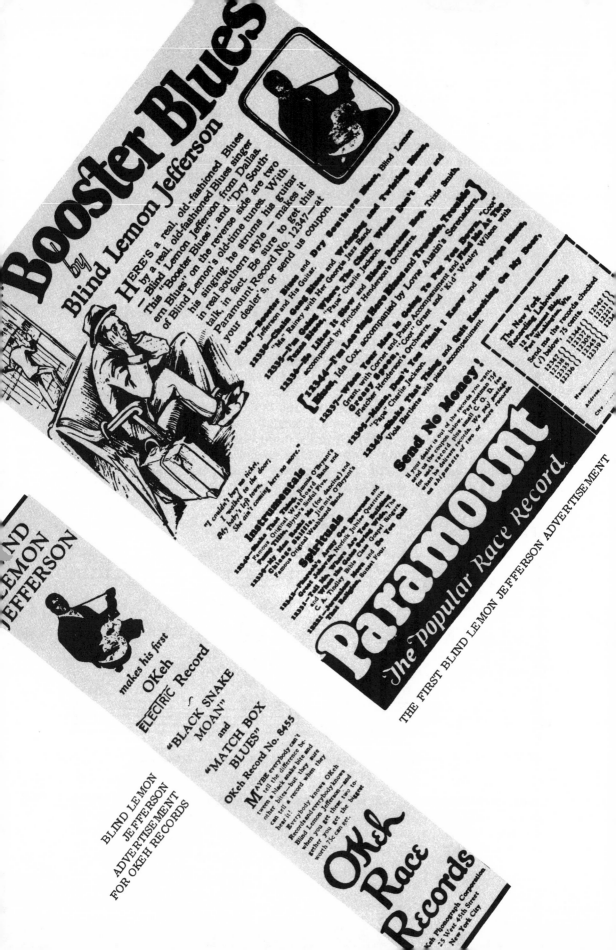

# Booster Blues

*by*

## Blind Lemon Jefferson

HERE'S a real, old-fashioned Blues by a real, old-fashioned Blues singer — Blind Lemon Jefferson from Dallas. This "Booster Blues", and "Dry Southern Blues" on the reverse side are two of Blind Lemon's old-time tunes. With his singing, he strums his guitar in real southern style — makes it talk, in fact. Be sure to get this Paramount Record No. 12347—at your dealer's, or send us coupon.

**12347—Booster Blues** and **Dry Southern Blues.** Blind Lemon Jefferson and His Guitar.

**12238—Chain Gang Blues** and **Weeping and Wailing** Blues. "Ma" Rainey with Her Georgia Jazz Band.

**12236—I'm Going Where The Chilly Winds Don't Blow** and **Texas Blues.** "Papa" Charlie Jackson.

**12320—Me Likes It Slow** and **Black Bottom Hop.** Trixie Smith, accompanied by Fletcher Henderson's Orchestra.

**[12344—The Leaving Race Blues and Trouble, Trouble.]** Ida Cox, accompanied by Lovie Austin's Serenaders.

**12327—When Your Man is Going To Put You Down**, "Coo" Grant, with Cornet and Piano Accompaniment and **Find Me At The Greasy Spoon**, accompanied by "Kid" Wesley Wilson with Fletcher Henderson's Orchestra.

**12306—Mamma, Don't You Think I Know** and **Hot Papa Blues.** "Papa" Charlie Jackson.

**12349—Shake That Thing** and **Quit Knocking On My Door.** Viola Bartlette with piano accompaniment.

## Send No Money!

If your dealer is out of the records you want, send us the coupon below. Pay postman 75¢ for each record plus small C. O. D. fee when he delivers records. We pay postage on shipments of two or more records.

### Instrumentals

**12169—Santa Claus Blues**, Jimmie O'Bryant's Famous Original Washboard Band and **Panama Limited Blues. Steal My Me** (for dancing) and **Chicago Stomp**, Jimmie O'Bryant's Famous Original Washboard Band.

### Spirituals

**12434—Trouble's Away** and **Barred Up** and **Cross Towards**, Norfolk Jubilee Quartette and **Will the Water Ate You While You De** and **Tell Me The Green River Bottom**, C. A. Tindley Bible Class Gospel Singers and **Sunset Four.**

**12351—Just Beyond** and **Be You Sad** That Bottom

# Paramount

## *The Popular Race Record*

THE FIRST BLIND LEMON JEFFERSON ADVERTISEMENT

---

"I couldn't buy no ticket, I walked to the door. My baby left town, She ain't coming here no more."

Elder Green's in town, Elder Green's in town,
    Elder Green's in town,
He's got it printed all over his automobile he's Alabama bound.

Don't worry me, don't worry me again.
When I get drunk and all down and out, don't worry me.

I've got a high brown and she's long and tall.
Lord, lord, lord, lord, boys, she'll make a panther squall.

Elder Green don't care, Elder Green don't care.
He's gonna tear down the old Church of God and build a
    barrelhouse there.

He also did his only recorded instrumental at the session, a ragtime guitar piece with the title "English Stop Time." Like "Elder Green's In Town," it was closely related to music from the older slave areas of the south east.

Example 26

Unlike Patton, however, he did not use much of the local countryside in his blues. In the town of Wortham three or four people still laughed over his piece that mentioned the nearby town of Groesbeck. A man standing in a small store warmed his hands over the coal stove thinking about Lemon's songs. "There was one he did about Groesbeck, about going to the penitentiary. I never did forget that one." The song "Blind Lemon's Penitentiary Blues," was one of the few in which Lemon referred to the towns near the farm where he had grown up.

Take Fort Worth for your dressing and Dallas (?) for your style.
Take Fort Worth for your dressing and Dallas (?) for your style.
But if you want to go to the state penitentiary go to
        Groesbeck for your trial.

I hung around Groesbeck, I worked in hard showers of rain.
I say I hung around Groesbeck, worked in hard showers
        of rain.
I never felt the least bit uneasy 'til I caught that penitentiary
        train.

I used to be a drunkard, rowdy everywhere I go.
I say I used to be a drunkard and rowdy everywhere I go.
If ever I get out of this trouble I'm in I won't be rowdy no more...

Lemon does not seem to have been in prison himself, but like every great singer his blues were a reflection of the emotional concerns of the people who were his audience. He was able, as the St. Louis singer Henry Townsend expressed it, to take "...sympathy with the fellow..." He sang a "Lock Step Blues," a "Hangman's Blues," a "'Lectric Chair Blues," and the brilliant "Prison Cell Blues," which kept the two line poetic form and the shouted melodic outline of the prison gang song.

Example 27

Many of his images were also taken from his country background, even though he had grown up without sight. Throughout his recording career he remained a Texas singer, despite the years he spent in Chicago and his trips to Memphis and Jackson.

He sang every kind of song, and his blues were an expression of nearly every aspect of the life that went on in the cabins along the winding stream beds and the oil blackened dirt roads, but there was also a personal emphasis in his music. He was as tormented with sexuality as the young Robert Johnson. His women, his "rider," his "brown," or his "pigmeat," dominated his blues. Desire with Lemon was hurried and impatient.

> ...I'm crazy about my light bread and my pigmeat on the side.
> I say I'm crazy about my light bread and my pig meat on the side.
> But if I taste your jelly roll I be satisfied.
>
> I want to know if your jelly roll's fresh, if your jelly roll's
> stale.
> Well, I want to know if your jelly roll's fresh, if your jelly
> roll's stale.
> I'm going to haul off and buy me some if I have to break it loose
> in jail...
>
> (Bakershop Blues)
>
> I feel like jumping through the keyhole in your door.
> I feel like jumping through the keyhole in your door.
> If you jump this time, baby, you won't jump no more.
>
> (Mean Jumper Blues)

His sexual blues were often intense performances, and their physical yearning was expressed with a repetitive insistence. His most successful recording was a vivid sexual blues. In May, 1926, a young girl singer from north of Dallas, Victoria Spivey, recorded a piece that she called "Black Snake Blues" for Okeh Records in St. Louis. Miss Spivey insists that the song had no sexual overtones, and that it described something that had happened to a girl friend when a black snake, a common field snake in Texas, crawled into the cabin where the girl was living. When Lemon recorded it six months later as "That Black Snake Moan" she remembers, with some resentment, that "...he changed it into a sex song." He included the image of the black snake crawling into his room, but he changed the verse, and with the change the song became a crying sexual lament

> Um - um, black snake crawling in my room.
> Um - um, black snake crawling in my room.
> Yes, some pretty mama better get this black snake soon.

> Uum - what's the matter now?
> Uum - what's the matter now?
> Yes, some pretty mama better get this black snake soon.
>
> Well, I wonder where this black snake's gone.
> I wonder where this black snake's gone.
> Lord, that black snake, mama, done run my mama home..

His obvious reference to the penis was more openly sexual than was usual in the early blues, and the record was also one of his best performances. He used a direct, assertive melodic line and his voice was even more intense than on many of the recordings he had done earlier in the year. It was the success of his first "Blacksnake" that led to OKeh's efforts to get him away from Paramount and the recordings of "Elder Green's In Town" and "English Stop Time." He was recording for Paramount again within a few weeks of the OKeh sessions and in June, 1927, he did a second "Blacksnake" piece, "Black Snake Dream Blues." In 1929 there was still another piece using the same imagery, "That Black Snake Moan No. 2." In these later pieces he consciously used the sexual symbolism of the snake, unlike the first recording which has some of the feeling of a spontaneous improvisation while he was recording. Paramount, however, never intimated in their advertising that Lemon was talking about anything but a snake. There were even drawings of Lemon and the snakes to make the point more strongly. To the people who bought the records, though, the symbolism was obvious.

> ...Uum, better find my mama soon.
> Uum, better find my mama soon.
> I woke up this morning black snake was makin' (just a) ruckus
>     in my room.
>
> Black snake is evil, black snake is all I see.
> Black snake is evil, black snake is all I see.
> I woke up this morning he was moved in on me.
>
> Uum, black snake was hanging 'round.
> Uum, black snake was hanging 'round.
> He occupied my living room and broke my (folding bed?) down.

> (That Black Snake Moan No. 2)

During his years of recording Lemon also seems to have traveled extensively, although his movements were vague and difficult to trace. He still went back to the farm at Couchman for visits, although his family saw little of him after he began working in Chicago. He had become one of Paramount's most established singers, despite the uncompromising roughness of his style. In the spring of 1928 the company even issued a birthday record for him, with a beautiful gray and yellow label that had his picture and a streamer saying "Happy Birthday,

Lemon." The necessity to find new material sometimes left him with thinly derivative verses, or with blues that were confused and incomplete. In a piece like "Balky Mule Blues" he began with verses about a balky mule and then included verses from a "Bear Cat Blues" before he was finished. Also he was sometimes used to "cover" successful recordings by other artists. Like most singers who were recording extensively during this period he did a flood blues, "Rising High Water Blues," to cover Bessie Smith's "Back Water Blues." It was one of three blues that he did with the pianist George Perkins as accompanist. He also did a "Chinch Bug Blues" to cover Lonnie Johnson's "Mean Old Bed Bug", and a "How Long How Long" after Leroy Carr's recording. In all of his recordings, however, despite the thinness of some of the verses, the musical level was consistently high.

Some singers drift like clouds over the flat landscape, changing with every movement of the wind. Lemon changed very little during the years when he was recording. He used the three line verse form for most of the blues and there was a consistency to his melodic and rhythmic approach. He left the folk songs and the hymns in their original form, and there were occasional pieces like "Bad Luck Blues" that are difficult to fit into any category, but the rest were strongly stamped with his individual style. "Bad Luck Blues" had some of the style of a play party song or a medicine show piece.

> Sugar you catch that Katy, I'll catch that Santa Fe,
>> Doggone my bad luck soul,
> Sugar you catch that Katy and I'll catch that Santa Fe.
> I mean Santy, speaking of Fe,
>> When you get in Dallas, pretty mama, look around for me.

He used only a handful of melodies for his blues pieces, one of the most distinctive melodies one with a final phrase in the accompaniment moving to a harmony on the VI of the scale. Blues with this melody included some of his best performances, among them "Tin Cup Blues," "Mean Jumper Blues," and "Sunshine Special." He also used a melodic phrase that descended from V to IV in the last line for blues like "Oil Well Blues" and "Pneumonia Blues." His more or less conventional three line verse forms differed most importantly in the phrasing of the second line. In some blues - "Big Night Blues" and "Peach Orchard Mama" - the last word of the second line was delayed as a kind of halting resolution, in others the phrasing was more regular.

Although Lemon largely remained outside of the main areas of development of the Texas blues he sometimes used many of the elements which were to become part of the mature style. In "Stocking Feet Blues" he used the rythmically insistent guitar bass and the elaborate upper string patterns that were also characteristic of some of the pieces of Henry Thomas, and he developed a rudimentary compound verse, a verse form that was to become almost a characteristic of the later blues of men like Lightning Hopkins. The harmonic resolution was still unsettled, but the verse itself was almost the fully developed compound stanza.

> She got up this morning,
> Come a tippin' 'cross the floor,
> Said mama,
> In her stocking feet,
> Honey, fare thee, sweet papa, fare thee well.
> I done all in the world I could, trying to get along with you.

"Tippin'" is a country term for "tiptoeing."

The scale in Lemon's blues was usually an open pentatonic, but in some of his strongest pieces the scale used only the first, an altered third, a fifth, an altered seventh and the octave. For the more song-like pieces, even a prison song like "Prison Cell Blues," the scale was fuller, omitting only the second.

Lemon seems to have done his last recordings for Paramount at the Gennett Studios in Richmond, Indiana, on September 24, 1929. He did eight blues, all of them among his finest performances. The Gennett Studio had a much better sound than the thin and poorly balanced sound of the Paramount Studio in Port Washington; so there was also much more immediacy and presence on the releases than on some of his earlier recordings. There was Lemon's usual sexual preoccupation in "Bakershop Blues," with its elaborately developed jellyroll image, and a bitter infidelity blues, "Pneumonia Blues." Perhaps one of the most moving of all Lemon's songs was the fourth blues of the session, "That Crawling Baby Blues," which expressed a disturbed, muted anguish over the confused personal relationships around him. He began, as usual, with the specific moment,

> Well, the baby crying, up to his mama's knee.
> Well, the baby crying, up to his mama's knee.
> Cryin' about his sweet milk and she won't feed him just his cream.

but the moment was left unfinished, not as a narrative, but as an emotional reality which could justify the generalized verse which usually followed the opening verse in Lemon's blues. There was also some ambivalence in his use of terms that could be mistaken for sexual imagery, "sweet milk," "she won't feed him just his cream." He extended his description in the second verse, however, definitely setting the blues into an infidelity context.

> Well, he cryin' in the fireplace and stops in the middle of the floor.
> Well, he cryin' from the fireplace and stops in the middle of the
> floor.
> Say mama, ain't that your second daddy standin' back there in the
> (?) door.

And with the third verse he finally set the emotional moment in one of the few blues verses that considered the effect of infidelity on the children growing up in the emotional confusion of casual promiscuity.

186

Well, she grabbed my baby and spanked him, I tried to make her
leave him alone.
Well, she grabbed my baby and spanked him, I tried to make her
leave him alone.
I tried my best to stop her and she said the baby ain't none of mine.

The fourth verse, the generalized statement, was built from the emotional situation of the other verses.

The woman rocks the cradle and I declare she rules the home.
Woman rocks the cradle and I declare she rules the home.
Many man rocks some other man's baby and the fool thinks
he's rocking his own.

The final verse was obviously padding to round out the performance.

Well, it was late last night when I learnt the crawling baby blues.
I said it was late last night when I learnt the crawling baby blues.
My woman threw my clothes out doors and now I got the crawling
baby blues.

There were few blues which so completely controlled the emotional elements in the blues form, and it was as effective melodically as it was textually.

Example 28

Lemon was also to be part of a Paramount release using several of the company's most popular blues artists - a "hometown skiffle" record advertised in the *Defender* on February 22, 1930 - but he died sometime before the recording session. There is still considerable confusion over his death, and it will probably always be difficult to reconstruct the events that led to it. Son House has said that he met Lemon in the studio in Port Washington the day before Son recorded in July, 1930, and that the next morning, when he, Patton, and Louise Johnson came to the studio to begin recording, they were met by the recording director, Art Satterlee, who shook his head and said, "I've got some bad news for you. Lemon was killed in a car accident early this morning." Four months before this, however, Walter Taylor and John Byrd recorded "Wasn't It Sad About Lemon?", and Reverend Emmett Dickinson did a "Death of Blind Lemon," both released on Paramount 12945 in the early spring, so Lemon must have been dead for several months before Son went to Chicago. A Paramount employee named Aleatha Robinson remembered that Lemon was recording on the afternoon before his death, but he may only have been in the Paramount offices on business. "Wasn't It Sad About Lemon?" suggested that the story the family was told of his death was probably true.

> Blind Lemon was born in Texas,
> A state we all know well.
> 'Twas on the streets of Chicago,
> Was where poor Lemon fell....
>
> The weather was below zero
> On the day he passed away,
> But this is the truth we all know well.
> That's a debt we all have to pay...

The family and friends in Texas heard that he froze to death in Chicago, and John Steiner, the Chicago jazz historian and business man who bought the Paramount property in the 1940's, heard from people associated with the company that Lemon had left the studios late in the afternoon, gone to play for a party, and been found dead on the street early in the morning with the snow drifted over his body. No one was able to tell him what happened to Lemon during the night although there was a suggestion that Lemon might have had a heart attack as he was waiting for his car and driver to pick him up. There was also a story that Lemon left the party drunk and got lost as he tried to make his way through the streets in the cold winter night. The wind sweeps in on Chicago from the lake, and on bitter winter nights it will almost turn a man around as he walks, stinging his face with fine driven crystals of ice and numbing his body through the heaviest clothes. Paramount hired a Texas pianist who was working for them, Will Ezell, to go with the body back to Dallas, and the funeral was held in Wortham with Lemon's family and neighbors walking across the cold, frozen fields to get to the services. He was buried in a country cemetery outside of Wortham, and, like Patton's, his grave was not marked. The neighbors remembered, however, that his mother had been buried next to Lemon when she died in 1947. Her headstone, a simple concrete monument, is under a small tree just inside a rusting barbed wire fence in the lonely cemetery, only a rusting metal marker in the wild grass growing over the space beside her grave.

# 13. HENRY THOMAS, "RAGTIME TEXAS"

The songster tradition was as deeply rooted in the spindly valleys of east central Texas as the work songs and the blues of Lemon Jefferson. Most singers in the South were called "songsters" by their neighbors because they usually could be prevailed upon to make music at almost any occasion, from a church picnic to a children's party. Nearly every blues singer did this kind of entertaining in his own community and had a few church songs and party songs in his repertoire. The difference between these songs and his blues was that he usually sang these pieces more or less as he had learned them, unlike his personal blues. It was the easy familiarity of the other pieces that made them effective for little dances and parties. The singers, also, were often brought to white affairs, when they would be surrounded by an audience that had to have old songs and considerable servility. In nearly every southern community there is an older performer who can be hired for white parties and social occasions like debuts and horse shows. Usually he is also his own community's "songster," and he knows dozens of songs like "It Ain't Gonna Rain No More," "My Blue Heaven," and "The Wreck of the Old 97." Because of the influence of local speech patterns and guitar techniques the style often has many of the characteristics of the blues style of the area, even though the songs are known everywhere in the South. In Texas the songsters had the high, tense sound of the blues singers, and their songs, like the weeds along the winding, dry stream beds near Austin or San Antonio, had the smell of the Texas dust and wind.

One of the most extensively recorded of the early Texas male singers was a songster named Henry Thomas, also called "Ragtime Texas" on some of the records. He was skilled performer, often reminiscent of one of the best known of the Memphis medicine show singers, Jim Jackson. Nothing is known of Thomas' life, and, as is often true with songsters, nothing can be learned from his songs. The blues singer has to expose himself as a person in his blues, but the songster is more a reflection of an area's musical interests than he is of his own concerns. Thomas mentions the town of Huntsville in the song "Run Molly Run," using the verse,

I went down to Huntsville, I did not go to stay,
I just got there in good old time to wear that ball and chain.

Huntsville is on Route 75 north of Houston, and there is a state penitentiary there, but the verse is a conventional one in the area. It could even refer to the Huntsville in northern Alabama. Thomas was one of the first artists used by the recording director Mayo Williams after he left Paramount Records and moved to Vocalion in 1927. The sessions were done in Chicago between July, 1927, and October, 1929. The releases were well advertised, but the copy material had no personal information. In the picture used for the ads he looked in his late thirties or early forties, his hair graying, his expression guardedly professional.

Thomas was an interesting singer for the range of his songs as well as his accompaniment styles, and he was also interesting for his use of the instrument known as the "quills." He was probably the first singer to record using the quills, even though they were at one time widely played throughout the South. The instrument is also known by the technical term "syrinx," but it probably is most widely known as "panpipes." Each "pipe" is a cross blown cane reed, held against the lips while the player blows across the opening in the top, just as a child blows on an empty bottle. The pitch of the reed is determined by its length - the shorter the reed the higher the sound - and usually the player binds a group of them together in a row, holding them together with pieces of stick. They are usually tuned to the local folk scale, and Thomas tuned his to a e-#f-a-b-c#e' scale, even though most of the songs he did were in a more generally diatonic mode. In the picture that was used in the advertisements the quills seem to be enclosed in a dark colored box that hangs around his neck on a rack similar to the arrangement that harmonica players use. Some of the finest of his recordings were characterized by the light piping sound of the quills alternating verses with his voice.

Thomas seems to have been almost a pure songster. Once he'd learned a song he didn't change it, even if he'd only half learned it at the beginning. In a song that seems to be derived from an earlier recording by one of the city women singers, "Woodhouse Blues," he even left the terms of endearment unchanged, and sang "Daddy, daddy .." instead of changing it to something which would make more sense. In some of the songs that he learned from white sources he had difficulties with the harmonies as well. In "The Little Red Caboose," which sounds like a minstrel tune, and "Honey, Won't You Allow Me One More Chance," which sounds like a vaudeville piece, he missed obvious chord changes, and in one of the country pieces, "When The Train Comes Along," he sounded in places as though he were singing in one key and accompanying himself in another. He does not seem to have had a strong musical sense. A songster, however, is important for what he remembers, rather than what he creates, and some of the songs Thomas remembered had the loose, noisy exuberance of the country picnics or the church suppers where he must have heard them.

Nearly every folk blues from the Texas - Louisiana area found its way into the songs he recorded. One of his pieces, "Bob McKinney," is a medley of folk blues, beginning with a version of "Stackolee," using Bob McKinney as the hero; then it goes into "Take Me Back," "Make Me A Pallet On Your Floor," and "Bully Of The Town." However, he didn't record "Jack O'Diamonds," even though it was widely known in Texas. He tended to turn away from the darker glints of Texas music, as though he were concerned more with a country white audience than with a blues audience. He must have played for dancing, and in his "Old Country Stomp" there were even verses with dance calls.

> Get your partners, promenade, promenade all around now...
> Oh boy you started wrong, take your partners, promenade...

One piece he remembered, "Shanty Blues," might have been from one of the states to the east, and it had a heavier sound than some of his other pieces. For the accompaniment he used an open tuning and played with a knife or a bottleneck. Most of the verses were conventional, but there were other verses which must have been from part of an older work song. The melody was a four line strain like the country dance pieces, but the work song fragments stuck to it like a burr caught in a man's overalls as he moves through the dry autumn brush along the banks of the Trinity River.

> Dogs on my track, man on his horse,
> Make it to my shanty if I can,
> If I can, if I can,
> Make it to my shanty if I can.

His voice was the high, less intense Texas voice, the tone produced further forward in the mouth than the Mississippi singers, the melodic line with little embellishment. His tone was a little heavier than some of the other Texas singers, perhaps because he was a little older when he began to record. Many of his pieces were the kind of song that Huddie Ledbetter, a Louisiana singer who spent years playing in Texas, called "sukey jump" pieces, little repetitive melodies that had an almost childish simplicity and innocence.

Example 29

(Run Molly Run)

♩=150

Run Mol-ly run, run Mol-ly run,

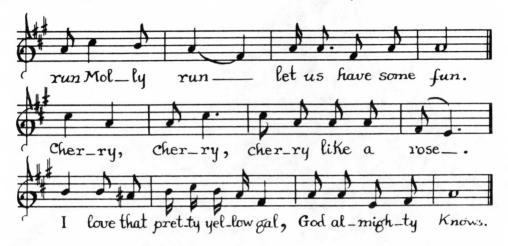

run Mol_ly run ___ let us have some fun.

Cher_ry, Cher_ry, cher_ry like a rose___.

I love that pret_ty yel_low gal, God al_migh_ty knows.

In the best of his blues there was this same musical brightness, even though the texts were often sombre.

Example 30

( Texas Easy Street Blues )

♩ = 180

Um _ m ___ what's the mat _ ter now.___

te _ ll ___ me ma _ ma what's the mat_ter

now. ___ I'm goin' back to Tex_as,

live on ea_sy street.

His accompaniments were generally as simple as the songs. For pieces like "The Fox And The Hounds" he used a "frailing" accompaniment, letting the excitement come from his yipping voice, the little melody of the pipes, and the verses of the song. On the pieces in which he used the quills the accompaniments were even less complex. He usually limited himself to "wrapping the guitar" - playing in straight beats - and the sound was often discordant, as though he were using unconventional finger positions. Like most Texas singers he kept the guitar close to standard pitch, instead of slackened considerably below it, as in

HENRY THOMAS ADVERTISEMENTS

Mississippi. Also he played in the middle strings to a great extent. There were other techniques that he also shared with later Texas singers, and he could be considered one of the earliest Texas blues men as well as a songster. Three of his recorded pieces, "Texas Worried Blues," "Cotton Field Blues," and "Texas Easy Street Blues," had nearly all the elements that became part of the emerging Texas blues style. The voice was unforced, and the melody, although close to the conventional city blues melody, was faster and lighter. The accompaniment technique was one of the first to completely define the Texas guitar style. There were elements of it in some of the Lemon Jefferson recordings, but in the Thomas pieces the style was more fully realized. The thumb played a repetitive 4/4 on the tonic of the key, the sound light and insistent. Usually there was the brush back on the upper strings with the first fingers, and a melodic figure was picked against this background up the neck of the guitar. Thomas might have been the first to play in this style, although it seems unlikely that he could have created it. It was probably a blues that the songster remembered, just as he remembered his other pieces.

Little of what Thomas sang continued in the Texas blues traditions, and he is a half-forgotten figure in the development of Texas music. Through Thomas, however, it is clear that the music of Texas has its own line of development going back almost as far as the earliest Mississippi style, going back, at least, to the point when the songster Henry Thomas first heard and remembered it.

TEXAS ALEXANDER

# 14. "TEXAS" ALEXANDER

Lightning Hopkins first met his cousin Alger Alexander in the early 1930's at a baseball game in a small town not far from Lightning's town of Centerville.

*Well, I met Texas Alexander in Leon County at a place you call Normangee, Texas. They had a little old do down there, what you call, I don't know, a picnic, and they had a ball game, see. Well, Normangee was playing Leona, so that's the way they had them named, they didn't, you know, no special big names like they got now ... just Leona playing Normangee. So I got down there and ... I seen a man standing up on a truck with his hand up to his mouth and, man, that man was singing. That was Texas, my cousin, I didn't know. Alright, I goes on there and that man was singing so and he like to broke up the ball game. People was paying so much attention to him instead of the ball game. Well, he had been gone. All his people was living in Normangee, most of them, you know, his mother and them at that time was living, and he had been gone kind of like I did and stayed for a while and he come back. That's the way he come back, you understand, he come back ready. I mean he come back ready with that singing. He couldn't play no music. He never played an instrument in his life. But he'd tote a guitar. He'd buy a guitar, and he'd tote it in case that he'd run up on you or me or somebody could play and he'd sing. And he kept a guitar 'cause if he asked could you play a guitar and you said, "Yeah," well, he got one, see. And then you all come tear it off. And that's when I met Texas Alexander many years ago in Normangee, Texas.*

*I accompanied him for quite a bit there in Crockett, Texas, Grapeland, Patterstein, Oakwood, and Buffalo and Centerville, Normangee, Flynn, and Marquez and back in them places. I*

> *never followed Texas no further than Houston for a long way,*
> *'cause he was a man to get up and go. First Cadillac that I*
> *ever known to be, you know, one of them expensive, bad cars -*
> *he went somewhere and he come to Normangee in a Cadillac*
> *and it was the longest old ugly car, old long Cadillac, one of*
> *them there old first made. But it was new! He got over there*
> *and everybody admired him, you know, because colored people*
> *didn't have nothing. They didn't even have T-Model Fords*
> *then and you know he come in a Cadillac. Yeah, Texas was*
> *doing all right for himself...* [1.]

Texas Alexander's music, like Blind Lemon Jefferson's and Henry Thomas's, was distinctly a part of the Texas landscape, but his singing was an individual expression. Many of his pieces were strongly influenced by the conventional city blues recordings, but in his most characteristic blues there was a rich imagery and a melodic expressiveness derived from one of the root sources of Texas music, the work songs and prison chants. Like Lemon he was commercially directed by the blues market, and he did few of the country play songs or ballads of a songster like Henry Thomas, but unlike Lemon he had developed his vocal style without accompaniment, so the work songs had undergone fewer rhythmic changes in their adaptation to the blues. He was in prison in the '30's, but it is not known if he was a convict before he began recording. Some of the work songs that he used were sung in the hilly countryside around Normangee and he could have learned them as a young man working in the fields. Others may have been derived from the "lead line" songs sung by the caller working the steamships as he dropped his weighted line from the ship's bow to find out how much water was under the shallow hull. There was a use of words and phrases from the river songs which could have come from the men working the landing stages on the rivers, or from the work gangs that were building levees for flood control.

It was the long, almost chanted melodic line of the holler which left the deepest imprint on his style, rather than the stronger gang shouts. The rhythm was a sensed pulse that was very difficult for an accompanist to follow, even though there was a consistent accent pattern in each of the verses.

Example 31

198

mur—der, mur—der    I have—n't harmed a man ——

Lord, they 'cused me of mur —— der ———, I have—n't

harmed a man ———, Ooh ——————, they have

'cused me of mur—der, an' I have—n't harmed a man ——.

The verses themselves were often taken directly from specific field songs, and his soft, often hummed vocal tone had some of the feeling of a man singing as he bent over a cotton chopping hoe.

> I been working on the section, section 32.
> I'll get a dollar and a quarter, and I won't have to work hard as you.
> Lord, I'll get a dollar and a quarter and I won't have to
>      work hard as you.
>
> Oh nigger licks 'lasses and the white man likes it too.
> Lord, I wonder what in the world is the Mexican going to do.
> Oh the nigger licks 'lasses and the white man likes it too.
>
> Oh captain, captain, what's the matter with you.
> If you got any battleaxe please, sir, give me a chew.
> Oh captain, captain, what's the matter with you.
>
> Water boy, water boy, bring your water 'round.
> 'Til you ain't got no water, fetch your bucket down.
> Water boy, water boy, bring your water 'round.
>
> Oh captain, captain, what time of day.
> Oh he looked at me and he walked away.
> Uum, oh captain, what's the matter with you?
>
> If you got any battleaxe, battleaxe, please, sire, give me a chew.
> Uum.
> Uum, lord, oh lord, oh lord.

(Section Gang Blues)

199

His style of singing, with its close relationship to the holler, enabled him to use the field songs almost without change. In the literalness of the "Section Gang Blues," it was clear that he was using verses that had been "worked up" by a gang that was laboring for pay, "I'll get a dollar and a quarter, and I won't have to work hard as you." At a wage scale of $1.25 a day there wasn't much reason to work very hard or to take the work very seriously, and in the verses there was a suggestion of some light chaffing of the boss, asking him for chewing tobacco and the time of day. With the reference to the Mexicans the song was also tied to the Texas landscape. His style was so fully developed within the area of the holler work song that he was able to sing other material from the prison gangs that was in strong contrast to the easy joking of "Section Gang." In "Levee Camp Moan," which he might have learned from the convict gangs working along the banks of the Brazos River, there was a despairing sombreness to the verses.

> Uum,
> Lord, they 'cuse me of murder, murder, murder.
> I haven't harmed a man.
> Lord, they 'cuse me of murder, I haven't harmed a man.
>
> Uum,
> They 'cused me of forgery and I can't write my name.
> Lord, they have 'cused me of forgery and I can't write my name.
>
> I went all around the whole corral,
> I couldn't find a mule with its shoulder (bare?)
> Lord,
>
> Uum,
> I worked all mornin' and I worked
> And I couldn't find a mule with its shoulder (bare.)
>
> Oh, she went up the country but she's on my mind.
> Oh, she went up the country but she's on my mind.
>
> Oh, if you don't come on the big boat she better not land.
> Lord, if you don't come on the big boat, big boat,
> I mean she better not land.

Nearly all of these verses had been used by a number of blues singers, but there were few recordings in which they were still so closely related to their work song form. These two blues, on OKeh 8498, were the first songs of Alexander's to be released, but through the rest of his career there were only a handful of releases with their distinctiveness. For nearly all of his early sessions the accompanist was the guitar player and blues singer Lonnie Johnson, who developed a free guitar style to accompany the slow field chants, and their first duets were richly musical. Before his early recording career ended Alexander had been accompanied by Lonnie, by Lonnie and the white jazz guitarist

Eddie Lang, the Mississippi Sheiks, a Texas guitarist named Little
Hat Jones, the pianist Eddie Heywood, and a trio composed of the great
New Orleans cornetist King Oliver, Eddie Lang, and the pianist Clarence
Williams. On these recordings the style was closer to the conventional
city blues, even though his phrasing still had some of the looseness
of the holler, and he often used the hummed interludes of the work songs.

Example 32

He generally stayed within the three line stanza form, and his texts
were not distinctive, but he was often very open in his sexual imagery.
The "Rolling Mill Blues" had the verse,

> When you gets to yoyoing you jumps it up and down.
> When you gets to yoyoing you jumps it up and down.
> But when you learn how to yoyo you turn it 'round and 'round.

and he elaborated on the image of the yoyo - a child's toy that moves
up and down a string-in pieces like "Peaceful Blues."

> "I'm going to climb my woman's belly like a yoyo do a string."

The singing for the more conventional pieces was clear and direct, but
in the pieces like "Awful Moaning Blues" there was considerable use
of the melisma on the hummed tones. He seldom used the mordents that
Lemon Jefferson had taken from the work song, but his holler style
was more controlled than Lemon's irregular rhythms and vocal phrasing.
For the country pieces he used a four or five note scale, often adding
the flatted seventh for the more conventional pieces. Also unlike Lemon
he was influenced by other singers, and a blues like "Double Crossing

Blues'' recorded in June, 1929, - once past Little Hat Jones' usual hurried introduction - became almost a complete imitation of Lonnie Johnson's style, even to the opening phrases of Jones' guitar solo. Lonnie lived in Dallas for months at a time during this period, and Alexander had been with him in New York and in San Antonio for a number of sessions so the influence was probably a direct one.

In 1934, despite the Depression, Alexander was able to interest Vocalion in recording some of his blues and there were three sessions, one in April with an inept rhythm group called the Sax Black Tams, and two in September with guitar accompaniment. Often the pieces were uncomfortably derivative, and in something like "Justice Blues" he seemed to be trying to sound like a singer with one of the local white country bands. There was even a moralistic sentiment that was difficult to reconcile with the easy sexuality of the earlier pieces.

> When you see a woman with a cigaret in her hand,
> When you see a woman with a cigaret in her hand,
> You can use her husband for a little kid man.

On "Easy Rider Blues," recorded on September 30, the lead guitarist sounded very much like the young Lightning Hopkins. There was the same picked rhythm in the thumb and the involved treble accompaniment figures that were characteristic of Lightning's style. This was after he and his cousin had met at the ball game in Normangee, so it could be Lightning in his first recording. In the differences between Alexander's unelaborated vocal line and Lightning's involved accompaniment melodies there were already the seeds of the fullest development of the Texas style.

When the war was over Alexander was again singing around Texas. He was a burly, dark man, with some aggressiveness still left from his prison experience. Lightning said that he had been sent up for "...singing them bad songs - 'Some works undercover like a bull hogs eye' - and they sent him down." In 1946 or 1947 he was living in Houston, and Mrs. Ann McCullum made an audition recording of his singing with Lightning accompanying him. The audition was for Alladin Records in Hollywood, and she had to travel to California with the artists that she chose. As Lightning remembers she asked "Do you want to make a thousand dollars?..." But she was uncomfortable around Alexander and took Amos Milburn with her instead. His last session seems to have been the Houston recording he did for Freedom Records in the spring of 1950, "Bottoms Blues" and "Crossroads," "Benton's Busy Bees," accompanied by Leon Benton on guitar and Edwin Pickins, piano. His style, by this time, had become almost indistinguishable from the dozens of other Texas singers who were recording at this period.

Alexander was perhaps too much involved with the commercial blues market to leave as distinctive a group of recordings as Lemon Jefferson, or the songster Henry Thomas, but the work song style, even when he first began recording in 1927, was no longer so closely tied to the blues. It was however, the seed from which so much had grown, and in his changing style there can be heard some of the changes in the blues themselves, as they moved from the dusty air of the country roads to the noise and the dim light of the roadhouses and the city night clubs.

# 15. SOME OTHER TEXAS SINGERS

Even in the relative sparseness of the blues recorded in Texas, the elements that were to become the mature Texas style were strongly marked. Columbia records did considerable recording in Texas in the late 'twenties, much of it with the great Texas religious singer Blind Willie Johnson, who was living in Waco. In Dallas the company worked with a number of blues men, among them Bobby Cadillac, Perry Dixon, Will or Bill Day, Billiken Johnson, Coley Jones, and Alex Moore, but the music was not strongly local in its styles. Cadillac and Dixon, who sang with piano or piano and guitar accompaniment, were influenced by the commercial city blues. Probably they were accompanied by the local musician Whistlin' Alex Moore, who also recorded for Columbia during this period. Coley Jones was advertised as "...the new Bert Williams," but he seemed to have learned most of his songs from the old minstrel stage or from white folk sources. He even did a version of the Child Ballad "Our Goodman," with the title "Drunkard's Special." He was probably also a member of the Dallas String Band, a country string band that Columbia recorded during this period. The band was rough and noisy, but they had considerable musicality and one of their compositions "Dallas Rag," has become popular as a folk instrumental piece.

In their singing the Dallas men represented the strong influences on Texas music, the country pieces, the city blues, and, to a lesser extent, the work song prison music. Johnny Head, a Texas singer who recorded for Paramount in late 1927 or early 1928, did a "Fare Thee Blues Part 1 and 2," but his style showed considerable white influence and there was even a kazoo-guitar Charleston section in the accompaniment. Willard Thomas, another young Dallas singer, was influenced by Lonnie Johnson's recordings on several of his Paramount releases, but his "No Baby Blues" showed a strong Lemon Jefferson influence. Even on songs like his "Hard To Rule Woman Blues," while the vocal influence was Lonnie Johnson, the accompaniment was in a more expressive knife style. His Mississippi blues, "Poor Boy Blues," also had a knife accompaniment. One of his most interesting pieces was a prison blues with some of the feeling of Texas Alexander's "Levee Camp Moan Blues," although it was more regular in its rhythmic structure and verse form. Thomas, who recorded under the name "Ramblin'" Thomas, played his own accompaniments and his style was rhythmically less related to the vocal chant than was Alexander's. Thomas's piece with the prison chant overtones was also a "moan," "Sawmill Moan," probably to cover Alexander's successful recording the summer before.

> Hey - hey, hey, hey.
> Heya - hey, hey, hey.
> And I had 'em all night and got 'em all again today.
>
> And I wish I had my same old good girl back.
> I wish I had my same old good girl back.
> 'Cause that's the only one that I ever did like.
>
> How can I love you? How can I love you?
> How can I love you, you stay out both night and day?
> How can I love you, you treat me most any way?
>
> I'm going to sing this time and I ain't going to sing no more.
> I'm going to sing this time and I ain't going to sing no more.
> 'Cause my girl have called me and I got to go.
>
> If I don't go crazy I'm sure goin' to lose my mind.
> If I don't go crazy I'm sure goin' to lose my mind.
> 'Cause I can't sleep for dreaming, still can't sleepwalk for cryin'.

The accompaniment was mixed, using strummed chords as well as finger-picked linear patterns, but for most of the verses he made considerable use of drumming single note repetitions in eighths on the lower strings. Melodically the piece moved from the freer hummed verse that opened it, to more conventional verse melodies for the last verses.

The elements of the developing Texas style were even more evident in the singing of younger men like Little Hat Jones - there was a young, nervous sound to his music - than it was in the older men like Lemon and Texas Alexander. Little Hat had some of Alexander's sound in his voice, and he was working as Alexander's accompanist when he began recording in the spring of 1929, but he was also moving toward a newer sound in both the voice and the guitar. Alexander recorded in San Antonio on Saturday, June 15, using Jones and a second guitarist as accompaniment. He did eight sides, including the fine "Awful Moaning Blues," and then Little Hat did two sides, "New Two Sixteen Blues" and "Two String Blues," released on OKeh 8712. Despite his obvious nervousness the pieces were distinctly marked with the Texas style. He used the same melody for both of them, singing in a high voice

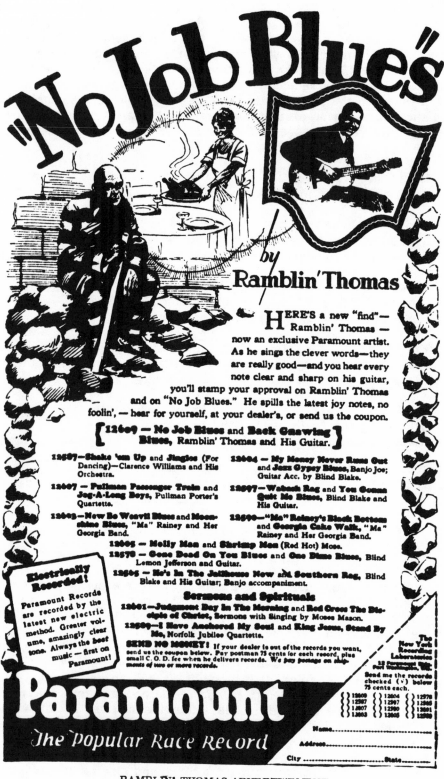

with the same mordent that both Lemon and Henry Thomas had used in their blues. The accompaniment was the alternate back and forth strum, rather than finger picking, with a melodic cadence that was surprisingly reminiscent of the pattern that the Virginia singer Luke Jordan used.

There seems to have been some interest in him by the OKeh field unit, and he recorded again the next Friday afternoon, June 21, doing four titles, and on these he was more assured. For ''Hurry Blues'' he used a Lemon Jefferson melody, but he was a little more adventuresome on the guitar than he had been the week before, alternating the finger strum with a picked melody in the thumb or forefinger. The vocal melody was begun high - an octave and a half above tonic - and the singing was very clearly phrased. The verses were undistinguished, but they were suited to his style

> I'm going, sweet baby, don't you want to go.
> I'm going, sweet baby, don't you want to go.
> I'm going somewhere's I never been before.

There was some use of nearly every element of the new Texas guitar style. On ''Rolled From Side To Side Blues'' there was a little alternate thumb work, with a doubled strum on the top strings, and on ''Little Hat Blues'' there was a hurried introduction like the openings he had used on some of the pieces he'd done with Alexander the week before, the tempo slowing when he began to sing. There was a girl's voice encouraging him on the last of the four sides he did, ''Corpus Blues'' or ''Corkscrew Blues,'' and he finally said, ''I can't pick it - I'm just learning how,'' and went into a boogie woogie passage on the bass strings.

OKeh was back in San Antonio a year later and Little Hat was recorded again. In the year his style had become more assured and all four of the pieces were strongly effective. ''Cross The Water Blues'' used a melody similar to one of Lonnie Johnson's standard melodies, but there was a syncopated boogie line in the guitar and a rich erotic description.

> I want you to take me home with you, baby, and ease me down
>     across your bed.
> I want you to take me home with you girl, and ease me down
>     across your bed.
> I want you to talk baby talk to me and then suck my tongue
>     cherry red.

''Cherry Street Blues'' was one of his best recordings, and it set the boogie bass patterns against an unvarying chord in the top strings and a rapidly moving rhythm. Although Jones had no opportunity to develop fully as a singer his music already had many of the elements that were to emerge in the Texas style as the long years of the 'thirties drifted into the Depression.

Dallas, like most southern cities, had small blues clubs that opened and closed in the Negro districts through the 1930's. The pianist Alex Moore worked steadily in the clubs through these years, and one of the singers who often worked with him was Willie Reed, one of the most interesting of the young Texas singers who managed to get onto record. He just managed to get on record, despite a number of sessions between 1928 and 1935. Of the fourteen titles listed in Dixon and Godrich only four were released, "Dreaming Blues" and "Texas Blues" from a 1928 session for Columbia, and "Some Low Down Groundhog Blues" and "All Worn Out and Dry Blues" from two Vocalion sessions in September, 1935. By the later sessions he had begun to fall into some of the styles that were popular on other recordings, but the 1928 session was unique in the Texas blues. He used one of the Texas vocal melodies, and the guitar accompaniment had some of the nervous movement of the alternate strum style, but he was finger picking in an open tuning. The guitar tone was hard, but there was a strength and inventiveness in the accompaniment patterns. He sang in a richer voice than other young singers like San Antonio's Little Hat Jones, and there was even some inventiveness in his verses. In "Texas Blues" he began,

"I'm gong out in west Texas where you can hear the wild dogs moan..."

It was unfortunate that Reed was unable to record more extensively, since he may have represented a less well-known Texas style. It was also unfortunate that two other Texas singers, Sammy Hill and Marshall Owens, recorded as little as Reed. Hill, who did two sides for Victor in Dallas in 1929, was more conventional in style than either Reed or Owens, but he sang with a sensitive and musical style, the voice clear and open with a slight vibrato on the held tones. On "Needin' My Woman Blues" he used the hummed chorus that was characteristic of most of the Dallas singers, its melody closely related to the same melody that Gertrude Perkins, Texas Alexander, and Ramblin' Thomas used in at least one of their Texas-oriented blues. Marshall Owens did four songs for Paramount in December, 1931, and there were elements of Lemon Jefferson's vocal melodies in his "Texas Blues," although his voice was darker and heavier. It was so much lower than the usual Texas blues voice that Owens may have been a northern Louisiana singer, or a Mississippian who was familiar with some of the Texas recordings. His "Try Me One More Time" was more in the songster tradition of Henry Thomas, or of the southern Louisiana songster "Rabbit" Brown. For both pieces the rhythms were very regular within a bar line pattern with a closer relationship to the "entertainer" guitar style than to the local blues styles.

Alex Moore was one of the most distinctive of the Texas pianists to record, as much as anything else for the piercing whistle on some of the pieces, as a break from his own singing. Moore was born in Dallas on November 2 , 1899, and began playing the piano when he was in his late 'teens. Some of his early recording was as an accompanist, but he also did six titles as "Whistlin' Alex Moore" for Columbia in 1929, and four more titles for Decca early in 1937. He was recently located in Dallas and recorded again for a small California blues company, Arhoolie Records, which is owned by the field collector and blues enthusiast Chris Strachwitz. His style has absorbed a number of influences since his earliest years and there is a florid extravagance to the melodic material in the right hand as he tries to crowd in as much of the new concepts as he can. His voice is not strong, but there is an insistence in the left hand rhythms, and he uses a variety of bass styles, from the walking bass and the ragtime bass of the older period, to the open chords of well-known performers like Albert Ammons and Pete Johnson.

Although a number of Texas pianists were recorded there was no highly idiomatic local style like Skip James'. Generally the music was deriva-tive. There has always been a tendency for some singers, especially men who do a lot of club entertaining, to pick up popular recordings and styles. Big Boy Knox, who recorded in San Antonio in March, 1937, had a great deal of this quality. He was another of the younger Texas pianists with some of the Leroy Garnett style, "Blue Man Blues" on Bluebird BB B-6952, was Bumble Bee Slim's "I Keep On Drinking," and "Eleven Light City Blues," on Bluebird B-6904, was derived from Kokomo Arnold's recordings, even to the use of Kokomo's distinctive compound verse melody. In "Texas Blues" Knox sang that he was born in Louisiana and moved to Texas, but there was nothing in his music that would re-late him to Louisiana. Black Ivory King, whose real name was Dave Alexander, had a more individual piano style, and his "Flying Crow," named for a southern train, had some of the feeling of the piano "train" pieces that were popular with the boogie pianists of the 'twenties.

> Flying Crow leavin' Port Arthur, why they come to
>     Shreveport to change their clothes.
> Flying Crow leavin' Port Arthur, why they come to
>     Shreveport to change their clothes.
> They don't take water in Texarkana, and for Ashdown they'll
>     keep on through.

> Twenty-five minutes from (Evelyn) for a cup of coffee and a
>     slice of cake.
> Twenty-five minutes from (Evelyn) for a cup of coffee and a
>     slice of cake.
> Flying Crow is heading for Kansas City and, boy, she just won't
>     wait.

> Yonder she goes she's gone, with a red and green light
>     behind.
> She's gone, she's gone, with a red and green light behind.
> Well now the red means trouble and the green means a rambling
>     mind.

Well, I hate to hear that old fireman when he tones the bell.
  (piano solo)
spoken: Oh ring 'em a long time.

Uum, Umm, Umm.

Other pianists, like Leon Calhoun who recorded for Vocalion as "Son Becky," or Harold Holiday, who was "Black Boy Shine" on Vocalion, were less individual.

The blues form for many Texas singers in the 'thirties became almost a constricting influence, and the music tended to cling to conventional three line melodic forms. There was, however, a development of the knife guitar style that may have been influenced by the "steel guitar" playing in the white country and western bands. The two best-known Texas blues men to use the heavy-necked steel guitar were Oscar Woods, "The Lone Wolf," who recorded for Decca and Vocalion in 1936, 1937, and 1938, and a younger singer who learned from him, Babe Kyro Lemon Turner, who recorded for the American Recording Corporation and for Decca in 1936 and 1937 as "Black Ace." Turner was born in 1905 in Hughes Springs, Texas, a small town in Harrison County. He grew up about seven miles from the Louisiana state line, and only about thirty five miles from the northern Louisiana town of Shreveport. The Depression forced him to try working in Shreveport when he was in his twenties and he met Woods there, an older man who was making a living playing at house parties and dances. Turner had already begun playing the guitar, but he learned the steel guitar technique from Woods, holding the guitar across his lap and using a glass medicine bottle as a slide. For both Woods and Turner the blues had become a fixed musical form, and there was little variation from the three line verse and conventional melodic material. Turner's pseudonym came from his Decca recording of "Black Ace," and he used the opening verse, "I am the black ace, I'm the boss card in your hand..." as an introduction to a radio program that he did for several months on Fort Worth's station KFJZ.

Even with the extensive recording of the 'thirties, however, the Texas blues style still lacked definition and focus. It was not until after the second World War, when local record companies sprang up in Houston and Dallas, that all the elements of the disparate Texas music environment finally were brought together and the Texas blues grew into the rich musical form that had been visible in the singing of Lemon Jefferson, Texas Alexander, and Henry Thomas.

# ROBERT JOHNSON—

# A NEW CONSIDERATION

So much has been written about Robert Johnson over the last 30 years that it's surprising for me to remember that in the introduction to *The Country Blues,* in 1959, I apologized for including a chapter about him in the book. I was trying to put the emphasis on the blues singers who had been important to the black audience that bought their records, and Johnson had done relatively few recordings and they hadn't sold in large numbers. As I wrote then, "It is artificial to consider him by the standards of a sophisticated audience that during his short life was not even aware of him, but by these standards he is one of the superbly creative blues singers."

In the chapter I wrote there was so little information about his life, and most of that was wrong—except that he was from northern Mississippi. Ironically, even the idea that the white audience was unaware of him turned out to be wrong. One of the most tantalizing artifacts from Johnson's short life is the original poster for John Hammond's "From Spirituals to Swing" concert, presented in Carnegie Hall on December 23, 1938. There, at the end of the next to last line in the paragraph listing the artists who were to appear, is Johnson's name. Hammond, who seems to have heard every important black musician playing anywhere in the United States in the '30s, had heard some of Johnson's records, and he'd asked Ernie Oertle, who had been the contact for Johnson's recordings, to find him for the concert. Oertle looked for Robert in Mississippi, but learned that he'd been murdered in the summer. The replacement for the country blues segment of the concert was another Mississippi singer, Big Bill Broonzy, who had moved to Chicago and was one of the most popular of the

211

new "Bluebird Beat" singers. As a tribute, Hammond played two of Robert's recordings from the stage, "Walkin' Blues" and "Preachin' Blues."

When I wrote the chapter about Johnson for *The Bluesmen* in 1967 it wasn't necessary any longer to apologize for writing about him. The emphasis in the new book was on what the growing young white audience considered to be the important blues singers, and Johnson was already becoming a legendary figure. Son House, who knew Robert when he was still a teenager, had been interviewed, and from House we had the outline of Johnson's life. In 1962 I talked with Henry Townsend in St. Louis, and in 1965 I met Johnny Shines in Chicago. Each of them was able to fill in some of the details of Robert's life after he'd left the plantation where Son House had known him. By the time I finished a book transcribing and annotating all of the songs in 1973—the book is titled, simply, *Robert Johnson*—I had spent weeks photographing the towns in the Mississippi delta where Robert had played for parties and dances, and the small cluster of shacks where he'd grown up. The researcher Gayle Dean Wardlow had found the death certificate, and there had been long interviews with Johnson's stepson, Robert Junior Lockwood. I was able to add all of this to what was already known in the long essay that introduced the songs.

On one level the mystery that was so much a part of the legend of Robert Johnson was slowly and patiently being unraveled. He was no longer a hazy figure standing in the dust at a delta crossroads. In the '70s two researchers working separately, Steve LaVere and Mack McCormick, found Johnson's surviving relatives, and after these interviews, although they are still unpublished, there wasn't much else to learn, except exactly what poison was used by the jealous husband who killed him. Sheldon Harris's monumental *Blues Who's Who*, published in 1979 (and now reprinted by Da Capo), included a short biography that had most of the details of Johnson's life—and finally in February, 1986, *Rolling Stone Magazine* printed the first of the photos that had been found. There was the face we'd wondered about for so many years. Robert looked very young, posed in his shirt sleeves with his guitar against a crude cloth backdrop. A cigaret was dangling from his mouth and he was almost smiling. His fingers, on the neck of the guitar, were—as one of the men who had supervised his first recordings remembered—very beautiful. On the cover of his book *Searching for Robert Johnson*, published in 1989, Peter Guralnick reproduced a second photo, which showed Johnson a little older and wearing a stylish suit, tie, and hat.

Robert Johnson's life, now that we finally can see who he was and how he grew up, isn't that much different from the lives of hundreds of other boys growing up in the rough plantation system that still controlled most of northern Mississippi. A likely birthdate is May 8, 1911, which would mean that he was between twenty-five and twenty-six when he did the first recordings in San Antonio. The father who was remembered around Robinsonville as Robert "Dusty," was a stepfather, who raised him when the family had moved to Commerce, a collection of shacks at the end of a dirt road where he spent his adolescence. When he was growing up there was some confusion about his name. His mother, Julia Major Dodds, had married Charles Dodds in Hazelhurst, which is south of Jackson, in 1889. She had ten children with him, then when Dodds—who made wicker furniture—had to get out of town, following a dispute with a local white family, she stayed in Hazelhurst with two small daughters. There was a story that Dodds had to flee Hazelhurst dressed in women's clothes, and he moved to Memphis to stay out of reach of the people who were pursuing him.

Dodds remained in Memphis for two years, using the name Spencer so he wouldn't be found. His wife was finally forced out of their house in Hazelhurst, and her eleventh child, Robert, was born after an involvement with a field worker named Noah Johnson. Julia wandered through the camps and small communities at the southern edge of the delta, picking cotton while her daughter Carrie, who was now eight, tried to watch out for Robert. There is a picture of Julia taken probably a year after Robert was born, and she is unsmiling, short and round-faced, in a broad brimmed hat and a loose dark dress with a bow at the neck and a wide cloth belt. There is nothing about her to suggest any of the confusion that had taken over her life.

McCormick told Guralnick that despite his mother's efforts to bring the family together Charles Dodds wouldn't accept the child she'd had with Noah Johnson. Finally he relented enough to move Robert up with him to Memphis, but he wouldn't let his wife come with her son. When Robert came to live with his stepfather he was three years old, and his stepfather now had all ten of the children he'd had with Julia with him. At the same time a woman he'd been keeping in Hazelhurst had moved in, with two children they'd had together. Robert, for the next few years, was Robert Leroy Dodds Spencer. His older brother, Charles Leroy, is supposed to have taught him something about the guitar, but Son House, who probably first encountered Robert around Robinsonville when Robert was fifteen or sixteen years old, remembered that he couldn't play the guitar at all then. Robert's mother finally married again, to a man named Dusty Willis, and when Robert was eight or nine years old she took him to live with them outside of Robinsville, where Son House saw him. Son moved to the town himself in 1930, and it must have been then that he saw Robert after he'd learned to play.

Commerce, where Robert lived until the end of his adolescence, isn't much more than two rows of shacks built to house the workers on the Abbay and Leatherman cotton plantation. A dirt road runs from the ramshackle houses back past the buildings of the plantation to the town of Robinsonville. The shacks were small and poorly built, without insulation against the cold, and without any ceilings or attics to keep off the searing heat. The bare earth around them was dusty in the summers and muddy in the winters. There wasn't any kind of shop. When Johnson was growing up there the workers got most of what they needed from the Leatherman store, and they could buy the other things in Robinsonville. When I traveled from Memphis down to Commerce in the early '70s I had the feeling that the small community must have looked almost the same way when Robert was growing up. The only real difference would have been the style of the cars parked alongside the buildings.

Commerce isn't far from Robinsonville, only $4\frac{1}{2}$ miles west of the town. Unless you ask somebody there's no way to know that you've gotten to Commerce, since there's no sign telling you that you're there. If you go on past the end of the houses you can leave your car and climb up on the levee, and you can see small communities looking a lot like it scattered in dust colored clumps over the flat delta countryside. Commerce has a small wooden church, but most of the places don't even have that much.

On a work day most of the men who live in the shacks are working in Robinson-ville or on the farm. There are usually children in muddy overalls playing out-side and they gather behind you when you walk up on one of the weathered porches and knock on a ragged screen door. Usually you see a child's face first, looking up at you wide-eyed, then the face of a young mother or a teenage girl who's helping to take care of the children staring at you warily through the rusty screen. It doesn't do much good to ask about Robert Johnson. Nobody lives very long in places like Commerce. The women answer you nervously, "No, I don't know nobody been here long. This is Commerce, alright, but nobody been here long that I know of."

As you walk along the row of buildings you wonder how they could have stood up to more than a winter, more than a growing season. They aren't much more than boxes made out of cheap pine boards, and for foundations there are two or three concrete blocks piled up at the corners and under the steps. The houses have been covered with sheets of laminated building paper that's been scored to look like bricks, but corners have torn away on most of the houses, and edges of the paper flap in the wind. The only things with any permanence along the road are the brick buildings of the Leatherman farm. When people in Robinsonville remembered Robert's stepfather as the short man they called "Robert Dusty," his clothes covered with dust when he came into town, they were remembering his fast, striding walk on the dry, rutted stretch of road from Commerce.

When I went back on a Sunday afternoon there were more people around, most of them still in their best clothes from the church service. Robert wouldn't have been much different from the other adolescents who were talking in a loose group behind one of the board storage sheds. They were thin and gawky, and their Sunday best was a carefully ironed white shirt and dark trousers that had a line across the knee from the hangers where they hung for the rest of the week. They glanced at me shyly, but mostly they were laughing and joking with each other.

Robert went to school for a short time at the Indian Creek School in Commerce before eye troubles forced him to stop—and these boys sounded like they were telling each other about what had happened during the week of classes. When the laughter took on a different tone it was obvious they were talking about girls. It was the kind of easy talk that Robert would have fit into when he was living in one of the shacks. The boys looked about the same age Robert would have been when he left to get away from his stepfather, and in a few years most of them will leave as well, to go on to a life that offers more than the work in the cotton fields that waits for them in Commerce.

Robert's stepfather was short, like Robert, but he was stocky and strong, with none of his stepson's look of young sensitivity. He and Robert didn't get along, and he was against music as a way of making a living. Robert first learned to play the harmonica, but he and Willis quarreled, and when he left, as Son House remembered, he still couldn't play the guitar. He probably went to stay with one of his sisters. When he came back he had the guitar hanging down his back that Son described. As Son said, after Robert had taken over his seat at the dance where he was playing, "He's gone now . . .!" There never was a question about Robert going to work in the fields. For the rest of the few years that he had to live he traveled with his guitar.

There were involvements with many women, and there were several children, but there were also periods of his life that were more or less stable. He married while he was still in Robinsonville, and he and his young wife moved in with a married sister in another of the small communities outside of town, but his wife died in childbirth when she was only sixteen. In May, 1931 he was married again, to an older woman named Calletta Craft, who already had three small children with a previous husband. He moved in with her back at his mother and father's old town of Hazelhurst, and while he was there he met an older guitarist named Ike Zinnerman who seems to have been the strongest influence on his musical style. In these Hazelhurst years he spent most of his time playing the guitar and learning songs, and when he began traveling again he was a professional musician. He moved north to Clarksdale with Callie and her children, but the life there was too lonely and hard for her, and when Robert left her to begin his wanderings she called her family to take her back to Hazelhurst.

For the next four or five years he had a long relationship with an older woman named Estella Coleman, who lived in Helena, Arkansas, just across the Mississippi River. She was probably fifteen years older than Robert, and her son, Robert Junior Lockwood, who was only three years younger, was also a blues musician who sometimes traveled with his stepfather. The blues singer Big Joe Williams remembered that there was always work around the saw mill at West Helena. "I used to go there to play and I could always pick up something, people there, you know, had most of them just come out of Mississippi anyway, so they wanted to hear the blues."

Robert hung around Helena for the chance to pick up some money singing whenever he was in town, and he had Estella's house to stay in as long as he was there. She could have been the woman that he sang about in the first song he recorded, "Kindhearted Woman Blues."

215

I got a kind hearted woman do anything in the world for me
I got a kind hearted woman do anything in the world for me
But these evil hearted women, man, they will not let me be.

When I left Commerce and Robinsonville on the trip to see Johnson's part of the delta I drove across the Mississippi to look at Helena and West Helena. The only bridge that crosses the river between Memphis and Greenville, 165 miles further south, rises above the line of levees at Powell, Mississippi, and puts you onto the road between Helena and West Helena. Like most of the river towns along the Mississippi, Helena has seen better days. The stores in the old business district are small and shabby, and even the white section up on the bluff has a run-down look to it. The black section of town is a row of dirty one-story brick buildings on Walnut Street, and some more worn buildings straggling along the railroad tracks on Mobile. In the '70s a battered restaurant called The Kitty Kat Cafe still had a large sign painted on one of its windows, "Colored & Mexicans."

West Helena, the section of town that Robert mentioned in the blues "I Believe I'll Dust My Broom"—"If I can't find her in West Helena, she must be in East Monroe I know"—is about five miles further west, up on the high ground. The lumber mill that Big Joe Williams remembered, the Chicago Mill and Lumber Company, still dominates the small district of one-story houses around its tall chimneys and its chemical cylinders. The logs that come in from the hills to the south and west are stacked in long heaps inside the high fence, dark with the water playing on them to keep them from splitting as they dry. Boys who live in the houses outside the fence pick through the scrap pieces for slabs to burn in the family stoves. Most of the houses are made out of boards cut from the same logs, and they have the same forlorn sense of weathered impermanence as the shacks in Commerce. The streets are still unpaved, but there are grocery stores now, most of them with Chinese owners, and the stores are in the same kind of run-down frame houses, with only dilapidated metal signs advertising cigarets and soft drinks and overhanging roofs out to the street to make them look any different from the rest of the town. It was in the black communities like West Helena, around the scattered mills or railroad yards and warehouses where there was some work, that Robert spent most of his time after he left the farm in the delta.

Even in the worst of the Depression years, when Robert was doing most of his wandering, the record companies that worked the blues market were still trying to find new singers. They didn't pay very much, and royalties were almost non-existant, but most of the singers who were working in the juke joints or the small local clubs managed to get onto one of the major blues lines. The talent scout who sent him to ARC, the American Record Corporation, was a music store owner in Jackson, H. C. Speir. Johnson's older sister Carrie, who had taken care of him when he was a baby, was living in Jackson, on Georgia Street, and he probably stayed with her when he was in town. He could have come into the store and auditioned for Speir, who held regular auditions when the musicians came to stand in line and play for him, or one of the other people who also were looking for talent may have heard him and sent him down to Jackson. The ARC liason man was the young white record salesman named Ernie Oertle.

Robert did his first recordings for ARC's Vocalion label in San Antonio on Monday, November 23, 1936. The A & R director for all of the ARC recording on this trip was veteran Art Satherley, who had done the same job for Paramount Records in the '20s, when he'd worked with their artists like Ma Rainey and Blind Lemon Jefferson. He had set up a studio on the mezzanine of the Gunter Hotel in downtown San Antonio. The producer in the studio with Robert for the sessions was another young white employee of ARC, Don Law, who was responsible for finding someplace for Robert to stay, then getting him out of jail after the police picked him up.

After Robert recorded "Kind Hearted Woman Blues," he continued to do a series of blues, all in the same afternoon session, that were among the greatest songs any blues artist ever was to record. One following another, he sang "I Believe I'll Dust My Broom," "Sweet Home Chicago," "Ramblin' On My Mind," "When You've Got A Good Friend," "Come On In My Kitchen," and "Terraplane Blues," then finished with a minor title, "Phonograph Blues," a weak song that wasn't issued until the 1960s.

In these songs was everything that the other musicians had talked about in Robert's blues, the startling instrumental technique, the moody imagery, the heavy, brooding emotions, and the feeling that he was possessed as he sang. Three days later, on Thursday, November 26, he recorded a single blues, then the next day began the session with an inconsequential jump song, another weak blues, and then came "Crossroad Blues," "Walkin' Blues," "Last Fair Deal Gone Down," "Preachin' Blues," and "If I Had Possession Over Judgement Day." On "Preachin' Blues" his emotionalism drove him to a performance that was almost incoherent in its intensity.

Oertle and Law were recording a number of other artists at the same time that Johnson was in their improvised studio—almost every style of music that was popular in San Antonio, from Mexican guitarists to Western Swing—but they recognised his uniqueness. Seven months later they brought him back to Texas to record again, this time to a studio they'd set up in an upstairs room in a warehouse in Dallas. Again, ARC was recording a number of other artists. On the first day, Saturday, June 19, 1937, Robert only recorded three titles, but one of them, "Stones In My Passway," was one of his masterpieces, and the last song, "From Four Until Late," was as quiet and understated as it was impossible to forget.

The next day, on Sunday, he began with "Hellhound On My Trail," then the session drifted through a number of styles and derivative blues until the fifth song, "Me And The Devil Blues," one of his most distinctive compositions, and the next to last song was the haunting "Love In Vain." The legacy of Robert Johnson is this body of songs he recorded in improvised studios in the middle of crowded recording schedules supervised by A & R men who were responsible

217

for almost any kind of music and style. What he did in the studio was completely his own achievement. Don Law and the engineer did little more than turn on the recording machine and tell Robert when to start. It isn't surprising that elements of the songs often can be traced to other blues singers who were popular at the time, and that parts of the guitar style or the use of falsetto, sometimes the songs themselves, have a more or less obvious source. What is still so startling is that after so many years the greatest of his songs fuse together into a stark, magnificent musical statement, that is unlike anything anyone else in the blues has created.

The first record that was released was "Terraplane Blues" with "Kindhearted Woman Blues" on the other side. "Terraplane" was imitated by dozens of young bluesmen, and for years the song was associated with him in Mississippi. He was excited at being a recording artist, and he took copies around to most of his family, including some of his children. He even met his father again, Noah Johnson, who had heard about his son's success. Since he was now a recording artist he extended his traveling, and it was at this point that he went north to Chicago and Detroit with Johnny Shines, and Shines remembers getting as far as Canada and New York with Robert, despite the uncertainty of not knowing where Robert was liable to be at any moment. Certainly Robert would have gone on recording, and if he'd performed for the "Spirituals to Swing" concert he would have become part of the popular commercial blues scene in Chicago. With his death his music was passed on to a younger of generation of artists who only heard him on record.

He was so casual about involving himself with other men's wives and girl friends that the musicians who knew him expected he would get into serious trouble sometime. He was playing in a road house called Three Forks outside of Greenwood and he became involved with the wife of the man who ran the local juke joint. On Saturday night, August 13, 1938, he was playing at the road house with Sonny Boy Williamson, and when they were taking a break somebody sent him an opened half pint of whiskey. Sonny Boy had some idea what was happening and he knocked the bottle out of Robert's hand. Robert protested, and when somebody handed him a second bottle, already opened like the first, he went ahead and drank it.

The bottle had been laced with poison, probably strychnine, which was commonly used to kill rats. He tried to go on playing, but he was in too much pain, and he was taken back to Greenwood in the middle of the night. He managed to survive the poisoning, but he was too weak to fight off an sudden attack of pneumonia. He died in the stifling heat a few days later, on August 16, 1938. If the May, 1911 date for his birth is correct, he was 27.

The interviews that have been done with his family will fill in more details, but essentially there isn't any real mystery now about Robert Johnson's life. If we don't know what he was doing on a particular day in 1933 or 1934, we know most of the places he might have been, and what he would have been doing sometime on a day like it. There was never any mystery about the songs.

All of them were finally released, and it was possible to listen to everything he recorded, even the unissued takes that were done at the sessions so there would be a safety master in case something happened to the first wax disc.

Sometimes, though, it seems that trying to find the essence of Robert Johnson is like trying to peel an onion. There always seems to be another layer of skin under the layer you've just peeled away. We've peeled away the mystery of his life and his songs, but what's left is the mystery of the handful of compositions that are unlike anything else in all of the blues. Without being able to ask Robert himself, we'll never know how he conceived "Hellhound On My Trail," "Come On In My Kitchen," "Love In Vain," or "Stones In My Passway," and we'll never be able to follow the steps that led him to develop the voice and guitar interplay in "Walkin' Blues." We will go on pursuing the image of the Robert Johnson we can imagine in West Helena or Friar's Point because of the singer who created some of the blues' most haunting and magnificent moments. It is these moments which will always be the mystery.

Perhaps the best way to remember him is to think of him getting out of bed in the middle of the night to pick up his guitar. Sometimes the girl he was staying with would wake up and see him sitting by the window, silently fingering the guitar in the moonlight. If he turned around and saw she was watching him he would stop.

# THE BLUES MAKERS
## Part II

# Sweet
# as the
# Showers
# of Rain

## PHOTOGRAPHS

# Contents to Part II

# Memphis and the Singers of Tennessee

# 1.
# Memphis and the
# Singers of Tennessee

There isn't much left to Beale Street now. You walk along the main street in downtown Memphis, and you turn away from the river, down the sloping blocks to what is now called W.C. Handy Park, and before you've gone a hundred yards you realize that the next time you walk down Beale Street it may not be there at all. It's been many years since Beale was the wide-open, roaring center of bars and honky-tonks that was as well known throughout America as New Orleans' Basin Street—but the buildings were still there. You could stand on a corner and look at the old brick facades, at the old high windows with dirty shades still pulled down late in the afternoon. A whole section of Beale had been taken over by pawnshops and cheap variety stores, but they had a ragged charm of their own, and you could still see blues and gospel records tacked up in some of the window displays. Further on, past the park, there were still some of the old pool halls and barbershops that had been part of the street's life. And beyond them you could walk along the lines of crumbling mansions that once had a more colorful history.

But now, a block down Beale Street, you begin to pass boarded-up store fronts, the elegant nineteenth century brickwork fronts behind the peeling plywood looking as though they're standing on their toes, trying to see over the obstruction. Beyond Handy Park there are only gaping openings where buildings once stood, and the corner where you might still have heard a struggling bluesman or a ragged street band is now the green boundary of a freeway. First Prohibition came to Beale Street, then reform politics, and finally urban renewal. Now there isn't much left except a name on some old records, the title of a blues song, and Handy Park, which seems just an extension of the ground beside the freeway since it's become a park without people. There are not even many old men who still remember it, except as something as dim and unlikely as their own childhood.

Nearly every Southern city was a center for some kind of blues—except maybe

Richmond or New Orleans, which were too close to the edges of the South. But of all these cities, Memphis emerged as one of the most important centers of the blues. Part of the reason was the city's importance as a center of business and industry on the Mississippi River. It sprawls behind mud bluffs along the river's edge more than 400 miles north of New Orleans and more than 300 miles south of St. Louis. It's the largest city on the river between the two. It was always known as a cotton center, but it's also an important market for timber. It has a cluster of railroads feeding into it, and there's endless shipping making its way up and down the Mississippi's muddy current. It has a population now of about a half million, of whom about a third are black, and it was a large city even in the period when Beale Street was booming.

Even more than its general personality as a trade center and a river town, Memphis was a center for music because it was close to the farms and the back country of the Mississippi Delta, which opens out about fifteen miles south of the city. It was in the Delta that the blues first began, and most of the Delta bluesmen came in and out of Memphis at one time or another. With a whole blues culture close to it—and the barrooms and honky-tonks of Beale Street to give the singers a place to gather—Memphis for years had an incredibly rich musical life, and because of the activities of the record companies who visited it regularly much of the music found its way onto records.

But Memphis is even better known for its own blues style than for the Mississippi blues that was also there. Memphis had its jug bands: small street groups using guitar and harmonica, a jug and a banjo, to accompany the blues and the country dance songs found everywhere along Beale Street. The two best known groups were the Memphis Jug Band and Cannon's Jug Stompers, but there were others who also got onto records—as well as ones that played for only a month or two along Beale Street and then drifted back to the countryside. It was the jug bands, whose music was mixed with the blues, that gave the city's music much of its style; but its bluesmen as well, including Furry Lewis, Frank Stokes, and Jim Jackson, added to the burst of sound that could be heard any night along the sidewalks of Beale Street.

Because of the range of Memphis music it is difficult to make any stylistic generalizations. The singing was usually rather straight and simple, without melismatic embellishment and with the melody tones clearly enunciated, as in much of the singing in northern Mississippi. There was a sophisticated approach to older material, so the harmonic range was larger than in much of the Delta blues, though the vocal scale tended to group itself around the blues modes using a flatted third and seventh. Often, as with Furry Lewis and Will Shade and other singers from the Memphis Jug Band, the singing had almost an amateurish hesitancy about pitch and phrasing, but this only enhanced the loose and informal feeling of Memphis music.

It's fortunate that most of the important recording in Memphis was done by one of the most brilliant artist and repertory directors working in the South in the twenties, Ralph Peer of Victor. Peer was from a middle-class background— his father owned a record store in Kansas City— and he had two years at North-western University before starting with the Columbia Phonograph Company of Kansas City in 1911. In 1919 he came to New York as director of production with General Phonograph Corporation, but the next year he became recording director for their subsidiary, OKeh Records. With OKeh he began the first "race" series, and in fact invented the name used to describe black material in the period. With OKeh he recorded the first blues record, Mamie Smith's "That Thing Called Love," early in 1920, and he went on to record a wide range of black music, both blues and jazz—including some country artists like Sylvester Weaver. As early as 1923 he traveled to Atlanta with a portable unit to record white country music there. He recorded the fiddler Fiddlin' John Carson, and then went on and recorded black singers working in the city, among them Lucille Bogan and Fannie Goosby. It was the first field trip by any of the companies, and it set a pattern that Peer was to continue for several years, traveling regularly to Atlanta, where the wholesale distributor Polk Brockman was scouting for him, to New Orleans, and to St. Louis, where a local record shop owner named Jesse Johnson was the scout. In St. Louis he found Lonnie Johnson and with him had one of the most successful of the male blues artists.

Late in 1926 OKeh became part of the American Recording Corporation's group of labels and in effect became a subsidiary of Columbia Records. Peer would have become part of a larger artist and repertory staff under the direction of one of his most serious competitors, Frank Walker. Instead, he left and went to Victor Records, which had been struggling for years to establish a blues line. At the same time Peer had begun to realize the potential in song copyrights, and in 1928 he and Victor established, together, the Southern Music Publishing Company. Peer almost immediately began working in Memphis, probably because no one else had to any extent, and he realized that if he wanted to establish a blues catalog he would have to find artists in areas where no one had looked before.

Of all the important artist and repertory directors working in the South, Peer was the one best suited to Memphis and its musicians. He didn't have the best ear for the sudden, large selling records—Mayo Williams at Vocalion was the most successful at that; and he didn't have Frank Walker's rougher hand with country artists. But he had a sensitive and intelligent ear, and perhaps because he was concerned with the songs themselves, as well as with the artists, he seemed to bring out depths in his artists that other people recording weren't able to get. The range of artists that he worked with was very wide, and the Memphis music, with its distinctive shadings and its quiet lyricism, fit into his careful approach. In a publicity release by Southern Music, published some years after Peer's death, there was an effort to list Peer's artists.

*It is well known that Peer discovered and recorded the legendary Jimmie Rodgers, father of the country field, as well as the legendary Carter Family. It is not so well-remembered that he recorded many other notables in the country, blues, gospel, and jazz categories. These include Ernest Stoneman, Rabbit Brown, Sleepy John Estes, Blind Willie McTell, Frank Stokes, Luke Jordan, Furry Lewis, Bennie*

*Moten, Jelly Roll Morton, Fats Waller, Cannon's Jug Stompers, the Memphis Jug Band (Will Shade), the Dixieland Jug Blowers (Clifford Hayes), Noah Lewis, Jim Jackson, Jimmie Davis, the McGravy Brothers and the Carolina Tar Heels. Too, he recorded the great blues singer, Mamie Smith, in her first recording, "That Thing Called Love," on OKeh.*

Largely because of his activity in the city we have an unparalleled glimpse of the musical activity in Memphis in the late twenties.

Beale Street is gone now, but the old neighborhoods north of the town center still have their rows of one-story wood houses behind straggling patches of grass and the uneven sidewalks under the spindly trees. Children play in the water-filled gutters after a rainstorm, and old men gather to talk on benches beside the grocery stores. Along one of the streets, if you know which grocery store to look for, you can find Bukka White sitting on one of the old chairs he's put out as his "office." Along another, if you know which weathered door to try, you can find Furry Lewis sitting beside his bed, his guitar on the wall, as he smokes a cigarette and looks quietly out at the houses across the street. The blues is still living in Memphis, even if the buildings that nursed it have been destroyed to make way for a future that perhaps will have forgotten that the blues was once there.

Beale Street today.

13

The only known photo of the Memphis Jug Band: (left to right) Ben Ramey, Will Shade, Charlie Polk, and Will Weldon.

# 2.
# The
# Memphis Jug Band

What people seem to remember most about Beale Street is its looseness—its lack of fuss and pretense. It was a wide-open neighborhood with a lot of music in the clubs or on the street itself, a lot of casual drinking, and a lot of sex that didn't cost much money. Memphis itself wasn't a formal town. It was still part of the surrounding country, a place where people growing cotton came in to do business, go out to a restaurant, stay over in a hotel, then go back out to their farms. It wasn't Chicago or New York—not even Atlanta or New Orleans. Loose —easy without much sophistication, but open and responsive to everything. The music of the Memphis Jug Band, perhaps the most typical of all the city's groups that recorded, had a little of all of these factors in its music, and in their way they reflected their surroundings as much as the Delta singers reflected theirs. It was part of the blues they did, with some of the casual drifting sound of men just in town for a long Saturday night—it was part of their minstrel songs, songs they played for Memphis whites—it was part of the classic blues they did with Hattie Hart, sounding a little like the Chicago recordings of Ma Rainey and her Tub Jug Orchestra—it was part of the folk songs and comedy songs they did when they went off in the picking season as part of the traveling medicine shows.

The Memphis Jug Band was part of Beale Street, and it seemed to reflect its rows of garish saloons and shabby stores, the dirty streets in back of it with their crumbling mansions and peeling wood boarding houses. Their music often had a rumpled sound to it, as though they were tucking in their shirttails as they played. Then at other times, other sessions, when somebody had a new song or a new arrangement, it all came together with a sudden smoothness, almost an elegance. Then on a session the next day they'd begin a song with a kind of one-by-one uncertainty, get confused in the instrumental choruses, then have to rely on their shouted enthusiasm to get them through the piece. This is what Beale Street was by this time—and this was Beale Street's music, the music of its jug bands.

15

The Memphis Jug Band was almost this loose and casual about its music, despite the players' seriousness and their complete involvement in what they were doing. Their sincerity, their complete honesty about the music came, as much as anything else, from the man who was responsible for the band, an open, warm singer and harmonica player named Will Shade—though he was always called Son by everybody in the band, since he'd been raised by a woman named Annie Brimmer and called Son Brimmer by the neighbors. He was still part of Beale Street and the jug band until his death in the 1960s. He lived in a crumbling tenement off an alley behind Beale, with a guitar under his bed and his harmonica shoved into a pocket and a book with painfully jotted phone numbers of the musicians around that he could still count on to come for a party or a session.

Son's band was the first jug band to record in Memphis, but it wasn't the first jug band to record. Clifford Hayes had started to record for Ralph Peer in the early twenties with his Louisville jug bands on OKeh, and with the name the Dixieland Jug Blowers they'd been very successful on Victor. They'd even added the great New Orleans clarinetist Johnny Dodds for one session, and one of the pieces—called, for no reason in particular, "Memphis Shake"—was put on the other side of a brilliant band release by Jelly Roll Morton and the Red Hot Peppers. But Son's music wasn't like the disciplined jazz of the Hayes group. His music was blues and country minstrel songs, and this is what his band played—with their own warmth and loose excitement.

Son was one of the few Memphis musicians who was born there (on February 5, 1898) and he grew up as one of the crowd of small boys who hung around the fringes of Beale Street. He played more harmonica with the jug band than he did guitar, but the guitar was his first instrument. He remembered learning enough to get started when he was still in his teens. He followed a singer named Tee-Wee Blackman around on the streets, watching his fingers when he played. The first song he learned from him was "Newport News Blues," a blues about the troops leaving Newport News, Virginia, for France in the First World War. Tee-Wee showed him enough so he could play in the key of A and the key of E, and he decided he didn't need any more lessons, but he couldn't figure out any other keys by himself and he had to go back to Tee-Wee again. By the time he'd reached his early twenties he was going down into Mississippi with the medicine shows, and he was singing with a small, young, pretty girl named Jennie Mae Clayton who was living with him just off Beale Street. It was from the two of them and the music they were doing that the Memphis Jug Band had it start.

From an earlier account discussed in *The Country Blues* of their first recording session:

> When Son came in from a show in 1926, he and Jennie started play-
> ing and singing in the bars along Beale Street. One night a man
> named "Roundhouse" came up to them and asked if he could join
> their band. Son said it was alright and Roundhouse started blowing

*on a bottle. Everybody at the bar started shouting, "Jug Band! Jug Band!" and they went along the street from bar to bar shouting and laughing. The next day Son decided to get up a band "... something like the boys in Louisville." He was talking about ... the Dixieland Jug Blowers. He got a friend, Ben Ramey, to play kazoo, and another, Charlie Polk, to play jug. (The jug isn't actually played as a musical instrument. The player makes a buzzing sound with his lips and holds the jug up close to his mouth. The jug acts as a resonator for the sound.) They were both young, about Son's age, with more enthusiasm than experience. Son played harmonica or guitar, so they needed a second guitar player. They talked an older, more experienced musician, Will Weldon, into joining them and they started playing along the street. Charlie Williamson, at the Palace, heard them and got them an audition with Ralph Peer. Peer came down to the theatre on Saturday morning and they played for him on the stage. He liked them and told them to have four blues ready for him when he got back from a recording trip to New Orleans.*

*On February 24, 1927, they made their first recording for Victor. They had been up all night rehearsing, but after a little to drink, Peer got them relaxed enough to play. In the middle of their second song Williamson came into the studio to hear how they were doing. Son remembers that Charlie was always a fancy dresser and that morning he had on a gray suit, gray spats, a green paisley waistcoat and a white derby. Charlie strolled in, took off his derby and put it down on the piano. There was a hollow bang when he put it down and Son was sure the test was ruined. He looked at the control room window and Peer was standing there laughing at the whole scene.*

They did four blues in their morning session, with Will Weldon singing the first two, "Son Brimmer Blues" and "Stingy Woman Blues." Charlie Polk —whose jug was almost inaudible anyway—sang the lead on the third song, "Memphis Jug Blues," with Will and Son singing harmony. Son had moved from harmonica to guitar and the two guitars had a string band flavor, with one of them capoed up high like a tenor guitar. Son sang his old "Newport News Blues" for the fourth song. The beginnings were ragged on their songs—usually Son starting it off, then Weldon coming in a beat or two later, and finally Ben and Charlie. But once they all got started the band had a good beat and the instrumental sound was strong. Ben could play almost cornetlike choruses on the kazoo, and Son's harp playing had a soft wistful charm. The singing was tight and nervous—Will didn't have any of the assurance he was to develop years later as the successful Vocalion artist Casey Bill, and Son was always more of an instrumentalist than a singer, but the harmony was good on "Memphis Jug Blues," and some of the best things they recorded later used vocal harmonies. Despite the nervousness of all of it— they were all young and unsure about what they were doing—the records had a kind of friendly appeal to them. Peer seems to have been satisfied enough to offer Son a contract and to bring the band up to Chicago to record four months later, on June 9, 1927.

Their Chicago trip was one of their few stays outside of Memphis, and it was also one of their most exotic brushes with success. They had decided to bring another harmonica player up with them so Son could play guitar, and they used a friend—a tall, thin musician called Shakey Walter. It was after this session that they had an offer to play at the Grand Central Theatre in Chicago with the Butterbeans and Susie review. Butterbeans and Susie were a blues duet team whose real names were Joe and Susie Edwards. They did some singing and some comedy and added acts like the Memphis Jug Band for variety. As Son remembered it in *The Country Blues*, their life in the theater was short but exciting.

They decided to do a jungle act with everybody in jungle costumes and Shakey Walter holding a large rattlesnake. They got the snake and pulled its fangs, but when they were having a dress rehearsal the snake got loose and started for a rat hole in the wall of the auditorium where they were rehearsing. Shakey caught it behind the neck and they finally got it back into its box, but they decided that they'd better not feed it so much so it wouldn't have the strength to wiggle. They opened at the Grand on Monday, June 20, 1927, wearing grass skirts and playing their guitars. Shakey and a girl from the chorus took turns holding the snake and singing. Son sang "Newport News" and they played some instrumental numbers and the audience seemed to like it very much. Ma Rainey heard about the act and booked them into Gary, Indiana, for her show the next week.

At Gary the act came to a disastrous close. One of Ma's chorus girls was from the country and she felt sorry for the snake because nobody was feeding it. She gave it some food without bothering to tell anybody. In the middle of the show th e revived snake began inching out of the hand of the little chorus girl who was dancing with it. It finally got its head free enough to turn around and nip her. It didn't have any fangs, but it had small teeth, and she screamed and let go. The snake immediately started for the footlights, since everybody was on stage, and the theatre panicked. The first ten rows of the audience climbed over the back of the seats, the orchestra scrambled under the stage, and Ma, fat as she was, jumped on top of the grand piano. Shakey made a dive for the snake and got it just as it was going into the orchestra pit. He scrambled to his feet, waving the snake, pretending to talk to it in a nonsense dialect. He started to dance around the stage with it and Son finally came to enough to start playing. After a moment of hesitation the audience gingerly started back to the seats and finally decided it was all part of the act. They got a rousing ovation. From Ma, herself, they got considerably less than an ovation. "If you bring that——snake on this stage again I'll have everyone of you put in jajl." Without the snake their act wasn't very exciting and they went back to Memphis.

They didn't have a lot of jobs in Memphis; there was a little scene around

Beale Street and the clubs but not enough. So they scuffled up whatever they could. An agent named Howard Yancey was getting them jobs for country dances and the kind of white society jobs that black groups could get in the South. They were mostly expected to play familiar songs for dancing, to get drunk and act foolish, and to look grateful for getting the job. They came in and went out the same door as the kitchen help, and whatever eating and drinking they did was back in the kitchen. The jug band did a lot of these jobs in Memphis, some of them at the Chickasaw Country Club, others in the Peabody Hotel, where they played for businessmen's stag parties. The tips were good, even if the jobs were unpleasant, and if they played at a party for somebody like Mayor Crump they got ten dollars apiece before the job started. The clubs on Beale Street were noisy and crowded, and most people in them were there to drink or gamble or look for women; in all the confusion and the casual drifting there wasn't any way for a country jug band to cause much of a stir.

They had recorded blues in Chicago, but they'd also recorded a swaggering version of the old English folk song "Bully of the Town," starting with a Charleston chorus for kazoo, two guitars, and jug. The vocal was a haphazard unison chorus with everybody singing as much of the words as they knew, and there were instrumental "jazz" breaks for kazoo and jug. Shakey Walter was a fine harp player, and he was very strong in the instrumental chorus of the "Sunshine Blues" that was recorded at the same session. They were selling enough records for Victor to do a little advertising. An ad in the Memphis newspapers showed a picture of the band. Son and Will Weldon were sitting in front with their guitars, Son grinning broadly. Ben Ramey was behind Son's shoulder, wearing a coat and tie, holding a long kazoo in his hand. Charlie Polk was in a jacket, a button sweater, and a shirt with a loose, open collar, holding a large earthenware jug and smiling almost to himself. A drawing made from the photograph—putting neckties on all of them and buttoning Charlie's collar— was used in the advertisements for the *Chicago Defender.*

Peer only waited until the end of the summer, then he brought them to Atlanta to record again. They did two sessions—on October 19 and 20, 1927. There were changes in the band for the six pieces they recorded. Charlie Polk didn't make the trip, and Son had added Vol Stevens to the band. Vol was born outside of town, but like the others he'd grown up in Memphis; he was living with his sister on Springdale when they were playing together. He played banjo/mandolin and sang. For this trip Son also brought along Jennie Mae, and she sang three blues, "I Packed My Suitcase, Started to the Train," "State of Tennessee Blues," and "Bob Lee Junior Blues." They finished the first session with the popular "Kansas City Blues," then did two songs the next day with Vol Stevens singing "Beale Street Mess Around" and "I'll See You in the Spring, When the Birds Begin to Sing." Vol used a six-string banjo for his own songs, and the rhythm had some of the surging swing of the Louisville bands which also used six-string banjos. Jennie Mae didn't sing again with the band for recording; she sounded very girlish and nervous on her songs, but she had a special quality of her own that added to the band's sound. The words to the songs were stronger in these sessions as well. The texts had been generally put together out of familiar verses, but Vol could put together verses in a stronger sequence, and in one of the first day's songs there was a verse that hasn't turned up in many other blues:

I got a voice like a radio, it broadcasts it everywhere,
I got a voice like a radio, it broadcasts it everywhere,
Now you can find a wild woman, boy, by broadcastin' in the air.

"I'll See You In the Spring" was another folk song, with a chorus that ended:

I'll see you in the spring,
When the birds begin to sing,
It's fare thee, honey, fare you well.

It's always hard to look back and remember something. Years slide into each other, days stretch and dwindle, hours stay in the memory, and whole months—at the same time—have gone completely. Even when the face, the sound of the voice are clearly there it's sometimes impossible to remember when the person first came through a door, or walked down a street. For Son, trying to remember all the musicians who were in and out of the Memphis Jug Band over the years was a long and difficult job. He sat in his shabby room looking down at his hands, drinking cheap wine as he thought back. There was one man he was trying to remember—it was Charlie Burse, who was sitting in the room with him, a thin, well-dressed man with a pencil moustache and a worried expression. They couldn't remember when they'd first met—only that it had been sometime after the Atlanta sessions in October 1927. Finally, as the afternoon got later and the gray winter rain slackened outside the window, he decided that he must have met Charlie before the next sessions, in Memphis three and a half months later. He knew that they'd met one night when he had a session coming up the next morning in the McCall Building Studio. In a club on Beale Street, Yardbird's, he heard a man entertaining in the back room, singing and playing a four-string tenor guitar. The man had on flashy clothes and he laughed as he sang, and he often called himself Laughing Charlie. He was a country musician just in from Decatur, Alabama, and he had a whole repertoire of the kind of songs you could hear at county fairs or farm auctions.

Charlie and Son became close friends, and they were friends until they died within a few months of each other. They both remembered that they had met that way, but they couldn't remember just when it could have been. The band did six songs in February 1928, but Charlie wasn't with them. He didn't do his first recording with them until the next fall, on September 11. But the sessions in February showed already how far the band had come in only a year. They had a style, a sense of professionalism. The songs started with a rush and kept up their excitement. There were little musical figures worked out in the arrangements, and the singing—even if it wasn't on a level with the greatest singers of the twenties—was strong and musical. The band that Charlie came into was a tight musical group, with a uniqueness and raw musicality in everything they did. Charlie himself added a last dimension—a noisy, uninhibited country dance rhythm, some new songs, and his irrepressible laugh. The engineers had trouble recording him—he tapped his foot too loud, so they put him up on a high stool, but he kicked the legs of that too. They finally had to put a pillow under his feet to keep the noise down.

As far as Victor Records and Ralph Peer were concerned, the Memphis Jug Band—with whatever musicians Son brought to the studio—was a successful recording act, and Son was early put on a royalty advance basis. For nearly four years he was paid $25 a week, which was a reasonable sum for the 1920s, and he was expected to arrange the sessions, write the tunes or use tunes that someone else in the band had written, and take care of rehearsals. Son took the job seriously, and he was always ready when the Victor recording unit was in Memphis, even if they didn't record the band on every trip. When the band was in the studio they were paid $50 for each side they recorded, and they split the money up among themselves. For their usual four blues sessions they got a total of $200 advance. Son had composer royalties, and they could go as high as six cents a record if he'd written the songs on both sides; even higher royalty rates were paid if there were sales in Europe or Canada. Between the royalties, the session advances, and the band's jobs, Son had more money than he needed for everyday expenses; so Peer talked him into buying some Victor common stock, and Son and Jennie Mae bought a house in Memphis.

As the band became more professional they were also useful to Peer in other sessions, as he could expect Son to get something together with the other musicians. They were behind a number of lead singers, from Memphis Minnie, who had just started recording when she did "Bumble Bee Blues " and "Meningitis Blues" with them in May 1930, to Hattie Hart and Charlie "Bozo" Nickerson. Hattie Hart was a Memphis woman who sang in the style of the popular New York blues artist Sara Martin, and she had a heavily dramatic style that didn't fit comfortably into the band's informality. Charlie Nickerson was a piano player and entertainer from the "Steamboat Bill from Louisville" show, touring black theaters in the South, and he recorded a vaudeville-flavored "Everybody's Talkin' about Sadie Green" in another May 1930  session. Son and one of his close friends, a piano player named Edward Hatchett who was playing at the Midway at 4th and Beale, accompanied another friend, Kaiser Clifton, when he did four blues at still another session in May 1930. Son even played guitar and harmonica for a religious group, the Memphis Sanctified Singers.

Peer usually wrote ahead to Son and gave him about two months to get ready for a recording date. The band always worked at Son's house, and they'd work all day on a song, going over and over it ten or fifteen times until they had it right. Son never was insistent on a hard, tight arrangement, but he knew how he wanted the arrangements to go, and he stayed with a song until they had worked something out that he liked. Jennie Mae would write down the words and when they'd played it and timed it Son would write his "OK" on the words; then he'd write in the title at the top and his name on the bottom so that Peer's Southern Music Corporation could copyright it. He tried to be as careful as he could with the copyrights, and nearly thirty years later, when I was able to write Southern Music and tell them I'd found Son living in Memphis, they were able to renew all of his copyrights. At the same time they sent him an advance on what they hoped might be some further earnings.

In the last year of the Victor contract, 1930, Peer had the Memphis Jug Band in the studio for nine different sessions, and in that year alone they recorded twenty titles. There was so much material that some of the things recorded late in the year were released under other names—like the Memphis Sheiks or the Carolina Peanut Boys—or under Charlie Nickerson's name. There were fifty-seven songs recorded for Victor over the four years of the contract, and Son used fourteen or fifteen different musicians, from his old guitar teacher, Tee-Wee Blackman, who played with them on their fine train blues "K.C. Moan," to friends like Hambone Lewis and Jab Jones, who played jug on different sessions. There were so many different people singing that it's difficult to say that any kind of blues was typical of the Memphis Jug Band. They even recorded two instrumental waltzes, "Jug Band Waltz" and "Mississippi River Waltz," in September 1928.

The financial crash of the early thirties ended Victor's recording activities in Memphis, even if it didn't end the Memphis Jug Band. The last sessions, in November 1930, had to be done in a banquet room at the Peabody Hotel, since the old studio in the McCall Building had been closed up. Peer settled accounts with Son, and he said goodbye to all of them as they left the studio. Son had managed to buy nearly $3000 worth of Victor stock with his royalties, but he had to sell it at a fraction of its face value and he and Jennie Mae had to give up the house. He kept struggling to keep the band going. They went to Chicago in 1932 and managed to get a session with Champion at their studios in Richmond, Indiana. Vol Stevens and Will Weldon were on the trip, and Jab Jones was on piano now—playing jug only some of the time. Otto Gilmore played drums. They did five songs that were released under various names, among them the Picaninny Jug Band and the Jolly Jug Band. They were in Chicago again on November 6, 7, and 8, 1934, with a slightly different band. Vol Stevens had been replaced by a violinist, Charlie Pierce, and Charlie Burse's brother, Robert, on washboard, had replaced the drummer. They managed to get three days of recording with OKeh, and they did twenty sides, the last releases by the Memphis Jug Band.

The sound in 1934 was different from the things they'd recorded for Ralph Peer. There were none of the gentle folk blues like "K.C. Moan" or "Stealin' Stealin'." With the washboard and Jab Jones's rolling piano style they were more of a country skiffle group, and there were more instrumentals and a jazz feeling to a lot of the solos. Son played fine harmonica and Robert Burse had a wide range of objects to hit on his washboard, including a large orchestra cymbal that he used on "Gator Wobble." They did wild, exciting versions of songs like "Take Your Fingers Off it" and "Boodie Bum Bum," with verses like:

Oh, the black cat told the white one,
let's go 'cross town and clown.
I said the black cat told the white one,
let's go 'cross town and clown.
And that white cat told the black one,
you better set your black self down.


It was exuberant, rough music. Most of the pieces were issued first on OKeh and then later on Vocalion, but nothing was selling much in 1934 and Son couldn't keep it going. Charlie Burse had two sessions in 1939, recording twenty titles with a larger swing-type group called Charlie Burse and his Memphis Mudcats that used a conventional piano, bass, and drums rhythm section. The days of the jug band were over.


The Depression had finished off what was left of Beale Street, and the years drifted by. There were odd jobs at the country club and at the homes of some of the white society people. Whoever got a job would call up people to get them to come play too. Laura Dukes—known as "Little Bit"—a close friend of Son and Jennie Mae, played the ukelele or ukelele banjo and did a lot of singing. Will Batts, a violinist, ran a band that included Milton Robie who'd once been in the jug band, and usually Laura Dukes and Robert Burse, and for parties there were other musicians always ready, including Son and Charlie. The jobs were usually an hour's entertaining—most of the time in a side room, while a dance orchestra played for the social side of things in the main room. They were a kind of souvenir of the old South, and as always there was a lot of drinking and a lot of clowning. A white man named Jim Strainer was often responsible for getting them home, and the jug band did a blues for him, "Jim Strainer's Blues."

But as the years went by there were fewer people interested in what they were doing. Charlie had always been a house painter, and he just went back to his regular job. Will Batts kept his band going until 1956, when he died of a stroke. Son had even learned to play the string bass a little and he was working with the band as well. Howard Yancey booked a lot of the jobs for the musicians—though Will Batts did his own bookings—and a woman named Mrs. Wagner used to book them for jobs outside of Memphis.

In November 1956, on a drab, wet morning, I found Howard Yancey still in his old office upstairs at 316 Beale Street. "You interested in those old jug bands? They're still playing." It wasn't much of an office, and times were hard for Yancey, as they were for the musicians. Son was working on and off in a tire-recapping plant—a large, cluttered garage—a few blocks off Beale Street. He'd always had trouble with a strained back from his youth, and with that and his drinking he wouldn't have kept the job except that the man who owned the garage liked his old records. He and Jennie Mae were living in a small, poor room in an unpainted building on Mulberry Street. He was excited to talk about his music and about recording again. He still looked like the man in the old advertisements; he had the same smile, though his face was heavier. He was wearing a sagging sweatshirt and trousers stained from his job. He hadn't seen Gus Cannon for nearly a year, but he had Burse's address, on a small street in South Memphis.

When we went over that evening Charlie was looking at television, but like Son he was excited to talk about music and his newest band. He even had an acetate test of a song that he'd made the summer before with the band—a rhythm and blues group with Son on washtub bass. He said he'd be over at Son's in the morning and they'd try to find Cannon. The next morning all three of them were there. A friend of Son's had seen Gus going into a laundry and he'd told him Son was looking for him. After a few minutes they decided they wanted to record again, and my portable machine was brought in from the car. I didn't have much money left—about 12 dollars—but they split it up and spent some of it for whiskey and a harmonica for Son. Cannon and Burse came back first with a cheap American harmonica, but Son said it wasn't good enough and they finally went back and got him a Hohner "Marine Band," the instrument most of the bluesmen use. For the rest of the afternoon—until the last light had dwindled in the winter afternoon—they sat in Son's room and played. They didn't stop until it was too dark to see the instruments. From the first description of the session in *The Country Blues*:

> . . . *At first they were tight and nervous, but Son, despite quite a bit of wine, began to pull the group together, just as he must have done at many recording sessions thirty years before.*
>
> *It was exciting to feel his influence on these men, who in the world outside of the dingy, cold room were more successful than he had been. It was not his musicianship—he was a limited musician. It was his earnest, deep sincerity. He had never been a great harmonica player and he hadn't had a harmonica in twenty years, but he began with fierce determination, sitting in a low chair, the harmonica almost hidden in his scarred hands. Before the afternoon was over, he and Charlie created the wonderful "Harmonica-Guitar Blues" that was included in the Folkways record of the session. While the others were outside, he played on an old guitar that Cannon had brought until he was able to re-create some of the magnificent blues he had recorded years before.*

It wasn't as it had been in the twenties, when there were a dozen musicians to call up, and there were new songs and new ideas to try. There wasn't much music left, but Son still could play as much harp as ever, and he was one of the finest of the country harp players. And he could still sing one of his most poignant blues:

What you going to do, Mama,
When your troubles get like mine.
Take a mouthful of sugar
And drink a bottle of turpentine.
I can't stand it.
I can't stand it.
Drop down, Mama,
Sweet as the showers of rain.

He got an old guitar after that, and he worked a little with Charlie. Milton Robie was still living on College Street and Charlie's brother Robert was still living off Beale, but the others from the band were dead. Son and Charlie were part of a television tribute to W.C. Handy in the spring of 1958, and they kept going with what they could scuffle up. But by 1959 Son wasn't able to work much anymore. He'd gotten a little money from Southern Music, and now he got welfare checks, and there were things like his Christmas job with Charlie. As he said in 1956:

*Me and Charlie work up and down the floors at the McCall Building. Every Christmas we play it, you know, for contributions. This year we didn't hardly make more than $12.*

Son and Jennie Mae were living in a crumbling wood building in a muddy open space behind Beale. It was a bad building, and the room they had upstairs was open to anybody who was around. Some of the people hanging out in the hallways and on the stairs were drunk, stumbling neighborhood thieves, and late at night Son was sometimes afraid when someone came to see him. Bo Carter had a small house down the alleyway, and he was living in almost the same squalid poverty as Son and Jennie Mae. He sat blind in his darkened room, talking a little whenever Son brought visitors around. It was still possible to use Son to help find musicians, and for a few dollars he'd try to get people over to his room to play. He recorded his "Newport News Blues" again for Decca in the summer of 1960, and there were young musicians like Charlie Musselwhite beginning to hang around for lessons and a chance to talk. But Son wasn't well, there was too much wine, and the poverty was too oppressive to fend off. The last effort I made to get a session together with him in the spring of 1961 wasn't successful. Laura Dukes came up, and for the first time Memphis Willie Borum turned up from his factory job, and Charlie came around with his tenor guitar. But everyone else from the building pressed into the room, too, and there was angry, drunken wrangling almost drowning out the music. Only Memphis Willie, who was sitting on the edge of the bed close to the wall, was able to keep out of it and go on playing. Laura Dukes and Son couldn't get away from the people around them—and the situation finally got so bad that the best thing to do was leave.

Both Charlie and Son died five years later, in 1966. Charlie had gone on working as a house painter, so there hadn't been the desperation of Son's last years, but for both of them their last efforts to play their music were hard and disappointing. Somehow it kept eluding them—the brilliance of the music they'd made thirty years before. But it was all still there, on the phonograph records they'd made, and for both of them, in wry thoughtful moments, it was almost enough to have it to remember.

Advertisement for Gus Cannon.

# 3.
# Cannon's
# Jug Stompers

Sometimes, as the years drifted by, Gus Cannon had the same wry moments as he thought back to the twenties and the brief period of his life when he was making records. Almost in his nineties now, Gus is still a tall, lean, wiry man, and, though his hair is grizzled and thin, his high laugh is as clear and sudden as always, and his eyes still brighten when he remembers those years. "White folk," he says loudly, using his ordinary expression for anybody who's come to talk to him, "we made us some music." He still gets around along Beale Street by himself, in his gold-rimmed glasses, a suit coat and an open shirt, supported by an elaborate stick that he made himself. In 1956, at the rough session at Son's old apartment on Mulberry Street, he was still playing the banjo and jug, though he couldn't do some of the old songs he could still remember. He sat in the chair close to the window and tried things over and over, shaking his head emphatically from side to side as his fingers fumbled with the strings. His biggest number had ended up with his swinging the banjo back and forth as he played, holding it by the fingers of his left hand around the banjo neck. He tried it a little standing in the half-light by the bed, half turned away while he tried to get it right, but his hands didn't have the feel anymore, and he almost dropped the banjo. His fingers have stiffened now, and the banjo sits in its case in his room, but he still can play the jug and talk with the same abrupt enthusiasm.

The long, still years were easier for Cannon—as the other Memphis musicians always called him—than they were for Son and Charlie. For Son the jug band had been the first important thing in his life, and he'd thrown himself into the business of rehearsals and recording and song writing. It was more important to him, for one reason, because he was so much younger. He was only in his late twenties, and he found himself in the hungry years of the Depression without any other skills to get him through. Cannon was forty-four when he started recording, and when the excitement was over he was still living just about the way he'd been living before. His music was from the pre-blues period, and his repertoire—like other musicians the same age, Jim Jackson among them—was a

27

collection of comedy songs, minstrel show songs, instrumental breakdowns, and interminable, usually bawdy, routines of jokes and stories. These were performed with the broadest gestures and mugging—usually in blackface. Some of the expressiveness of Cannon's face must come from those old days. As he sits talking his face changes from the wide grinning pleasure of something he's just remembered to a petulant shake of his head and a deep frown, with the corners of his mouth almost sagging in his unhappiness; then his lips purse in sudden anger and he shakes his head; then without the slightest hesitation his head is thrown back and he is laughing loudly. A moment later he stops talking and glances carefully at you to see what the effect of it all has been.

An important aspect of the life of men like Cannon is that careful glance after a moment of clowning. Cannon addresses most of the people who come to see him as "white folks" because for him the white world has always been a distant, but continually threatening, aspect of his life. Son was an adolescent during the outbreak of racial violence in the Memphis area in the first years of the World War—when southern whites attempted to slow the rush of black field workers to northern cities with a wave of lynchings and beatings—and as an adolescent he was able to minimalize some of the emotional effect of it. Cannon, however, was older, and he'd spent most of his life as a sharecropper, and since he'd already left Mississippi, where he was born, he was the kind of man who was suspect. He has never said if there were specific instances when the antagonism that was always present between the races in the South singled him out as a victim, but the white man has continued to be the same threat to him, despite the "hilarity" of his shrewd blackface performance, despite the grinning face every black man of his generation learned to present to his watching white neighbors.

For the countryside that he came from, and by the standards of the period when he started playing, he was a professional musician—even if it wasn't the kind of full professionalism that we associate with music today. There wasn't enough money for a performer to spend his time singing and playing in the American rural areas—especially in a period when the absence of recordings or radio meant that there was someone who played an instrument and sang in almost every house. All the performers, white and black, lived and worked as part of their small towns or farm areas, and they did their playing when they weren't working their jobs or on their small farms. It was exceptionally talented men like Cannon who were considered "professional" and who brought their own standards to the music they created. It was this quality, as well as the repertoire, that gave the jug band recordings that Cannon did their distinctiveness. His experience and his musicality—and the experience of his old partner Hosea Woods—gave their performances a brilliance and a coherence that much of the country instrumental recording of the period lacked. Even when they were rough, and some of their songs were uncertain, the broad humor kept everything together. Cannon and his group made an important contribution to the picture we have of Southern music of this early period, and their recordings are still some of the most exciting that came out of the wealth of Memphis music in the 1920s.

Of all the Memphis characteristics in Cannon's style, perhaps it's Memphis as a kind of musical crossroads that's most evident. Like many of the other singers he came out of Mississippi, but without any close identification with the Mississippi blues style which developed after he'd left. He was born in northern Mississippi, in Red Banks, on September 12, 1883, working in the fields when he was a small boy on a poor farm. He always liked music—loved it as a boy—and he wanted to learn the banjo, which was still a popular folk instrument at this time. He made his first instrument himself out of a bread pan and a guitar neck. His mother gave him the bread pan, and he put holes through the sides of it to hold the guitar neck. He covered it with a raccoon skin that he scraped thin. The only problem with this kind of head was that there was no way to tighten it since the instrument didn't have the metal frame and drumhead ring of commercial banjos. He remembers that he always traveled with his pockets full of crumpled newspaper, so he could make a fire before he was going to play. He held the banjo over the flames until the skin head was tight enough so it had a banjo "ring" to it.

He started playing when he had his first banjo and, as he remembered in 1956 during the interviews for *The Country Blues*:

> . . . *The music he learned was that of the old dance songs and reels. The first song he learned was the little dance song "Old John Booker You Call That Gone," and he "strummed" it on the banjo. That is, it was played with a syncopated finger-picking, down-stroking and thumb-picking style that is similar to the older banjo frailing style. Then he followed around after one of the men who could really play, Bud Jackson, from Alabama, and he learned to finger-pick a little jig in 6/8 time. Cannon laughed. "When I had them two songs down, you couldn't teach me nothing, 'cause I knew it* all.

He was able to get himself a real banjo after he'd been playing a short time, and when he was fifteen he was already working small dances in the local countryside. He was living in the Delta at this time, and it's possible that he might have recorded then. From *The Country Blues*:

> *About 1901, when he was seventeen or eighteen, he was in Belzoni, Mississippi, a small town between Yazoo City and Clarksdale. Some people came to his cabin and asked him if he wanted to make a record. He didn't even know what they meant. They told him to bring his banjo and they took him into town where a man had a cylinder recording machine. After getting over his nervousness, Gus played a dance song, singing into the crude metal horn. He remembered the picture of the dog looking into the horn, and he thinks it was somebody from the old Victor recording company. He was paid for his playing and went back to his cabin, still wildly excited at having heard himself play. The early catalogs of Victor, Columbia*

*and the Berliner gramophone companies do not list anything specifically as by Cannon, but there are cylindrical recordings of banjo songs and dances one of which could be his cylinder. He may have been recorded by a pioneer field collector whose recordings have been lost, but if the material should ever be found, it would be a priceless collection of black country music.*

Even today, as an old man, Cannon still gives an impression of energy, of restless movement. He always has some little job going on, something that he's planning to do somewhere. He seems to have moved as much when he was a young man. He worked in the cotton fields up and down the Delta, sometimes on shares, sometimes for somebody else. He was in and out of most of the small towns, and he still kept playing and singing. He got up to Memphis for the first time just before the war, in 1913, and for the first few days he stayed down on the docks watching the stevedores doing their heavy, hot work carrying and lifting back and forth from the river steamers. He found a small job so he could stay in town and tried to take some music lessons from Professor Handy, but Handy couldn't understand the kind of music Cannon played and he couldn't understand the kind of formal music Handy was trying to teach him, so the lessons ended after a few hours.

He still kept moving around after he got to Memphis. He "made a cotton crop" on some land out on the Macon Road, but the land didn't give much, so he went across the Mississippi the next year and worked a crop outside of Chatfield, Arkansas. The next year he went out of the South, for the season, and put in a crop outside of Cairo, Illinois. He didn't like the cold weather, and he went back to Tennessee at the beginning of the winter. By this time he was playing the banjo almost as much as he was farming, so he was traveling most of the summer, even when he'd gotten a little farm started. In 1916 he was working some land outside of Ripley, about forty-five miles northeast of Memphis, on Route 51, the main highway down through the Delta to New Orleans. Ripley was a small town, a straggling section of stores and feed shops, the small farms coming close to the dirt back streets. It was a quiet town, but like every small place in the South during these years it had its own local musicians. The best of them, and now the best known of them, was the harmonica player Noah Lewis, who was one of the musicians who helped give Cannon's recordings their excitement a dozen years later.

The neighbors around Ripley—and around Henning, the small place a few miles closer to Memphis where Noah was born—still remember him, and they remember his music. The researcher Bengt Olsson even found members of his family. In Henning he found a cousin, Emma Green. "Noah was my cousin. He was born on Glimpse Farm in Lauderdale County, outside Henning, around 1890. His dad was Daniel Lewis. He was a farmer and didn't play no music. Noah started blowing the harp when he was nothing but a kid."

Sleepy John Estes remembers that Noah moved to Ripley with his wife when he was about seventeen. She was a cook and they lived at a small place called Minglewood. It was just outside of Ripley, a box factory at a little crossroads called Ashport. He spent most of his time playing the harmonica for whatever money he could get, and he's remembered as having a belt with harmonicas in different keys stuck in it. He'd also learned the local trick of playing two harmonicas at the same time—one with his nose—and most people remember him for this as much as anything else. Shakey Walter Horton, who lives in Chicago now but learned to play around Memphis, can still do it. Noah was a small, dark young-looking man, and his music had a deep personal sensitivity. Cannon remembers when he first met him: ". . . Noah was just a country boy from Ripley. He just played alone on parties and in the streets. Noah really could blow the harp through his nose. He had a son around Ripley by the name of Noah too  who was supposed to play the harp too." When they met Cannon was thirty-three and Noah was twenty-six.

Although Noah was doing a lot of playing by himself when Cannon first went up to Ripley, there was another Ripley musician who was also playing for parties and dances with Noah, the guitarist Ashley Thompson, who's recently been found still living quietly in the country. The three of them formed a small band that played regularly around Ripley for the next three or four years, mostly on Saturday nights for country balls and suppers. Cannon, as restless as ever, went back to Memphis in 1918 and took a job as a plumber's helper, but he still kept going up to Ripley whenever there was any music to be played. But he was spending as much time on the road with the medicine shows and the small carnivals as he was playing dances in the country. By the early twenties he'd become a well-known personality for the "doctor shows," and he was on the road most of the summer, through eastern Arkansas, western Tennessee, and northern Mississippi.

The shows that Cannon traveled with were loose and informal. The "Doctor" usually had a flatbed wagon or a truck that was painted with his name and his advertising slogans, and the rest of the show straggled after the truck in their cars. They didn't travel that far—only from one small town to the next—and there wasn't much of a show to set up. The wagon worked as the stage, and if it was an afternoon show they didn't need any lights. At night they had lanterns to hang up over the show area. The show always started off with one of the singers who came out in blackface and did some blues and some jokes, or did some of the popular minstrel show songs. If there was a dancer with the show there was usually some dancing. Almost anything worked on the shows, as long as it kept people entertained. When they'd gotten enough of a crowd gathered the Doctor would come out with his product and the sales pitch would start— and it was expected to be as entertaining as the show. The Doctor promised and pleaded and harangued and argued and, sweating and shouting like a revival preacher, he dragged the money out of the crowd around the wagon. Sometimes the singers had to stay close to the audience to pass out bottles and collect money, but most of the time they went off to somebody's house, played more music, and got drunk.

Cannon toured for years, through the summer and into the big season when the cotton was coming in in late August and September and the people in the country had a little money. He was with Dr. Stokey, Dr. Benson, Dr. C.E. Hangerson, and Dr. E.B. Milton. Most of the time he played with Hosea Woods, and they had a whole repertoire of songs and jokes, but he had his own specialty number as well. It was the banjo trick he tried to do in Son Brimmer's apartment thirty years later. He'd start off playing "Old Dog Blue," then he'd suddenly swing the banjo out in front of him, over the heads of the people pressed in close to the wagon. He was still holding it by the neck, and he'd change chord as it swung back, strum it with his right hand and swing it out again. He'd finish the number with the banjo waving in front of him like a flag and the crowds usually liked it a lot. As he tried to do it later he looked down at the banjo very seriously and said that in the beginning he'd practiced for weeks to get it right, and he'd had to put a mattress down on the floor of his house so the banjo wouldn't get too damaged every time it slipped out of his hands and banged to the floor.

Hosea Woods—Cannon always called him Hosie—was about his age, from Stanton, Tennessee. They always worked out their show with a few days of rehearsals before the season started, then waited for one of the shows to get in touch with them. Hosea was a good singer and comedian and kazoo player, but he could play a little on almost every instrument. Cannon thought he was best on guitar, violin, and cornet, and they usually worked everything into the show. They did mostly old duet pieces, but Gus heard a man named Chappie Dennison playing on a piece of pipe, and he and Hosie decided to start their own jug band. At first they had a third musician who blew into a railroad coal-oil can, but Gus insists that the man blew so hard into the oil can that he kept bulging the bottom out and finally split the seams of the can. To do this a man would have to have the lung power of an air compressor, but to judge from the songs and stories coming out of that period of Southern history there would seem to have been a lot of strong men then. Whatever happened Cannon decided to play jug himself, and he had a small jug made out of sheet metal that was held in a harness that went around his neck so he could play it while he played the banjo. When he played a jug on a harness years later he usually had a kazoo stuck beside it so he could go from one to the other. The new sound gave an even more raucous noise to their songs, and Gus remembers that he would come back into Memphis at the end of the season with a new suit, in the latest box-back style, new patent-leather button shoes, and a gold watch chain hanging in front of his lapel. In a photo taken of him in Memphis about 1925 he's wearing his suit—with the belt buttoned in front—a high buttoned sweater, a dress shirt, and a fancy tie. He has the look of a cool sporting type, with none of the raffish grins of the Memphis Jug Band.

By the mid-twenties Gus had become fairly well known on the show circuit, and with one show or another he traveled from central Mississippi as far north as Virginia. He was usually called "Banjo Joe," and when the enthusiasm for country recordings finally reached the musicians in Memphis he kept the name. As Gus said years later, "I give myself the name Banjo Joe!" Son Brimmer seems to have been the person that got him interested in recording when he

32

heard him playing on Beale Street. Gus went up to Chicago with Jim Jackson and Furry Lewis in October 1927 and auditioned for Mayo Williams at Vocalion. Williams seems to have liked his playing enough to send him over to Paramount, even though he wasn't interested in using him on his own series. Cannon remembers that when he'd auditioned for Paramount they told him they liked his playing, and they brought in Blind Blake—one of their biggest sellers and a fine guitarist—and told him to work out some pieces with Cannon. They went to Blake's apartment and spent the next three or four days rehearsing. As Cannon remembered in 1956:

> *We drank so much whiskey! I'm telling you we drank more whiskey than a shop! And that boy would take me out with him at night and get me so turned around I'd be lost if I left his side. He could see more with his blind eyes than I with my two good ones.*

They finally got some pieces worked out and they went into the studio the first week of November. The first song was one of Cannon's blues, "Jonestown Blues," and he recorded it without Blake's guitar. Then they did three songs together, Cannon singing and playing the banjo and Blake playing his own distinctive guitar style as accompanist. The first was another blues, "Poor Boy, Long Ways from Home," then they did Cannon's wild banjo piece "Madison Street Rag," which was as much a spoken story as it was a rag, and they did an instrumental duet, "Jazz Gypsy Blues," with Cannon playing kazoo as well as banjo. Blake did one of his own songs, the widely sung minstrel show number "He's in the Jailhouse Now," and Cannon played banjo behind his singing. They finished with two of Cannon's medicine show songs, "Can You Blame the Colored Man?" and "My Money Never Runs Out." Paramount issued his songs as by "Banjo Joe with guitar accompaniment by Blind Blake," and they did some advertising for the releases. The *Chicago Defender* ran one of their mail order ads for "Madison Street Rag," with a drawing of a street scene and a photo of Cannon:

> *Just hear him strum that mean banjo—as the Queen looks on, and the double-jointed boy dances a jig! Here is a sensational new record by the new exclusive Paramount artist, Banjo Joe. There are some snappy words to this Blues, and a red-hot whistling solo part. In addition, Blind Blake and his Guitar do some real accompanying. All in all, it's a great record—we mean it. Be sure to ask your dealer for Paramount No. 12588, or send us the coupon.*

These first Paramount recordings that Gus did are remarkable for being almost the only recordings by a black musician playing the five-string banjo, an instrument that by this time had been taken over by the white musicians who'd learned if from the black performers around them. The recordings he did for Victor were jug band music, and his banjo playing was part of the larger instrumental sound. The first song he did for Paramount, "Jonestown Blues," had only banjo accompaniment, and his playing is a virtuoso display of what can be done with the blues on a five-string instrument. It has a high, clear sound, and the strings have little resonance, so the accompaniment is much busier than a guitar accompaniment would be, but he was enough of a musician to use a wide variety of rhythms and pickings. He was nervous, and the singing sounds stiff, but he wasn't a blues singer, and the text of the song wasn't distinctive.

> Said I left Lula, goin' to Jonestown
> Man I left Lula, goin' to Jonestown
> Those Jonestown browns, boy, make you turn your damper down.
>
> I cried Jonestown, boy, too small a burg for me
> I cried Jonestown, boy, too small a burg for me
> Said I left Jonestown, boy, goin' back to Tennessee.
>
> Say I got to old Memphis I laid my banjo down
> Well I go to old Memphis I laid my banjo down
> I got full of my good whiskey, my good gal made me clown.
>
> Then I left Memphis, goin' back to Jonestown
> Well, man I left Memphis, goin' back to Jonestown
> Said them good old browns, boy, sure have made me clown.

It's the banjo playing that gives the record its uniqueness. He plays instrumental choruses between verses and ends with two choruses, the second in a softer picking—he introduces it by saying "Hush now, banjo"—with a kind of floating sound, like someone carrying a suitcase down a hallway as he walks on tiptoe. His banjo choruses are free, open melodies, shaped by the instrument's own distinctive sound. The banjo doesn't sustain a tone, so the slower lines of the guitar won't work on it. What Cannon has developed is a melody that uses the banjo's high brilliance, its distinctive instrumental technique using what are called "hammering-on" and "pulling-off," and the surprise of hesitations and bursts of chord. To "hammer-on" with a banjo, a string is plucked, then the left hand presses on the string with a sudden sharpness, usually a fret above the note already struck. If the finger hits the string sharply enough it will give another tone. To "pull-off," the left-hand finger lifts from the fretted string, but it lifts off with a sideways pull and plucks the string as it comes off it. He accompanies the vocal phrase with understated chording, then ends the phrase with the same melodic phrase in the banjo that he used to begin the piece. It is interesting to have Cannon's blues, if only to have this small glimpse of what the earlier banjo styles might have been as the blues was developing.

When the sessions were finished Cannon put his banjo back in its case and returned to Memphis. He and his wife had a house at 1331 S. Hyde Park, he had his job as a plumber's helper, and he had his music for the summers and falls. Chicago didn't mean that much to him. Charlie Williamson called him as soon as he was back to tell him that Victor was going to be in town to do some recordings in January, and they were looking for more jug bands. The first records by the Memphis Jug Band had been out for several months and Ralph Peer realized that he had something he could sell. As far as Cannon was concerned he'd had the first jug band in town, and he was ready to do more recording. As he said later, "There's some fellows say they started this here—I won't 'spute 'em—but I had the first jug band was heerd in Memphis." He didn't have to get the music together; he just drove up to Ripley in January and brought his old band down—Noah Lewis and Ashley Thompson. They stayed at his house, rehearsed some of their old numbers, and went into the studio the next day, a Monday, January 30, 1928. They did four songs, Ashley singing the first two, "Minglewood Blues" and "Big Railroad Blues," and Gus and Noah the two others "Madison Street Rag"—the same banjo piece he'd done with Blind Blake three months before—and "Springdale Blues." He was playing his metal jug; by this time the Victor engineers had learned how to get the sound onto the discs, and his enthusiastic puffing can be heard behind the singing.

It was a short session, but it was exciting music, and everything they played had its own distinctive character, from the sensitive "Minglewood Blues" to the rousing medicine show hokum of "Madison Street Rag." The three of them were so pleased with the session that they bought a gallon of corn whiskey and went out south of town—probably to Bunker Hill, the loose collection of run-down shacks close to the Mississippi line where a lot of the blues men hung out. They drank so much all three of them passed out, and the next morning they woke up on a cabin porch, lying on the cold, hard boards, instruments and instrument cases scattered around them, and their clothes looking as if they'd spent most of the night crawling through the dirt.

The country dance music they'd played so long flavored what they did as a jug band, and their experience gave their recordings a close, tight sound. The rhythm was built around the banjo, with its short, pungent tone, and they played in a faster 4/8 rhythm instead of the usual blues 4/4. Cannon played with a simple finger-picking, plucking one of the middle strings with his forefinger, playing the two outside strings with his thumb and second finger. It was the same kind of picking that was used by many white bands of the period, and it gives the music a heavy center to the rhythm. Cannon was looking for the rhythm in the music, and he also liked a strong bass line, stronger than he was getting from Ashley, who played a gentle, introspective finger-picking style. Peer contacted Cannon again the next summer about doing more recording, and he was out on a show with a friend, Elijah Avery, who had moved up to Memphis from Hernando, Mississippi, and was living around the corner from Cannon in Hyde Park. Elijah played a vigorous six-string banjo for the session, and Noah Lewis came down from Ripley again to play harmonica.

Their first day, September 5, 1928, they were a warm, noisy, excited country dance band—sometimes settling down into the blues, but just as often breaking out into some country ragtime or an easy shuffle. All the pieces they did were instrumentals, "Ripley Blues," "Pig Ankle Strut," "Noah's Blues," and "Hollywood Rag." Listening to them with the phonograph turned up high and a little hard liquor to drink gives you some of the feeling of what it must have been like crowded into a store or a saloon in Ripley, dancing a little, shouting to friends, the lantern hanging from the ceiling shaking with the noise and the excitement. They came back to the studio four days later, September 9, and this time they did two songs, one of them Cannon's strong, hard comment on racial differences before and after the Civil War, "Feather Bed." It was still in the forced language of the minstrel stage, but he sings it with a complete seriousness, the band hurrying behind him. Noah Lewis was playing a version of the melody "Lost John" for the chorus, and he played it with a fierceness that matched Cannon's. It was an edgy, fast, completely honest performance, and it was one of the most exciting recordings the band made. The words were hard to understand at the fast tempo they used, but enough of the bite came through, even if some of the details were lost.

> I remember the time just 'fore the war,
> Black man was sleepin' on shucks and straw,
> Now, praise God, old massa's dead,
> Black man sleepin' on a feather bed,
>
> Ooh, ooh, my dear Henry,
> Over the road I'm bound to go,
> Ooh, ooh, my dear Henry,
> Over the road I'm bound to go. . . .

It wasn't until later in the month, on September 20, that Hosea Woods finally got into town and had a chance to work with his old partner. He played kazoo with the others, and they did two instrumentals, "Cairo Rag" and "Bugle Call Rag." Their version of "Bugle Call Rag" is in the best medicine show tradition of doing burlesque versions of popular favorites. They traded the usual jazz breaks back and forth on kazoo and jug, with Cannon almost out of breath in all the excitement. Noah did one of the songs on the session, his beautiful "Viola Lee Blues," and there was an obscure medicine show song called "Riley's Wagon." They had done ten sides in the month, some of their best recording. Lewis was the finest harmonica player around Memphis, and his plaintive, lonely sound was a strong contrast to the brittle insistence of Cannon's banjo, and the clear, firmly outlined bass lines that Elijah Avery played. The music they did with Hosea on the last day was a suggestion of what was to come when the band got back into the McCall Building Studio the next year.

In the summer of 1929 Cannon and Hosea went out with the shows, just as they'd been doing every year; then they decided, when the season was over, to go to Chicago and see if there was anything for them there. The companies were beginning to record less, but the two of them managed to get a session with Brunswick and did two songs, "Last Chance Blues" and "Fourth and Beale" as "Cannon and Woods (The Beale Street Boys)." The session was in mid-September, and they were back in Memphis at the end of the month. Peer was in town again for Victor, and he wanted more material from the jug band. This time Cannon and Hosea stayed together, and Noah came down from Ripley again. They did four songs on October 1, "Last Chance Blues," "Tired Chicken Blues" with its interesting major-minor modality, "Goin' to Germany," and "Walk Right In," then finished their recording for the year with four more songs on October 3, "Whoa! Mule, Get Up in the Alley," "The Rooster's Crowing Blues," "Jonestown Blues," and "Pretty Mama Blues." Most of the material was from the medicine show routines that Cannon and Hosea had been doing together down in the little Mississippi towns on the hot nights at the end of harvest season. The music was noisy and exuberant, and they were so excited to be doing all of their numbers that Cannon, later, couldn't remember that Noah had come down from Ripley to record with them. He had to listen to the records, and he shook his head, finally: "I believe that boy *is* on there after all." But there were some blues, as well as the comedy songs, and Noah sang his beautiful "Goin' to Germany." The "Jonestown Blues" was the same song Cannon had done for Paramount two years before. One of the songs was to become popular later, the country ragtime duet that he and Hosea did called "Walk Right In," though at the time it was just another one of their old songs. The text was confused but it was basically about a woman telling her man to come in and sit down and think about things for a while. As Cannon explained it in *The Country Blues:*

> I went to an old lady's house one day, and she told me, "Walk right in." I said, "I thank you." She said, "Well, will you sit down?" Said, "Thank you, ma'am." She says to me, say, "Well, how long you gonna be here?" I said, "I'll only be here but a little while." And so that night, some way or another, I commenced to dreamin'. Got up there about twelve o'clock, one night there, 1913. So I got hold of my old banjo. I said, "You know one thing, Bessie? You told me to walk in here. Now you know I'm gonna get somethin' or other on that. And this is the way it went:

Now you walk right in,
Sit right down,
Baby, let your mind roll on. . . .

By the time the records were released the stock market had crashed in the United States and the long misery of the Depression had begun. But no one knew, in the first months of it, how long it would go on, and Peer was in Memphis to record again a year later. Cannon and Hosea had come in from a show again, and, as always, Noah came down from Ripley. They did two songs on November 24, 1930, "Bring It with You When You Come," and "Wolf River

Blues," and there were two final songs on November 28, the first, ironically titled, "Money Never Runs Out" and the other "Prison Wall Blues." Hosea sang three of them—all except "Money Never Runs Out"—but he wasn't a blues singer. His voice had the high-pitched nasal tenor sound that was popular on the minstrel shows. The songs, however, were strong, musical performances, and they rounded out the series of recordings that Cannon had been doing since 1927. Cannon's Jug Stompers did twenty-six titles over its three years together—brilliant, irascible, sensitive, irrepressible, and musical. The band was all of these things, and the records have managed to catch the feeling that they had, from the sudden wailing of Noah's harmonica, to Cannon's rowdy jug playing, all of it showing their deep-rooted response to the music of the little towns and country crossroads where they did their playing.

The long years of the Depression settled over Beale Street, and what had been left of the district when the reformers cleaned it up was shut down by unemployment and poverty. There were still little jobs, street cleaning, laboring, house painting, whatever a man could find to keep going. The old wooden buildings behind Beale Street were left unpainted, and they began to have a weatherbeaten look. The larger houses back in the old neighborhoods were crowded with people living four or five to a room, and the dirt of the front yards was left untended. Fences were nailed together out of packing case boards, broken windows mended with cardboard and newspaper. The Memphis summers were still hot and drowsy, and you could go out to Bunker Hill, or back up toward Brownsville and get corn or watermelon for pennies. The bands went on working little jobs for society parties or in the country clubs. Cannon still went out with some of the old shows, though there wasn't much money when he got back in town. He was forty-seven now, he'd lived a hard, full life, and it was just as easy for him to keep his little job as a plumber's helper. Hosea still went out with him on the shows, though he sometimes worked with another friend his own age, Willie Williams.

By the forties Cannon was working as a general handyman and gardener for a white family who had a large house on South Park, one of the wealthier parts of South Memphis. There was a large garage twenty or thirty yards behind the house, and he had the apartment upstairs. The stairs went up the front of the low building, and his door was off a small balcony. He had filled every corner of the space with things he'd picked up and was going to repair or thought he might use sometime. Like all handymen he had an idea of what he could do with all of it. His banjo was in its case back by the window, next to a table piled with things he'd accumulated. He had an old picture of himself up on the wall, but he didn't have any of his old records. They'd all slipped away from him over the years. The family knew about his life as a musician, and they let him live in the apartment for a small amount of work. He spent a lot of his time working around the neighborhood cutting grass and doing general gardening. He was a familiar figure around the neighborhood, usually with a straw hat pulled down over his eyes to keep out the sun, his tools wheeled in front of him in a homemade cart. He was still the same, tall, lean, hard-muscled man he'd been for forty years and could work for hours in the long Memphis sunlight.

He was still living in the same crowded rooms when I first met him in late 1956. After the session at Son Brimmer's apartment I took him back to the house and we talked about his early years. When the record of the session came out—on Folkways in 1958—we spent a few days together and there was another chance to talk, and the people he was working for had a family party for him with the first copy of the record. Cannon sat listening to the phonograph—hearing himself talking—and he nodded his head, agreeing with everything he had to say. "That's right," he said and got out his banjo and played along with his solo. In 1959 a record was put together to go with the book *The Country Blues*, and one of the pieces on it was the old "Walk Right In." Cannon had listened to it again with the woman he'd recently married at the age of 75. "Is that my hubby on there?" she kept asking. Cannon shook his head and smiled at the song. "Me and Hosie sung that song more years than I can name. We had something in those years then."

"Walk Right In" still had some of its old excitement. In 1963 a folk group recorded a new version of it and it was suddenly a number one record, a major success. The company that had recorded it, Vanguard Records, was unsure about the copyright, and the whole problem suddenly became very complicated, with the Southern Music Corporation—Ralph Peer's company—claiming it outright. It became necessary to find Cannon, and a small group of us flew down from New York, with Maynard Solomon of Vanguard and a copyright lawyer. It took me a little time to find Cannon, since the family had left the house on South Park and Cannon and his wife had gotten their own little house on the edge of town. The son of the family knew approximately where he was, and the neighbors were watching for someone to come down. The song had been on the Memphis radio and everybody knew it was Cannon's. The house he was in was small and drafty, white painted, with two rooms. It hadn't been an easy winter for him, and he'd had to pawn his banjo. Solomon went to Beale Street, got his banjo for him, gave him money to get some coal for the house, then Cannon came to the city courthouse with us to make statements.

The interesting thing that emerged from the long, and frustrating, struggle with Cannon's copyright for the song was the glimpse it gave of Peer's method of operation in the South. Some of the singers, like Son Brimmer, had been on a royalty basis, and their songs were protected for them by Southern Music. For many other singers, however, the compositions were filed as "works for hire," which meant that the music had been written by someone working as an employee of the publishing company. With material of this kind it's always very questionable how much of it will ever earn any kind of royalty, and the companies often simply paid the performer a flat fee for the rights to the songs. Generally the writer got a larger sum this way than he would have through a royalty arrangement. Jazz musicians were notorious for selling away rights to songs for the money to pay a bar bill or a hotel account, and Fats Waller, in 1929, once signed away the rights to nine songs, including some of his biggest successes, for a few dollars each to help pay a debt. The contracts for many of Peer's artists were simply handled in the "works for hire" category. When "Walk Right In" became successful there was suddenly a great deal of money involved, and Southern's first concern was to protect their claim to the song.

Then, through the efforts of, among others, Dorothy Morrison, who had been with Southern since 1928, when the company was only Peer, herself, and a bookkeeper, an arrangement was made for Cannon to get his composer's royalties for the song, and he's gotten a small income from it over the years.

Cannon kept working through all of it, and for a time in the early sixties he had a job taking care of the lawn and the garden for a church not far from his little house. As he described it, "I got my little job cleaning up gumballs in the summer, but it don't come to much in the winter." He was one of the artists appearing in the film *The Blues*, when I was in Memphis filming in 1962, and in 1963 he was one of the three Memphis artists who came to New York for a concert with the Friends of Old-Time Music. He and Furry Lewis and Memphis Willie Borum came up in the spring on a Greyhound bus, with chicken and cake that Willie's wife had packed for them. There was an unforgettable moment when Gus first climbed the stairs of the Times Square subway one night and found himself in the middle of the lights and the hustle of 42nd Street and Broadway. He looked around shaking his head and finally said, "I never thought I'd see anything like this in all my born days." At the concert he did some of his old songs, even doing a moment of banjo juggling, and the three of them sang together as a casual jug band while Furry and Gus did their old comedy routines.

Cannon still gets around in Memphis, but he's ninety now, and even his strong arms have begun to feel a little tired. Bengt Olsson and Bill Barth, who was also doing research and playing a little music in Memphis, took Cannon up to Ripley to see Ashley Thompson, and they shook their heads a little when they saw each other, saying, "You done got old." Cannon can't play much, and he was hit in the throat when some boys tried to rob him on Beale Street, so he can't sing very well either. He is as tall and straight as ever, and in his suit jacket and horn-rimmed glasses he doesn't look as though he might have been a bluesman. But it's there in his sudden burst of laughter when he sits down, sips from a beer can, and thinks back to Ripley and Beale Street and all the other places and times he's played in his long life. "White folks, them was some times, I tell you."

# 4. Other Memphis Singers

Memphis wasn't a big town, and most of the musicians working along the street were with one jug band or another, but there were also some bluesmen who were brought into the studios the companies had set up in town. One of them, Jim Jackson, recorded one of the biggest blues records of the twenties, "Jim Jackson's Kansas City Blues." Jim was an older, bald singer and entertainer who was born in Hernando, Mississippi, but at the time he recorded he was living at 1150 Grant, in North Memphis. He spent most of his time with the medicine shows, and he went out with the Silas Green show, the Abbey Sutton show, also the Red Rose Minstrels, and the well-known and popular Rabbits Foot Minstrels that toured out of Port Gibson, Mississippi, every year. Most of the other Memphis musicians knew him well, played with him, and all of them knew his song "Goin' to Kansas City." Gus Cannon has said that he was in Chicago with Jim when he recorded it, but he wasn't allowed to play on the session with him. Mayo Williams had moved to Vocalion after his own blues label, Black Patti, had failed, and Jim was one of the first artists to record for him. The record was released on Vocalion 1144, Parts 1 and 2, in December 1927.

In the chaotic blues market of the late twenties it was often difficult to predict what would sell, and the companies had to put out a lot of releases to get results. Jim's song was one of those that hit. It was more of a medicine show song than a blues—a simple collection of verses like:

> If you don't want my peaches, don't shake my tree
> I ain't after that woman, but she sure likes me

followed by a refrain:

> I've got to move to Kansas City, mama, sure as you're born
> I've got to move to Kansas City, mama, sure as you're born
> I've got to move to Kansas City, honey, where they don't 'low you.

Advertisement for Jim Jackson's Kansas City Blues.

Sometimes he sang it:

I'm gonna move to Kansas City . . .

and that's the way most of the Memphis musicians remember it. The record
sold and sold. On March 17, 1928, there was a full-page advertisement for it in
the *Chicago Defender*, with a drawing of Jim and illustrations for all the verses.
He did a second session for Vocalion—recording Parts 3 and 4 of "Jim Jackson's
Kansas City Blues"—but about the same time he also began recording for Victor
in Memphis. His first session for Peer was on January 30. For a brief time there
was a struggle between Vocalion and Victor over his services. On April 21,
1928, only a month after the full-page ad for Vocalion, Victor announced his
first two records for them, "The Policy Blues" and "Bootlegging Blues" on Vic
21268 and "My Monday Woman Blues" and "My Mobile Central Blues" on Vic
21236. The advertisement also announced that he was now an exclusive Victor
artist. In May, three weeks later, Vocalion advertised its new record—"Jim
Jackson's Kansas City Blues, Parts 3 and 4" on Voc 1155, but he stayed with
Victor for the rest of the year, doing eighteen titles all together over the nine
months he was with the company. The next year he went back to Vocalion in
Chicago and did a series of recordings for them over the next year and a half.

None of Jim's records was as popular as his "Kansas City," but because it was
so successful he had a chance to record an extensive repertoire of medicine
show songs and blues. He'd spent his life as a country entertainer—he was probably in his late forties when he recorded—and he knew every kind of song. The
thirty-one songs he recorded are a priceless glimpse of the kind of material it
took to get a crowd in a country town—the kind of humor and broad slapstick
that got them up to the stage and got them laughing. He wasn't a blues singer
so much as he was a country songster, even though his "My Monday Woman
Blues" was also sung by other Memphis blues singers. On a song like "This
Mornin' She Was Gone," he could even throw in theatrical sobbing, and it only
added to the loose mood of the song. He used an assumed minstrel dialect, with
its conscious "gwine" and "hyar," and there were outrageous comedy songs
like "I Heard the Voice of a Pork Chop," with its chorus "I heard the voice of
a pork chop say, come unto me and rest."

But Jim was more than noisy country humor and tent show routines to keep
the crowd listening while the next act got ready. He was a shrewdly talented
man, with a deeper sense of the music he was doing. He had taken the old song
"Old Dog Blue," and for years he sang it almost as a free poem, extending its
imagery in the finest folk traditions. It was so startling that the one serious reviewer of the twenties, Abbe Niles, mentioned it in his column in the literary
journal *Bookman* in its issue for September 1928: "Old Dog Blue . . . a wholly
fascinating story of a hound who treed his possums anywhere he found them,
from a holler stump to Noah's Ark." The accompaniment Jim used for it was
almost a banjo picking, instead of his usual steady strum.

Had a old dog his name was Blue
You know Blue was mighty true
You know Blue was a good old dog . . .
Blue treed a possum out on a limb
Blue looked at me and I looked at him,
Grabbed that possum, put him in a sack,
Don't move, Blue, 'til I get back.
Here Ring, here Ring here,
Here Ring, here Ring here . . .

When old Blue died and I dug his grave
I dug his grave with a silver spade.
I let him down with a golden chain
And every link I called his name.
Go on Blue, you good dog you,
Go on Blue, you good dog you.
Blue lay down and died like a man
Blue lay down and died like a man
Now he's treein' possums in the promised land.

I'm going to tell you this to let you know
Old Blue's gone where good dogs go.
When I hear old Blue's bark
When I hear old Blue's bark
Blue's treed a possum in Noah's Ark
Blue's treed a possum in Noah's Ark.

There was still another dimension to Jim's skill as a performer. For a poor share cropper, in town for a Saturday's shopping, standing in a dirt street in his overalls and his sweat-stained straw hat, there would be an immediate sense of identity with something like a hound dog who finally went to heaven and treed his possums with the angels. In many of the songs that he did there was an even more direct identification of the subject of the song with the determined sense of life in his audience. The blues had to function as the language of a culture that was almost deprived of a language, and in it there was a whole range of expression that went beyond the simple response to loneliness or poverty. To a white who happened to come along and stand back of the crowd to listen to someone like Jim Jackson, it would sound like the usual "darkey" songs he'd heard all his life. Stealing  chickens, getting in trouble with the police, getting run out of town—all the clichés of the minstrel shows. And the singers were usually wearing blackface  with white-painted mouths, so there wasn't much to make him think any differently. But Jim was saying more; he was saying that the black man will keep on going, he won't be beaten, that he'll somehow get through it.

Jim's songs weren't the only ones that had this deeper intention—there are well-known examples like "The Gray Goose, " who couldn't be cut or eaten, or "Long John Green from Bowling Green," who couldn't be caught. But he was able to do it in the guise of something else, and the most obvious comic song could become a sudden sharp comment on something that was much larger. He did a version of the "traveling man" song and he presented it as a simple minstrel song. The man made his living "stealin' chickens," which immediately established his color, since in the popular songs of the period the black man's life was spent stealing chickens. The policeman went after him, but

> He didn't care how fast that a freight train would pass
> This man would get on board.

Jim went on singing in a cheerful voice, with a simple strum on the guitar, for the next verse reciting a well-known "brag" story about the man.

> Well, they sent that old travelin' man one day,
> I asked for one pail of water,
> And where he had to go was two miles and a quarter.
> He went and got that water alright, but he stumbled and fell down.
> He run three miles and a half and got another pitcher,
> Caught the water 'fore it hit the ground.

His last verse was more specific, and on the words "white ladies" he sang with a little mincing lilt, to make it even sharper, to make it even more clear that in the contest between the two the black man was going to come through.

> He ran and jumped on this Titanic ship
> And started up that ocean blue.
> He looked out and spied that big iceberg, and right overboard he flew.
> All the white ladies on the deck of the ship
> Said that man certainly was a fool,
> But when that Titanic ship went down he's shootin' craps in Liverpool.
>
> Don't you know,
> He was a traveling man. . . .

He repeated the last two lines, as a kind of insistent reminder.

> And he wouldn't give up and he wouldn't give up
> 'Til the police shot him down.
> And he wouldn't give up and he wouldn't give up
> 'Til the police shot him down.

Though he had veiled it in the most obvious minstrel show terms, his audience, in the small Mississippi towns where he did most of his playing, had no difficulty understanding what he was saying.

For Jim, as for almost everyone else, the bleak first months of the Depression finished the recording sessions. In the early winter of 1930, probably February, Vocalion was in Memphis to record and he did two songs, "Hesitation Blues (Oh! Baby, Must I Hesitate?)" and "St. Louis Blues," that were released later in the year on Vocalion 1477. The local musicians don't remember seeing him after this—they don't remember that he was in town much after the success of his first record. Sometime in the thirties he seems to have gone back to Hernando, and he died there in 1937.


Another singer that the musicians knew from the tent shows and from Beale Street was a tall, heavy man named Jack Kelly. Furry Lewis remembers him living in Orange Mound, but Willie Borum, who played with him a lot in the thirties, remembers him living in town. "Jack Kelly smoked a cigar all the time. It was never lit, it just always was there. . . . He would play the guitar and I would blow the harp. Doc Higgs was with us on jug." Although he worked along the street, he had a steady group that was managed by Howard Yancey. Will Batts played violin and was as much of a leader as the band had. Sometimes Stokes and Dan Sane played with them, sometimes a banjo player named Ernest Motley, and later the guitarist Milton Robie. Mary Batts, Will's widow, remembers that they rehearsed at their house all the time and that most of their jobs were for Memphis white people, who brought them out to picnics or the country club and then relied on Jim Strainer to drive them back when they got drunk. She would tell him just to "Bring him up there on the porch," and she'd let Will sleep there until he was sober enough to come in the house. Will had played violin on Frank Stokes's last session for Victor, and though he had a day job all through the years, he went out and played along Beale Street with the rest of them when he got through with work.

As the thirties ground on there was an effort to revive the record industry, and the labels manufactured by the American Recording Corporation continued to release blues material. Kelly, with the band, got a session in New York on August 1, 2, and 3, 1933. Dan Sane made the trip, with Will Batts and "Doctor" D.M. Higgs, who was playing the jug. Mary Batts remembers that Will played the guitar with Jack on the first song, "Highway No. 61 Blues," and after Jack had sung five numbers Will sang two. The next day Dan did the first song, as in the Memphis Jug Band days when everybody got to try a blues. Even Doc Higgs sang a "Bad Luck Blues," but the titles he and Dan sang on were never released. The singing on the third day was by Jack and Will. Will was a slight, dark, good-looking man who had been playing and singing in Memphis for most of his life. He was born on January 24, 1904, in Benton County, west of Michigan City, Mississippi, but he moved to Memphis with his family when he was fifteen. His father played the violin, as well as his older brother Robert, and Will started playing at country suppers when he was nine. They had to put him up on a chair so people could see him.

There was still enough interest in the jug band sound for ARC to call them a jug band—"Jack Kelly and his South Memphis Jug Band"—but what they played was mostly solid, strong blues with a heavy accompaniment. They did one instrumental that was released, "Policy Rag," but the rest of the songs were blues. Kelly was a deep-voiced singer, with a kind of stolid feel for his music. There wasn't any of the kind of instrumental arranging that Son Brimmer had tried with the Memphis Jug Band. They recorded blues with a thick texture and an insistent rhythm, loping along after Doc Higgs's jug playing. The records were released on the ARC low-price labels.

Jack recorded again in Memphis in the late thirties—for Vocalion on July 14, 1939. He did ten sides, and six of the songs were finally released. There was another guitar and a violin with him, but no jug. The band never made much money from their recording, but Mary Batts remembers that Will came back from the first New York trip with " . . . a whole fruit jar full of money!" The Swedish researcher who talked to Mrs. Batts, Bengt Olsson, has also suggested that Jack recorded again in 1950 with the harmonica player Walter Horton, who was living in Memphis during this period—before he went to Chicago to join the Muddy Waters band. A Sun release, Sun 174, is listed on the label as by "Jackie Boy and Little Walter," and one of the composers credited is Kelly. Horton insists that they recorded together, so the Sun record probably is the one he remembers. Only the label has been found, but a copy, if it ever turns up, should make it clear whether or not it is Jack Kelly. Willie Borum remembers that Jack was an old man, gray-haired, when he died. Will Batts had died earlier, of a stroke in 1956, and Mary gave Jack Will's guitar. Jack died in Memphis, probably around 1960.

Son and the Memphis Jug Band used nearly every musician in town for their sessions, but Vocalion was interested in getting something for themselves out of it, and on their last Memphis session—the same trip when they recorded Jim Jackson's last songs—they recorded a tent show entertainer named Jed Davenport and his Beale Street Jug Band. Not much is known about Davenport except that he was working the shows with Dub Jenkins on saxophone and Al Jackson on bass. He'd recorded two harmonica solos the fall before for Vocalion and they might have suggested that he come in with a jug band on their next trip. They did six sides in January 1930, with two different harmonica players, two guitars, and a jug. The songs were loose and uninhibited. Someone played mandolin on one of the songs; there was a kazoo on "Piccolo Blues" but it's impossible to tell who could be playing. They probably played with Memphis Minnie on a session the next summer, in August, but there were only two titles—"Grandpa and Grandma Blues" and "Garage Fire Blues"—and the band was called Memphis Minnie and Her Jug Band. Davenport was said to have picked up the trumpet and by the late thirties he was working in local clubs. He left Memphis for a time—it's been suggested he was drafted during the Second World War—but was back along Beale Street in the 1960s.

At the same time, however, another Memphis bluesman was creating music that came from other sources and tied itself more closely to older song tradition. Furry Lewis had been part of the jug band crowd. His own music was distinct and individual, adding his own mood and style to the music in Memphis.

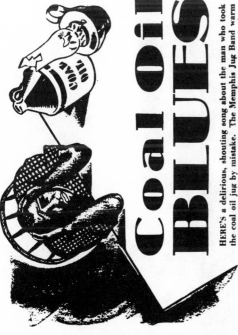

Three Early Advertisements for Memphis Jug Band

CANNON'S JUG STOMPERS. left to right, GUS CANNON,
ASHLEY THOMPSON, and NOAH LEWIS.

Material from the N.Y. Public Library

GUS CANNON

Photo by Ann Charte

BARBECUE BOB                                    Contemporary advertising photo

MEMPHIS WILLIE B., FURRY LEWIS, and GUS CANNON in Greenwich Village, 1964

Photo by Ann Charters

# 5.
# Furry Lewis

Furry Lewis is a small, gentle man who spent most of his life sweeping the streets of Memphis. If you saw him working along Beale Street, or Hernando, or Vance—the streets he swept for more than forty years—you wouldn't have thought of him as a bluesman. He pushed a can in front of him on a wheeled metal cart, sweeping as he went, leaving full cans at the street corners for the city trucks to pick up, and taking empties where they'd been left for him. In the summers he usually wore a short-sleeved shirt, wash trousers, and a baseball cap. He limped a little; he lost a leg in a railroad accident in 1917 and he swept Memphis streets for more than forty years on an artificial leg. It was a morning job, and he started out before there was much traffic, always seeing the same few regulars along the streets, people who, like him, had something to get ready for a new day. He was usually through by eleven or twelve. In the summers he worked as much as he could in the shade, to get away from the sun, and in the winters he stopped off a lot in buildings where he knew somebody who'd let him sit for a moment to warm up.

He moved around a lot during those years, and if you came into town and had to find him you went down to the city garage, where the sanitation crews were dispatched. Once you tracked down the crew boss in the empty, echoing building, he would look at his chart and tell you where Furry was. "He's got Beale Street to do again—let's see, it's about 9:30, he should be right about here now"— and he'd show you a point on his city map, and off you'd go looking for Furry. When you found him, usually not far from where the crew boss said he'd be, he kept working as he talked. He just worked a little slower and stayed close to the curb so he could hear what you were saying. It wasn't much of a job, but it kept him going through all the lean years, and he finally had a small pension out of it at the end.

When Furry went to work for the Sanitation Department in 1923, his other life, in a way, was over, and after he'd worked many years there his other life was

49

almost lost in the shadowy days people thought of when they reminisced about Beale Street. When you'd find him in whatever furnished room he was living in and you'd bring over a guitar and something to drink so he could play again, most of the people living in the house with him would hang around the door looking at him with surprise. They'd never known he was anything but a street sweeper. If they had heard anything about his old life they hadn't really believed it. But there had been the other life, and for a few scattered days in the late twenties, he took time off from his job and took his guitar to the studios set up in Chicago or Memphis, first recording for Vocalion, then for Victor. There weren't many sessions—four of them—and there weren't many recordings—only twenty songs—but they were enough to give Furry a secure place in the history of blues.

The songs Furry sang were distinctly personal, while still, in many way, characteristic of the blues in Memphis. He's almost an archetypal figure in the development of the blues in the city, even though it was the street bands, rather than solo blues artists, who were the most obvious along Beale Street. Even Furry, when he remembers the old days, usually remembers playing on Beale Street with a group. As he said in a conversation with Bengt Olsson years later:

> When I was eighteen, nineteen years old, I was good. And when I was twenty I had my own band and we could all play. Had a boy named Ham, played jug. Willie Polk played the fiddle and another boy, call him Shoefus, played the guitar, like I did. All of us North Memphis boys. We'd meet at my house and walk down Brinkley to Poplar and go up Poplar to Dunlap or maybe all the way down to Main. People would stop us on the street and say, "Do you know so-and-so?" And we'd play it and they'd give us a little something. Sometimes we'd pick up fifteen or twenty dollars before we got to Beale. . . .

The blues in Memphis didn't have the intense, raw loneliness of Mississippi music. It was a softer, talkier blues—mingled with the medicine show songs and folk songs and ballads that were popular in the country when the musicians left town to play the little shows. The other Memphis bluesmen who did a fair amount of recording—Jim Jackson and Frank Stokes—like Furry mixed minstrel songs with their blues, and their ragtime songs were as popular as anything else they did. All of them were from Mississippi, and they heard the blues there, but Memphis was different, and its music was different. Furry had been born in Mississippi—his name is Walter, and he's still not sure why other children at school gave him the name Furry—but he left it when he was still a boy, and his life has been spent in Memphis, most of it in the run-down neighborhood of old wood-sided houses lining narrow, badly paved streets north of the business section. He thought for many years that he was born in 1900, and he stayed on his job until he thought he'd gotten to retirement age. But one of the young blues enthusiasts who was taking guitar lessons from Furry, Jerry Finberg, went through old school records to help Furry get Medicaid and found that he'd been born seven years earlier, on March 6, 1893. Occasionally Furry himself will forget and give other dates, but this seems to be the correct one. When he finally stopped sweeping the streets he was in his seventies. He was born south of Jackson, in Greenwood, Mississippi, but he, his mother, and his two sisters moved to Memphis when he was six. She'd separated from his father before he was born, and Furry never saw him. His life was spent in Memphis, with occasional small trips out of the city. As he told Bengt Olsson:

> My mother had a sister lived on Brinkley Avenue. Call it Decatur now. We stayed with her. They a housing project there now, but I could still show you the spot. I was raised right there and walked a few block to the Carnes Avenue School. Went to the fifth, and that's as far as I got. Started going about, place to place, catching the freights. That's how I lost my leg. Goin' go down a grade outside Du Quoin, Illinois. I caught my foot in a coupling. They took me to a hospital in Carbondale. I could look right out my window and see the ice-cream factory. That was in 1916. I had two or three hundred dollars in my pocket when that happened, too. I had just caught a freight 'cause I didn't feel like spending the money for a ticket.

It was Furry's Memphis background that helped shape his blues, that gave him the kind of straightforward singing style, without embellishment or stress, that was characteristic of most of the blues records the Memphis men made. The same quiet, almost thoughtful understatement was part of everything they did, from blues to minstrel show songs, to folk ballads. They sang all kinds of material for the little shows, and Furry will probably always be remembered best not for his blues but for his brilliant reworking of the great ballads "Casey Jones," "John Henry," and "Stackerlee." But his first two sessions were blues, done for Jack Kapp, who was director of the Vocalion race series that Mayo Williams was auditioning talent for. Furry remembers that he had been out with a show singing with Jim Jackson, and Vocalion brought them up to Chicago because Jim's song "Goin' to Kansas City" was very popular locally. Furry feels they went up in May together, then they were auditioned separately; but Jim didn't record his "Jim Jackson's Kansas City Blues" until a fall session, when Furry did his second group of blues for Vocalion, so he probably has confused the two trips. He does, however, remember the first afternoon he was in the studio and described it when we first talked in 1959:

> The first recording session, when I was around, goin' around then, you know, gettin' people could play, and we was goin' to Chicago, you know, to make records. And so I went on there and I met Mr. Jack Kapp. He's a fine fellow, Mr. Jack Kapp was a fine fellow, and so I made two or three records there with Mr. Jack Kapp. When I first went in there, you know, he know'd what I like and so he had a whole gallon of whiskey sittin' there and he said, "Well, you drink a little, but just don't drink too much until you get through with the record because you get so drunk you can't play." So, I like to got drunk anyway, but I made the record. . . .

51

Furry did five blues his first session, "Rock Island Blues," "Everybody's Blues," "Jelly Roll," "Mr. Furry's Blues," and "Sweet Papa Moan." They seem to have been well enough received for Vocalion to bring him back again with Jim Jackson in the fall, and all of the releases were advertised in the *Chicago Defender*; so Furry, in a quiet way, had begun his recording career. Jim Jackson did his "Kansas City Blues" at his session, and it became one of the biggest blues hits of the twenties. Furry, at the same time, was recording another group of blues, but he began the session with the first of his great ballad versions, "Stackerlee," which was titled "Billy Lyons and Stock O'Lee." This time the blues didn't do well enough for Vocalion to bring him up the next spring, but Ralph Peer was in Memphis the next summer—recording, among other people, Jim Jackson, who had moved from Vocalion—and he did a session with Furry. On August 28, a Tuesday, Furry took the afternoon off from his job, changed his clothes, and went down to their studio in the McCall Building. It was a long session, and he did seven blues and a magnificent reworking of the ballad "Casey Jones" that was released on both sides of Vic 21664 with the new title "Kassie Jones"—probably so Peer could published the version with his own publishing house.

The blues he did for Peer were also interesting, among them the brilliantly accompanied "I Will Turn Your Money Green" and his "Dry Land Blues," but they don't seem to have sold well since Peer didn't use him again. But Vocalion was in Memphis again the next fall—in 1929—and Furry did his last session in the twenties. The first two sides were another ballad—this time his "John Henry," released on Voc 1474 as "John Henry (The Steel Driving Man)"—and he finished with two more blues, "Black Gypsy Blues" and "Creeper's Blues." Furry's first recording career, and to a large extent his creative years as a bluesman were over with these sessions; he never was able again to create songs with the vividness and the uniqueness of the finest recordings he did then.

All of the blues that Furry did were interesting, and everything was a skillful example of setting an accompaniment to a melody, but the three ballads were especially his own. For "Billy Lyons and Stock O'Lee" he used a repeated line that seemed to sum up the song: "When you lose your money learn to lose." As he explains it, "That means don't be no *hard* loser. That's what this song is about." That *is* what "Stackerlee" is about, but few singers have been interested in any dimension to the song beyond Stackerlee and the murder of his friend Billy Lyons. It is this sudden, quiet summing up of a song that makes his ballads stay in the memory. He's been able to find the essence of the songs, the feeling of quiet melancholy that threads through them, tying the details of the story into a broader, deeper, more human narrative. The gentle sadness is part of the wistful, almost tentative quality of his singing, and he emphasized it with the guitar accompaniments. The finger-picking he used for "Kassie Jones," with a slide on the lower strings, suggest some of the feeling of the train and even has the quality of a second melody of its own—sad, in its way, and lonely.

In both "Kassie Jones" and "John Henry" he changed the emphasis of the songs by focusing on the women and the other people around the central figures. In the usual versions of "Casey Jones" he's presented as a brave but reckless engineer who tries to make up for lost time, wrecks the trains, and dies ". . . with his hand on the throttle," scalded with steam. Furry, instead, talks about Casey's wife and a dream she had that she never explains. "Mrs. Casey says she dreamt a dream, the night she bought her sewing machine . . . " He talks about Casey and his troubles with the police almost as though he were reminiscing about the times he ran into Casey himself—in barrooms or on the street—or as though he were simply repeating things someone else had told him. He repeats the last line of each verse almost thoughtfully—and the lines still linger while he plays the sad little guitar melody before the next verse. "This mornin' I heard someone was dyin', Mrs. Casey's children on the doorstep cryin'." The mood isn't broken, even when Casey's widow tells the children not to worry, there will be more pension money for them. Instead, you hear over and over again the same little refrain, the same mood of quiet reminiscence. Furry has humanized, personalized the long story of Casey Jones—taking away the trappings of heroism and the religious clichés that were standard in the versions he heard around him.

His "John Henry" had the same quality, and he again stripped the ballad of its heroic overtones. He makes it clear that it was a human being who dies—and left sad people behind him. There were women in other versions of "John Henry," and he includes them all, but there is a poignant sadness in the image of John Henry's woman going to find him. "I'm going where John Henry fell dead. Please take me where my man fell dead." Like John Hurt, who recorded his version of the ballad as "Spike Driver's Blues," Furry finds the story more tragic than heroic. As in "Kassie Jones," he repeats the last line of each verse, emphasizing the mood, and again the accompaniment follows what he's doing with his voice and in the text. The accompaniment is done with a slide, in the Mississippi bottleneck style, and the guitar states the melody in a lingering minor version of it while the thumb, alternating on the first and third lower strings of the guitar, relentlessly drives the rhythm. He still plays it the same way, and his fingers seem to dance on the strings. Watching him play it is almost like watching a ballet done with his hands, as Chaplin had done his ballet with two buns on forks.

The imagery of Furry's blues, in his first sessions, was a hard contrast to the soft melancholy of his ballads. The images in song after song were rough and cruel, the relationships with women described in angry recitals of infidelity and disappointment. In one blues he sang:

> I believe I'll buy me a graveyard of my own,
> Believe I'll buy me a graveyard of my own.
> I'm goin' kill eve'body that have done me wrong. . . .

Even though this verse, as well as almost every other verse he used, came from earlier blues sources, he seems to insist on saying this over and over again. His relationships with women seem to have been as disappointing for him.

> I'd rather see my coffin rollin' from my door,
> Rather see my coffin rollin' from my door,
> Than to hear my good girl says I don't want you no more. . . .

Again, from another blues:

> I'd rather hear the screws on my coffin sound,
> I'd rather hear the screws on my coffin sound,
> Than to hear my good girl says I'm jumpin' down. . . .

He could say with sudden bitterness:

> If you want to go to Nashville, mens, ain't got no fare,
> Want to go to Nashville, mens, ain't got no fare.
> Cut your good girl's throat and the judge will send you there. . . .

> I'm goin' get my pistol, forty rounds of ball,
> Get my pistol, forty rounds of ball.
> I'm goin' shoot my woman just to see her fall.

Verses like these, of course, were standard material for many blues of the period, but it was Furry's insistence on them that gives them an emotional weight. Often his songs, like "Falling Down Blues," were simply loose collections of verses, and most of the verses he used were part of the standard Memphis repertoire, but he could put them together with a close sensitivity to the verse's inner meaning. He didn't do it with any kind of intellectual preconception. When I asked him about it as part of the research for the book *The Poetry of the Blues* in the summer of 1962 he said:

> *Well, one thing, when you write the blues and what you be thinkin'*
> *about, you be blue, and you ain't got nothin' hardly to think about*
> *you just already blue and jus' goin' write.*

In answer to a question as to how he put the verses together he said:

> *Well, you just rhyme 'em up. See, the time when you just get a blues,*
> *what you call the blues sometimes you just haven't come out like*
> *you 'sposed to and it don't be right you have to go all over again until*
> *you rhyme it. It got to be rhymed just like it is 'cause if you call*
> *yourself with the blues or anything else, if it ain't rhymed up it don't*
> *sound good to me or nobody else, do it.*

He didn't feel there was any principle of structuring in the way he developed his texts. Asked about his choice of a first verse he said:

> *Well, the way that'll be, the first verse is just—the first verse could be the last. You know, just any old verse I wanted that could have that to the first, then go right on from there and just rhyme up from it, and make them all kind of match, you know, the same like that.*

His only general consideration was that every verse should be ". . . talking about the same thing." But he interpreted this very loosely, and each of his songs contained verses that seemed to have been chosen almost by accident. But often it's possible to sense a sequence even in a blues that seems to have little inner connection. In one of his songs he moves from a verse dealing with a "graveyard of my own," to the cynical verse about killing a woman to get to Nashville; then he uses a verse about shooting his own woman—which brings it a step closer to him, since the second verse was a general reference to "mens." He follows this in the next verse by saying that he'd rather hear the screws on his coffin than hear that his woman is "jumpin' down"—leaving him. These first four verses have been related by their general mood of anger at his woman's leaving him. The next three verses seem to bring it even closer to him. He says that he's going to sit down and write a letter, " . . . back to yon' town." Then:

> This ain't my home, I ain't got no right to stay.
> This ain't my home, must be my stoppin' place.

The reason for the letter becomes clear—he's left home and he's writing back. The song ends:

> When I left my home you would not let me be,
> When I left my home you would not let me be.
> Wouldn't rest contented 'til I come to Tennessee.

With this he seems to clarify the entire text. He's angry and bitter as the song begins—angry because his woman is leaving him. And her leaving him is even harder because she forced him to leave home—to "come to Tennessee"—and she's left him alone there. In another place, and another time—perhaps even a few minutes later—Furry might have sung it differently and used different verses in a different order, but what he sang here seems to have been conceived with some inner coherence in mind, even if it wasn't consciously articulated.

As a guitarist Furry had few peers in Memphis in the twenties and he seemed to have learned every kind of picking and tuning in his wanderings into the countryside. "Falling Down Blues" was played with a slide, with the same alternating thumb bass he used for "John Henry," barring across the frets with a finger to make the change to a subdominant harmony. His "Mean Old Bedbug"—a cover version of Lonnie Johnson's big success—was finger-picked with a kind of banjo style that used a pull-off with the left hand to give it a little halting rhythm. "Why Don't You Come Home"—his version of the Memphis song "Goin' to Brownsville"—was played with a bottleneck, the guitar respondins to the vocal line in a beautiful interrelationship between the voice and the sliding "song" on the guitar that followed it. Of all his pickings probably the most interesting was the complex accompaniment he used for "I Will Turn Your Money Green," the second song he recorded for Ralph Peer on August 28, 1928. The text was one of his less coherent assemblies, with the second verse, the well-known "If you follow me, baby, I will turn your money green . . ." used almost arbitrarily for the title. But the picking was distinctive and inventive. The guitar was tuned to open D, which is D-A-D'-F#-A'-D''—and the rhythm was a strong counterpoint to the simple melody.

In most of the blues he sang in the twenties, he'd been harsh and angry about the women he'd known, but there were other verses, other glimmerings of relationships that had been happier, of love that hadn't ended with such bitterness. It was one of the women who'd known him and been happy with him then who led me to the small room where he was living in Memphis in 1958. It was winter, and it was cold along Beale Street, and I didn't have any recording to do, but I still took the chance to stop by and talk to Will Shade again in the shabby room where he was living with Jenny Mae. After an hour or so of talking about the city's bluesmen, Will went out of the room to get his guitar and Jenny Mae came close to the old iron stove against the wall. "Those other men you asked about," she said in a quiet voice, "Furry Lewis doesn't live too far from here. I saw him on the corner yesterday. He's working for the city." She and Furry had lived together before she was with Will and they still talked whenever she saw him on the street.

The city garage was empty when I stopped in later in the afternoon—all the crews had gone home for the day—but the office suggested calling the Memphis city personnel office. After two or three phone calls a girl said she had an address that she thought was current. Late the same afternoon I found Furry sitting in his room in the house the girl had given me the address for, a frame house on one of the North Memphis back streets. The street was lined with other houses like it, a few straggling trees, automobiles along the curb, straggling bits of lawn, the houses shabby and unpainted—here and there one of the older ones torn down and a new brick apartment unit up in its place. He was surprised that someone had finally come to talk to him again, but he was easy about it, too. It had been a long time of sitting in rented rooms and getting up before dawn to go out and sweep the streets. The next day I had an old Epiphone guitar I'd rented from one of the Beale Street pawnshops when he got back to his room from the job. He took the guitar, checked the tuning, and asked me what I wanted to hear. I was surprised that he didn't want to try the guitar first, but I asked, after a moment of uncertainty, for "John Henry" the way he'd played it thirty years before. It didn't have all of his old presence or sense of drama, but his fingers were almost as fast as ever, and his voice still had its gentle, soft plaintiveness.

Furry and I were able to do a considerable amount of recording over the next two years. A few songs were recorded in February 1959—then the rest of an LP for Folkways was completed in his room in October. He had told his neighbors in advance and the recording was done with the door of the room left open so people could stand inside and listen. He was pleased and excited to be recording again—as much for the chance to show everyone that he was one of the old Beale Street bluesmen as for the money or the chance to be on record. Two years later, in the spring of 1961, Ken Goldstein, who was in charge of the Prestige Bluesville series, asked for two more albums. There was time to write Furry in advance, and when I got to Memphis he had a guitar ready and a carefully lettered list of songs. As he got into the car to go to the studio he stopped and waved the guitar to everyone from the neighborhood who'd come out on their porches to watch. "Goin' to do some recordin'," he said several times, then got into the car with a pleased smile.

The Prestige sessions were held in Sun Studios, the modern recording facilities that Sam Phillips had built after his success with Sun Records and his group of artists that included Elvis Presley, Jerry Lee Lewis, Carl Perkins, and Johnny Cash. The engineer for the sessions was Scotty Moore, who had been the guitar player on all of Elvis's first recordings and was still working with Elvis whenever he was doing a film. If Furry felt any nervouness at the empty studio and the elaborate control room he never showed it. His only worry was whether or not he had enough songs to fill two LPs. He'd been working on the guitar, and he could do all of his old pickings except the accompaniment to "Turn Your Money Green." He still sang many of his old blues, but they had become gentler, and there wasn't so much anger in the verses he used.

The sessions went slowly, but it wasn't Furry's fault. Scotty was as much a musician as he was an engineer, and at almost every song they stopped so Scotty could ask him what tuning he was using, and how he was picking the accompaniment. Unlike so many white guitarists who have come to Furry with the same questions, Scotty wasn't trying to learn something he could use himself. It was just his quiet appreciation of what Furry was doing as an artist and a musician. Furry used every kind of tuning, usually working with open tunings so he could get the sound of the open string vibration. This is a fuller sound than a fretted string, and the fullness of his open tunings added to the depth of his guitar sound. Also he kept the guitar tuned low, sometimes almost a fourth below concert pitch, again for the fuller resonance he got with the slacker strings. He was able to take one day off work, but the second afternoon he had to come after he'd finished sweeping the streets. There was more money for him after the sessions, but it was still the chance to  be a musician again that meant the most to him.

In 1962 the film *The Blues* was conceived, mostly because of Furry and the flashing pattern of his fingers as he picked "John Henry." It seemed that film was the only way to capture what he was doing. In July it was possible to film him working out on his job—sweeping along one of the sidewalks not far from Beale. Then he did his "John Henry" in front of his house with his new wife, Versie, and his friends, in their best clothes, listening to him play. He had a small, old guitar that he'd decorated with a ribbon on the neck and the ribbon and the movement of his fingers created the same kind of free dance that I'd first seen three years before. It was still difficult to find a way for him to get out and play more, but the new recordings were selling a little, and in the early sixties there was a growing interest in the country blues.

In the spring of 1963 Furry, along with Gus Cannon and Memphis Willie Borum, rode a Greyhound up from Memphis to play a concert in New York City sponsored by the Friends of Old Time Music. It was intended more as a jug band concert than a blues concert, so they played as a group for most of the evening—for an audience of about two hundred that had gathered in one of the small lecture halls at New York University. But there was a completely unplanned and unforgettable moment in the Village Folklore Center on MacDougal Street in Greenwich Village earlier in the day. All three of them had come into the shop, and they were standing toward the back talking with Israel Young, the owner. A boy came in with his girl, both of them in their teens, and he picked up one of the shop's guitars. He told her he was going to play a Furry Lewis picking for her—completely unaware that Furry was also in the shop. As he played Furry came closer to him, listening, and as the boy looked up and hesitated, Furry reached out without a word, took the guitar, and showed how the lick *really* should be played. He finished with a medicine show buck and wing, tapped twice on the body of the guitar, handed it back, and with a half smile pushed his hat down on his forehead and walked back to Gus and Willie, leaving the boy with the guitar and a very confused expression on his face.

In the years since then Furry has finally retired from his job and taken his small pension. He moved from room to room for a while, as he and Versie quarreled and separated and made up and came back together. As the blues revival became more widespread he began to travel more and there was some more recording. He's become part of the small folk and blues music scene in Memphis, appearing at the Memphis Blues Festival, and working for occasional club jobs. He hasn't changed, and he's still the same gentle, small man he was, though he remembers more of his old medicine show jokes now, so there's more laughter in his room. His fingers have finally gotten slower, but his voice still has it quiet plantiveness. He had never completely stopped playing, thinking that sometime, somehow, the music might come back. It has now, in ways he never thought it would, and it brought him a new life and vitality, at a moment when he thought his life was almost over. As he told an interviewer who talked with him later,

> . . . *All those years I kept working for the city, thinking things might change, Beale Street might go back like it was. But it never did. . . . Sometimes, nothing to do, no place to play, I'd hock the guitar and get me something to drink. And then I'd wish I had it, so I could play, even just for myself. I never quit playing, but I didn't play out enough for people to know who I was. Sometimes I'd see a man, a beggar, you know, playing guitar on the sidewalk, and I'd drop something in his cup, and he wouldn't even know who I was. He'd think I was just a street sweeper.*

# 6.
# Frank Stokes

Now listen baby, you so good and sweet,
Hey, little baby, you so good and sweet,
I want to stay 'round you, if I have to beg in the street.

For many of the bluesmen of the twenties there's no way to tell what they looked like—only occasional handbills and leaflets, a badly reproduced photo of a face in a faded old record catalog—a guitar, a stiff expression, and an uncomfortable suit. Paramount Records used a photo of Frank Stokes and Dan Sane—'"The Beale Street Sheiks"—on an advertising leaflet in 1928, in their suits, holding their guitars. But even though their faces were hard to see, there was still a sense of their presence, their strength, despite the stiff pose and the uncomfortable clothes.

> *You just can't help it, the way the Beale Street Sheiks play their big time numbers on Paramount Records tempts you to get every one of them. They have some new records waiting, ready to give you more than your money's worth.*

But there's still another photo of Frank Stokes—from the Victor catalog the next year—and this seems to be more the way he's remembered by the people who knew him in Memphis. He's in his shirt sleeves, with light-colored suspenders, a cloth cap pulled down over his forehead, and the inevitable guitar in his hands, but it's held out there in front of him as if he really were going to play it. His face is dark, with a thin moustache, intent eyes, and a strong, set mouth. Will Batts was the violinist on Frank's last sessions for Victor, and Will's sister, Maggie Tuggle, still remembered Frank when being interviewed by Bengt Olsson.

*Frank Stokes? He was very tall. He used to play for picnics. Once I was giving a party and Frank Stokes was playing there. Just when he began playing everyone began dancing. There was a fat woman who stomped, so that a floor-seal popped! Stokes played with a beat that was very good for dancing. Him and Will used to play "Sweet Georgia Brown." Will played the violin. I loved to hear them play that.*

Despite the differences between them in age and temperament the Memphis musicians were a group. They lived and played and hustled together. Every bluesman from the twenties remembered Frank, and they all describe him as a tall, strong man, older than they were, who had a blacksmith shop and did most of his playing with Dan Sane (or Sain), a close friend who was with him until the late forties when Sane moved to Caruthersville, Missouri. Stokes lived south of the city—southeast, toward the Mississippi line—and his blacksmith shop was in Oakville, on the corner of Democrat Lane. There are different opinions about his age. Some of the people who knew him said he would have been over sixty when he had his picture taken for Paramount. Willie Borum, who played with both Frank and his son in the thirties, thought that Frank would have been in his fifties. Part of the confusion is that he didn't come into town until the twenties and he went back to Mississippi before his death. Mary Batts, Will Batts's widow, knew him very well and she thought he must have been born about 1880, which would make him in his late forties when he was recording. The people who were close to him knew him as a musician, and his age wasn't important.

It wasn't only their loose association playing on Beale Street that bound the musicians together. They were just as much joined by their Mississippi background. An old friend, Lizzie Wise, said that Frank came from Tutwiler, south of Clarksdale, where he was raised by a Fred Carbin. From Tutwiler he moved to Hernando, Mississippi, a kind of center for drifting singers and guitar players, where he played with Jim Jackson, Elijah Avery, and younger bluesmen like Robert Wilkins and Garfield Akers. People still remember him working for the Doctor Watts Medicine Show with Akers—both of them with their faces blacked up, except for the usual painted white mouth. Dan Sane, who was to work with him later, was also from Hernando, and their association probably began there. Hernando isn't far from Memphis—just a few miles below the state line—and most of the musicians found their way into the city at one time or another in their careers. Fred Carbin moved into Memphis, and Stokes, who was still living with him, came in as well, and they had a house in Bunker Hill.

Bunker Hill is still a section of wooden houses with tumbledown fences straggling along the pitted roads. Stokes always was a traveling man, and he was gone a lot—two months a year back in Olive Branch, Mississippi, and down into the Delta for picking season—but Bunker Hill was what he thought of as home, and he had a wife there named Lula. She still is living, and she remembers that they moved together when he went to Oakville and started the blacksmith shop there. She said that he played every Saturday night in Oakville—outside the J.J. Arnold Grocery Store. "If you was there on Sat'day night you just couldn't get through in no way. The place was crowded as could be . . . white folks too; they was crazy 'bout Frank—called him lots of times 'cause they wanted him to play for 'em. Played all those foxtrots and waltzes for 'em."

Frank also sang a blues about Bunker Hill, where they first lived, but Bunker Hill was well known to Memphis bluesmen, and there was an even earlier recording of a song about it by Ollie Rupert, who sang in 1927:

> Out on Bunker Hill, where the people have their fun,
> Out on Bunker Hill, where the people have their fun,
> I can lay down on the green grass and look up at the sun.

Frank did play all those "foxtrots and waltzes," and he also sang medicine show songs as well as blues—old street pieces like "Chicken You Can Roost behind the Moon" and "Mister Crump Don't Like It," known and sung the length of Beale Street. It's even been suggested that he wrote "Mr. Crump," but it was an old song, and it's unlikely that a Hernando bluesman would have made up a song to perform on his occasional trips to Memphis. When W.C. Handy described writing "Memphis Blues" he talked about another song called "Mister Crump," which he says was the basis for "Memphis Blues," and it was probably one of the versions of this that was the root source for Stokes' song. Stokes seems to have been well known on the medicine show circuit, as well as for his street singing, and in the summer of 1927, with Dan Sane, he did his first recording. They did seven titles for Paramount as the Beale Street Sheiks. The titles reflected the kind of near-minstrel material they were doing—"Beale Town Bound," "Jazzin' the Blues," "Half Cup of Tea"—but Stokes had a rich blues voice, and there were none of the minstrel show mannerisms in the way they played. It's difficult to say how they got up to Chicago to record, since Paramount didn't have much contact with Memphis. It was the largest blues company going at the time, and often singers went up on their own to audition; so they could have gotten with the company that way.

There seemed to be some interest in what they were doing at Paramount and they were in Chicago to record again the next month. Two of the pieces they did were remakes of things they'd done the month before, but at the same time they did three new pieces, including "Mr. Crump Don't Like It" and a "Blues in D." A friend from the medicine shows was up at the same time, Gus Cannon, who was recording for Paramount with Blind Blake. Paramount didn't follow up with them, however, and the next session was for Ralph Peer, who came into town in February 1928 to record the Memphis Jug Band. On February 1 Frank and Dan did four titles, including their brilliant "Downtown Blues," which was released on Vic 21272. They were in the improvised studio in the McCall Building the same day that the Jug Band did "Snitchin' Gambler Blues" and "Evergreen Money Blues." The week had started for Peer with the first four pieces that Cannon recorded with his Jug Stompers.

The sound on the Victor sides was much better than on the Paramount recordings, and Stokes's compelling, almost harsh voice came through with immediate clarity, and their guitar duets were brilliantly exciting. The next summer he did two short sessions by himself, doing four songs on August 27, 1928, and two more the next day. Sane joined him again on August 30, and they did four more titles, including the fine "T'Ain't Nobody's Business If I Do, Part 1 and Part 2," which was rather popular for them. Peer was recording Furry Lewis at the same time, and Furry did his classic "Kassie Jones" the same day that Stokes returned for his second session, Tuesday August 28th. Stokes's two pieces were done in the middle of Furry's session. The next year he recorded again, both for Paramount, with Dan Sane again as the Beale Street Sheiks, and for Victor. The Paramount sessions were done in Chicago in March 1929, and Victor recorded him in Memphis in September. These sessions were his last and he played without Sane. On six of the songs he used Will Batts on violin, but for his final two blues, on September 30, he played alone again, recording pieces with evocative titles, "Frank Stokes' Dream" and "Memphis Rounders Blues."

In the three years that Frank Stokes was a recording artist he did thirty-nine songs—a large number for the time and more than someone like Robert Johnson was able to do seven years later. He wasn't an imaginative singer—his style was simple and direct, and his texts were usually assemblages of familiar local verses. In their simplicity his texts matched his singing style.

> Now listen baby, I want to come back home.
> Now listen baby, I want to come back home.
> Then I'll tell you what happen, baby, since your man been gone.

There was a kind of flat literalness in his songs, and there was little use of complex imagery.

> I ain't no rounder, but I stays at home,
> I mean I ain't no rounder, but I stays at home.
> If you don't like my treatment you sure can leave me alone.
>
> Baby, someday you'll come to be my friend.
> Baby, someday you'll come to be my friend.
> Then we'll be alright, be back on the road again. . . .

But there was something that Stokes and Sane had that gave their blues their fresh excitement and their sauntering nonchalance. The verse could be something like:

> Hey listen mama, the world is done gone away,
> Hey listen mama, the world is done gone away,
> I got a bad luck deal give me trouble every day

sung in Frank's heavy voice, but behind the words he and Dan were playing some of the most marvelous two-guitar ragtime duets ever to get onto record. And it wasn't just for one or two songs—they did it on piece after piece. Sometimes, as in "Hunting Blues," the two guitars had a little of the sound that Henry Thomas had in his guitar part for "Fishing Blues," but most of what they did can't really be compared with anything else. Garfield Akers and Joe Calicott, who had known Frank when they were first starting out, did guitar duets with some of the complexity of Stokes and Sane, but they were doing music that had developed out of the field holler forms, and it had a more ambiguous harmonic structure. What Stokes and Sane were playing wasn't the kind of classic ragtime of Scott Joplin, but it had its own excited exuberance.

Most of their songs were blues, even if there were minstrel show elements woven in. Some were ragtime songs, and the verses fit the relaxed rhythm of their fingers.

> I never never never
> Can forget that day
> When you called me baby,
> How long, how long.
> I ain't had no lovin'
> How long, how long
>
> Have you seen my baby baby baby
> Tell her hurry home
> I ain't no good baby,
> How long, how long.
> And I'm on my way, babe,
> How long, how long.

In their accompaniments Frank took the simple rhythm, though he used changing c h o r d positions to give his playing more variety. Around this Dan wove a loose, syncopated line, sometimes melodic, sometimes harmonic. Sometimes he emphasized what Frank was doing—and there would be a moment of strutting rhythm as both of them picked out a bass lick—and sometimes he wove a filigree around it, as if he was so pleased with what Frank was doing that he didn't want to get in the way. All of their recordings had verses left open for the guitars; on some, like "Rockin' on the Hill Blues," they played verse after verse of pure country ragtime, without a vocal. It was the kind of music that people had to dance to—they couldn't keep their feet still. A musician named Lincoln Jackson —who played the second part with Frank when Frank came out to his little town of Cordova, outside of Memphis,—remembered this kind of irresistible rhythm as an integral part of Frank's style, and he told Bengt Olsson:

> . . . In them days we had what you call moonlight picinics, you know.
> They'd last for three days straight! Out in the woods, you know; lots

*of shade and ain't no one goin' bother you out there. People came in
buggies or horseback from miles around. In the night we'd light rags
with oil so everything'd be fine . . . barbecued hogs, goats an' chicken;
had lots of moonshine whiskey an' crap games. Man, we had our-
selves a time! That's the kind o' occasion Frank'd play for us. Sometimes we had drum and fife bands playin' all 'em marches an' stuff,
but everyone was jus' wild 'bout string music. Frank sure could make
'em do the Charleston 'n' Shim Sham Shimmy! He had a good
rhythm, you know. I'd second him most of the time—we were pretty
close; he'd stay at my place every time he came aroun'."*

This is what you hear in the irresistible guitar duets that Frank and Dan recorded. If you can just imagine dancing along with it a little you can get the
feel of a country picnic and a smoky fire cooking the barbecue, and the taste of
homemade liquor still burning your tongue, and people around you picking up
their feet and dancing. Sometimes couples dancing, sometimes a man doing his
own buck dance to show off a little, sometimes a woman dancing alone with a
baby in her arms, the baby's laughter joining in the enthusiasm.

The Depression finished recording for Frank, though he went on playing for
years afterward. Dan took part in one more group of recordings, the sessions
that Jack Kelly did in New York on August 1, 2, and 3, 1933, with three or
four of the Beale Street regulars, including Will Batts, as the South Memphis
Jug Band. In 1930 Frank was living with his father again not far from Will
Batts's house. Willie Borum played with Frank and his son Roosevelt when
they went out on the streets in the late thirties. Frank was living on Carnes
Avenue at this time, and there was a daughter, Georgia, as well as a son. He
was an old man now, though he kept traveling and playing a little. He seems to
have left his wife and gone back to Mississippi, and he died in Clarksdale about
1960. He is said to have eaten meat accidentally sprinkled with DDT in the
Snow Cafe on Esaquina Street. A woman, Viola Miller, said that her man used
to play with Frank when he would come down to Clarksdale, even though
mostly he was there to pick cotton. She was the one who described his death
by poisoning, although no death certificate has been found. But she remembered his music. "He had a heavy voice and played with a heavy beat." That
was Frank Stokes.

# 7.
# Some Singers
# Outside of Memphis

If someone wanted to get to Brownsville he had to go east, away from downtown Memphis, then when the highways divided he had to stay on Route 79—the right-hand road. The left-hand road—Route 51—led up north through Henning and Ripley. All of them were as much east as north of Memphis, country towns in the rolling, tree-covered land that had been cleared down to its yellow-red soil, then planted in cotton and soybeans. The soybeans are recent; when the land was first cleared it was all used for cotton, with a little space left around the cabins for vegetables, some of the land left for a few rows of corn. On the hillsides and back in the ravines there is a heavy growth of trees and brush, and on a fall day, walking back along the fences under the shadows of the trees, you kick away piled oak leaves, as deep brown as the dirt under them. You can smell smoke from cabin fires—through the lowering light a man walks ahead of you with his shotgun and his dog, doing a little hunting while there's still some light.

West Tennessee wasn't like the Delta, only 65 or so miles to the south. It didn't have a concentrated black farm population; it didn't have the crowding and the isolation of the Delta shack communities. The musicians coming out of the small towns and off the farms tended to drift into Memphis and become part of the rough crowd of singers and bluesmen working along Beale Street. But there was a country tradition, a style for all of them to draw on, even if it wasn't clearly identifiable—like the Mississippi bottleneck style, or the guitar rhythms of the Texas men. Most of them finger-picked the guitar, with the kind of loose raggy feel on the uptempo pieces that Frank Stokes and Dan Sane had. On the slower blues they often chorded behind the vocal phrase, then filled in the measure after it with small runs on the upper strings. There wasn't a lot of the unison guitar-voice melodies that were used in the Delta. If a slide or a bottleneck was used it was for a special piece—like "John Henry." The singing was also lighter in texture, the voices pitched higher, and the tone shaped farther forward in the mouth. It was a vocal tone a step closer toward a country white intonation. Often there was some uncertainty in the vocal phrase and the dominant phrase was anticipated by an upward tone shift that was slightly awkward.

Not all of the men that came into town stayed in Memphis. They liked life better back in the small towns where they'd grown up. One of the singers that Willie Borum played with a lot in the thirties was a guitarist and singer from Henning named Allen Shaw. They went to New York on September 17 and 18, 1934. Shaw is remembered as a tall man by the people in Henning that Bengt Olsson talked to, tall and well-built. Willie Borum just remembers that he was always traveling; there was no way to keep up with him. He had a job in Memphis when Willie met him, but he never stayed long on any job. He was a skilled guitarist, but his playing didn't have a strong individuality, and of the five blues he recorded only two were issued, "I Couldn't Help it" and "Moanin' the Blues" on Vocalion 02844. He played a lot with Noah Lewis when Noah was living in Henning, and in the late thirties he was more or less settled down in the small farm town, working at the C.S.O. Rice cotton gin. He died in Henning in 1940, at about the age of fifty.

These towns weren't very far out of Memphis. About forty-five miles. Noah Lewis could come in to work with Cannon, then go back up to Ripley or Henning the next day. In Memphis Noah was always with people like Cannon or Willie Borum—who learned how to play the harp with help from Noah—but in the country he worked at little grocery stores, or for picnics or dances. He's remembered in 1925 at a store called Orysa just outside of Henning with a guitar player named Jim Garrison. Many guitar players filled in with him, including Norman Haliburton and Cordelius Treadway. Eddie Green told Bengt Olsson:

> I played with Noah here in Henning. We had a band. I played guitar and Allen Shaw was in the band too. Occasionally Son Green played in the band. We played songs like "Joe Turner," "Big Fat Woman," "Casey Jones," "C. C. Rider" and others. I remember when we played at Cherry. A woman came in at a party and found her boyfriend with another woman. She grabbed Son's box and hit the boyfriend over the head, busting the guitar, and got the strings hung under his nose and ears! On another occasion my girl slapped me with a pocketbook. I hit her over the head with my guitar. On the Crutcher farm we had a party that lasted two days. There were many fights but the party never ceased. They just kept on drinking, playing and fighting. . . .

Noah had a son in Ripley who also was named Noah and played the harmonica. He'd lost his wife after they'd moved to Ripley, and his son died in Ripley as well. He stayed on in Ripley through the years that he was recording, just going down to rehearse with Cannon before they had to go into the studio. His life went on after the sessions, and he stayed up in the country, in the last years working as a farmhand for Willie Smith at Henning. It wasn't far from where he'd been born about 1890. His music stayed as pure and as expressive for years—and the people around Henning and Ripley still remember the sound of his harmonica. But in the last years he was in poor health, he couldn't play, and he was living in a small shack outside of town. It was under a large tree, a wood building with a narrow door, a windowless front, a board step out into the weeds. He was still there in 1960 when he died. He lost his way, was out all night, and was nearly frozen when he was found. His feet were amputated at the hospital, but he couldn't be saved, and he died in the hospital in Ripley.

Brownsville was on the other highway leading out of Memphis, but there were dirt roads going back and forth between Ripley and Henning and Brownsville, and all the singers knew each other. Brownsville's larger than the other two, and it had its own musical life in the twenties and thirties. It had its younger musicians like Hammie Nixon, who played harp, and Yank Rachel, who played mandolin. It had its younger blues singers, Charlie Pickett and "Brownsville" Son Bonds, who made recordings in the thirties. For Pickett there were only two sessions, August 2 and 3, 1937, but Son Bonds had three sessions in 1934, one in 1938, and a last in 1941. He wasn't a strong singer, but he had a commercial style and the songs he did were young but effective. He was a good guitarist and his voice had the usual rural Tennessee nasal sound. Pickett was more interesting as a singer, but he did only four blues. One of them, "Down the Highway," is almost free rhythmically, with the guitar playing in unison with the voice, then following with its own musical phrase. His voice is high and his singing is in a uniquely personal style. It is a startling blues—a suggestion of a country style that has had little representation on record and now is completely lost. But there is "Down the Highway"—first issued on a Decca single 7707—as a brilliant example of it.

But it was another singer who gave Brownsville its place in the blues, one of the greatest country bluesmen to record in the years of the Depression, Sleepy John Estes, who spent almost his entire life in the town.

# 8.
# Sleepy John Estes

I was raised in Lawdry County, you know I was schooled on Winfield Lane.
I was raised in Lawdry County, you know I was schooled on Winfield Lane.
You know what I made of myself, it's a cryin' shame.

It was a verse John Estes sang often in the first few months after he'd been found still living near Brownsville, Tennessee. It was his flat, hard comment on the reality of the years he'd spent there, living in a harsh poverty that was deeply disturbing to see. Winfield Lane was a rutted, unpaved farm road running through the red-brown clay earth outside of Brownsville, Tennessee. Most of the farms had been abandoned and there was only a scattering of houses along the road, some of them deserted cabins with fallen-in roofs and peeling tar paper. There were small stretches of cotton, some grazing land, but most of the land was overgrown with brush and trees. The cabin John lived in was about a mile and a half from the turn into Brownsville, a sagging wood shack that had once been painted red. The ground in front of it was bare of grass, an open mud space with a refuse of dirty dishes, old clothes, a chair that had gotten broken and left outside the door. It had only two rooms, one of them empty except for a bundle of rags on the filth of the floor, the other room with a chair, a rusted wood stove, and two beds piled with the same rags that were on the floor of the other room. A metal plate with bits of food stuck to it had been left on the chair, and flies clustered around the rest of the dishes left in a bucket on the floor. There was no electricity or water. In the daytime most of the light came in through the cracks between the cabin's warped planks. It looked like any of the abandoned cabins left in the fields, but John Estes was living in it, with his wife and five small children.

Many of the old bluesmen who were found still living in the 1950s and 1960s were living in ghetto buildings, or in shabby houses in small towns in the South, but Estes's poverty had a desperateness to it. He'd long been troubled with his eyes, and he'd finally become completely blind. Even knowing that he was in poor health, blind, and living in a poor shack, I still wasn't prepared for the sight of him, a gaunt, tall figure in dirty farm clothes, a shapeless straw hat on his head, sitting alone on a bare wooden chair in front of the cabin of a neighbor. Because he'd been told someone wanted to see him, he had an old guitar across his lap, the strings rusted, a pencil tied around the neck as a kind of capo. One of his sons, who was about nine years old, led him back and forth from his house to the Meaux house, and it was painful to watch him stumbling along, holding his guitar, his feet scuffing with uncertainty over the dirt and stones.

A few months later John was able to move into Brownsville, and with the earnings that came in from concerts and recordings he was able to add to the welfare check he received from the state of Tennessee, but the years of darkness and poverty on the country road left their marks on both his health and his spirit. The man across the road, a sharecropper with a family of his own to feed, had tried to do what he could for John, but he felt that it was John's blindness that had left him so helpless. "People cheats him, you know, when he goes and buys things. If he gets some butter they makes him pay four times what it says on the counter; then they don't give him his right change." He had grown blind when he was older, and he hadn't developed any of the ways to deal with his blindness that someone younger learns. He was only fifty-eight years old, that afternoon at the cabin on Winfield Lane—but he looked and moved like a man in his seventies.


A handful of the bluesmen of the twenties seemed to sum up the intense emotionalism and strong musicality of this early blues period, when it was a music of unique individuality and a clearly sensed personal expression. It was not blues bands or groups, or the interplay of one instrumentalist with another. All of that was to come later. In the twenties it was still largely a music coming from the country to the city—it was still a music of singers living in small communities and functioning as the expression—and the entertainment—of the people in these communities. Of the hundreds of blues singers who recorded during this period, Estes was one of the most individual. During a time when there were many great blues artists, he was one of the greatest. It was his way of using his materials that gave Estes his greatness. Many singers were using the same verses, many had used the melodies, and the forms he used were generally clearly within the blues idiom of the period he was recording—but he was like a stream from the farm country where he grew up. It picks up its materials from the banks that it washes against; then it leaves them farther downstream spread out in new patterns and arrangements.

John was born John Adam Estes—friends in Brownsville still call him John Adam—in Lauderdale County, outside of Ripley. It comes out as "Lawdry" when he sings about it. He was born on January 25, 1904, one of sixteen children. His father was a sharecropper and played a little music. John started on his father's guitar when he was still a child. When he was eleven they moved into Brownsville, in 1915, and he did get a little time in school in a wood frame school building on Winfield Lane, not far from where he was living when he was found. About this time he was hit in the eye with a stone in a baseball game and he was never able to see well again. He worked a little in the fields along with the rest of his brothers and sisters. This was still the old farm life of the rural South. Cotton all year around, with its hours of digging and chopping and weeding and picking. John didn't like field work, and when his father died in 1920 he started making his living with his music. It wasn't much of a living, just the usual country picnics and parties, playing for dances. Long hours sweating in the lantern light, singing the blues until his voice was gone and he couldn't do much more than strum the guitar. Memphis wasn't far, but he didn't come in. He wasn't an entertainer, and he wasn't a street singer. He had his own blues, and he had his own life in the small town where he'd grown up.

Brownsville, like most small towns in the South, had its little square, its court-house, its line of one-story shops looking hopefully at the courthouse for any sign of business. Their plate-glass windows were filled with cheap watches and cotton dresses, kitchen utensils, lanterns, car parts, and tools. It also had a few other musicians. John was soon playing with James Rachel—who was usually known as Yank and had been in Brownsville all of his life. He was younger than John—four years younger. He was born on March 16, 1908. He learned the guitar from his uncle, Daniel Taylor, but he was also a brilliant mandolin player, and it was the mandolin that he played with John. They met at a party where John was playing, and, though Yank had managed to get through the sixth grade in school, he didn't see any kind of job he could do in Brownsville and he drifted into music. The other musician closely associated with Browns-ville and John is his harmonica player, Hammie Nixon. He was nine years younger than John, and he was only fourteen the first time they met. He was born in January 1913 in Ripley and he grew up playing the harmonica. "I don't know when I started. I just played it since I was a kid." John heard him at a country supper and got his mother to let him live in Brownsville. And they've been close friends ever since.

The years in Brownsville before he recorded gave John's music its individuality. He was a great singer, with a high, thin, crying voice that had almost a child's despair—but he wasn't much worried about the guitar, and he depended on the musicians with him to give his songs their final structure. Yank was with him on his first sessions—Hammie was too young—but when he began recording again five years later Hammie was with him too. His harmonic ideas were so loosely developed that it was only musicians who knew his style that could really work with him. Hammie knew his music so well that he could play a harp line almost in unison with John's voice, and Yank had worked out a compli-cated mandolin style to go with John's strummed guitar rhythms. John was twenty-five when he came into Memphis and auditioned for Ralph Peer and did his first session on September 16, 1929, during an extended field trip that Victor made during that month to record the Memphis Jug Band, Cannon's Jug Stompers, and Frank Stokes.

Estes worked with one of the Memphis Jug Band men, Jab Jones, on his first Victor sessions, and he knew the songs well enough to record versions of some of the jug band songs later, but he was something that they weren't. He was a country bluesman in the classic sense. His music had come out of the field singing and the country breakdowns of the countryside around Brownsville, and he was able to build a creative structure—the way a person builds a house—out of the materials of his life.

John Estes—"Sleepy John Estes" as he was called on record labels, because he'd gone off to sleep on the little bandstand at a country dance and his friends started calling him "Sleepy"—was to have a long, and eventually successful, recording career in the years between 1929 and 1941, even if his life in Brownsville wasn't changed much by it. When he did go to record he was gone only a few days—at most a few weeks. There wasn't much money for the sessions—someone as successful as Memphis Minnie was getting only $12.50 for every side she recorded, and that was a flat rate. Any royalties had to come from compositions. Hammie Nixon recorded ten songs as accompanist for Little Buddy Doyle on a session for Vocalion in Memphis in 1939 and his total payment for the session was $10. If any Chicago musicians remembered John they remembered him as one of the Southern bluesmen who came in town, made some sides, spent the money, and got back home as best they could. With the amounts of money he was making it wouldn't have taken him long to go through it, and he sings about riding freight trains and jumping off at hobo jungles with a depressing sense of reality.

In the twelve years that he made records in his early period he recorded forty-four blues for first Victor label, then Decca, and finally Victor's lower-priced label Bluebird. At his final session, on September 24, 1941, he recorded first with two Brownsville musicians, Son Bonds and Raymond Thomas, as The Delta Boys. They did six songs, including "When the Saints Go Marchin' In" and "Every Time My Heart Beats." Later the same day John recorded three blues, "Lawyer Clark Blues," "Little Laura Blues," and "Working Man Blues." Thomas again played imitation string bass, but Son Bonds had switched from kazoo to guitar. John's first Memphis session, on September 16, 1929, was more of an audition than a session. The engineers did only one song, "Broken-Hearted, Ragged and Dirty Too," and it was left as an unissued test. He had Yank Rachel with him, and Yank worked well with him, but Jab Jones, the pianist, was working with the Memphis Jug Band and he probably wasn't familiar enough with John's individual rhythmic style. They came back in the studio eight days later and this time—on September 24—they got a usable song, the fine version of the "Goin' to Brownsville" melody that was titled, probably for copyright purposes, "The Girl I Love, She Got Long Curly Hair."

They seem to have recorded slowly, and they didn't get more than two songs a day at any of the sessions. They came back two days later and got two of their best blues recorded, a second version of "Broken-Hearted, Ragged and Dirty Too " and "Diving Duck Blues." There was a last session for the year the next week, on October 2, but Jab had dropped out and there was a harmonica player added. They again got only a single blues, "Black Mattie Blues," The next May Victor was in Memphis again and they got the three of them together—Jab back on piano—for four different sessions. The first day, May 13, they got

"Milk Cow Blues" and "Street Car Blues." May 17 they recorded again, but this time Yank Rachel did the singing on the first song, "Expressman Blues." Four days later there was another two-song session, this time with John singing; then Jab dropped out again and there were four songs recorded on May 30, two of them with Yank singing. Victor 23318 was released with two of Yank's vocals—the "Expressman Blues" and 'Sweet Mama"—but John was listed on the label as the singer, and for some time the different voices with the same name caused a little confusion.

The Depression deepened after the last Victor sessions, and John's life in Brownsville went on pretty much the way it had before. He went on playing the little picnics and the auctions and dances—a thin, withdrawn man who played his guitar with a kind of repetitive loping rhythm and sang with a kind of emotional possession. Hammie Nixon was working with him, and they managed to keep something going. Gennett Records had tried to continue their race label with a cheap series called Champion, but the early thirties were too hard for them to get through. They sold the copyright for Champion in June 1935 to the new Decca label. John and Hammie had been going up to Chicago for occasional trips, trying to play their blues and trying to get another session, and for a period after 1931 they stayed in the city. Big Bill Broonzy, whose memory was colorful, if not entirely reliable, described a blues contest between himself and Memphis Minnie, with John and Richard M. Jones as the judges. They decided Minnie had won it and carried her around the room on their shoulders, while Bill walked off with the prize, a bottle of whiskey. If it did happen it would have been sometime during this period that John was in the North. He managed to get to know Mayo Williams, who went from Vocalion to the new Decca series, and it was for Decca that John recorded again, two sessions with Hammie, done in Chicago on July 9 and July 17, 1935. Their first release, "Down South Blues" and "Stop That Thing," was the first release on the new Champion race series—it was Champion 50001, and all three records that they did came out first on Champion. But the 5000 series wasn't strong enough, and all of the releases were moved over to Decca's very successful 7000 series.

But it still wasn't time for John to reach his audience. The Champion releases were loose, surging blues, but they were on the wrong label. It wasn't until he recorded for Decca again in 1937 that he began to get a solid popularity. He did eighteen blues in three sessions in 1937 and 1938, then six more in 1940, and the next year he was recording for Victor's very popular Bluebird line. It was only the Musicians Union's ban on recording and the wartime shellac shortage that ended his early career. He was popular enough to have his photograph on the front of the "Decca Race Records" catalog, his face set and unsmiling, between the broadly grinning photos of Peetie Wheatstraw and Georgia White. Victor, to cash in on his popularity, even released some of the first recordings they've done with him in 1929 on their Bluebird series. It was a long, rather prolific, and successful recording career—and that made the poverty of the years afterward even more difficult to accept. Out of all the music that he recorded, all the songs he composed, there should have been something to keep him out of that crumbling cabin in the overgrown fields outside of Brownsville.

The blues that John recorded are a brilliant expression of the depth of the blues as a poetic expression. In his singing and in the songs that he wrote there is a complete expression of himself as a human being, a portrait of the people living around him, and an insistent commentary on the reality of life in western Tennessee in the shabby, dusty years of the Depression. It's possible to see—to understand—something of this life because of John's blues about it—because of his own unsentimental, clear-eyed understanding of it that he was able to express in the wistful reflection of his songs. He was one of the greatest singers of the early blues period—with a sensitive, intense voice that seemed almost to cry in its sadness and its ruefulness. It was a clear, high voice that was almost free of the limits of the blues verses and had its own sensed rhythms. It wasn't a sensual voice—John wasn't particularly concerned with physicality in his blues—but it was an emotional, powerful voice that hung in a fierce clarity over the sound of his guitar.

The form of his songs was on one level generally simple, and on another stubbornly complex. He usually worked within standard blues forms, but he kept placing them in a rhythmic context that forced the music into new, and often awkward, dimensions. The first sessions were remarkable for their rhythmic ambiguity. Because of his limitation as a guitarist, John had developed a kind of doubled rhythm that he strummed as he sang, using only simple melodic figures at the end of a vocal phrase. Yank had learned to play along with him by emphasizing the lyricism of his voice, and on the mandolin he played long melodic lines, interspersed with rhythmic elements that doubled John's strumming. Jones, playing the piano, was left in the difficult position of accompanying a voice that was singing in standard blues progressions, while the guitar was playing a simple strum in a kind of double time. He was able to work something out, and the tension between the two rhythms gave the best of their performances a rich, textured sound that moved in sudden emphasis under the directness of the voice.

John was to use the "Brownsville" melody for most of his recording career, but it's difficult to tell where he learned it. It had already been recorded before his version of it, and one of the recordings is very similar to his in the general shaping of the phrases—particularly the third phrase—and in the emotional "feel" of the voice. This version of it is a strange, clumsy recording by an accordion player and singer from—probably—Cleveland, Mississippi, named Walter Rhodes. Rhodes was a street singer who worked in small Mississippi towns like Cleveland and Bobo, but when he recorded for Columbia in 1927 there were two guitarists on the sessions with him. Their names were Maylon and Richard Harney, brothers from Arkansas who were called "Pet" and "Can" on the recording. Rhodes seems to be playing a simple, archaic kind of accompaniment on his accordion, which sounds like the kind of square, simple instruments that the Cajun musicians used, while the Harney brothers are attempting to play a fairly modern and skilled blues duet. No real rhythm emerges out of the jumble of styles, but it is possible to hear Rhodes voice, and his version of the melody is strong and effective.

Goin' to buy me a roos-ter___ put him in my back door.___

Goin' to buy me a roos-ter___ put him in my back door.___

See a stran-ger com-in' he lost his way be - fore.

Charley Patton also seems to have heard the record—or heard Rhodes—and he used it as the basis for his "Banty Rooster Blues" recorded two years later. Although it's difficult to follow the chord progression in Rhodes's recording, the harmony he is singing is a standard twelve-bar blues, though—from the inflection of the second phrase—he would seem to be singing in a modal scale rather than a diatonic. Also the rhythm of his version is regular—that is, within a standard twelve-bar, 4/4, form. In his first recording of it Estes's version is significantly different. It still has the initial introductory vocal tones—two beats before the beginning of each sung phrase—that were a carryover from the old phrasing of the field holler. But instead of a steady 4/4 beat there's a kind of suspended rhythmic jog—like a man running two steps in place—as the phrase picks up again. But in other respects the melody is very similar.

Now I'm goin' to Browns-ville take that right hand road.

Now I'm goin' to Browns-ville take that right hand road.

Lord I ain't goin' stop wal-kin' till I

get in sweet ma- ma's door.___

John's vocal is in the purest holler tradition, and it would be as effective if he was walking on a dirt road singing it to himself—a way singers often had of letting their women know they were on their way in from the fields. The tension in the rhythm comes from Jab's efforts to sort out the involved relationship between the double strum of the guitar and the freely shifting melody of the voice and the mandolin. John essentially is singing in 4/4, while the accompaniment is in 8/8. Jab was forced to fill the space with considerably more piano than bluesmen of the twenties usually did, and the rhythmic complexity comes from his shifts of phrase and harmony. John's guitar is heard as an almost inaudible strumming in the lower strings.

The other songs from the first sessions were generally within the standard twelve-bar form, and it was only for this version of the "Brownsville" melody that John kept the holler phrasing. When he recorded it again more than thirty years later it still had this same structure. On one of the other songs, "Street Car Blues," the phrase length was irregular, as he added beats in his guitar strum to the line endings, but the other blues either had a twelve-bar form or were in a recitative form that kept the twelve-bar structure but used a doubled first line in a kind of recited vocal phrase. It's the same form that someone like Lightnin' Hopkins has used for dozens of blues. As John used it in his first sessions it was a clearly defined melodic root he used repeatedly for later blues.

Now look-y here, ba-by, see what you done done. done made me love you, now yo' man done come, 'cause... Need more,

Despite the uncertainty of some of the details of these early performances, they were in their own way magnificent, and there's nothing in the blues like them. Even if Jab Jones wasn't sure how to follow what the other two were doing, he never faltered, and on something like their "Diving Duck Blues"— when all three of them were working within a clearly understood pattern—the instrumental texturing was brilliantly effective. Jab had worked out a piano version of the melodic phrase John played on the guitar and all three of them played it in a kind of unison at the end of the vocal phrase, though each of them played it with his own rhythmic shading and his own scale mode. They were some of John's greatest blues, and they still, after all the years since they were made, have the freshness of excitement and surprise.

Brownsville, even though it is a small town, is on a major highway—it has radios and records. Whatever was going on in the blues made its way to Brownsville's flat, drab black section, and even John's music showed some of the changes as the years passed. It wasn't John's singing or Hammie's harmonica playing—it was the young musicians from Brownsville who recorded with them that made most of the change. John has had the same style for most of his life, and his guitar playing hasn't changed since his first days in the studio, but his recordings seem to have more variety—because of the different sound of his accompaniment and his slight adjustment of vocal rhythm and phrasing to the new sound. It was only on the first six sides for Champion—in the summer of 1935 when he and Hammie were in Chicago—that he was his own accompanist, and it's clear that he needed other musicians with him. He had found a kind of jogging, dancelike strum for his songs, and often there seemed to be almost no rhythmic connection between his voice and the accompaniment. The songs were exciting—with his voice at its most emotional, and the texts brilliant blues poems. Some of the best of his recitative blues were from these sessions—the fine "Drop Down Baby," with its refrain:

> Well, my mama she don't 'low me to fool 'round all night long.
> Now I may look like I'm crazy,
> But poor John do know right from wrong

and his "Someday Baby," which influenced some of the Chicago singers when it was released the same year. But in a simple blues, like "Married Woman Blues," the limitations of his guitar playing begin to interfere with the effectiveness of the performance. He used his same strum for the blues, but in a more usual 4/4 tempo. The strum was unobstrusive, in itself, and his singing was always stunning enough to overcome the clumsiness of the background, but the harmonic structure of his playing was always uncertain. He seemed undecided as to how he wanted to play the simple tonic, subdominant, dominant harmonies that he was singing. Instead of the usual chord pattern of

I - I - I - I (sometimes IV for the second measure)
IV - IV - I - I
V - IV - I - I (or the V chord was held through the second measure)

John sometimes began with a measure of tonic and subdominant, two beats of each, though his subdominant wasn't a definite IV chord, and he divided the measure sometimes with the kind of subdominant chord coming first, sometimes second. His dominant chord in the last phrase was often used only for a single beat—not long enough to establish the harmony, but sudden enough to throw off the harmonic movement of the piece. After the beat—or two beats—he hurriedly went back to his little rhythmic strumming on his basic open chord. The guitarists who worked with him later—the Brownsville musicians Charlie Pickett and Son Bonds—sometimes found themselves haplessly following along, and there is some of the same confusion in their duets, with the guitars beginning a verse with the harmonic changes for the second line of the verse. The uncertainties of the guitar work wouldn't have been so obvious if John hadn't been so effective as a singer. He *sang* all the harmonic changes for the standard progressions—he just didn't bother to play them. And as a singer he was so brilliantly effective that for his best recordings the inadequacies of the accompaniment seem to be wholly wound into the texture of the song. On one of his late sessions, June 4, 1940, for Decca, the guitarist on some of the pieces sounds like another musician and there's a startling modernity in songs like "Jailhouse Blues." With its careful, melodic guitar work it's a recording that could have been made in the mid-1950s, and it emphasizes the effect that John's music had on the development of the blues in the years before the war.

It wasn't only as a singer that John Estes made a place for himself in the history of the blues. The verses he wrote have a directness and an immediacy that few singers can match. He could write the simple blues love songs that most of the singers of the thirties wrote by the hundreds, but he had much more on his mind. He had seen much more, and he wanted to tell about it. He had some of Patton's involvement with the place he lived in, and the people of Brownsville find their way into his blues—as people, not as symbols or standard blues types he's given a name. His blues about the mechanic Vassie Williams, who had a garage in nearby Durhamville, was a song about somebody he knew, somebody he was close to.

> Now Vassie can line your wheels, you know poor Vassie
>     can tune your horn.
> Now he can line your wheels, you know poor Vassie
>     can tune your horn
> Then when he set it out on the highway you can hear
>     your motor hum.
>
> Now my generator is bad, and you know my lights done stopped.
> Now my generator is bad, and you know my lights done stopped.
> And I reckon I'd better take it over to Durhamville, and I'm goin'
>     to stop at Vassie Williams' shop.

Sometimes he changed the names, but you can hear him mention the grocer Pat Mann and his son, who was a lawyer; another lawyer, Mr. Clark, had a whole song; most of the Brownsville police force comes in at one time or another; and even the mortician Al Rawls turns up in a song, as well as the local liquor store owner Peter Albert. As he said in one blues:

> Now Brownsville is my home, and you know I ain't goin'
>     to throw her down.
> Now Brownsville is my home, and you know I ain't goin'
>     to throw her down.
> Because I'm 'quainted with John Law, and they won't let me down.

His songs had this sense of a place and people, and he could write a blues that had the kind of details you hear in a country story. He had the literalness of Bukka White, but he had a stronger narrative sense, and in some of his blues you could follow what he was singing almost as a story, even if it wasn't a ballad song in the usual sense.

Now when I left Chicago I left on the G & M
Now when I left Chicago I left on that G & M
Then after I reach my home I had to change over on that L & N.

Now came in on that main west, and I put it down at Chicago Heights.
Now when I came in on that main west I put it down at Chicago Heights.
Now you know then poor John gone, and that's why I stayed all night.

Now if you hobo through Brownsville you better not be peepin' out.
Now if you hobo through Brownsville you better not be peepin' out.
Mr. Winn will get you and Mr. Guy Hare will wear you out.

Now out east from Brownsville it's about four miles from town.
Now out east from Brownsville it's about four miles from town.
Now if you ain't got your fare that's where they will let you down.

One of his songs was a personal ballad about a near drowning, the well-known "Floating Bridge," and in his description of what happened and then his song about it there's a clear illustration of the immediate relationship between his life and his music. As he told me:

*I was travelin' in Hickman, Kentucky, and the car went in the high water, the '37 flood it was. Got going to my cousin's home and had to go across one of them floating bridges tied to the cable there, you know, to keep it from floating away, and we got on that bridge and hit that pretty rough, you know, the way he was driving. He lost control of the car and it went off to the left. I was sitting on the far side putting some strings in my shoes and I was the last one. There's two-three on the other side of me and that made me last getting out on the bridge.*

*Well, my cousin, it knocked him in the head scuffling in the car. He cut hisself and he's sitting up there on a log and he asks, "Everybody out?" "Unun, John's still in there." By that time I had come up the third time. He jumped off that board and saved me. He got me and put me under his arm and treaded water up to the bridge and pulled me up on to it.*

Out of this John selected the details that were the most emotionally vivid for him and set them to the old melody usually known as "Two White Horses in a Line." He recorded it the next summer, August 2, 1937, in New York.

Now I never will forget that floating bridge.
(three times)
Tell me five minutes time in the water I was hid.

When I was going down I throwed up my hands.
(three times)
Please take me on dry land.

Now they carried me in the house and they laid me 'cross the bank.
(three times)
'Bout a gallon and a half of muddy water I had drank.

They dried me off and they laid me in the bed.
(three times)
Couldn't hear nothing but muddy water running through my head.

Now my mother often taught me quit playing a bum.
(three times)
Go somewhere, settle down and make a crop.

Now the people standing on the bridge was screaming and crying.
(three times)
Lord have mercy while we gwine.

It was in details like "Couldn't hear nothing but muddy water running through my head" that his blues found some of their greatest power.

John had also the rare ability to find sudden images, small phrases, that left an immediate impression of what he was trying to suggest in his song. He had phrases like "Now, went upstairs to pack my leaving trunk . . ." giving a complete sense of leaving, packing up, getting out, in the simple "leaving trunk." The verse goes on with a more obvious but still strong phrase, "I never had no whiskey; blues done made me sloppy drunk." He could give a whole sense of a crowded town and a loose Saturday's confusion in a phrase like "Now, I know the people is on a wander everywhere." And he summed up a woman in one of his most striking phrases, "Some of these women sure do make me tired, got a handful of 'gimme,' got a mouthful of 'much obliged.'" He had the poetic range to describe a relationship in simple but direct emotional terms:

Now asked sweet mama, let me be her kid.
She said, "I might, but I like to keep it hid."
Well, she looked at me, she begin to smile,

Says, "I thought I would use you for my man awhile.
Just don't let my husband catch you there,
Just don't let my husband catch you there."

And in another blues he could give the government advice on how to end the Depression.

Now you ought to cut off so many trucks and tractors, white folks,
    you ought to work more mules and men.
Now you ought to cut off so many trucks and tractors, white folks,
    you ought to work more mules and men.
Then you know that would make, ooh babe, money get thick again.

He was one of the strongest and most effective of the blues poets of the twenties and thirties, and some of his most striking phrases and images have become part of the language of the modern blues song.

It was Big Bill's book that stopped people from looking for John. Bill said that Estes had been a very old man when he recorded and that he'd been dead for years. Bill was actually eleven years older than Estes, so it's unlikely that he ever saw him at all, but John's singing style had such a unique, quavering quality to it that he sometimes did sound like an old man on his recordings. But other musicians knew of him and occasionally they mentioned him. In 1957 Big Joe Williams told Robert Koester, who owned Delmark Records and operated the Jazz Record Market in Chicago, "Sure, Sleepy John's still alive. He lives on a farm outside Brownsville, Tennessee." Koester hadn't known Big Joe long enough to sort out from what he said what was true and what was clearly not true. In 1959, when his shop was on South Wabash, a man working next door said, "My name is Sam Estes from Tennessee," but Koester thought he was making a kind of joke on the name Sleepy John Estes, and it wasn't until years later that he learned it was John's brother. It was finally Memphis Slim who led to John. He'd heard about him from Big Joe, and when he was asked by a young filmmaker, David Blumenthal, if he knew of any old bluesmen in that part of Tennessee, Slim told him to look for Estes. Blumenthal was making a film documenting some aspects of the new black freedom movement under the title *Citizen South, Citizen North*. He went to Brownsville, found the ruined shack where John was living, filmed it, and came back to Chicago. When he got back to town he decided he should film a modern jazz group in a nightclub, and he was sent to one of Koester's employees, Joe Segal, who knew a lot about the Chicago jazz scene. Joe talked to Blumenthal for a minute, then he went upstairs to get Koester. "Bob, there's a guy downstairs who claims he's located a blues singer named Sleepy John Estes."

Within a few weeks John was in Chicago for a first short tour. Koester had called a man named Odell Saunders who answered, "If I had known you were going to call I would have had John Estes stay around here—he was here an hour ago." Koester went down to Brownsville, immediately bought John some clothes—"slack britches" as his neighbor Phil Meux recalled—helped him get a guitar, and arranged to bring him up north. Since then he has managed John's business affairs, handled his recording sessions, and done what he could to help John find his way out of the poverty of the years when he was living on Winfield Lane. There was a second film documentary done a few weeks after John returned from his first trip. He and his family were still living in their cabin and I was able to film them there for *The Blues* in the early summer of 1962. It was stifling and hot, and it wasn't possible to work in the heat for more than a few moments at a time. John sat stilly through it all, his eyes closed, his face without expression. The children moved around him a little, but they were almost as silent, and for a sequence of the family on the porch they sat almost without movement, the sun glaring on the hard-packed dirt in front of them, the boards of the porch squeaking if anybody shifted from one foot to another.

At the Newport Folk Festival in 1964 John was as silent as he had been in the Tennessee sunlight. Many young blues enthusiasts milling around behind the stage area before he sang almost missed seeing him. He was in a jacket and slacks, wearing a shirt and tie. He had on an ordinary businessman's hat and he was wearing dark glasses. There was some of the same reserve when he sang, but Hammie Nixon, as always, was with him, and Hammie's stubby figure filled the stage as he went from harmonica to jug, doing his best to keep the crowd entertained. Yank Rachel was with them as well. He'd been found living in Indianapolis and he'd also begun recording for Koester's Delmark label. The three of them seemed a little unsure of themselves, on a low stage in Newport's steady gray drizzle, playing for a large crowd—almost four thousand people watched their afternoon workshop appearances—that was scattered across the grass in blue jeans and sweat shirts. But the music was still there—the cry was still in John's voice—and their songs were a moving glimpse of the world of Brownsville, and the people who lived in it, thirty years before. It was all there, in the blues that John Estes had built out of the simple materials of his life.

(See page 90.)

# 9.
# Memphis Minnie

It is, of course, a misnomer to speak of the country blues artists as "bluesmen" since there was a scattering of women who played and sang the blues throughout the South, but the masculine element in the country blues was so dominant, and the male singers so completely identified with the style, that the term "bluesmen" is very useful. The generalization of the urban blues in the early period as dominated by women and the country blues by men holds generally true, despite occasional exceptions. There was no male singer who was as significant in the urban blues scene as Bessie Smith, Ma Rainey, Clara Smith, Ida Cox, or Sara Martin, just as, in the country blues, there was no woman singer with the influence of Lonnie Johnson, Lemon Jefferson, Leroy Carr, or Big Bill. This generalization, however, has to give way a little in the thirties, for in the middle of the masculine country blues world there was the exultantly feminine figure of Minnie McCoy, a handsome, vibrant woman known to the people who bought her records as "Memphis Minnie."

Her professional name is misleading in some ways, because for most of her career she—along with most of the other commercial blues artists—was living and working in Chicago, and a point could be made for excluding her from a discussion of regional blues styles. As the blues became more and more of a marketing phenomenon in the thirties, almost all of the regional groupings broke down in Chicago. But she had many years of playing in Memphis before she began recording, and even at the end of her career there was still a suggestion of the Memphis vocal tone and the kind of earnest rhythmic movement that was characteristic of that city's style. Also she was part of the Beale Street scene for many years, and it seems important to include her in a discussion of Memphis music, even if much of what she sang and played was done elsewhere and reflected many other influences.

Like nearly all of the city's blues artists, she wasn't born in Memphis, but unlike them—most were Mississippians—she was born farther south, in Algiers,

Memphis Minnie.

Louisiana, across the river from New Orleans, on June 3, 1896. Her family's name was Douglas, and she was the first of thirteen children. Her name was Minnie, but she was so active when she was young that her parents nicknamed her "Kid," and she was always known as Kid Douglas in her years in Memphis. When she was still young, only seven, her family moved to Walls, Mississippi, which is just over the Mississippi line, about fifteen miles southwest of Memphis on Highway 61; then a year later they moved into Memphis itself. Her first instrument was a banjo that she later remembered she learned to play in two weeks, and by the time she was fifteen she had gotten herself a guitar and was "serenading" along Beale Street.

She was part of the crowded, hectic life along Beale Street for nearly twenty years, usually playing and singing with a small group or with one of the local bluesmen. She was well known by all the singers and she seems to have learned most of their finger-picking techniques, as well as the blues and songs that were popular in the city. She was especially close to the musicians of the Memphis Jug Band and for some time lived with Will Weldon, who was one of the band's original members. By the late twenties, however, she was living with a Mississippi singer named Joe McCoy, and much of her early recording was done with him. She remembers that a scout for Columbia heard her singing in a barbershop and sent them to New York to the studios there. Ralph Peer seems to have missed her, even though he'd tried recording some other women singers on his trips away from New York. The interest was in male singers at this point, and even Columbia recorded only one song with Minnie singing and didn't release that for some time. Probably their pseudonyms of "Kansas Joe" and "Memphis Minnie" were given them by Frank Walker at Columbia, since she was still called Kid Douglas by the other Memphis musicians, and the people who remember Joe usually refer to him by his own name. His records were also released under the name Big Joe, Hallelujah Joe, Mud Dauber Joe, Georgia Pine Boy, and Mississippi Mudder; so there would seem to be a basic confusion as to his stylistic identity.

In some ways there is some of the same confusion in the music they were doing together in the late twenties since so many influences were present in the Memphis musical scene. Other people close to them were recording, including Will Weldon and the Jug Band, and many of the Mississippi singers with stylistic similarities to what Joe was doing were coming into Memphis to record; so there was a great deal of music to choose from. Everything seems to have made some impression on what they were playing on the streets, and certainly Minnie, by this time in her mid-thirties, was a completely assured performer. But this early Memphis period, even though it covered so many years of her life, is perhaps not so crucial in considering Minnie's career, since she became one of the most successful of the commercial performers of the next period of the blues.

It's difficult to make any assessment of the artistic development of a commercial singer like her. For one thing there are so many recordings, and in their larger patterns of expression they reflect more of a response to the popular blues market than they do any changing artistic attitudes. She was successful at the beginning because of her voice, her muscianship, and her songs, and she stayed successful by making changes in the music she was creating—changes which kept what she was doing closer to the line the blues was taking as a popular music. She was able to continue her career for almost twenty years, and if she had not suffered a stroke at the time when there was a new interest in the older blues artists she would have been performing and recording again. She made more than two hundred recordings, and they reflect almost every kind of blues that was popular in the thirties, from love songs, to the kind of party blues that the Mississippi Sheiks and Tampa Red were doing, to a raucous celebration of Joe Louis's success, "Joe Louis Strut." But it's still possible to trace a kind of overall pattern in her blues and to follow some of the techniques that led to her large success.

A popular music—and the thirties blues had certainly become a popular entertainment form—has to be clearly identifiable and on a larger level comprehensible. People have to be able to recognize it and understand it, which means it has to be simple. But its simplicity means that it can easily degenerate into a facile manipulation of the elements that are immediately effective. The first problem for an artist who wants to be successful is to learn how to use these elements—which isn't difficult to do, since they have to be simple or they lose their larger acceptance. The second problem for the artist is credibility—what he sings has to be believable. It has to become more than a manipulation of forms. The singer has to create an impression of being a symbol of the emotions that are at the center of the forms. Minnie began by using whatever forms she found around her, and she quickly found a way to express her own attitudes through them—or to create the impression this was what she was doing. In the popular arts this is good enough. At the height of her career she had found a clearly identifiable image which she was able to project as the center of her blues. Her career faltered when she couldn't project this image any longer and had to fall back on the forms around her, as she'd done twenty years before. The new styles and new attitudes didn't fit any longer, and what she was doing became obviously forced. This pattern can be superimposed over the career of any popular artist, white or black, since it is repeated over and over again with a relentless predictability. The surprise with Minnie is that she was able to continue it for so long, and she had one of the longest and most successful careers of any commercial blues artist of her time.

At the first session she and Joe did together she was overshadowed by his blues. Columbia brought them to New York and recorded six songs on June 18, 1929. The material was scheduled for release on their 14000 race series, and the first single was on sale on August 2. It was "That Will Be Alright" and "When the Levee Breaks," Col 14439, by "Kansas Joe and Memphis Minnie," though Joe sang both numbers. It sold as well as the other blues recordings Columbia was releasing at the time. The initial pressing order was 2950 copies, and there was an additional pressing of 3000 copies, a total of almost 6000 records. A Bessie Smith record issued two weeks earlier sold a little more than 8000 copies. "When the Levee Breaks" was one of Joe's finest recordings, a sensitive, emotional song that grew out of Mississippi floods of 1927—or out of other songs written about them—and their guitar accompaniment was a raggy duet finger-picked in the best Stokes and Sane style. They got confused in the first instrumental chorus following the vocal, when Minnie changed to the subdominant chord one beat too soon, but Joe changed to simple chording and held the rhythm until they got it together again for the next chorus. As a text the song was a clear example of what Joe could do as a blues writer—and what he couldn't do. The first verses were strong and direct, though their effect was weakened by standard lines like "Thinkin' about my baby and my happy home" and "I ain't got nobody to tell my troubles to." None of the details was strong enough to give the song a vividness that it lacked, though there was a clear overall mood. The thing that was most lacking was a definite self that dominated the song. The use of common verse material and the failure of the song to become more sharply visualized kept it from being a more successful blues text. These were habits that were to follow Joe through his career, and must have been among the reasons that his career lagged behind his wife's despite his early success.

If it keeps on rainin', levee's goin' to break
If it keeps on rainin', levee's goin' to break
And the water goin' come and we'll have no place to stay.

Well, all last night I sat on the levee and moaned
Well, all last night I sat on the levee and moaned
Thinkin' about my baby and my happy home.

It if keeps on rainin' levee's goin' to break
If it keeps on rainin' levee's goin' to break
And all these people will have no place to stay.

Now look here, mama, what am I to do
Now look here, mama, tell me what I can do
I ain't got nobody to tell my troubles to.

I works on the levee, mama, both night and day
I works on the levee, mama, both night and day
I ain't got nobody to keep the water away.

Oh cryin' won't help you, prayin' won't do no good
Oh cryin' won't help you, prayin' won't do no good
When the levee breaks, mama, you got to move.

I worked on the levee, mama, both night and day
I worked on the levee, mama, both night and day
So I worked so hard to keep the water away.

I had a woman, she wouldn't do for me
I had a woman, she wouldn't do for me
I'm goin' back to my used-to-be.

Oh, mean old levee caused me to weep and moan
It's a mean old levee caused me to weep and moan
Caused me to leave my baby and my happy home.


Columbia followed the first release with a second single several weeks later, on September 27. It was again two of Joe's vocals, "Goin' Back to Texas" and "Frisco Town," on Col 14455. They still had two titles, one of them Minnie's "Bumble Bee," but they held off on the release. Joe and Minnie had come back to Memphis, and they were there through the winter and spring of 1930, living just as they had been before the short New York trip. But Vocalion and Mayo Williams came into Memphis in February, and Mayo, with his usual commercial sense, realized that it was Minnie that should be recorded. In a series of sessions he recorded duets, with both of them singing and playing, and also songs of Minnie's, including her "Bumble Bee." The first thing he released from the sessions was "Bumble Bee" and "I'm Talking about You," on Vocalion 1476. "Bumble Bee" came out also on the other Vocalion labels—Banner, Oriole, Perfect, and Romeo. It was one of the year's most successful blues recordings, and it was one of Minnie's best known songs for several years. There were many copies of it and songs that used its imagery and its effect was wide-reaching. She recorded it again with the Memphis Jug Band on May 26 for Victor; then Columbia, realizing their mistake, put out their first version, with Joe's "I Want That" on the back of it, on August 15. But they'd waited too long, and it sold only 1100 copies, about the same sales they were getting on most of the country blues releases by this time. Minnie, by this point, had already moved to Chicago, and in July, a month earlier, she'd recorded "Bumble Bee No. 2" and a "New Bumble Bee." The song was a sexual blues, but it was fresher than most of them had been for some time, and there wasn't the heavy elaboration that dragged down the sexual blues the New York writers were turning out at the time. There was even a kind of innocence in her image of the bee as the male, the stinger as the penis, and the sting as the sexual embrace. In her different versions of it she usually described her bumble bee with a kind of loving admiration.


I got a bumble bee don't sting nobody but me
I got a bumble bee don't sting nobody but me
And I tell the world he got all the stinger I need.

And he makes better honey, any  bumble bee I ever seen
And he makes better honey, any bumble bee I ever seen
And when he makes it, lord, how he makes me scream.

She even recognizes his casual amorality—"He get to flyin' and buzzin', stingin' everybody he meets"—but it doesn't anger her.

My bumble bee got ways just like a natural man
My bumble bee got ways just like a natural man
He stings somebody everywhere he lands.

As much as anything else it was the lack of even the pretense of anger that gave the song much of its freshness. As the blues was shifting closer to white popular song it was losing some of the desperate unhappiness that had characterized the infidelity theme in the twenties. Her lighter touch had a newer sound to it.

With 1930 came the beginning of America's slide into unemployment and chaos, and with this came a change in almost every aspect of American life. The twenties and everything they represented were swept away by the lines of unemployed on the streets, by the overloaded cars trying to get out of the South to jobs West or North—anywhere, by bank failures and drought, and a sudden realization that perhaps the United States hadn't found the answers to everything. The new seriousness of mood affected the blues, and it affected blues advertising. Almost overnight the caricature drawings on the advertisements disappeared, and the singers and performers who had been part of this period were swept away with them. The stereotype of the black entertainer at the beginning of the twenties was the blackface banjo player who told funny stories; by the end of the decade it was the chorus line of the musical *Shuffle Along*, Duke Ellington, and Louis Armstrong. The blues, at the edge of this tide, was dragged along with it. The most creative artists—who were still developing their blues out of their own experience—changed very little, but the newer popular blues artists, like Minnie, were to take the blues closer to popular music than it had come before.

Mayo Williams recognized Minnie's gift, and despite the financial crisis she was still selling records. He had her and Joe in the studio in Memphis in February; then, after Minnie had done the two sides with the Memphis Jug Band and some duets with her sister and her brother-in-law for Victor in May, she and Joe moved to Chicago and Mayo recorded them in June, July, August, and October. Minnie was just as active in the first few months of 1931—she did seventeen songs between January and May. With so much recording they had to use whatever kind of material they could find, and they did instrumental duets—like the Stokes-and-Sane-styled "Let's Go to Town" they recorded in March. Some of the songs were folk-like complex songs, similar to the kind of material the Memphis Jug Band was using—songs like "After While Blues," recorded in May. They did the old vaudeville blues "I Called You This Morning" as a duet, using the same melody that they'd used for the "Frisco Town" that Joe sang on their Columbia sessions in 1929. It was in this first period of her career that Minnie was successful simply because she was talented. She was working in the accepted styles, and she brought to them a clear, sincere voice, a great sense of song structure. There was also the same freshness to her imagery. She did songs with wonderfully light, expressive humor, like the talking story she did of a pet hog called Frankie Jean that wouldn't come unless it was whistled to. Williams released it as "Frankie Jean (That Trottin' Fool)" on Vocalion 1588 in the early fall of 1930.

Minnie and Joe were both fine guitarists, and their duets were interesting. Much of what they did came from their years of playing along Beale Street, but they'd also listened to recordings, and Minnie's single string melodic leads often sound like Lonnie Johnson. Both of them seem to be finger-picking; if they're using a flat pick they're very fast with it. The accompaniments were usually in first position chords, with a lot of string resonance and an emphasis on chord root tones that Joe played with his thumb. He played the second part, very strongly and fully, usually alternating a thumb bass note on the first and third beats of the measure and a strummed chord on the second and fourth—all of it set into a frame of runs and fills that doubled behind Minnie's more melodic leads. Most of this disappeared from her style when she learned barred chords and began using a flat pick a few years later, but at this period what she was doing was still close to the kind of music she'd been going when she was still called Kid Douglas and was living with Will Weldon not far from Beale Street.

In this period she still hadn't found the kind of self-projection that came later in her career, but she did one strong blues after another. She had the vividness of detail, the sense of personal identity in her songs that Joe didn't have. A song like "Crazy Cryin' Blues," with its high "crying" melismatic passages at the end of the lines, and its hummed choruses with an almost Mississippi-style intensity, shows clearly what she could do with the blues, and it shows how she was able to achieve much of her success. The verses are tightly interwoven, the musical setting is distinctive enough to set it apart as a song—the accompaniment is a wonderfully textured duet—and the sense of her place in the song, which she achieves by the careful use of details, gives the text something that Joe's "When the Levee Breaks" didn't have—the necessary feeling of personal identification, of an immediate personal credibility.


> I been goin' crazy, I just can't help myself, uumh
> I been goin' crazy, I just can't help myself, uumh
> Because the man I'm lovin', he loves that someone else.
>
> (The second verse is hummed as a kind of crying chorus.)
>
> I was locked outdoors, sat on my steps all night long cryin', uumh
> I was locked outdoors, sat on my steps all night long cryin', uumh
> I was goin' crazy, crazy as I could be.
>
> I got up this morning, I made a fire in my stove, uumh
> I got up this morning, I made a fire in my stove, uumh
> And made up my grain and stuck my pan outdoors.
>
> I'm crazy, I'm crazy, just can't help myself, uumh
> Crazy, I'm crazy, I just can't help myself, uumh
> I'm as crazy , crazy, as a poor girl can be.
>
> (The last verse is also a hummed cry.)


It was in the middle part of her career that Minnie was able to project a self-image that was broadly appealing to her audience. It was an image that was immediately recognizable—it was the same mistreated woman theme that had dominated the city blues of the twenties. In song after song she described herself in terms of rejection or betrayal by the men in her life.

It's hard to be mistreated when you ain't done nothin' wrong
It's hard to be mistreated when you ain't done nothin' wrong
And it's hard to love a man when you can't keep him at home.

As she complained in one song, "Tell me, men, what do you expect us poor women to do?" Sometimes she tried to hold out for small favors:

I'm so glad that I ain't nobody's fool
I'm so glad that I ain't nobody's fool
If I give you a dime of my money you sure got to come under my rule

but usually her mood was of simple resignation:

It keeps me thinkin' and wonderin' all day time
It keeps me thinkin' and wonderin' all day time
Oh, people, it's so hard to please that man of mine. . . .

Last night he started a argument
He dared poor me to grunt
Then taken my last dollar
To get his girl friend drunk
That keeps me thinkin', wonderin' all day time
Oh, people, it's so hard to please that man of mine.

She was successful in projecting the sense of identity with her audience by her usual concern for small details that made the songs identifiable and by the sincerity of her own singing. Also the modesty of her accompaniments kept the feeling of shabby poverty that was the social context for what she sang. But it's also true that this was a self-image that she put on and off when she needed it. It's with performers like Minnie—as it was in the twenties with singers like Maggie Jones and Sara Martin—that the whole concept of the blues as a poetic, expressive art form breaks down. The blues she sang all through the thirties had little to do with the life she was living. She was a handsome, talented woman, with a successful career and an open enjoyment of the things of life she found around her. She made a comfortable living for the Depression years and she lived well in Chicago. Her marriage did end with Joe McCoy, but she didn't have the series of drab affairs that she described in her songs. The image which she projected of herself, however, was poor, often alone, often resentful—sometimes even pathetic in her need for affection.

This same love dream come a tippin' through my room
Same love dream come a tippin' through my room
I got a letter from my dad say he'll be home soon.

It was this use of material that came from a common store of accepted attitudes that characterized the blues as popular music rather than folk expression. She lightened  the image with a number of blues that expressed her pleasure with sexuality, and she responded to the lighter emotional mood of the thirties with a less tragic view of what was happening to her. She was resigned, but she could live through it. When she talks about an unfaithful lover in one of her more popular blues, she doesn't say that she's going to shoot him or throw herself in the river and drown. She simply shrugs and says, 'I'll hide my shoes somewhere near your shirttail." But her projection of this imagined self—this persona that she centered her blues around—was skillfully done. She was contintinually able to find verses with a newness and a freshness. It was her old skill with details and her sense of the verse image that somehow tied it together. In some of the blues the persona was so dominating that she even anticipated the situation and prepared for her lover to leave before he'd finally gone.

> Across the hill I built a lonesome shack
> Across the hill I built a lonesome shack
> So when my good man quit me I wouldn't have to beg him back.

She went on from this verse—which was almost self-defeating in its determination to avoid being defeated—to develop the other emotional suggestion in the verse—that she was going to find her way out of the situation with some degree of pride intact. She " . . . wouldn't have to beg him back."

> In the southeast corner that's where I put my cold iron bed
> In the southeast corner that's where I put my cold iron bed
> So when he put me out, have someplace to lay my head.

The whole determination to build some kind of place where she could get away does have a feeling of determination and pride to it, and the sudden detail "southeast corner" has a feeling of resourcefulness about it. She knows what she's doing.

> Buy my groceries and my stove where they are sellin' cheap
> Buy my groceries and my stove where they are sellin' cheap
> So when he starts beatin' me have some place to cook and eat.

The success of a blues text like this, of course, lies in its other levels of meaning. Most of the people who listened to her records were living, as she was, in cities; they certainly weren't going to build cabins anywhere, and most of them probably couldn't have pointed out a room's southeast corner in the slum tenements where they were living. But all of this was only an emotional metaphor for the deeper meaning, which was that a woman doesn't need to be helpless, that she can have her own strengths. Even if it's only a fantasy, she can retreat from the ugliness she can't get away from in her own life.

As a musician Minnie had changed considerably from the days when she had played along Beale Street. She learned to use barred chords, with their tighter, more choked sound, and she played a kind of suggested "swing" beat, a straight four chords to the measure with some emphasis on the off beat. It was much closer to the kind of rhythm that the popular black music had moved into, and it certainly helped her prolong her career. What she was playing was still danceable, even with the popularity of the new steps like the Lindy that came in in the mid-thirties. She did her first records without Joe in January 1935, and she recorded without a steady second guitarist until she married Ernest Lawlars, "Little Son Joe," and began recording with him in February 1939. In the four years that she was working alone she used a number of accompanists for her sessions. There were some brilliant piano from Black Bob, who did the instrumental solo on "Joe Louis Strut" in August 1935. Will Weldon— who was in Chicago now and beginning his successful career as Casey Bill— worked with her on steel guitar in October 1935 when she did four songs for Bluebird the same day he was in the studio. There's a second guitar on one of the songs he did, "Your Wagon's Worn Out Now," and it's probably Minnie.

For a brief period she experimented with small instrumental groups as accompaniment. The commercially oriented blues she was doing followed the trends in rhythm and accompaniments, even if the songs were left pretty much unchanged. Washboard Sam started recording not only with Big Bill on guitar and Black Bob on piano, but with an added clarinet, Arnett Nelson. The session was in June 1936. Five months later Minnie used a trumpet, along with Black Bob and a string bass player, for a session. At his next large group of sessions, in January 1937, Big Bill was using a trumpet also. It wasn't jazz, with the new instruments, but it wasn't as close to the blues as the simpler accompaniments had been. Even Casey Bill worked with a larger group for his sessions in the spring of 1937. The sophistication of the horns—despite the weakness of the trumpet player Minnie used—tended to work against the image that she, and the others, had been slowly building, and she stopped using heavier accompaniments after a session in December with Blind John Davis on piano, Arnett Nelson, clarinet, and a strong bass player. For her next sessions, in June 1938, she still had a piano and bass, but Charlie McCoy played mandolin. When she started recording in February 1939, she was with Little Son Joe, and they worked together for the next ten years.

There was a lot of recording during the entire period. The record industry was slowly pulling itself out of the worst of the Depression. It wasn't so much that there was more money anywhere—it was just that the companies, by price cutting, by placing records in corner variety stores, and by emphasizing more commercial material, had found new ways to get at what there was. If an artist, like Minnie, was selling, then they made sure there was always a new Memphis Minnie record for a customer to buy. Her Vocalion releases had been priced at 75 cents at the beginning of the thirties, but in 1935 they were selling for 35 cents, and everything she'd recorded for them was available. Between 1934 and the recording ban in 1942, there was a new Memphis Minnie record in the shops almost every month. Minnie wasn't getting rich from it—she was paid only $12.50 for every side she did—but there were some royalties from her compositions, and all the attention she was getting from the records kept her working steadily as long as she felt like playing. With this kind of pressure to turn out songs, all of the major artists of this period began to sound like each other as they went in and out of the studios with the same accompanists, and often the same kind of material, month after month. Minnie was the only woman with this kind of popularity, although Decca had Georgia White, who played the piano and had some of Minnie's success.

In 1941, after twelve years of recording, Minnie had another big success, like the "Bumble Bee" that had started everything off for her in 1929. She did a little song with a delayed verse form—a kind of sexual tease that suggested more than it actually said when she finished the verse. It was her "Me and My Chauffeur Blues," which she recorded on May 21, 1941. It was released with Can't Afford to Lose My Man" on OKeh 06288. She was still with the same record company, but the labels were being shifted, and her releases had been coming out on Okeh since the previous year. "Me and My Chauffeur" kept her career going for another ten years. It could have been the simplicity of the song that helped sell it, since it dealt with things like her not wanting her chauffeur to be riding those girls—which finished as riding those girls around—and was instantly memorable and earthily funny.

The melodies Minnie used for most of her blues in the 1934 to 1941 period, when she did much of her recording, were much simpler and less varied than the country song forms she and Joe had worked from in their first sessions. She still used the old "Sitting on Top of the World" melody—others turned up from time to time—but she'd stopped using the songs with repeated final refrains that she liked early in the thirties. Instead she was into a rather straight blues that was completely regular in its rhythm and harmonic changes. She used it over and over again, or with slight variations, for blues after blues. As always, with any artist who has recorded a great deal, there was considerably more variety in the texts than there was in the melodies.

With her warm, open voice, and the steady musicality of her guitar playing, she was able to bring a personal sense of identity to it. It was everybody's blues during these years, but Minnie could make you think, as long as you were listening to the record, that it was her blues, and she was still capable of recording songs that were as close to her own beginnings as songs she'd recorded back in Memphis with Kansas Joe.

> I was born in Louisiana
> I was raised in Algiers
> And everywhere I been the peoples all say
> "Ain't nothin' in ramblin', either in runnin' around"
> Well I believe I'll marry, oh Lord, and settle down.

And occasionally she even allowed herself a larger comment on the social situation around her.

> The peoples on the highway
> Is walkin' and cryin'
> Some is starvin', some is dyin'
> Ain't nothin' in ramblin', either in runnin' around.
> Well I believe I'll marry, oh Lord, and settle down.

In a large measure she deserved the success she had in her years living in Chicago.

She probably would have been able to pick up her career again after the blues revival began in the mid-fifties, but her husband, Ernest Lawlers, had a heart attack in 1957 and he had to stop playing. They went back to Memphis and she played occasionally around the city, but she wasn't well herself, and she didn't want to be away from him for long trips. She suffered a stroke in 1960; then he died a year later, leaving her in the care of her sister. She spent some time in a nursing home, in poverty and relative obscurity, even though there were friends in Memphis who were still in touch with her. Chris Strachwitz, of Arhoolie Records, reissued a number of her early recordings and was able to get royalties to her from the sales. The income helped her both financially and psychologically. When she suffered a third stroke she was moved from the nursing home back to her sister's house, and it was there that she died on August 7, 1972. She had outlived nearly all her contemporaries and, of all the musicians she had known and sang with along Beale Street, only Furry Lewis was there for the funeral. It was another reminder that the last days of the old Memphis blues styles had come after so many years of rich excitement and variety.

# Atlanta

Atlanta.

# 10.
# Atlanta

Sometimes, driving through the rolling hill land to get to Atlanta, it seems difficult to believe that the city will be there. There doesn't seem to be any reason for one of the South's major metropolitan areas to be sprawled in this scrub forest on the bank of the Chattahoochee River in north-central Georgia. The Chattahoochee isn't a major river, the city isn't close to any important mineral resources, and there's no feeling of the geography of the land leading you to any kind of natural site. The trees on the rolling hills north of the city suddenly thin out, the houses of the first suburbs begin to line themselves alongside the highway; then the density of houses and cars thickens and you're in Atlanta. Of all the cities in Georgia that could have been important, it would seem that Savannah, on the Atlantic, and on the Savannah River, would have been the state's dominant city, but Savannah is almost a backwater, hot and sticky and a little crowded in the summers, quiet and a little out of the way in the winters.

Even with the relentless efficiency of modern highways and newer train systems, geography still holds some kind of sway over us, and Atlanta's position perhaps reflects a little of this. It feels, as you come to Atlanta, as if you've been hugging the edge of the Appalachian Mountains. If you want to go west from the coastal states, the mountains push you away, and if you want to go east from the southern countryside of Alabama or Mississippi, the lower lip of the mountains holds you off. Atlanta is a kind of corner— a place where you can turn. As you come down from the Carolinas on your way to New Orleans or Jackson, Atlanta is the place where you swing from the eastern slope of the mountains down to the southern hill country. If you're on a train coming east from Birmingham on your way to Richmond you'll be routed through Atlanta to get under the mountains. The mountains are more easily crossed now—the roads are better and the train systems service the whole mountain area—but Atlanta was built in an earlier period, and it has kept its position and grown and stretched itself into the South's most modern and prosperous city.

Atlanta, in its central city, isn't much larger than Memphis. Each of them has about half a million people. Atlanta, however, is the center of a large suburban area, and its total population is closer to a million. Outside of Memphis, you're into the red earth/timber/farm country before you've gone too far. Around Atlanta you're still in the suburbs. Also, Atlanta's period of growth came later; so it's a more modern city. But as musical centers, both of them were small, and there was no center of recording or musical activity for either of them. Each of them had a theater that was important to the black community—the Palace on Beale Street and the Bailey Theatre on Decatur Street, the center of Atlanta's black neighborhood. The theaters brought them into contact with the touring reviews and stage shows, as well as using local talent for occasional presentation, but the recording companies came through only on an irregular basis. The musicians themselves, in both cities, came in from the surrounding countryside. Memphis had the Mississippi Delta to draw upon for its bluesmen, so there was a clearer definition of sources for much of the music recorded in Memphis. Atlanta, in contrast, seemed to be centered in an area without a dominant rural style; so the blues recorded there seems only fitfully to glimpse back to an earlier songster or work song tradition.

This doesn't mean that Decatur Street, sloping down into the lowland off Peachtree Street, with its line of shabby storefronts and barbershops, had no local blues style. The Atlanta singers were distinctive in everything they did, from the way they played the guitar to the way they conceived blues rhythms to they way they sang, but it seems to be a tradition developed more in the back streets in Atlanta and influenced by the phonograph record in a way the Memphis tradition was not. This seems to be most clearly reflected in the rhythmic pulse, which in the blues of other areas is closely related either to a songster tradition or to the work and gang songs. The Atlanta musicians often used a kind of strumming that had no clearly defined rhythmic character. The older ones, like Peg Leg Howell, were closer to a folk orientation, and some of Howell's best blues were half-remembered songs from the earlier period, and he used a number of finger-picking styles, as well as the strumming beat. Also his recordings with his "Gang," a loose street group in the eastern skiffle tradition, had some of the rough exuberance of the country dance. It's in the singing of the younger men, such as Barbecue Bob (Robert Hicks), that the lack of a strong relationship to a larger area style is seen most. This didn't affect his popularity in any way, and he was one of the most successful bluesmen of the period, but it does seem to hem in his creativity at moments. The Atlanta style is a fascinating hybrid of irregular chantlike rhythms and uniquely personal harmonic and structural forms. It is perhaps best typified by Robert Hicks, but other singers, less well known, such as Willie Baker and Curley Weaver, could sing in the style with considerable effectiveness, and their "Atlanta-styled" numbers, such as Baker's "Weak Minded Blues" or Weaver's "No No Blues"—probably learned from Hicks—are distinctively part of the blues along Decatur Street.

There also seemed to be a predilection for the twelve-string guitar in Atlanta, which also is unusual in rural blues since it's very difficult to choke the third string for the kind of modal tonalities that are common in blues from other areas. The harmonic forms are generally derived from the urban twelve-bar form, though often there is a distinct pause at the vocal phrase ending, emphasizing the harmonic change, and often there are unrelated tones included in the chord grouping. The vocal tone is generally very strong and somewhat low in pitch, the sound coming from the back of the mouth with the throat rather tight. It isn't one of the prettiest vocal sounds in the blues, but it has a harsh effectiveness against the twanging tone of the twelve-string. The vocal scale has many elements of the urban blues scale—that is, with a conscious use of the flatted third and the flatted seventh tones—but often the voice treats the third as a more neutral tone, with its modality more ambiguous. The mode is closer to the white scale of much Southern singing and may reflect a closer musical relationship between the races at the point when the vocal style was forming. This tonal ambiguity, set against the irregular phrase rhythm of the voice, and the hard, rough vocal tone contrasting with the doubled jangling of the guitar's upper strings are the dominant elements of the Atlanta style, and for a brief period, because of Hick's popularity, the style became rather widely known.

It was such a unique style, however, and so closely identified with a local area, that it didn't have a long life, and it has almost completely been lost, even in Atlanta itself. Some of the vocal intonation is still there in Atlanta singing, and sometimes there's some of the old twanging strum, but it's the Piedmont guitar style that's dominant throughout the area—or at least dominant to the extent that traditional blues survive at all in Atlanta. It's now a modern city, rushing into the new American future, and it doesn't seem to be a future that includes the older blues.

As in Memphis, the character of the recording done in Atlanta reflects the personality of the recording director who was most responsible for that recording. In Memphis it was Ralph Peer; and in Atlanta it was Columbia's recording director, Frank Walker, who most shaped the picture we have of Atlanta's music. Walker was interviewed by Mike Seeger in 1962, and, although he didn't have detailed recollections of the recordings he did there, his answers suggested some of the attitudes he brought to his sessions. Walker, unlike Peer, was born in the country, on a farm in Fly Summit, New York, and his father died when he was six, forcing the widow to put him with another family. He worked as a farmhand until he was eighteen; then he went into Albany to a business college to learn shorthand stenography and later worked as a secretary to the president of a local bank. He worked other jobs, moved to New York City, then was in the Navy from 1916 to February 1919. He found himself in the record business a few months later, mostly by accident. As he told Seeger:

> *Well, it so happened when you got out of the service in those days there was very little happening in the line of work. My concern was liquidated. There were no jobs available. Soldiers and sailors were selling apples on the streets of New York and all over the country. There were no such things as jobs. I had offered my services for as low as fifteen dollars a week. I couldn't find a job.*

*So finally one day I happened to run into a man on the street whose name was Frances S. Whiten. He was a Commander in the Navy, a position above mine, and I had done something that he had admired very much that had gotten him written up in the Congressional Record. He asked where I was working and I said, "I wish I were."*

*"Well," he said, "I am a nephew of the Duponts and we own Columbia Phonograph and Dictaphone Corporation and you're coming over and work for me." I said, "I don't know anything about a phonograph record," and he said, "Neither do I, so you can be my assistant."*

He trained in Columbia's Bridgeport factory, then left Columbia for a brief period to run a concert management agency in Detroit. In 1921 he was back at Columbia and ready to begin his work as an artist and repertory director. As he told Seeger, he first went into the South with portable equipment in the twenties largely because of his "first love" for country music. Columbia began their 15000 white folk music series to accommodate the material he was bringing back with him. At the same time, as he didn't tell Seeger, he had become one of the most important figures in the blues recording industry, and artists he worked with included Bessie Smith, most of the other major urban blues artists of the period, and jazz artists ranging from King Oliver to the New Orleans Owls. Clarence Williams, who was an assistant of Walker's during some of this period, recalled that he had almost complete freedom in his choice of artists and recording. The Columbia race series, the famed 14000 series, began in November 1923—first it was a 13000 series but, after eight releases, worry over the implications of the number 13 induced Columbia to change the numbering. For the next ten years Walker was recording for both series, the country and the race series, on regular trips through the South.

*. . . As business grew, we made periodical trips to the South and at least two trips a year. We had a rather bad time of it if we recorded less than two hundred masters on each trip. Now, not all of these found the market. It's not like today, with the taping and so forth. In those days the recording was done on solid wax and you had to bring containers of the waxes you used. So you were very careful and choosy. . . .*

Walker sent word ahead to local distributors or retailers who were working with him as scouts, and they got out word to any musicians in the area that Columbia's unit would be in town to record. Walker himself made all decisions on both artists and their repertoire, unlike Paramount, which often let their scouts send the artists on to Chicago, where the decisions were made. He worked, roughly, on an alternating weekly basis, recording country artists one week, then black artists the next, though sometimes the two necessarily overlapped. About Atlanta he remembered, in his interview with Seeger:

*We recorded in a little hotel in Atlanta, and we used to put the singers up and pay a dollar a day for their food and a place to sleep in another little old hotel. And then we would spend all night going from one room to another, and they kept the place hopping all night in all the different rooms that they were in. You would have to go from one room to another and keep your pen working and decide we won't use this and pick out the different songs that they knew, because you couldn't bring songs to them because they couldn't learn them. Their repertoire would consist of eight or ten things that they did well, and that was all they knew.*

*So, when you picked out the three or four that were best in a man's so-called repertoire you were through with that man as an artist. It was all. It was a culling job, taking the best that they had. You might come out with two selections or you might come out with six or eight, but you did it at that time. You said goodbye. They went back home. They had made a phonograph record, and that was the next thing to being President of the United States in their mind.*

*Then, out of it, there were a very few who could learn or could adopt something that somebody else might be able to do but not record. So you might put those two together, so that one might be able to teach the other and you came up with a saleable or recordable product. . . .*

Walker came to Atlanta to record his country artists, such as Riley Pickett and Gid Tanner and the Skillet Lickers. These were the names he remembered from the artists he worked with there, and the things he'd recorded that he remembered best were the raw country vaudeville sketches like "Corn Likker Still in Georgia" that he wrote for them with a man working at the Atlanta radio station, Dan Hornsby. They were broad, obvious, rural humor, and they sold, as Walker remembered, ". . . in the hundreds of thousands." Nothing he did with his blues artists was as successful, even though the artists he recorded included Peg Leg Howell, Barbecue Bob, Charley Lincoln, and Blind Willie McTell. The Atlanta blues that we have on record are—to a large degree—the material he decided to record on those long nights before the sessions when he tried to "cull" what would sell best. Perhaps this, as much as any other factor, has shaped the musical picture that emerges of the Atlanta bluesmen.

# 11.
# Peg Leg Howell

Of all the voices from Atlanta in the twenties, the one that seems to come out of the oldest tradition—the one that seems most closely tied to a half-forgotten, quietly introspective music from the farm cabins and the still crossroads—is Peg Leg Howell. He was the the first country bluesman to be recorded for Columbia's race catalog, and there was something in his music that was deeply entwined with the Georgia countryside, with its soft sunlight and hazy sky and lingering summers. In the fifties on trips to Atlanta, it didn't seem possible that he could still be living, and questioning people along Decatur Street was sourly discouraging. But people in a hard, poor neighborhood can be silent with a stranger, until they have some idea what he's asking about. A man would stop and think a minute. "Yes, I 'member that old man, but he hasn't been 'round here for a long time." But by the sixties the interest in the older blues had spread even to Atlanta. Three young enthusiasts, George Mitchell, Roger Brown, and Jack Boozer, stopped in one of the noisy, crowded barbershops on Decatur Street where the response in 1958 had been only guarded stares. As Mitchell wrote later, in the notes to an album of Howell's blues:

> *When we stopped at Shorters' Barber Shop, one of the oldest establishments on Decatur Street, we decided to ask about additional blues singers as well. After mentioning Peg Leg Howell, ten men gathered around us offering to lead us to him.*

> *Finally after the confusion had subsided and we had gotten over our shock, we picked two of the men to take us to Howell. We rode about a mile past Capitol Square, turned into a dirt road and pulled up in front of Howell's small and shabby house. Our guides were knocking loudly on the door when we heard the faint voice of a very old man telling us to come in. The house was dark and musty, but the moment I saw Howell sitting in his wheelchair in the back room,*

*I recognized him from his pictures. He appeard to be very old, was unshaven, and had no legs. Just seconds after I introduced myself, he eagerly reached for the guitar I was holding. He took it in his large, worn hands and immediately began singing and playing. He sang in a deep, moaning, almost inaudible voice, but we could still make out the words:*

> *Some folks say them worried blues ain't bad,*
> *Yes, some folks say them worried blues ain't bad,*
> *But they's the worst old feeling that ever I had. . . .*

Peg Leg—his real name was Joshua Barnes Howell—was seventy-five when he was found again in Atlanta, and the years of lonely poverty had left their mark. After a month of practicing with the guitar he recorded again in an Atlanta studio, but the music was only fitfully reminiscent of what he had created thirty-five years before. Of greater importance was the opportunity to learn more from him about the early period of Georgia music. As he told Mitchell:

*. . . I was born on the fifth of March in 1888. I was born in Eatonton, Putnam County, Georgia. I am 75 years old.*

*My father was a farmer. When I was a child I went to school in Putnam County; I went as far as the ninth grade before I stopped. After that I worked on my father's farm with him . . . plowed. Worked on the farm until 1916, when I was about 28.*

*Then I worked at a fertilizer plant in Madison, Ga., on the Georgia Road to Augusta. I had lost my leg in 1916 and had to quit farm work. I got shot by my brother-in-law; he got mad at me and shot me. That's how I lost my leg. I worked at the fertilizer plant for a year. After that I didn't do much, just messed around town. I came to Atlanta when I was about 35 years old. I just got tired of staying in a small town. I didn't do much of anything in Atlanta when I came there either.*

*I learned how to play the guitar about 1909. I learnt myself—didn't take long to learn. I just stayed up one night and learnt myself.*

*The men from Columbia records found me there in Atlanta. A Mr. Brown—he worked for Columbia—he asked me to make a record for them. I was out serenading, playing on Decatur Street and he heard me playing out on the street. This was around 1927, I think, but it could have been earlier.*

Peg Leg Howell (right) and his gang, with Eddie Anthony playing violin.

It was probably Frank Walker who supervised Peg's first session, on November 8, 1926, during one of his visits to Atlanta to record country artists. He'd been recording black artists in Atlanta, but they had been gospel groups or the popular preachers, like Rev. J.M. Gates, who had recorded for him earlier in the year. Peg did four songs for the first sessions, "Coal Man Blues," "Tishamingo Blues," "New Prison Blues," and "Fo' Day Blues." The last two songs were released first, on Columbia 14177-D. The day of release was the 30th of December 1926, and the record was listed in the February 1927 advertising supplement. It was relatively successful for the period, with an initial pressing of 5250 copies and a second pressing of 4000 copies, but the sales didn't compare with either the best of the gospel groups or the established blues artists. A record by the Birmingham Jubilee Singers released the same day sold 16, 725 copies, and a Bessie Smith record issued two weeks later sold 23,700.

For the next two and a half years Walker continued to record Howell, but his career, like his songs, was modest. Walker decided to record him with a group, and for the next two sessions, in April and November of 1927, he recorded him with his friends Eddie Anthony, who played violin, and Henry Williams, who played guitar. The first of their releases by Peg Leg Howell and His Gang, "Jelly Roll Blues" and "Beaver Slide Rag"—which went on sale on May 30, 1927, on Columbia 14210-D—was his most successful record, and it sold a total of 12,950 copies. It was a fresh, raucous country stomp, played with noisy enthusiasm, and it deserved to be successful. Peg's own songs were softer, more subtle, often tracing motifs and scenes from a country life that was almost forgotten by the new audience in the cities. He recorded by himself again on November 9, 1927, and he did his beautiful "Skin Game Blues," with its evocation of the work camps and their endless, fierce card games. There was another solo session the next spring, on April 20, 1928, where he did four songs, but the rest of his recording was with other instrumentalists. Eddie Anthony sang and played with him the next October; there was an unknown violinist for his session on April 10, 1929; then he and a friend named Jim Hill did four last songs three days later. These records were released over the next eighteen months, but there was no further work for Peg. He hadn't made much money from his music, but they'd paid him $50 for the first record, and there had been steady advances and royalties, and he had some chances to sing in the bars when the records were coming out. When his recording career was over he was forty-one, and he drifted back to the life he'd been leading before Columbia heard him on the street.

Where did Howell's songs come from? He had a much wider range of song than other Atlanta artists, and his guitar playing, despite its limitations, used a number of techniques, from complex finger-picking, to more standard picked blues, to exciting work with open tunings and a metal finger slide. On his recordings he sounded like a quiet, introspective performer, and certainly he had almost none of the sexual assertiveness of other bluesmen of the period. There is little specific erotic content in any of his songs. He could even be awkwardly self-pitying, in songs like "Rocks and Gravel" or "Please Ma'am." "Please Ma'am" has a kind of desperate hopelessness to it.

Please ma'am, please ma'am please,
Take me back, try me one more time,
Please ma'am, please ma'am, please,
Don't you want no more to take me back,
Please ma'am.

Been begging you all night long,
I'll acknowledge I've done wrong,
Please ma'am, please, take me back,
Try me one more time, please ma'am

Begging you all night long,
I'll acknowledge I've done wrong,
Please ma'am, take me back,
Try me one more time,
Won't do wrong no more, please ma'am,
Please take me back,
Try me one more time,
Please ma'am. . . .

Some of his songs seem to suggest that he came out of a tradition that was losing ground in the country areas even when he was young, and some of what he recorded has no clear antecedent in either of the area's cultures. He says that he wrote some of the material he recorded, and, since he clearly remembers the source for many of his songs, his claim to have written others has to be taken seriously, even though all of his songs have considerable cultural reference. Like many other country artists of the late twenties he was influenced by other recordings, and there is considerable eclecticism in his blues pieces, just as there was in the work of the other Atlanta musicians. Songs like "Low Down Rounder's Blues" and "Doin' Wrong" use melodic lines and guitar patterns influenced by Blind Lemon Jefferson; on other songs, among them "Broke and Hungry Blues," he tries to imitate Lonnie Johnson's distinctive guitar style. He'd been singing on the streets with a mandolin player—Eugene Pedin, who never recorded—when Columbia first heard him, and he seemed to work well with other musicians, so Frank Walker was justified in using Eddie Anthony to work with him on many of the pieces he did. There was a photo of Peg in the 1927 Columbia catalog that reflected the mood of his music. He was portly, half smiling, with a careful moustache, and—for some reason—a white skull cap. He was wearing a white shirt and tie, a striped sweater, and a dark suit jacket. The text was the usual string of clichés.

*When "Peg Leg" Howell lost his leg, the world gained a great singer of blues. The loss of a leg never bothered "Peg Leg" as far as chasing around after blues is concerned. He sure catches them and then stomps all over them.*

*Nobody ever knows just what will happen when "Peg Leg" Howell is let loose with a guitar, but it always is sure to be good.*

When he talked about his music in 1963 he confirmed that much of what he'd learned came from the country and that much of the music outside of the city was sung without accompaniment. This would seem to explain the problem some of the Atlanta singers had of relating the vocal melody to their guitar style. "I learned many of my songs around the country. I picked them up from anybody—no special person. Mostly they just sang, didn't play anything." Other songs that he did were derived from his own experience. He heard the "New Prison Blues," his first release, when he was in prison himself. "In 1925 I had been in prison for selling whiskey and I hear the song there. I don't know who made it up. As for selling the whiskey, I would sell it to anybody who came to the house. I bought the moonshine from people that ran it and I sold it. I don't know how they caught me; they just ran down on me one day." The "Jelly Roll Blues" came from a man named Elijah Lawrence, who was singing it in the country.

Of all the songs he recorded, however, some of the best were things that he wrote himself. "Some of the songs I made up. 'Too Tight' was one; 'Rocks and Gravel' was another. That's really about the blues, that 'Rocks and Gravel'. Just made 'em up and played 'em. 'Coal Man Blues'—I wrote that too. 'Skin Game Blues'—that's about gambling. Skin game is a card game.''

"Rocks and Gravel" was one of his less interesting pieces, but the last two songs he mentioned are perhaps his most interesting. They seem drawn from a large cultural area, and they have elements of urban white material as well as rural black. "Coal Man Blues" is sung to a complex finger-picked accompaniment, the guitar following the voice over and over in its hurried sixteen-measure verses. The harmony is unusual; what is outlined in the finger-picking is a repeated patter of I - IV - I - IV, I - I - V - I. The song has ballad elements, coal vendors' street cries, and blues verses, all of them somehow merging into the song's overall dimensions. It begins with a sharp image of city life, seemingly outside of the kind of experience that was part of Howell's own life.

> Woke up this mornin' 'bout 5 o'clock,
> Got me some eggs and a nice po'k chop,
> Cheap cigar and a magazine,
> Had to run pretty fast to catch the 5:15.

The next verse is related to it, but it has some of the character of a street ballad, half remembered in its details.

> Let me tell you something that I seen
> Coal man got run over by the 5:15
> Cut off his arms and it crushed his ribs.
> Did the poor man die? No, the poor man lives.

This is followed by another verse about the accident, giving a different train number and making it clear that the coal man is dead. The fourth verse is a street vendor's cry.

Hard coal, stovewood man,
Hard coal and the stovewood man,
I ain't got but a little bit left,
If you don't come get it gonna burn it myself.

There are more street vendor cries, then the song shifts again and begins to take on a blues tinge.

Sell it to the rich and I sell it to the poor
Sell it to the rich and I sell it to the poor
Sell it to the rich and I sell it to the poor
Sell it to the nice brown that's standin' at the door.

Furnish your wood, furnish your coal
Furnish your wood and I furnish your coal
Furnish your wood and I furnish your coal,
Make you love me doggone your soul.

By the end it has become a blues, still repeating over and over its breathless melody.

Let me tell you, mama, what's the matter now
Let me tell you, mama, what's the matter now
Let me tell you, mama, what's the matter now
You don't want me, take me anyhow.

The verses seem to come from such diverse sources that much of the song is clearly not original, but he has put it together with a naive excitement, and with the distinctiveness of the finger-picking it is a remarkable performance.

"Skin Game Blues" is a unique masterpiece, and in it all the things in his style that were most individual contributed to the effectiveness of the performance. The guitar is in an open tuning, and he plays the same kind of running rhythm that he used on "Please Ma'am." He uses a slide on the upper strings and the guitar plays a unison melody with the voice. The verses are richly textured in a complex structure that uses spoken interjections, a balladlike refrain, and a series of references to other gambling songs sung everywhere in the rural United States. In its overall form a verse melody is used at the larger division points in the song, and it is followed with a subsidiary verse melody that is sometimes used without the opening verse, and there is a refrain that alternates with them.

I (Guitar tuned open; accompaniment picked on chord tones.)

When I came to Geor-gie mon-ey and clothes I

had, babe, All the mon-ey I had done gone, my Sun-day clothes in

pawn, Sun-day clothes in pawn, Sun-day clothes in

pawn, lo- vin' babe, my Sun-day clothes in pawn.

After the spoken interjection "Hold the cards, dollar more, two more a half," recited in rhythm with the guitar, the singing returns with the same melody as "Sunday clothes in pawn."

Dollar more, the deuce beat a nine,
Dollar more, the deuce beat a nine, lovin' babe,
Dollar more, the deuce beat a nine.

When I (did?) the skin game last night, thought I'd have some fun,
Lost all the money that I had, babe,
Had to pawn my special gun.

Had to pawn my special gun,
Had to pawn my special gun, lovin' baby,
Had to pawn my special gun.

(refrain)
Say, you better let a deal go down, skin game comin' to a close,
And you better let the deal go down.

Well, gambled all over Missouri, gambled all through Spain, babe,
Police come to arrest me, babe, and they did not know my name.

And they did not know my name,
And they did not know my name, lovin' baby,
And they did not know my name.

(refrain)
Better let a deal go down, skin game comin' to a close,
And you better let the deal go down.

110

Spoken:
   Hold the cards, dollar more, deuce beat a nine,
   Add more, two, put up over there, nigger.

(refrain)
   Better let the deal go down,
   Said you better let the deal go down.

   Gambled all over Missouri, gambled through Tennessee, babe,
   Soon as I reached ol' Georgie, the niggers carried a handcuff to me.

   The niggers carried a handcuff to me, babe,
   The niggers carried a handcuff to me, lovin' baby,
   And the niggers carried a handcuff to me.

(refrain)
   Better let a deal go down, skin game comin' to a close,
   And you better let the deal go down.


The last verse is difficult to interpret since during this period no black man in the South was performing a police function, but within the context of the song it seems to have an emotional extension from the first reference to "Georgie" in the opening verse. It was not the kind of song that was selling to blues audiences, and, although the record had an initial pressing of 2310 copies and a second of 2000, it is difficult to believe that it was in any way possible for a recording like this to be made in a commercial context. It's performances like "Skin Game Blues" that give the early country blues its importance in the history not only of American song but also of American folk culture.


The recordings ended for Peg in 1929, and a few years later he stopped playing completely. His friend Eddie Anthony died in 1934, and he didn't want to play without him. "After my last record, I just stopped recording. Didn't make no more. After I stopped recording, I just played around town. I went back to selling liquor. Then I ran a woodyard for about two years around 1940. I lost my other leg in 1952. Through sugar diabetes.

"Through the years I have lived all over the city, moved all over. I haven't done much playing over the years until recently. After Eddie Anthony died, I just didn't feel like playing any more. . . ." There was no more recording after the album that George Mitchell did in 1963, and except for some reissues of his older songs Peg is still a lesser known figure in the blues. But he occupies a significant niche in the development of the Atlanta blues, and in his finest songs he was able to add a small, but personal, dimension to the blues itself.

# 12.
# The Hicks Brothers-
# Barbecue Bob and
# Laughing Charley

*"What you laughin' at, Charley?"*
*"Well, I done laughin' at you how you tryin' to barbecue that meat."*
*"I don't see anythin' funny about that."*
*"Ain't you 'fraid you'll get burnt?"*
*"Oh no, I know my stuff on that, I'm makin' it good and juicy. That way the people like it, you know, these days, with the gravy runnin' out."*

> Barbecue Bob and Laughing Charley,
> Atlanta, November 9, 1927.

The music of the Hicks brothers is remarkable for its lack of roots in a local blues tradition. They were among the early country singers to be extensively recorded, and over a period of three and a half years there was a great deal of recording, particularly of Bob. If there were a strongly identifiable blues style from rural Georgia it would have been evident in the material they recorded, but the sense is more of a broad eclecticism than of a clearly defined response to the life in the small farm towns they grew up in. What they shared with the other Atlanta singers was a sound in their voice, a halting, inner centering of the vocal rhythm, and the sweeping ring of their guitar playing. But even if their music doesn't have an immediate textual identity, or a feeling of a shared body of song material that they drew from—as the Memphis musicians had with their medicine shows—there is a sad, lingering, haunting plaintiveness in what they sang, and it transcended the occasional dated humor and the stiff imitativeness of some of Bob's recordings. If there is any one thing that characterizes their music it's their sometimes embarrassed, sometimes clumsy, but deep and obvious sincerity. Whatever the response was to the music of the Hicks brothers, it was music that stayed in the ear, and even if it was overshadowed by the greater brilliance and musical depth of singers from other parts of the South, their music wasn't forgotten.

Like the other Atlanta musicians, they came in from the country. They grew up on a farm in Walton County, about twenty-five miles east of Atlanta. The country is flattening as the land drops away from the last hump of the Appalachians, and east of Atlanta it's rolling country, with brush in the stream beds and a deep, loamy quality to the earth. The soil is still red-brown, but there isn't so much of the raw erosion that has gouged out the hill country to the northwest. There's a greenness to the land all year round; even when the leaves fall from the hardwoods the grass is still thick and green, and there are sprays of leaves on the spiny brush. The farms have spread over the best of the land, and the fields have been deep plowed to get the last bit of richness out of the soil. When the Hicks boys were growing up it was still cotton country, though there weren't the oppressive flat miles of dusty fields as in the Mississippi Delta. But even though the farms were smaller they were just as poor, and it was the same relentless yearly circle of planting, weeding, picking in the long months of spring and summer.

Charley was the older brother, born about 1899. Bob was two and half years younger, born in 1902. And they were close, as brothers—there's a warmth between them on their recordings together, a feeling of things lived through together. Charley started playing first, and Bob picked it up from him when he was fourteen. A sister still lives in Atlanta, where she was interviewed by George Mitchell, and she felt that Bob was the better guitar player, but Charley had a better voice. Their closeness is evident on their first recording together, "It Won't Be Long Now, Parts 1 and 2," Columbia 14268-D. After their self-conscious dialog about Bob's job in the barbecue shack and their troubles with their girls, they sing a blues together, and the style they sing in is Charley's—a difficult, irregularly structured blues, with a complicated vocal melody. They sing and play in unison, something almost unheard of in blues duets, but Bob's affection for his older brother would seem to have extended to his brother's music, and he could remember what he'd learned well enough to match the guitar playing and the vocal inflection almost exactly, in a rumbling, steamy, dark sound.

Charley had earned the money for his guitar by picking cotton, and both of them were used to hard work. Their sister said that they came into Atlanta about 1920. Bob was just eighteen. He worked as a yardman for a time, then when the Biltmore Hotel was completed he went to work there, and from the hotel he started working as a carhop at a barbecue shack in Buckhead, a rich white neighborhood in Atlanta. When it wasn't too busy he played for the customers while they ate and they took him out to play for parties when the barbecue shack closed for the night. He got his nickname from the job. He started there about 1925, and he'd been there two years when Columbia records heard of him and sent a man out to find him. The companies had only been recording country blues for a little more than a year when he went into the studio, and in Atlanta there'd been very little earlier recording. Peg Leg Howell had done four songs for Columbia the November before, and there'd been enough interest for Columbia to try to find new artists in the area.

Bob was the first of the brothers to record. He did "Barbecue Blues" and "Cloudy Sky Blues" on Friday, March 25, 1927, during a two-week period of recording that Frank Walker supervised in Atlanta. All the recording was done in a downtown hotel and there were more than two hundred songs recorded, all but thirty of them by Columbia's white artists. Bob's recording was released on May 10 on Columbia 14205D, with an initial pressing of 10,850 copies. In this first enthusiam over the country blues the new recordings sold very well; it was still a new style of blues—as far as the people buying records were concerned—and there weren't that many recordings. The record was advertised in the June catalog supplement, and there was an additional pressing of 5000 records. This was a total sale of nearly 16,000 copies of a first record of a new artist who was completely unknown outside of Atlanta. A fine Bessie Smith record issued a month later, "Send Me to the 'Lectric Chair," sold a thousand copies less. Walker was pleased enough to bring Bob to New York a month after the record was released to record again. Bob's sister says that he went to New York by train with a manager and that they wrote the first song he recorded there, "Mississippi Heavy Water Blues," on the train on the way up. It was one of the many songs about the Mississippi River floods of the winter before, and it was probably his best known recording, though its sales weren't exceptionally high. Copies of the record—on Columbia 14222D, with "Mama You Don't Suit Me" on the other side—turned up for years in junk shops and Salvation Army stores everywhere in the South, and almost all of them were gray and worn with endless playing.

Bob stayed with the well-known OKeh artist Mamie Smith, who had a large house in Harlem, and he did two sessions in New York. On the first, June 15, 1927, he did the "Mississippi Heavy Water Blues" and "Mama You Don't Suit Me " and two other blues, "Brown-Skin Gal" and "Honey You Don't Know My Mind." The next day he did four more songs, but since Walker was always looking for other kinds of songs he thought he could sell, two of the songs were gospel pieces. Bob did the blues "Poor Boy a Long Ways from Home " and "Easy Rider, Don't You Deny My Name " and the gospel songs "When the Saints Go Marching In" and "Jesus' Blood Can Make Me Whole." The religious pieces were his next Columbia release, on August 20. To keep the two styles of music separate Columbia used his own name, Robert Hicks, for the religious recording, while the blues releases were always by Barbecue Bob. The two religious songs sold almost as well as the blues pieces—there was an initial pressing of 6775 copies and a second pressing of 4000—but he was a blues singer, not a guitar evangelist, and he didn't record religious material again.

For most of the bluesmen who went north to record, the cities were too difficult to deal with, and when they'd finished with the work in the studio they went back to the South. Bob was back in Atlanta for the rest of the summer, and he recorded for three days when Walker and the Columbia engineers were in town in November. Charley also started his recording career at the same group of sessions. He did six blues on November 4, the next day Bob did four songs, on the ninth they did their duet, and the next day Bob did two final blues. Probably it was Bob who got his brother the studio sessions, since the companies always asked their artists if there was anybody else they knew about who could come in and sing. Peg Leg Howell was recorded during the same group of sessions, along with the popular Columbia white artists who were centered in Atlanta.

The duet "It Won't Be Long Now" was the first release from everything that they'd recorded. Frank Walker rushed it into the stores, and it was released only a few weeks after they'd sung it, on December 20, 1927. Whether it was the season, or the song, or just the new sound of their Atlanta music, the record was a big success. With two pressings it sold 16,750 copies, more than any other release on the race series in this period. To follow up on its success Charley's first recording was released only three weeks later, on January 10, and a new record of Bob's came out on January 30. Charley's—under the name Laughing Charley, because of the laugh he used to start some of his songs—was his "Hard Luck Blues" and "Chain Gang Trouble" on Columbia 14272D. At first his records sold as well as Bob's. The two releases in January each sold about 12,000 copies, Bob's 11,295 and Charley's 11,600. They each had a record out in April, but this time Bob's sold 14,425 and Charley's only 9300. Charley's record was later to be one of his better known ones, "Jealous Hearted Blues" and "My Wife Drove Me from the Door," because copies continually turned up when collectors went through the South digging out the old blues recordings, and most of the copies were virtually unplayed.

In the next trip to Atlanta, in April 1928, the same month they each had a record out, Walker recorded both of the brothers again, Charley on April 11— he did four songs—and Bob on April 13 and 21—he did eight songs in the two sessions. Only two of Charley's were released, one with the startling title "If It Looks Like Jelly, Shakes Like Jelly, It Must Be Gelatine," which sold poorly, only 6350 copies. He was recorded only twice again as a solo performer—once the next fall and in the spring of 1930. They did another duet together at the same time, a minstrel show recording of "coon" material, "Darktown Gamblin'—the Crap Game" and "Darktown Gamblin'—the Skin Game." It was released under their own names, Robert and Charley Hicks. It had some similarities to the kind of skits Walker had been successful with using his "hill-billy" artists, but it came too late to sell to the vanishing blues audience in 1930.

Bob had gone on to become an established artist and he was recorded every time Columbia was in Atlanta. Over the three and a half years he was a Columbia artist he did sixty titles, and his releases sold almost 200,000 copies—198, 365 were pressed and usually all copies were shipped to stores during this period. He consistently outsold every artist on the Columbia race series except Bessie Smith, Ethel Waters, and Blind Willie Johnson for the years he was recording. It's difficult to tell what he might have earned in royalties from his recordings. There are no composer credits on any of his songs, which usually meant that the performer was paid a flat fee for the copyright. Record royalties were sometimes a flat fee, but usually for someone like Bob there was a regular royalty paid, often 1½ cents a side. This would have given him an income of almost $6,000 if he was being paid this royalty. Certainly his sister remembers it as a time when her brother lived a "fast life." Columbia had posed him at the barbecue pit with his cook's apron and hat for a publicity photo, grinning broadly and playing his guitar. He had another photo taken for himself, still with a grin, but wearing a carefully tailored striped suit, a white shirt and white necktie, and a stylishly soft felt hat. He's holding his guitar, but the grin is more of assured success than it is a performer's effort to be agreeable. His face is warm, open, friendly, with deep-set, smiling eyes.

It's easier, in some ways, to understand Charley's relative lack of success than it is to understand Bob's consistent ability to sell records. It was the impression left in their music of the lack of a tradition that limited what they were able to achieve as bluesmen. The music of the black countryside was a functional music, and one of its most important functions was as dance music. Charley's music, and almost as often Bob's, wasn't danceable. They'd worked out a way to add a guitar accompaniment to their singing, but they had trouble fitting all of it into a rhythm, and the guitar followed with its rhythm, and the two halves of the music never quite came together. Bob, at least, worked out some simple guitar strums for accompanying some of his songs, but Charley continued to sing his short vocal line, then followed it with a short guitar figure that sometimes worked against the vocal rhythm. Charley was also a limited guitarist. In some of his pieces, such as "Country Breakdown," he uses two chords, but in most of his blues he only uses one, alternating two rhythmic figures at the same places in the verse. If it had been a music for dancing there would have been a stronger pulse, as there was for the music from Mississippi or from the Carolinas to the north.

Even in the vocal melody there was no feeling of it coming out of a wider dimension. Early black singing was generally in unison, and there were specific rhythmic units shaping the music. Most commentators from the prerecording period stress the communal aspect of the singing, and in most areas of the South there are still elements of the group song in the solo singing that came from it. The most conspicuous example is from Mississippi—the delayed beat of the melody, still allowing time for the fall of the axe that had measured the time of the phrase as it developed out of the work song. Charley and Bob, instead, seem to be singing almost to themselves, with the same kind of introspective, melodic sensitivity that still can be found in the cabin songs from the area. It was a personal expression, with a still plaintiveness, despite its awkwardnesses and hesitations. And there was an assurance to what they did—even if Charley was only playing a one-chord blues with repetitive accompaniment patterns he played it with a strong insistence, and the guitar's twelve strings rang out under his heavy voice. Despite the rhythmic monotony and the limited harmonic color, his performances had their own identity.

Both of the brothers were eclectic in their music—influenced by the recordings they heard and the other singers they hung out with. Bob, because he was a better musician, picked up more than Charley, but Charley often has echoes of other singers in what he does. Each of them assembled verses from other sources, instead of writing new songs. There was some originality—and often they had arresting figures in what they did—but there was little of the inner linking that weaves disparate verse material into a strong emotional fabric. Almost any of Charley's songs shows his difficulties in this area, and the widely distributed "Jealous Hearted Blues" includes almost all of the things he could do, both the aspects of his style that were effective and those that weren't. The song form is the simple narrative blues, with the first line doubled and the third and fourth lines functioning as a refrain that repeats throughout the song. The first verse is a direct, strong statement:

You can have all my money, all I own,
But for God's sake leave my girl alone,
Oh, I'm jealous, jealous, jealous hearted, see,
So jealous, I'm jealous as I can be.

But the second verse, instead of developing this idea—illustrating it or continuing it—falls back on one of the standard erotic verses used in dozens of blues from the period. It could be related to the concept of the first verse—the loss he feels is specifically sexual—but the use of a cliché instead of a verse more directly concerned with the song weakens the effect.

I got a range in my kitchen bakes nice and brown
All I need someone to turn my damper down
'Cause I'm jealous, jealous, jealous hearted, see,
So jealous, I'm jealous as I can be.

The next verse is another standard idea, but the fourth is one of his strongest, and he used it in other blues as well.

I know the mens don't like me 'cause I speaks my mind
Oh the women crazy about me, 'cause I takes my time
Oh, I'm jealous, jealous, jealous hearted, see,
So jealous, I'm jealous as I can be.

The sexual boast implicit in the verse has little relationship to the point where the song started, but it still has its own vividness; it is something you remember him saying. The rest of the song continues with overused verse material, and the effect of the song's strongest material is weakened in the context.

Charley, however, had effective moments as a bluesman despite his limitations. His voice was dark and plaintive, the rhythmic uncertainties of the Atlanta vocal style intensifying the mood of emotional vulnerability. Even in his sexual assertiveness he sounds like a man who could be hurt emotionally, and verses like the "I know the mens don't like me" are strengthened by this sense of unhappy bewilderment. There are moments in each of his blues where his limitations—the awkward guitar accompaniments, the pleading inflection of the voice, the diffuse verse structure—work to make the emotion more deeply expressive.

Bob, with his ability to use other singers' material, had a much broader range than his older brother. His sister remembers that he spent his time with the other Atlanta musicians, Curley Weaver, Buddy Moss, and Willie McTell, and he was conscious of the trends and the styles that were popular at the moment he was scheduled to record. He was consistently able to write songs like his "Mississippi Heavy Water Blues" that mirrored the mood of the blues audience. Often the texts were the same loose assemblages of worn verse material, but sometimes he was able to create a strong blues text. There was a vividness and a directness in the text to "Mississippi Heavy Water Blues."

117

I was walking down the levee with my head hangin' low,
Lookin' for my sweet mama but she ain't here no mo',
That's why I'm cryin', Mississippi Heavy Water Blues.

I'm sittin' here lookin' at all this mud,
My gal got washed away in that Mississippi flood,
That's why I'm cryin', Mississippi Heavy Water Blues.

I think I heard her moan on that Arkansas side,
Cryin' how long before sweet mama ride,
That's why I'm cryin', Mississippi Heavy Water Blues. . . .

He was a more versatile guitarist than his brother, though he played in a style
that was as individual and often as arhythmic.

Both of them had a unique harmonic innovation in the opening phrase of a
verse. In many of the songs the guitar continued to strum the chord ending the
previous verse through the middle of the new first line—then the rhythm
paused and the chord changed to a subdominant harmony, with the voice continuing its phrase. There was also a strong modal sense in much of what Bob
sang, even when it was material he seems to have gotten from someone else. It
would also seem clear that Frank Walker influenced his choice of material to
some extent—there are thin songs that seem to have been recorded only as momentary entertainment. His borrowings from other singers are often almost entirely masked by the uniqueness of his own style. A verse like

Uumh, uumh, lord, lord, lord
Uumh, uumh, lord, lord, lord
You women in Atlanta treated me like a dog

from "She's Gone Blues " has some of the assertiveness and the vocal phrasing of Willie McTell, but these elements have been almost absorbed into his own guitar playing and his own melodic forms. He didn't play twelve-string guitar on all his sessions—"She's Gone Blues" was recorded on a six-string instrument—but his accompaniment style was the same on either type of guitar. In "She's Gone Blues" there's no steady pulse in the accompaniment—only an understated vocal rhythmic unit. The guitar is almost silent when he sings, then it answers the voice in a jumping figure, alternating notes two octaves apart.

Certainly he was effective as an entertainer, whatever limitations he had as a musician. He had new songs ready for more than twenty different sessions, and he did fifty-six blues during his short career. His voice was young and rough, but with a sensitive appeal. Whatever he wanted to sing about came across on the recordings with a freshness and immediacy. He had the ability to communicate, and in a popular song form this is the strongest requirement. When he had a strong song the performance was often hard and exciting. His "Yo Yo Blues" was one of his best later recordings, and it was a brilliant train blues, the accompaniment played with a knife on the strings. There were suggestions of train whistles in the accompaniment, and the song rattled along with a hopping syncopation similar to the older jig rhythm. The verses themselves weren't exceptionally original, but the last line repeated itself in an interesting way.

> Hey Mister conductor, let me ride your train
> Hey Mister conductor, let me ride your train
> I want to clear your yard,
> Clear your yard,
> Clear your yard again.
>
> You don't let me on I'm goin' ride the blinds
> You don't let me on I'm goin' ride the blinds
> You wants to yo-yo, Bob, but you know this train,
> You know this train ain't mine.

But the last months of 1929 hit Bob just as they hit every other blues artist. As he said in the title of a blues he recorded in April 1930, "We Sure Got Hard Times Now." The same day—April 18—Charley did his last Columbia session, "Doodle Hole Blues" and "Mama Don't Rush Me." They did their minstrel show duets the next week, on April 23. There was a last session for Bob the next December, in which he did six songs. The last of the material was released on Columbia 14614 on August 31, 1931, "It Just Won't Quit" and "Ease It to Me Blues." It was as strong as many of his earlier records, although it sold only 800 copies, and sold is perhaps not the word to use. The copies were pressed and shipped, but most of them probably sat in forgotten bins in half-empty general merchandise stores around the South.

Despite the sales figures, however, Bob had a wide audience, and he would have gone on recording as soon as the worst of the crisis had passed, but he became seriously ill in the fall of 1931. He died in October of pneumonia, already weakened by influenza. His sister thought it could have been tuberculosis, and she felt his hard living had aggravated it, but it seems to have been the combination of the two diseases that killed him. He was twenty-nine years old when he died. For Charley, it meant the end of the small world around him. He'd been so close to his younger brother that he couldn't think of going on with his old life. He stopped playing the guitar and doesn't seem to have played or sung again. The sudden laughter that had marked his records—and given him his name, Laughing Charley—ended. His sister said that he was an alcoholic for many years, and a researcher working in Atlanta, Bruce Bastin, learned that he was jailed in March 1956, when he was living on Old Wheat Street in one of Atlanta's roughest districts. He died in the state penitentiary in September 1963.

Blind Willie McTell, late 1920's.

# 13.
# Willie McTell

*I growed up down in south Georgia. Statesboro, Georgia, was my real home. I was born in Tompkins, Georgia, 134 miles from Atlanta, 67 miles west of Augusta. . . . I taken up music when I were quite a child, but in a period of time I quit for eight years. After the eight years I went back to playing as I entered into blind school, Macon, Georgia. I continued my playing up until 19 & 27, the 18th day of October, when I made records for the Victor record people, and from then up until 1932 I played for the Victor people, alone, by myself. But in the period of time, in 1929, I made records for the Columbia people, changing my name to Blind Samuel, and was the author of the song "Come Around to My House, Mama," "Cigaret Blues," and "Atlanta Strut," and so on. And after then I worked with the Vocalion people of 19 & 33, takin' up odd jobs payin' you a small sum of money of $50 a week, but they was getting all the records of blues that they can. And after the period of time I picked up another job with the Decca Record Company. They wanted the blues. They give you a small sum of money, but you get paid expenses. And after the period of time I returned back to Augusta, Georgia, where they had moved the machine, where they laid a gang of blues there in the summer, in June of 1936, and after the period of time I haven't made any more records, but I have lots to be released. . . .*

*transcribed from an interview with John Lomax, 1940*

Probably most country bluesmen would have summed up their careers as laconically as Willie McTell, though they usually didn't have as accurate a memory for dates. But behind the bare outline of McTell's career is the reality of McTell himself, one of the great classic bluesmen. It was true, literally, that he always did have "lots to be released," up to the day of his death in the middle or late

121

fifties. He managed to get himself recorded, he managed to have songs ready for session after session from the fall of 1927 until almost thirty years later, when he did a last group of songs for an Atlanta record store operator in 1956. Thanks to his persistence and his readiness to get into the studio whenever there was a chance to do something, we have an almost unparalleled chance to study the whole career of one of the most gifted bluesmen of the Atlanta school.

Not much more than the simple outline he gave John Lomax is known of his early life; only a few details have been added. He was born on May 5, 1901, and lived in the country until he was nine, when he and his mother moved into Statesboro, Georgia, a small city about halfway between Augusta and Savannah. It's hot, wet country, stifling in the summers and often muggy and oppressive in mid-winter. He wasn't blind from birth, but seems to have become progressively blind in his late teens. Ed Rhoades, an Atlanta record shop owner who met him in 1956, said that McTell had suffered from inflammation of the optic nerve which led to retinal detachment. He had increasing difficulty with his sight, then woke up one morning and everything was black.

Although he told Lomax that he took up traveling with the shows after he left blind school, he seems to have spent most of his teens wandering through rural Georgia with every kind of traveling show. He was most closely associated with the John Roberts Plantation Show in 1916 and 1917, but there's no way of knowing exactly what he did, since he was probably too young to do more than help out and play an occasional number. He was in and out of Statesboro, but still seems to have thought of it as his home until 1920, when his mother died and he moved to Atlanta. As he described those years himself, "I could go anywhere I wanted then without letting anybody know where I was—I didn't have nobody to write back to but a brother, three years old—and he wasn't able to understand."

It's difficult to sort out exactly what he was doing in the twenties, but it could have been during this time that he gave up playing for some time, and he certainly went to schools for the blind, in Michigan and New York, as well as in Georgia. All this suggests that total blindness came in his teens, forcing him to give up his wandering, and he tried to find some other means of support by studying in the blind schools until the popularity of the blues in the mid-twenties brought him back to music.

For whatever reasons McTell wasn't among the first group of Atlanta bluesmen to record. Perhaps he was still out of the city—or perhaps Frank Walker didn't think he'd sell. It was Ralph Peer who finally decided to record him in the fall of 1927, nearly a year after Walker had done the first Atlanta blues recordings with Peg Leg Howell. Peer had started with Victor at the beginning of the year, and he'd made his first trip to Atlanta, where he'd done a lot of recording in the early twenties for OKeh. He was in the city in February, and then when he returned in the fall he recorded McTell on Tuesday, October 18. There were four songs, "Writin' Paper Blues," "Stole Rider Blues," "Mama, 'Tain't Long fo' Day," and "Mr. McTell Got the Blues." When Peer was in Atlanta the following year, on October 17, 1928, there were four more songs recorded,

"Three Women Blues," "Dark Night Blues," "Love Talking Blues," and his well-known "Statesboro Blues." McTell went on recording after this, and there were dozens of blues and a long series of sessions, but he never again was able to sustain the mood of creative intensity that marked these first recordings. There were occasional moments later, scattered masterpieces in otherwise undistinguished sessions, but he seemed to find a peak of expression on these two days of recording in Atlanta.

It's impossible to say why McTell's music was so brilliantly honed in those sessions. It could have been a kind of young intensity; it could have been Peer himself, who worked slowly with artists when he was out with the Victor field unit, usually recording only a handful of sides during a day's work. Songs were timed in the studio, there were rehearsals, there was a chance for someone like McTell, recording for the first time, to get the feel of what he was doing. And Peer seemed to like singers with an individual style, who gave their blues a distinctive mood or form. Frank Walker, on the other hand, liked the rough and tumble of his country recordings, and he liked noisy country humor. When Walker took McTell into the studio on October 30 and 31, 1929, two years after his first Victor sessions, McTell recorded syncopated guitar pieces, medicine show songs, and talking blues. It could also have been that Walker was trying to give McTell some kind of direction. No sales figures are available, but there's nothing to indicate that his blues for Peer sold very well. McTell was recorded only once a year and only when Victor happened to be in Atlanta to do something else. With Columbia he began to make an effort to keep up with current trends, and he went on making the same effort for the rest of his career. Perhaps it was Frank Walker who was responsible for the change, perhaps it was McTell himself. There's no way, now, to tell.

But the first blues that he did—and the occasional masterpieces that he did in scattered sessions later—what was it in them that made them so unique? For the earliest sessions it was the plaintive quality of his singing voice that was immediately identifiable. His voice was high and rather light, sounding much younger than someone in his late twenties, and there was almost a pleading quality to it, a helplessness to his phrasing. He strengthened the impression with verses that emphasized his drifting and his homelessness. In "Statesboro Blues" he begins:

> Wake up mama, turn your lamp down low,
> Wake up mama, turn your lamp down low.
> Have you got the nerve to drive Papa McTell from your door?

The second verse, where he seems to be asserting his independence and his ability with women, only makes his vulnerability more evident since he says that he's orphaned and, even if he has a woman, he's already said in the first verse that he isn't staying with her.

> My mother died and left me reckless, my daddy died and left me
>   wild, wild, wild,

123

Mother died and left me reckless, daddy died and left me
  wild, wild, wild.
Now I ain't good lookin' but I'm some sweet woman's angel child.

The third verse continues with his mood of unhappiness:

She's a mighty mean woman, do me this-a way. . . .

And the fourth suggests that whatever good things have happened to him were at some other time, in some other place.

I once loved a woman better than any'n I ever seen,
I once loved a woman better than any'n I ever seen.
Treated me like I was a king and she was a doggone queen.


All of these things had been included in dozens of blues, but there was something in his voice that made it seem reasonable that the song at least came close to his own experience. All of this was accompanied with a restless, busy guitar background, with modal elements, and a sense of irresolution to what he was doing, as if he felt he had to keep hurrying on after something.

There was the same restlessness in the great "Mama, 'Tain't Long fo' Day," played with a slide on the six-string guitar he used for the first session in October 1927. It began with him again waking up a woman.


Wake up mama, don't you sleep so hard,
Wake up mama, don't you sleep so hard.
For it's these old blues walkin' all over your yard.

The person he described in this blues is the same one that he described in "Statesboro Blues."

Blues grabbed me at midnight, didn't turn me loose 'til day,
Blues grabbed me at midnight, didn't turn me loose 'til day.
I didn't have no mama to drive these blues away.


He follows the vocal melody with the slide melody on the guitar, still picking the bass strings with his thumb. The contrasts in the accompaniment seem to mirror his uncertainty as passages played with the slide alternate with measures of finger-picking on the lower strings. In one of the most beautiful verses, the guitar picks up a phrase at the end of the first line and repeats it with a kind of emotional extension that heightens the poignancy of his singing.


The big star fallin' mama tain't long fo' day.
The big star fallin' mama tain't long fo' day.
Maybe the sunshine'll drive these blues away.

Since these are the kinds of effects and the kind of mood that Peer got from many singers, it could have been his influence that gave the music some of its quality, and certainly McTell never did it consistently again although he continued to create occasional remarkable performances throughout his career.

It was also his guitar playing that was distinctively his own in these two early sessions. Certainly he used figures and patterns he'd taken from the recordings of Blind Blake and Blind Lemon Jefferson, but he wove them into a shifting, continually fascinating pattern. He's often been described as "free" in his musical approach, but this is an oversimplification. His singing generally remained in the standard blues patterns, and the harmonic changes are the standard I-IV-V 12-bar verse. Usually the guitar part accompanying the singing was also consistent and fairly regular. It was the extension phrases at the end of the line that were unpredictable in their form, even if the voice usually came in with the next line correctly in rhythm. Also between verses he often varied the bridge material both in length and style. On the Victor sessions, where he had time to work everything out, there is a highly effective tension between the regularity of the voice and the unpredictability of the guitar, and, since everything he played still had his own characteristic sound, the musical texture that resulted was very effective. In later sessions, where he doesn't seem to have had much time, the final result was often jumbled and unclear.

The change from six-string to twelve-string guitar between the first two sessions didn't seem to make much difference in his style. He was one of the few guitarists who could handle the more cumbersome twelve-string instrument with the same ease as the simpler guitar. But there was a wiry astringency to the sound of the twelve-string that also emphasized the plaintiveness of the voice. He usually played in standard tunings, most often in the keys of C and E, and retuned to open E for the pieces he played with a slide.

During this period of his life he was one of the crowd of young blues musicians hanging out on Decatur Street. He knew the Hicks brothers well, and he was close to Buddy Moss and Curley Weaver, a younger musician who worked with him on his later sessions in the thirties. McTell was a short, slight man, about 5'8", and in the one photograph of him from this period—his Victor publicity photo—he was in a suit and vest, with a watch chain, a white shirt and a necktie. He has a cap on over his boyish face, and he has a small moustache. He seems very small and very young, and the large Stella twelve-string guitar on his lap makes him look even smaller.

After the two sessions with Ralph Peer, released under the name Blind Willie McTell, Columbia became interested in him. In 1929 Walker was in Atlanta a month before the Victor unit got to town and recorded six songs on October 30 and 31. The first, "Travelin' Blues" and "Come on Around to My House Mama," was released on Columbia's 14000 race series, Col 14484-D, on January 3, 1930. Probably to avoid difficulties with Victor, the record was released under the name of Blind Sammie, the first of what was to be many pseudonyms for Willie. Columbia's allocation system was still functioning, despite the financial crisis, and the initial distribution for the record was 2205 copies, with a repressing of 2000, about standard for a lesser known artist at this point. A month later Peer was in Atlanta and did eight titles on November 26 and 29, but only two were released, "Drive Away Blues" and "Love-Changing Blues." Columbia was interested in him enough to do another session in April 1930, then, despite the financial pinch, recorded him on October 23 and 31 in 1931. His last two Columbia releases were transferred to the OKeh label, which had become a Columbia subsidiary, and he was given a new name, "Georgia Bill."

The Columbia sessions were mixed, musically and stylistically. There were some great blues, like "Broke Down Engine Blues" and "Scarey Day Blues," there were some racially distasteful medicine show numbers like "Razor Ball," some loosely shaped ragtime pieces, and some rather disorganized blues that showed more and more influence from other recordings. Clearly there's a groping for some kind of identity, and despite the moments of brilliance there's no sign that McTell ever found it. Walker says that he was responsible for choosing what he would record of an artist's repertoire; so it could have been his own indecision that caused the recordings to drift so perceptibly. But "Broke Down Engine Blues" was one of McTell's masterpieces, and he recorded it again at other sessions over the next twenty years.

The record was shipped to retailers on December 15, 1931, but the initial pressing was only 500 copies and there was no additional pressing order. It's difficult to say whether his records were reaching any kind of audience, since sales by all artists had reached the same grim levels. A Bessie Smith recording was released the same month with a pressing of only 800 copies for a "special release," and there was a note in the files to the production department: ". . . Manufacture against shipping orders only." He kept going, though, with the same kind of gritty determination that marked his long and tangled career. He and a woman named Ruby Glaze did four party blues for Victor on February 22, 1932. They were similar in structure to the blues that Lonnie Johnson had been doing with Clara Smith and Victoria Spivey. The woman sang the first lines:

> Oh, roll me on my belly, babe, feed me with your chocolate stuff
>   (McTell answers in the background, "I'll feed you with it, baby.")
> Oh, roll me on my belly, babe, feed me with your chocolate stuff
>   ("I'll give it all to you, mama.")

And McTell finished the verse:

> I want you to keep it all for your daddy and don't give nobody none.

There seem to be two guitars playing the rather heavy accompaniments, stylistically very similar to the duets he was to do the next year with Curley Weaver, but both guitars sound like twelve-strings and Weaver usually played a six-string.

The sessions the next year were for the newly reorganized Brunswick Radio Corporation and were released on Vocalion label, although of the twenty-three songs he did only twelve were finally issued. He went to New York with a group of Atlanta artists, including Curley Weaver, who sang and played with him on some of the dates, and Buddy Moss, who seems to have accompanied him on another of the sessions. Vocalion records sold for thirty-five cents, and they had a much better chance at the little market that was left than Columbia or Victor, whose records were still priced at seventy-five cents. The pressing quality was generally poor, and the sessions were hurried, but the difference in price was enough of a compensation for the average purchaser, who had very little money for anything by this time. McTell recorded on September 14, 18, 19, and 21, and redid two of his strongest songs for Columbia, "Broke Down Engine" and "Southern Can Mama," as well as a broad spectrum of other material, including, for the first time, religious songs.

The struggle for a clear identity was even more acute than it had been for his Columbia sessions between 1929 and 1931. By this time the music of the country male blues artists had become as much a standard commercial product as the urban blues of the women singers had become in the late 1920s, and there was a need for a singer to find a kind of self-projection that related to the concerns of the record buyer. It was the need for a kind of persona that Memphis Minnie, among others, had been so successful in projecting. McTell, clearly, had no strong identification with this kind of blues. His singing, during these sessions, was pleasant and musical, but not characterized by any strong emotion, and the two guitar duets were generally a little cumbersome. The strongest influence on him now seemed to be Lonnie Johnson as a blues singer and Blind Willie Johnson as a gospel singer. Blues like "Death Cell Blues" show the Lonnie Johnson influence even in the guitar playing. McTell seems to have absorbed almost all of Johnson's characteristic figures. The gospel songs were played in an open tuning with a slide, and there was a rough power to them, but they were disorganized and too similar to the Blind Willie Johnson records that were still somewhat popular. "Lord Have Mercy If You Please" and "Don't You See How This World Made a Change" were released on Vocalion 02623, with Curley Weaver playing the second guitar and joining him for the singing.

The Vocalion labels and the various A.R.C. labels were now under the control of the Consolidated Film Industries, who had bought out the two parent companies in 1930 and 1931, and if there had been any strong response to the Vocalion releases there probably would have been an effort made to get McTell into a studio again, but they let him go to Decca, an American subsidiary of the English Decca operation, which started its thirty-five-cent blues label in 1934. Decca's recording was under the direction of Jack Kapp, who had been the head of the old Vocalion race series, and he also brought with him Mayo Williams, who'd been working with him before in Chicago. They were interested in getting as much material as possible, and in 1935 they brought Willie to Chicago, where he recorded on April 23 and 25. His wife Kate was with him for these sessions, and the gospel duets they did are even more influenced by Blind Willie Johnson than were the duets he'd done with Curley Weaver two years before. There is some possibility that Kate McTell is the same woman who recorded the blues duets with him for Victor as Ruby Glaze, but their voices, while similar, seem to reflect different levels of professionalism, and they seem to be separate artists. Kate's contribution to the records was the kind of responsive vocal chorus that Angeline Johnson, and others, had added to Blind Willie Johnson's records.

It's certainly possible that Mayo Williams was influential in the sound of gospel recordings that McTell made. They were released under the name Blind Willie, with as much of Johnson's style as possible, and the idea may have been to convince some buyers that this was the original Blind Willie Johnson. All of the companies had begun a policy of doing only a single take of each number, which also worked to McTell's disadvantage, since he often was undecided about the structure of his pieces. Curley Weaver was with him for these sessions, and—as in New York—he did some solo pieces of his own, including "Tricks Ain't Walkin' No More." On the blues that McTell did, the Lonnie Johnson influence was even stronger on some pieces, like "Bell Street Blues," which had the same kind of careful literalness that marked all of Lonnie's recordings during this period.

> . . . That Bell Street whiskey make you sleep all in your clothes,
> That old Bell Street whiskey make you sleep all in your clothes,
> And when you wake up next mornin' feel like you done laid outdoors.
>
> I drank so much Bell Street whiskey they won't sell McTell no more,
> I drank so much Bell Street whiskey won't sell poor boy McTell no more.
> I've got the cans and glasses, boys, layin' all 'round my door.

The last session also included blues like "Cold Winter Day," in the style of Memphis Minnie, and there was almost an obsessiveness with death in the last titles, among them, "Lay Some Flowers on My Grave," "Death Room Blues," "Dying Doubler Blues," and "Cooling Board Blues," the last a reference to the "board" where a body was laid after death.

The Decca sessions seem to have been as poor in sales as the Vocalion sessions, and the company didn't record him again. But in October 1940, he was recorded by John Lomax for the Library of Congress Archives in an Atlanta hotel room, and the interviews and music he did that morning are a priceless glimpse of McTell as an artist. Lomax had been told about him by friends and only a short time later his wife noticed McTell at one of the "Little Pig" barbecue stands that they passed in their car. They stopped and asked him if he wanted to come to the hotel and he answered, "Business isn't so good, I'll go along with you to your hotel." Lomax couldn't remember the location of the hotel, but, as he remembered: " 'I'll show you,' said totally blind Willie. Between us and the hotel there were six or eight right-angled cross streets and two places where five or six streets crossed. Chatting all the while with me, Blind Willie called every turn, even mentioning the location of the stoplights. He gave the names of buildings as we passed them. Stored in his mind was an accurate detailed photograph of Atlanta."

McTell agreed to come back early the next morning and record for a dollar and cab fare, and he did a variety of material, from gospel songs to folk ballads, as well as some blues and the sketch of his life. Much of what he sang probably was at Lomax's request, since it's similar to the kind of material that the Library of Congress was looking for. But thanks to the monologs, the session did give a sense of McTell as a person, and there was also the first version he was to do of his song "Dying Crapshooter's Blues." This personal reworking of the old "Streets of Laredo" theme is one of McTell's masterpieces, and this version, which seems to have been recorded not long after he wrote it, since he didn't do it on earlier sessions, has a clarity of musical detail that the two later versions lack, even though the 1949 version recorded for Atlantic Records has the best sound of the three. McTell described it to Lomax as his own composition. "I am goin' play this song that I made myself, originated it from Atlanta. It's three different marches of tunes." The tempo is more relaxed than it became later, and all the details of the accompaniment are brilliantly clear. The gospel material was similar to what he'd been recording for the commercial companies, but the whole morning's recording was a clear portrait of McTell and his music. When he'd finished he wouldn't let Lomax call a cab, saying he'd just have that more money, and he set off from the hotel walking through the Atlanta streets he knew so well.

The wartime boom hit Georgia, just as it hit every other part of the country, but McTell was forty, and his music wasn't close enough to any kind of pop style for him to work in the local nightclubs. He sang for occasional parties, worked the streets singing for tips, and often went out to the Sea Islands to play for tourists in the summers. He was still with Kate, and the local office of the Lighthouse for the Blind seems to have begun helping him during this period. He did a lot of his playing in the crowded parking lots outside the nightclubs, and he was also a regular at the chain of Pig 'N' Whistle stands.

During all of this period he and Curley Weaver were still playing together, and he was still known as a blues artist; so it was only to be expected that the new labels looking for material in the postwar years would pick him up again. Atlantic Records did an extended session with him in 1949, after their Atlanta distributor had told Ahmet Ertegun—who with his brother Nesuhi had started the company in 1947—about McTell. It was one of McTell's more interesting sessions, with songs ranging from a wonderful new version of his "Broke Down Engine Blues" to some country ragtime, a second recording of "Dying Crapshooter's Blues," and some gospel pieces. Fifteen titles were recorded, but only two were released at the time, "Broke Down Engine Blues" and "Kill It Kid," which he'd recorded for Lomax as "Kill-It-Kid Rag." They came out on a 78, Atlantic 891, under still another pseudonym, "Barrelhouse Sammy (The Country Boy)."

The same year he also recorded more of his standard repertoire for Regal Records, a small independent company operating in New Jersey. He and Weaver traveled together to the sessions, and Curley did some solo things of his own at the same time, including his "Tricks Ain't Walkin' No More," which came out as "Trixie" on the Sittin' In With label. The material that came out on the Regal and Savoy labels was under still different names, "Pig 'N' Whistle Band," "Pig 'N' Whistle Red," as well as "Blind Willie" and his own name, the last two used for gospel material. As with the Atlantic session not everything was used, and the rest didn't appear until years afterward.

The pattern that had developed in McTell's relationship with other companies— a large group of songs recorded as part of a new blues line—repeated itself again, and there was no follow-up to any of the releases. He was still singing and playing as brilliantly as ever, but his style never caught on with the young blues audience, which was looking for something with more obvious theatricality. McTell's individuality and personal intensity obviously put some people off.

It got harder and harder for him to scuffle a living. People who saw him in the 1950s remember him as a short, stocky, grizzled man, always with his big Stella twelve-string, making his own way around Atlanta's streets. But there was to be a final session. In August 1956, a young Atlanta record shop operator named Ed Rhoades was playing blues records in the shop one night and someone said, "There's a guy like that singing in the alley." It was McTell, singing in the parking lot of the Blue Lantern on Ponce de Leon.

For the next few months McTell stopped by the store regularly. Rhoades remembers that he was often drunk and that he would drink anything anyone offered him. He was still dressed with the same kind of formality he'd had for his Victor portrait, and the photos Ed took of him show him in a suit jacket and a tie. At this point he was living in a cellar in a house two doors down from the Coconut Grill. He was still playing Stella twelve-strings, and if he broke one he always got a new one. In the fall of 1956 Ed decided to record him, and he sat him down in front of a tape recorder and asked him to sing for friends. What he got was McTell's street repertoire, from "Basin Street Blues" to "The Wabash Cannonball," but, as always, there were sudden moments of brilliance, like "Dying Crapshooter Blues" and still another version of "Kill it Kid," and the tapes are an invaluable last glimpse into the world of Willie McTell, including some introductions to the songs and some information about his own life.

In the spring of the next year Rhoades remembers that McTell began to lose his voice. His wife, a woman named Helen now, was in poor health, and McTell was receiving help from The Lighthouse for the Blind on a regular basis. Rhoades lost touch with them and heard later that she died in 1959 and McTell a year later, in October 1960, though no death certificate has been found—only a file card from The Lighthouse with the word "deceased" written across it. The tapes from the session sat in a closet in Rhoades's store, with other things in a cardboard box, and he had almost forgotten about them until he read *The Country Blues* about the same time McTell died. He flew to New York in 1961 with the tapes and we listened together on a worn Pentron tape recorder in a dark apartment on West 72nd street. The tapes were sad to hear, despite the insight they gave into McTell's last years as an artist, because they showed so clearly how little he had been able to use his great blues talent in his years of street entertaining. For Rhoades they had a particular poignance, for he was suffering from the same eye trouble that had blinded McTell, and as his own sight got worse he felt closer and closer to his memory of McTell. The songs were brought out by Prestige on their Bluesville series.

Willie McTell must be regarded as one of the great blues artists for the brilliant and sensitive musicality of his first sessions and for the scattered masterpieces that he was able to record over the next twenty-five years. Like all of the Atlanta men he had to struggle with the lack of a strongly defined local blues style to give his music a direction, but in a way more than the others he was able to develop a style that was often eclectic, but at its best moments fused all the elements into a direct and strong emotional statement. The thing that's important about the body of music McTell left behind isn't that much of it is weak—the important thing is that he created a handful of blues that are among the most moving of all the early country blues.

Blind Willie McTell, 1956.

# 14.
# Some Other
# Atlanta Singers

Most of the recording done in Atlanta was with white artists, and the recording of black music tended to concentrate on a relative handful of singers, but there were occasional other bluesmen who did record in Atlanta and there were also local men who managed to have a recording career despite the difficulty in interesting the companies there. Sometimes the Atlanta facilities were used to record singers from other areas, and musicians like Barefoot Bill and Pillie Bolling were brought in from Alabama for Columbia's 14000 series, and Bo Chatman was brought from Mississippi for OKeh. Peer even brought the Memphis Jug Band to Atlanta to record in October 1927. But there were also some recordings that seem to be by men singing along Decatur Street, even though they weren't part of the group around the Hicks brothers. In November 1927, Frank Walker recorded a singer named Emery Glen, and he sounds like an older man who had been close to the Atlanta blues style. There were four sides, "Back Door Blues" and "Blue Blazes Blues" on Columbia 14472, and "Two Ways to Texas" and "Fifth Street Blues" on Columbia 14283, all recorded on November 7. Despite the reference to Texas in the title of one of the blues, there are marked similarities to the other Atlanta men. He's playing a twelve-string guitar and there's the same kind of vocal phrase, with the guitar filling out the rhythmic unit in a kind of strum. His texts, however, were a kind of stage theatrical diction—mixed with more usual blues verses.

> I got the blue, blue blazes blues, it burns all night long,
> I got the blue, blue blazes blues, it burns all night long,
> I sits up wonderin' because my good gal's gone.
>
> Smoke go up the chimney, black clouds hangin' low,
> Smoke goes up the chimney, black clouds hangin' low.
> Where in the world did my good gal go?

Papa love mama, mama do love me,
Papa love mama, mama do love me,
Mama's in the graveyard, papa's in the pen.

You will have the blue, blue blazes blues, it burns all night long,
If you had treated your good gal wrong,
Well, you can't mistreat 'em, why she left me no one ever know.


Nothing is known of Glen except for these four sides he recorded on one of Columbia's trips to Atlanta.

One of the most interesting artists to record with some of the Atlanta style in what he sang was Willie Baker, who recorded for Gennett in Richmond, Indiana, in 1929. He did considerable recording, and there were six sessions between January 9 and March 11. For some reason Gennett recorded his first four songs over and over—two of them, "Weak-Minded Blues" and "Sweet Patunia Blues," were recorded four different times—so there were only eight blues, but they are an interesting musical group. "Weak-Minded Blues" was almost pure Hicks— with the same halting rhythms and vocal phrasing that made Barbecue Bob's records so distinctive, even though Baker was singing verses that had been done earlier by singers like Blind Lemon Jefferson, including the well-known "I wonder will a matchbox , mama, hold my dirty clothes. . . ." Something like "Rag Baby," on the other hand, was an older eight-bar blues with almost a sentimental minstrel show harmonic form and a kind of sentimental text, using only bits of phrases like:

    I have a baby,
    You have a baby,
    I ain't got no baby now.

And this was played with a kind of early finger-picking style that gathered momentum as he hurried through it.

Walker had recorded Eddie Anthony with Peg Leg Howell's gang and even had him sing on some violin/guitar duets Howell and Anthony did together in 1928, but Anthony appeared under his own name—at least as Macon Ed—on OKeh, recording with titles like "Tantalizing Bootblack" and "Warm Wipe Stomp." Since OKeh was under the general umbrella of Columbia at this time, the sessions may have been supervised by Walker, and the Tampa Joe, who played guitar with Macon Ed on the sessions, could even have been Howell, though there isn't a great stylistic similarity between these duets and the solo records Howell was doing at this time.

There were also younger men who were part of the scene, and their recording careers began later, among them Buddy Moss, who became one of the most important figures in the development of the Piedmont blues; the harmonica player Eddie Mapp, who recorded with Curley Weaver; Fred McMullen, who went on to New York to record with Weaver and Ruth Willis in January 1933;

and Weaver himself, who was a close friend of Blind Willie McTell's and had a lengthy recording career of his own. Little is known of McMullen, and Mapp was found murdered in an Atlanta street in 1931, at the age of twenty. Weaver began his career under the shadow of Barbecue Bob, and his first session, for Frank Walker, included a "No No Blues" that was very close, stylistically, to what Bob Hicks was doing.

It isn't surprising that they should have been close musically, since they had known each other for many years. Weaver, whose first name was James, was born in 1906 not far from the Hicks brothers and knew both of them before he moved into Atlanta in 1925. Weaver's other recordings were not so close to the Atlanta style, and he had become a Piedmont guitarist by the time he did his last session—for Regal Records in New Jersey in 1949. He was closely associated with McTell in the 1930s and worked with him on many of his sessions for A.R.C. He himself had some success with his version of the well-known "Tricks Ain't Walkin' No More," which he recorded under various names both for A.R.C. and for Regal. It was his first recording—the "No No Blues" on Columbia 14386, recorded on October 26, 1928—that was most fully in the Atlanta style, but there was a suggestion of the city's sound in many of the songs he did over the next twenty years. He was not a distinctive artist. He had a pleasant voice, not strongly individual, but his singing and his guitar playing were skillful and musical, and his music is an important addition to the story of the blues in Atlanta.

# The Atlantic Coast and the Carolinas

# 15.
# The Atlantic Coast and the Carolinas

The southern Atlantic Coast is the old coast line of North America—flat, swampy, a bedraggled stretch of trees, dunes, and mud. The coast is slowly sinking as the movements of the earth's crust pull it toward the west while the California coast rises higher behind its steep line of cliffs. As the level falls the ocean seeps into the hundreds of stream beds and shallow indentations in the shoreline, and the coast of the Carolinas or Georgia, up into Virginia, is a maze of twisting, stagnant tidal waterways and low islands. The land slowly rises, flattening across the alluvial plains of North Carolina and South Carolina, the Tidewater flatlands of Virginia and Maryland; then it heaves into lines of stony ridge, then into the raw wilderness of the Appalachian Mountains, dark and wood-covered in a sweeping mass hovering above the rolling inland country behind the coast.

The first settlements in the South were scattered along the coast—at first on the small islands themselves, but they were too disease-ridden, and the people surviving the fevers pushed their way inland along the banks of the rivers. The first Africans were brought to America to the coastal islands in 1622, only a short time after the first Europeans had arrived, and the two races grew up together in the new environment. Despite the differences in their status, they influenced each other in a complex interrelationship.

The coastal islands are still beautiful in their fringed cloak of trees and moss and the silences of their winding waterways, but they no longer have a dominant position in the culture of the area. Most of the people have left—except for growing clusters of summer vistors—and the people left from the older period have lost much of their distinctiveness. Only in the Georgia Sea Islands is there still a unique culture—the Geechee and Gullah cultures surviving from the pre-Civil War slavery period. It was the land away from the coast—which was turned to tobacco and cotton culture—that played a large role in the development of the blues, but along the coastal stretch the music had its own characteristics.

The blues of the Virginia and Carolina areas seem, in some respects, to reflect an earlier musical tradition than the blues that emerged from the Mississippi Delta. The earliest importation of slaves had been to these colonies, and the roots of Afro-American culture had been shaped here among the Mandingo and Wolof peoples who found themselves in the new world. The Wolofs brought the banjo with them—a small wooden instrument with a skin head called the halam— and the Mandingoes brought the playing techniques of their stringed instrument, the kora. The kora is played with an alternating thumb technique, the other strings plucked with the first finger, much as Gary Davis played the guitar. The last three fingers are used to support the instrument. The kora is a large instrument, rather difficult to construct, and requires a large, dried calabash for its body. Probably because of this the instrument didn't survive in the new environment, but the banjo spread rapidly and soon was played by slaves of every tribal group.

The characteristc sound of kora playing is a rather free finger picking, with a rhythmic center in the alternate thumb stroke. It is, however, considerably less structured than the later Carolinas guitar picking. This style first was transmuted to the banjo; then, as the banjo was taken up extensively by whites, the techniques were transferred to the guitar. The European bar line divisions became more clearly defined, and the stressed beat pattern became more dominant, as happened to other styles of African music when they were altered by European influence. By the time the guitar styles fully matured there was probably no real consciousness of an earlier tradition, and most of the musicians, if questioned, would have gone no further back than the banjo as a source for their style. Gary Davis, in fact, regarded it as a personal innovation and told Stefan Grossman he had learned it by listening to local piano players.

Except for the Piedmont guitar school that centered around Buddy Moss, Gary Davis, and Blind Boy Fuller, the recordings of the coastal bluesmen are scattered and inconclusive. They do point, however, to an older style that was dying out by the time recordings were first made in the region. Few of the coastal musicians even recorded in the area. Bayless Rose recorded for Gennett in Richmond, Indiana; William Moore, who was born in Georgia but grew up in Tappahannock, Virginia, recorded for Paramount in Chicago; Willie Walker, from Greenville, South Carolina, was recorded in Atlanta. Only Luke Jordan, who was from Lynchburg, Virginia, was recorded away from one of the major cities for his first session. Peer recorded him in Charlotte, North Carolina, on a field trip in 1927, then brought him to New York for a second session.

The scarcity of recordings by coastal artists probably wasn't simply because the field units missed them—though certainly many fine musicians were missed, despite the efforts of scouts from half a dozen companies. All of the companies were recording white artists in the Virginia and Carolina areas, and they would have recorded bluesmen if they'd found them. The answer seems to be that the coastal style was losing out to other kinds of music, and it was only in the Carolinas that a new style was emerging.

It is difficult to generalize from only a handful of singers and recordings, but certainly there is a unique quality to the coastal music. There was still a strong instrumental tradition, and there were many pieces that were called "rags" in their repertoire. Sylvester Weaver, who was one of the first country bluesmen to be recorded and sounds like a coastal artist, did two instrumental pieces, "Guitar Rag" and "Guitar Blues," for his first OKeh release in 1923. By "rag" what was usually meant was a medium tempo piece with a syncopated picking in eighth notes against a bass line that had many of the alternating thumb characteristics. The pieces generally were not melodic, but instead repeated their little picking patterns over changing chords, and the sense of a melody came from the progression of the chords themselves. There was considerable variety within each performer's "rags," but one of the most widespread chord progressions for rag pieces in the thirties was some variation on:

C — A — D7/G7 — C

One of the formulas used in the Piedmont area was to repeat this phrase twice, then add a bridge going to subdominant harmony:

C — C7 — F — Fm

An entire piece using this progression would be:

C — A (or A7) — D7/G7 — C
C — A — D7 - G7
C — C7 — F — Fm
C — A — D7/G7 — C


Many of the "rags" of singers like Fuller, and even of Chicago artists like Bill Broonzy, were built around it. William Moore's "Barbershop Rag" is a classic example of the chord sequence, with the slight twist of beginning his eight-bar phrase on the A chord; so it becomes:

A — A — D — D
G — G — C — C

This progression is so characteristic of guitar ragtime that it could almost be a definition of a certain kind of piece, just as the twelve-bar blues progression is part of the definition of the blues.

Most of the coastal singers appeared long enough to record, then dropped out of sight again; so not much is known about them. William Moore refers to himself as a barber in his "Barbershop Rag."

Old barber Moore on the box,
Only barber in the world can shave you and give you music
    at the same time. . . .

His Paramount recordings were done around January 1928, when he was in the studio on two different days. The first day he did seven numbers, including "Ragtime Crazy," "Ragtime Millionaire," and "Barbershop Rag." At the next session he did only two numbers, but both of them were instrumentals, "Old Country Rock" and "Raggin' the Blues," released on Paramount 12761. "Old Country Rock" seems to include elements of an even older style, and probably comes out of a kind of banjo—or guitar-banjo duet—style from the pre-blues period. It has a distinctive flavor to it and is one of the most brilliant examples of the genre. Moore lived out the rest of his life in Tappahannock and died there in 1955.

Bayless Rose recorded on two separate days for Gennett in Richmond, Indiana, but of the three pieces recorded the first day, May 24, 1930, two were recorded again on June 7; so his total output was six sides, of which four were never released. He sounds like a country songster who also knew some blues, and his singing and the texts are undistinguished. However, he did an interesting instrumental, "Jamestown Exposition," presumably named after the celebrations for the three-hundred-year anniversary of the founding of the British colony at Jamestown, Virginia. It has the same reflection of earlier banjo playing and refers to the even earlier style of halam and kora playing that the slaves had brought to the coastal colonies. It was released on the same record as his "Frisco Blues," a slide train piece very similar to Furry Lewis's accompaniment style for "John Henry."

Luke Jordan, like Rose, was a songster, but his blues had a beautiful sweetness and a kind of wry wistfulness that made them unforgettable. He was a good guitarist, but his accompaniments were kept simple, to emphasize his texts. His home was in Lynchburg, Virginia, a small city in the mountains. Peer recorded him first in Charlotte, North Carolina, on August 16, 1927, doing two blues, "Church Bells Blues" and "Cocaine Blues," and two minstrel numbers, one a version of a mountain folk song recorded by a number of people, among them Geeshie Wiley, called "Pick Poor Robin Clean." Neither of his blues was in the usual melodic pattern, but the guitar had a softly swinging rhythm, and the voice seemed almost quitely amused at the vagaries he was singing about. He was recorded again more than two years later, when Peer brought him to New York for sessions on November 18 and 19, 1929, but only six songs were recorded, and two were unissued. He returned to Lynchburg after the sessions and lived quietly there, making his living as a songster and working odd jobs.

Other singers from the area who seem to be stylistically related—such as Willie Walker and Pink Anderson, who was from Spartanburg, South Carolina, as well as Carl Martin, who was born in Virginia and moved to Knoxville, Tennessee— are more closely tied to the Piedmont school. The first of the Carolina men to record was Julius Daniels, who, Bruce Bastin learned, was born in 1902 in Denmark, South Carolina, then moved to Pineville, a small community outside Charlotte, North Carolina, when he was ten years old. Ralph Peer may have heard him on one of his trips through the area, and he recorded Daniels in Atlanta. There were two sessions, one on February 19, 1927, with Bubba Lee Torrence singing with him on two sides, and the other on October 24, 1927, with Wilbert Andrews playing second guitar and singing. Even though Daniels was still in his twenties when he recorded, he has the feel of an older songster, and his range of material went from blues like "My Mama Was a Sailor" to gospel songs like "Slippin' and Slidin' Up the Golden Street." His songs themselves reflect this eclecticism, and even his most interesting performances, like his "Crow Jane Blues" on Victor 21065, are more assemblages of other material than distinct personal compositions. His guitar playing already has some of the elements of the Piedmont style, though he never had the fluid rhythmic movement of the musicians who came later. Bastin has also located his death certificate; he died in Pineville from the effects of syphilis on October 8, 1947.

Probably the closest to a legendary figure from this early period of the Piedmont blues is Willie Walker, a blind musician from Greenville, South Carolina. People as diverse as Josh White—who, when he was a boy in Greenville, heard Walker and probably led him through the streets—and Gary Davis—who played with Walker in a string band in Greenville in 1912 and 1913—agree that he was the finest guitarist of them all, and he may have been one of the most facile of the musicians playing in this East Coast style. Walker fortunately was recorded by Frank Walker, and for once the legend and the reality bear each other out. He doesn't have Davis's flaring intensity or Fuller's irresistible swagger, but his technique is stunning. The playing is loosely rhythmic and swinging, with sudden busy runs picked with a startling assurance. Bastin took a copy of the Walker recording to Walker's old neighborhood more than thirty years after his death and found that people still remembered his playing with awe. He was born afflicted with congenital syphilis and was blind from birth. He was the same age as Gary Davis, both of them born in 1896, and came to Greenville when he was still in his teens, probably 1911 or 1912, since Bastin found a listing for the family on Elmford Street in the 1913 City Directory. Most of Walker's playing was in the ragtime style—usually in the key of C—and no one was considered his equal in that key.

Walker always played with another Greenville musician, Sam Brooks, as his second guitarist, and Brooks added an unobtrusive but solid and sensitive background to Walker's playing, leaving Walker free to play his flowing runs. Brooks was a carpenter who came to Greenville about the same time as Walker's family, and he's remembered for always having a large wad of tobacco in his mouth as he played. Both of them went to Atlanta for the Columbia session, recording four titles on December 6, 1930. Of the four only two were released, "South Carolina Rag" and "Dupree Blues," on Columbia 14578. The "South Carolina Rag" is really a little song called "That's No Way to Do," but for Walker the text and the song are almost secondary. He has four verses that he repeats throughout the record, after beginning with a partial verse referring to the guitar playing.

Hey, play that boy.
I want to tell you that's no way to do.

Asked for a drink of water, she brought gasoline.
Now let me tell you, doin' me mighty mean.
I want to tell you that's no way to do.

Talk about your gal, ought to see mine,
She's the sweetest gal in town.
I want to tell you that's no way to do.

Hey, hey, play that thing,
Hey, play that thing.
I want to tell you that's no way to do.

Music man, ain't it grand,
Play that thing, boy, long as you can.
I want to tell you that's no way to do. . . .

Walker was also a fine singer, with a warm, expressive voice, but his concern is certainly not with the text. His "Dupree Blues," on the other side of the record, is a version of "Betty and Dupree," which is more concerned with the story and the guitar playing is more restrained. Harmonically the rag was in the usual four-chord circle—an eight-measure verse of

$$A - A - D - D$$
$$G - G - C - C$$

though sometimes between the two guitars the chords are played in different inversions. It's unfortunate that Walker never had another opportunity to record. He might have had a chance to get into a studio again when the record business began to pick up, but he died of the effects of syphilis on March 3, 1933.

Pink Anderson and Carl Martin are excellent examples of the diversity of the Carolinas style. Pink was born in Laurens, South Carolina, south of Spartanburg, on February 12, 1900, but for many years he lived in the quiet black section of Spartanburg. You had to walk up the steps to his house, and if he saw you coming he usually had time to get out to the porch to say hello before you got to the door. He was a tall, gangling man with an easy personality and a skilled, relaxed musical style. He thought of himself more as an entertainer than a bluesman and, when I recorded a three-album cross section of his music early in the sixties, the songs he did for the blues album were well-known, standard pieces; the only thing really personal about them was his own warmth and his skill with the guitar. Most of Pink's life was spent entertaining with little medicine shows or at tobacco or stock auctions. He was away from Spartanburg every year, traveling from town to town with whatever show had hired him for the season. He and a friend named Simmie Dooley worked for years with Doctor Kerr's show, and they recorded together for Columbia in Atlanta on April 14, 1928. The pieces they did, "Every Day in the Week Blues," "C.C. and O Blues," "Papa's 'Bout to Get Mad," and "Gonna Tip Out Tonight," were certainly chosen by Frank Walker to emphasize the blues part of their repertoire, but the singing was in the entertainment style of the shows, with the two of them alternating verses and harmonizing on choruses. The recordings were a glimpse into the world of the Piedmont medicine show. After Simmie's death Pink worked for many years with a one-legged harmonica player named Arthur Jackson, or "Peg Pete," who always seemed to be on the road when I tried to locate him in the early sixties. Pink had to stop traveling because of his health by 1961, and he suffered a stroke in 1964, ending his playing career.

Carl Martin was only peripherally associated with the Piedmont scene, but he certainly was an excellent guitarist in the Carolina style, and he was familiar with the local repertoire. He was from Virginia, Big Stone Gap, where he was born in 1906, and he moved to Knoxville, Tennessee, in the center of the Appalachians, when he was a teenager. Brownie McGhee was also from Knoxville and they must have known each other when they were both playing in the small city. Unlike Pink Anderson, Martin is a bluesman, with a busy, insistent guitar style based on the kind of ragtime technique that was prevalent in the twenties. He recorded at a number of sessions in Chicago in the mid-thirties. He'd moved there from Tennessee in 1932. Much of what he did was in a more Chicago-oriented style, but he could also record pieces like his "Old Time Blues" and "Crow Jane" that he did for Bluebird on July 27, 1935. He was associated with musicians like Bill Broonzy and Tampa Red during most of this period, but he still had kept his roots in the coastal style.

Of all the coastal bluesmen, however, the best known certainly was Paramount's recording artist Blind Blake. He was one of the most brilliant guitarists to record in the twenties as well as a strong, workmanlike singer and composer. His style was a shaping force in the new blues developing in the Carolinas, even though he wasn't part of the local musical scene, and still is one of the most elusive figures of the early blues.

Blind Blake advertisement.

# 16.
# Blind Blake

In a way it's misleading to include Blake in a discussion of the coastal school of blues, since he did all his recording in Chicago and was closely associated with the music scene there, but his style seems to be characteristic of a whole way of playing that developed in the southeastern states, and he was clearly an influence on the musicians there. Like the bluesmen from Virginia, he's part of a regional style while still uniquely separate from it. There's still no way, however, to tell how or where his style was formed, since he is one of the handful of major early bluesmen about whom almost nothing is known. In a way it's difficult to believe that so little is known about him, despite years of patient research. There was even some conjecture over his name, since some of the composer credits for his recordings list the name Arthur Phelps, which sometimes indicates the artist's real name when he's recording under a pseudonym. In a song he did with Papa Charlie Jackson, however, he clearly says that his name is Arthur Blake.

It's especially difficult to understand how Blake could have stayed so elusive. He wasn't an obscure artist with one or two records done by one of the itinerant field units. He was one of the major artists of the twenties, and all of his recording was done for Paramount, one of the leading blues labels. Between 1926 and 1931 or 1932 he recorded more than eighty titles and worked with musicians as well known as Johnny Dodds and Jimmy Bertrand. The Paramount publicity department distributed a photo and he was included in their advertising promotion, *The Paramount Book of the Blues*. But despite all this, what little we know of his life is fragmentary and incomplete. *The Paramount Book of the Blues* said only, by way of biography:

> . . . *Born in Jacksonville, in sunny Florida, he seems to have absorbed some of the sunny Florida atmosphere—disregarding the fact that nature had cruelly denied him a vision of outer things. He could not*

*see the things that others saw—but he had a better gift. A gift of inner vision that allowed him to see things more beautiful. The pictures that he alone could see made him long to express them in some way—so he turned to music. He studied long and earnestly—listening to talented pianists and guitar players, and began to gradually draw out harmonious tunes to fit every mood. Now that he is recording exclusively for Paramount, the public has the benefit of his talent, and agrees, as one body, that he has an unexplainable gift of making one laugh or cry as he feels, and sweet chords and tones that come from his talking guitar express a feeling of his mood.*

One musician who certainly knew Blake was Gus Cannon—he worked with him in Chicago, when Cannon recorded for Paramount as Banjo Joe. When I met Cannon in 1956 he still shook his head and smiled when he remembered Blake.

*We drank so much whiskey! I'm telling you we drank more whiskey than a shop! And that boy would take me out with him at night and get me so turned around I'd be lost if I left his side. He could see more with his blind eyes than I with my two good ones.*

What little that's known of Blake comes from these years in Chicago, though a relative in Patterson, Georgia, says that he came from Tampa and played in the southern Georgia-northern Florida area. In Chicago he lived at 4005 S. Parkway, where his landlady, Mrs. Renett Pounds, tried to look after him as best she could, despite his heavy drinking. In 1929 the *Chicago Defender* reported that he'd gotten in touch with a friend, George Williams, who was managing one of the touring road shows called the "Happy-Go-Lucky" show, and he toured with them until late 1930 or 1931, when he may have gone back to Jacksonville.

As difficult as it is to understand how there could be so little known about him, it's in a way as difficult to understand his popularity. He was a brilliant guitarist, but only an ordinary singer, and his songs had no clear textual identity. He seems to have had two important advantages, one that he was so early on the male blues scene, the other that he could turn out an almost indefinite number of reasonably proficient blues lyrics whenever a session was scheduled. Like every important blues company, Paramount had to have a steady stream of records with the favorite artists recording new material every few months, so that there could be regular new releases. Blake, and the other steady Paramount male blues artist, Blind Lemon Jefferson, were in and out of the studio, recording session after session, and both of them were popular for as long as they continued to record.

Even though Blake was recorded rather early in the rush to country blues, his voice is still disconcerting. He had a careful, clearly enuciated style that had some of the flavor of the vaudeville stage. In a line like

There's one thing in the world I can not understand

144

the "can" and "not" are carefully articulated, in a manner that would have been awkward for someone like Blind Lemon and, to an extent, sounded awkward for Blake. On an occasional piece like "Blake's Worried Blues" the singing is a little more impassioned, and there's a suggestion of Blind Lemon's vocal style in some of the phrasing, but most of his blues are reminiscent of the stage blues recorded by revue artists like Mamie Smith, Rosa Henderson, and Sarah Martin. On pieces like "Stonewall Street Blues" he even breaks into the double-time "jazzy" effect that Mamie Smith's back-up group, Johnny Dunn and His Jazz Hounds, used to throw in, and he sings one verse over stop chords in the guitar in the early jazz style. For one of his blues, "Goodbye Mama Moan," he used a Charleston dance beat throughout. His harmonic structuring also showed the effects of the vaudeville stage more than it did the back country. His first recording, "Early Morning Blues," made sometime in the early fall of 1926, is a twelve-bar blues, but the harmonic form is rather sophisticated, using a I to VI progression at the end of the repeated line, before going to the resolution in the final line. The complete verse is:

$$I - IV - I/IV - I7$$
$$IV - IV - I/IV - I/VI$$
$$II - V - I/IV - I$$

The singing stays closely within the bounds of the form. He's one of the few successful artists who never took any liberties with the twelve-bar form; this takes a measure of excitement and drama away from his performance, since there isn't a sense of any emotional force shaping the style. He continued to stay close to the harmonic patterns he set up with "Early Morning Blues" and used the same accompaniment figures in most of his blues. The melodies were also the same for many of his blues and almost any verse can be taken as typical of his melodic style.

*Raise note slightly in pitch (but not enough for it to become an *e*).

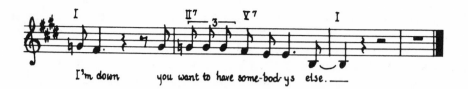

I'm down    you want to have some-bod-ys else. ___

The texts he assembled were effective, though lacking any strong individual quality. He used familiar verses, and the emotional situations he described were typical of the blues of this period:

> I'm worried now, I won't be worried long,
> I'm worried now, I won't be worried long.
> Brown I loved makes me sing this song . . .

or

> I'm goin' grab me a freight train, ride until it stops,
> I'm goin' grab me a freight train, ride until it stops.
> I ain't goin' stay around here and be your stumbling block. . . .

The uncertainties and instabilities of relationships with women were the continuing concern, and in the blues of the twenties the masculine role is almost completely passive, which could certainly be a reflection of the place in American society that the black man found himself, expressed as an almost helpless dependence on women and their emotional inconsistency. If there was an assertive text it was almost always specifically sexual, as in a song like "Hard Pushing Papa." This attitude was to change in the thirties, the newer blues perhaps in a way reflecting the beginning of a change in the way black men viewed themselves in the society. Blind Boy Fuller and Peetie Wheatstraw, who typify many of the new attitudes, both used many of the sexual boasts in their texts, but there was an overtone of self-confidence in what they were saying, even if often the texts included familiar verses. Blake, however, was still involved with the earlier concerns.

> Walkin', walkin', talkin' to myself,
> Walkin', walkin', talkin' to myself.
> Wonderin' if I die would my baby love somebody else.

A line from "Cold Love Blues" seems to express his feelings about the situation:

> Every day she treats me worser than the day before.

He usually was able to shape his material into a coherent statement, but the lack of originality often left a flatness to the complete text, and he sometimes borrowed verses from the vaudeville blues without bothering to make any changes, even if there were incongruities. One blues was clearly taken from a blues duet similar to the kind of songs that man and woman teams like Butterbeans and Susie, among others, were performing, but Blake sang it without seeming to notice that it was written as a dialog, especially in a verse like:

146

Tell me pretty Mama, where did you stay last night?
Tell me pretty Mama, where did you stay last night?
Ain't none of your business, daddy, since I treat you right.

Most of the bluesmen who used a verse with this construction usually added a "She said . . ." or a "She told me . . . " at the beginning of the final line to clarify the speaker.

But it's the other side of Blake's abilities—his guitar playing—that gives him his place in the development of the twenties blues style, and one of his best known solo pieces, "Southern Rag," also sheds some light on his own background. The solo was recorded sometime in October 1927, shortly after he did six blues earlier in the month. "Southern Rag," released on Paramount 12565, was the only piece he did at this session. The record begins with a brilliant display of what has come to be called "ragtime" guitar style—an alternating thumb bass, with a series of rhythmic clusters on changing chord harmonies. With decisive showmanship Blake delays some of the beats, anticipates others, catching a whole feeling of loose country dance and floating afternoon sunlight. Then he begins a spoken commentary that shifts suddenly into the coastal dialect of the Geechee and Gullah peoples of Georgia—a shift so easily done that it raises some question about Blake's background. Could he have spent some time on the Georgia sea islands? Perhaps he could even have some family background there—or was raised there himself—and Jacksonville, in northern Florida, was the city he'd come from last when Paramount asked him for some information. The accent is a hard one to imitate, but he seems so natural with it that it could be that it's his other accent that's not natural to him; that would explain the stiffness of his other singing on some records.

The great early black vaudevillian, Bert Williams, was a West Indian, and he had a similar problem with his speech pattern. His own English had a lilting West Indian accent, and he had to painfully learn an acceptable black "dialect" before he could successfully perform on the stage.

Blake's commentary begins in his usual accent:

*Now we're (doin') an old Southern Rag. Way out there in all that cotton fields, where them people plant all that rice, make sugar cane, and peas and so forth grow.*

Then he shifts into a Sea Island accent:

*"Hey mawn, I want a match so you can light my pipe, yeah."*
*"Go on, old Geechee, I ain't studyin' 'bout ya."*
*"No, I know you ain't studyin' me now. Soon's you get my rice though I bet you study me then. Fancy you that."*
*"(Let's get) back in the row now. I should help pick this cotton or dig potato either one."*

*"I strip more rows of sugar cane than you strip in ten years!" Now we goin' do the dawnce now they call the Geechee dawnce. I goin' give you some music they call the Geechee music now.*

The music he plays as Geechee music is a more freely rhythmed guitar picking, with less emphasis on the thumb stroke and a flowing arpeggiation in the upper strings. The Geechee people were felt to have retained more of the old African traditions, and playing in this manner is closer to the style of the older African instrumental music, particularly the playing of the kora. After the instrumental break he lapses back into the usual speech of his other recordings.

The rhythmic pattern for Blake's syncopated figures was not complex—usually a short sequence repeated on different chords. His own personal characteristic, however, was a double beat with his thumb, which he did by pulling the thumb over one string to make it sound, then hitting the next string with the thumb with the same continuous stroke. This gave the whole rhythmic figure a bouncing kind of anticipation, and his playing had an infectious lilt that was effective with everything from duets with Gus Cannon to his jazz recordings with Johnny Dodds.

He could also play a less restricted, more lyric style, and on at least one of his recordings—"Blake's Worried Blues," made at his first session in September 1926 and released on Paramount 12442—he played a solo chorus that was very similar in style to the guitar instrumentals on the records of Lonnie Johnson, who had started recording for OKeh ten months before. The solo is open and melodic, with a complete mastery of the instrument. There was this same sense of complete assurance in the three instrumentals he recorded in April 1928 with Dodds and Bertrand. Dodds, at this point, was one of the best known jazz musicians in Chicago. He was no longer recording with Louis Armstrong, with whom he'd done the immortal series of Hot Five and Hot Seven recordings between 1925 and 1927. Now he was recording with every important jazz name in the Chicago area, he was recording with his own orchestra, and he was leading a very successful band at the popular club "Kelly's Stables." Bertrand wasn't as well known as Dodds, but he was very active in Chicago, and in that city, at least, his reputation was as high.

In their trio session Blake more than holds his own. The three sides, "C. C. Pill Blues," "Hot Potatoes," and "South Bound Rag," were early collectors' items, not only for Dodds' presence, but because of the raw inventiveness and sheer drive of Blake's playing. Bertrand was a fine drummer and had recorded extensively playing the washboard, but for some reason Paramount had him play mostly slide whistle, with some wood blocks thrown in; so the entire rhythm was Blake's guitar. There was no feeling of rhythmic weakness. Blake was playing his alternating thumb style, with syncopated figures in the upper strings that he used as a contrast to Dodds' flowing, songlike style. Dodds seemed to feel completely free playing against his rock steady pulse, and it's the contrast between them, each playing at his best, that makes the records so memorable.

Some of Blake's recordings were released on Paramount's cheaper Broadway series during this period—though not the trio sides with Dodds. For these releases Paramount used the name Blind George Martin. Blake recorded steadily through the last years of the twenties, following a rough schedule of between six and ten songs in the spring—April or May—and another eight or ten in the fall—October or November. At his solo sessions he usually did several songs in one sitting. There was also a session with cornet and piano, and Jimmy Bertrand again, playing xylophone this time, in September or October 1928, when he did nine songs at once. After the trio sides with Dodds and Bertrand, Paramount used a number of other musicians with him for other releases, including a marvelous "Hastings Street Boogie" that he did with the Detroit pianist Charlie Spand at a session on August 17, 1929.

Despite the Depression, Blake went on recording, and he lasted longer than many other artists. There is some uncertainty about his final session, but he was still recording in 1932. His last recordings were released on the Paramount 13000 series, the last things pressed before the company slid into bankruptcy.

In the publicity portrait of him that Paramount sent out—the only photograph known of Blake—he looks thin and tall, long-legged and gangling. His eyes are closed, but he is smiling broadly, and his face has an open, broad warmth in its expression, as if he were pleased that someone was listening to him. As in the photograph of Blind Lemon that Paramount also sent out—which is the only known photo of him as well—Blake is dressed in a suit, his hair carefully trimmed, and the picture is taken against a bland studio background. Someone—probably an employee in the Paramount office—signed both photos "Cordially Yours" with a flowing signature. The picture, the recordings, and some hazy recollections are what we have of Blake as a person, but the bright, raggedy optimism of his guitar style was to change and develop in the hands of Carolina guitarists like Buddy Moss, so that what we have of his music is still a broad, echoing expression.

# 17.
# Buddy Moss

Cultural history is no kinder than any other kind of history, and there's no assurance that the names or descriptions of a musical style have any more reality than the names describing an historical epoch. Of all the blues styles, only one is associated with a single individual—the Carolinas school of guitar playing that's usually called Blind Boy Fuller style. Certainly calling it that gives Fuller his full measure as a commercial artist—he was the best selling of all the East Coast bluesmen—but it's hard on people like Buddy Moss and Gary Davis, who played a significant role in the development of the style and who sometimes— Moss especially—found themselves described as Fuller imitators. Moss not only was in at the beginning, he recorded earlier as well, and some of the performances that were described as "in the style of Blind Boy Fuller" were recorded long before Fuller even got into a recording studio! Moss is an angry, resentful man now, and there's considerable reason for him to be disappointed at the assessment that was made of his music and his career.

Moss, fortunately, has been found in Atlanta and is still playing as well as ever, though he has had little success beginning a new career. In recent years he's been interviewed by a number of people, among them Bruce Bastin, who talked with him in connection with his excellent study of the Southeast blues styles, *Crying for the Carolinas*. There has been some recording, but a session he did for Columbia has never been released, and the other tapes made of him in performance have circulated among other record companies without success. Only a concert recording from the mid-sixties has been released, on Arnold Caplin's Biograph label. Moss is as brilliant as ever on it, but he is still living in semi-obscurity in Atlanta, playing for occasional festivals or for small blues clubs. If he were living in New York, where there is a denser gathering of blues enthusiasts with access to magazines and record companies, Moss probably would have had more of a chance, but he's decided to stay in Atlanta, where he's lived for much of his life.

It was circumstances, more than anything else, that curtailed Moss's career. From the beginning he was part of the commercial blues world. He was born in Jewell, Georgia, on January 26, 1914, his full name Eugene Moss. Jewell is north of Atlanta, in the northern Georgia clay hill country. He was there only until he was four, when his family moved to Augusta, on the South Carolina border not far from Statesboro, Georgia, where Willie McTell grew up. When he came to Atlanta he was still a teen-ager, but he was already a strong harmonica player, and he was part of the crowd that hung out along Decatur Street, which included McTell and the Hick brothers. His first recordings were made in the summer of 1930—July and August—when he did four numbers with Curley Weaver and Fred McMullen as the Georgia Cotton Pickers. The sessions were done for Frank Walker of Columbia Records and were released on the 14000 race series. Buddy was sixteen and Weaver was only twenty-four.

At the same time Buddy was learning the guitar—he remembers getting some lessons from Barbecue Bob Hicks and listening to records by Blind Blake and Blind Lemon. He certainly listened to Blind Blake's work, as did most of the other Georgia and Carolina musicians. It was Blake who was to be the strongest influence on their own style. Buddy probably also learned from Weaver, since they were close friends and Weaver had been playing the guitar for three or four years when they met. Moss became a much better guitarist than Weaver, but both of them had the same basic style of fingerpicking.

The early years of the Depression drifted over Atlanta, and the level of recording activity dropped. McTell had occasional sessions, but most of the other Atlanta men were silent. However, when recording began to pick up, Moss began with A.R.C. The first session was in New York on January 16, 1933, ten days before his nineteenth birthday. It was a loose Atlanta session, and he was back in the studio the next three days as well, recording eleven blues of his own and also playing with Fred McMullen, Curley Weaver, and Ruth Willis, who had come up to record at the same time. His first three songs had only his own guitar for accompaniment, "Bye-Bye Blues," "Daddy Don't Care," and "Red River Blues." For the other songs there was usually a second guitarist, who was either McMullen or Weaver, though he finished the final session playing alone. In his discussion of Moss's first sessions, Bruce Bastin has pointed out that there are even close similarities between these first pieces and later recordings of Fuller's. "Daddy Don't Care" seems to have been the direct source of Fuller's later "You've Got Something There," and there are similarities in the two guitar styles at many points. Moss never developed texts that were distinctly his own, but he had a strong sense of image, and often the force of the language overcame the awkwardness of occasional verses. In a blues beginning

> Walkin' down the hard road done wore the soles off my shoes,
> Walkin' down the hard road done wore the soles off my shoes,
> My soles are ragged, I got those hard road blues . . .

the vocal rhythms are uneven, and the verses he ties to it are overfamiliar; but there is a vividness to the opening image, and, since he manages to refer again to the hard road, the blues does have an emotional effect. The image lingers through the rest of the performance, even with the limp repeated rhyme of the final verse.

> Have you ever laid down at night, thinkin' about your brown?
> Have you ever laid down at night, thinkin' about your brown?
> And get the hard road blues and ramble from town to town.
>
> Reason why I start, why I low down,
> My gal done quit me, I got to leave this town.
> I put some wheels on my boogyin' shoes,
> Goin' to roll back to my baby to get rid of these hard road blues.
>
> I lay down last night, a thousand things on my mind,
> I lay down last night, a thousand things on my mind.
> Goin' to walk down these hard roads, just to cure my low down mind.

But even with the ordinariness of his texts, Moss was an effective artist. His voice was warm and responsive, without the swaggering roughness of Fuller's on the loose swinging pieces that Fuller did later, but with some of the close, personal appeal of Brownie McGhee, who was later a close friend of Moss's. All of the men from the area were influenced by the Blind Blake techniques, but Moss was one of the first to be able to play the complex instrumental flourishes Blake used. Moss had the same double thumb roll, and he used the clustered rhythms that Blake used.

The blues that Moss did were released by A.R.C. on their cheapest labels—the Banner, Melotone, Oriole, Perfect, and Romeo labels—as well as on the better known Vocalion label. The cheaper labels all sold for twenty-five cents apiece, and each line was labeled for a different retail chain. Romeo material, for example, could only be bought at S.H. Kress stores, and each of the others had their own store identity. This kind of distribution was one of the factors that kept Moss's name from collectors. The pressings were done on the poorest quality shellac, and there seems to have been only enough pressing to fill immediate orders. It was the height of the Depression, and sales of everything were small. The Vocalion releases were usually under the name of Jim Miller, but he and Weaver and McMullen also did some trio pieces that were released under the name Georgia Browns.

Despite all the difficulties of beginning a recording career in 1933, Buddy's releases seem to have sold. He was back in New York to record again nine months later—and this time there were five sessions between September 14 and 21. Weaver was with him again, but this time the third guitarist was Willie McTell, and as with the first session it's sometimes difficult to tell who's playing the second guitar. In one group of matrixes McTell is the singer for numbers 14045 to 14051, Moss sings on matrixes 14052 to 14054, Weaver then sings for the next four, and Moss sings "B & O Blues No. 2" and "Some Lonesome Day" on matrixes 14064 and 14065. The sessions were so informal that it's difficult to sort out which of them was playing. The next matrix is McTell singing "B & O Blues No. 2." The long day's work ended with Moss singing five more of his own pieces. What A.R.C. was recording was clearly intended to be a reasonably consistent group of pieces that they could merchandize steadily in the dime store outlets. In four days of recording the three of them did forty-four sides—which not only means a lot of hard work, but also drains away any material they might have to use. It wasn't surprising that before the end of it they were singing each other's songs and that it's sometimes a little difficult to tell who is playing guitar.

A.R.C. continued recording Buddy; he had that ability, necessary in the thirties, of being able to come up with an unending stream of songs which, though they weren't markedly original as far as their texts went, were consistently musical, and he played with his usual technical brilliance. In 1934 and 1935 he recorded thirty-five blues, enough to keep the stores in new releases on a regular schedule. But after the last session on August 28, 1935, his career virtually ended. At this time he was living in Greensboro, Georgia, and he went to jail there, dropping out of the musical scene for six years

Bruce Bastin also interviewed the white businessman J.B. Long, who was managing Blind Boy Fuller and other artists during this period, and Bastin described what happened to Moss in the late thirties in his book *Crying for the Carolinas*.

> *. . . His successful recording career was terminated, although he was finally permitted to work as janitor at the County Courthouse in Greensboro, a post given to trustees there. Art Satherley of ARC wrote to Moss requesting that he write to J.B. Long, to see if he could get him out on parole. Long drove down to see the parole board and put a strong case for Moss's release on parole. Long was willing to offer Moss a job on a 70-acre farm that he had near Burlington and give him $30 a week plus rent and board—no mean sum in those days. At this time, Long was mayor of Elon, where he still lives, and the local chief of police lived only three doors away! On top of this, he could promise that Moss would get a further recording session with ARC; and he would be living out of Georgia anyway. Although that particular parole board was soon discharged for selling pardons, Long put his case to the new board and parole was granted. Moss travelled to stay with Long in Elon, working two or three days a week at Long's home and in the store at weekends. It was here that he got to know Brownie McGhee—with whom he is still in touch—as well as the Trice brothers. He did in fact record again for OKeh in 1941, using Sonny Terry and Red to accompany him, while on some tracks Brownie McGhee played piano, for example Joy Rag. However, the war and the resultant economic and union restrictions on the recording industry meant that Moss dropped out of sight until his re-discovery in Atlanta in the mid-'60s.*

The years that he spent working for Long also meant the end of his reputation as a bluesman. Fuller began recording for A.R.C. a month before Moss's last sessions, and he became immediately popular. His records sold well, and they sold in larger and larger numbers as the economy began to drag itself out of the worst of the Depression. The pressing quality improved, the distribution widened, and Fuller's records were sold by the thousands. This doesn't mean that Fuller didn't deserve his success. He had an ability to project himself and his whims and his excitements and his unhappiness that Moss had never had, even at his best. But Fuller's style was certainly the same style that Moss had begun recording years earlier. The reason collectors called Moss a Fuller imitator was that they found Fuller's records first. There were more of them, and they came much later than Moss's. Fuller records were among the first blues records you found when you junked for old blues records in the South. Moss's turned up later—they weren't so well recorded, and they were usually worn. It was easy to categorize him as a Fuller imitator.

It's hard to see, after so many years, why Moss wasn't recorded again while he was working on Long's farm, especially since it was A.R.C.'s recording director who had asked him to write to Long. It might have been that the terms of Moss's parole didn't leave him free to travel as far as New York—but probably it was the success of Fuller that kept him doing his odd jobs. Fuller had become so well established for A.R.C.—selling mostly on the higher-priced Vocalion label— that Satherley didn't need Moss, especially with a style that was so similar. Perhaps Decca could have used Moss for their blues series, but as long as Long was managing Fuller there doesn't seem to have been a chance for Moss. He didn't record again, in fact, until after Fuller's death, and after his enforced silence he didn't sound as individual as he had six years earlier.

Moss, today, is still resentful over what happened to him, a chunky, dark-skinned man, with an intense expression, still a brilliant guitarist and musician, and almost restlessly looking for a chance to get back some of the success he had in his early years. At least he's no longer considered simply one of the many followers of Blind Boy Fuller—but there's still been no major reevaluation of his importance in the development of the Carolina blues style.

# 18.
# Blind Boy Fuller and
# Blind Gary Davis

When you come into Durham, North Carolina, on back roads—in from the rolling, flat countryside around the small city—you get the feeling that most of it must be warehouses. The long, windowless shapes of the tobacco warehouses line the back streets. Durham has other sections—it's as modern a city now as you can find in North Carolina—but there is always that lingering impression of those rows of warehouses. Tobacco has always dominated North Carolina's economy, from its first years as an English colony, and it still is a tobacco town, with the countryside around divided into the careful fields that are characteristic of tobacco culture. With the tobacco there were jobs and money, and that meant that Durham swelled in the first decades of the 1900s—growing at the expense of the surrounding farm country. It meant a growing black population with some income, but still close to the country roots of their own culture. It also meant—since one comes on the heels of the other—bluesmen, drawn to the city's streets and taverns, struggling to make a living from the country people still hungry for the blues.

The streets of Durham—and the other cities of the North Carolina tobacco country, like Winston-Salem or Rocky Mount—are silent now. Only passing traffic, people lounging in open doors on hot summer afternoons, children playing along the street—the bluesmen who used to sing along Durham's streets have been gone now for long years. But, as the Durham musician and writer Bill Phillips described in a spring 1974 article in the Atlanta publication *Southern Exposure:*

> *In 1935, if one were to travel one block south from Main Street in Durham, across the railroad tracks, one would see the proud store fronts and bustling enterprises of Durham's black business section. The black middle class was pushing for whatever heights were attainable in a segregated society. The Biltmore Hotel played host to the*

155

*likes of Cab Calloway, Count Basie, and Bessie Smith. A few doors down, the Bull City Barber Shop catered to the vanities of fashionable folk, and the* Carolina Times *in the next block chronicled the passing events.*

*This is where the action was—and where Blind Boy Fuller and friends could be found. Possibly Gary Davis just walked around the corner eluding his social worker (always curious if Davis made money on the streets) and taking some time off between his frequent visits at church meetings. Street singing during this time was an art practised throughout the South by urban blues singers. Although nobody got rich at it, a surprising amount of money could be made by a talented musician. Since the city viewed it as begging, a letter sanctioning the activity was periodically sent from a welfare official to the police chief. For example:*

*April 8, 1933*

*Mr. G.W. Proctor*              *In re: Fulton Allen (Col.)*
*Chief of Police*                  *606 Cameron Avenue*
*Durham, N.C.*                                  *City*

*Dear Mr. Proctor:*
    *If it meets with your approval we are glad to recommend that the above named man be allowed to make music on the streets of Durham at a place designated by you.*
    *Assuring you that we are always glad to cooperate with you, I am*

*Your very truly*

*W.E. Stanley*
*Supt. Public Welfare*

The Fulton Allen referred to in the letter was, of course, better known as Blind Boy Fuller, and he eked out a living in Durham by singing on the streets, with a relief check of $23 a month, and with the income he earned, from 1935 to 1940, as a prolific and successful recording artist. He felt completely at ease playing in the streets. Another Durham musician, Willie Trice, talking to Bruce Bastin, remembered Fuller playing on the New York streets in 1937:

*On the day following their arrival in New York to record for Decca, Willie Trice remembers being woken about 11 a.m. by Fuller, already neatly and smartly dressed as always. He never wore dark glasses or shades and his cap was always on his head; he never went bare-headed*

156

*nor wore a hat. Fuller was impatient to get out on the New York streets—by no means unfamiliar to him by this time—and he dragged Willie out of bed to take him down, where he played for about an hour before coming back into the hotel.*

It's difficult to tell with any exactness when they all got to Durham. The letter asking the police to let Fuller sing on the streets of Durham is useful, because it makes it clear that he was there at least before April 1933. In the late thirties there seem to have been days when Fuller, Gary Davis, and Sonny Terry—the great Carolinas harmonica player who was also blind—played together along Pettigrew Street, or close to the tobacco warehouse gates when the workers were getting off. These moments must have been some of the most electrifying that could be found in the blues in the thirties. Fuller with his solid, steady rhythm and brilliant picking, Gary Davis with his startling runs and complex rhythmic variety, and Sonny with his "whooping" harmonica style. Fuller usually worked on the street with his washboard player, Oh Red (George Washington), so he would have been there as well, adding his percussive, rushing beat to all of it. If they didn't make a good living at it, it was only because times were hard, and the men coming out of the factory gates in their sweat-dark shirts and sagging overalls didn't have much money either.

But this was the late thirties, and it had been a period of years before they got to know each other and started playing together in Durham. Davis seems to have moved into the city about 1935—he's listed in the city directory for the first time that year—though he might have been there even earlier. Sonny Terry might have come in about the same time, though he probably met Fuller the year before and stayed at Fuller's house when he first came to Durham, so it could have been in 1934. Davis was considerably older than the other two—39—and Fuller was in his mid-twenties, a year or two older than Sonny.

Of the Durham musicians—and of all the guitar players and singers in the Carolinas—the dominant musician among them probably was Gary Davis. It wasn't only that he was older and that he'd had a longer involvement with the kind of East Coast finger style that Blind Blake represented. Gary Davis is one of the great blues performers—even if he stopped playing the blues at an early stage. There are only two blues recorded by him in the thirties—as part of a session he did with Fuller when he also recorded a group of gospel songs—but they are uniquely brilliant. They represent a fusion of a localized style—the Southeast guitar ragtime technique—with the individual genius of a great performer. It isn't a style that would be popular with a general blues audience. It's too startling, too sudden in its changes and inflections, too free in its technical flashes—as he lets himself respond freely to the implications of his material. There's no sign that his two sides ever made any impression on the thirties record buyer, any more than the recordings of Skip James, the Mississippi singer who seems most like him in a kind of personal genius, made an impression—but Gary was a guitar player's guitar player, and his influence can be heard on the whole body of Carolinas music recorded in the thirties. His influence in later years—on New York's young folk guitarists—was so pervasive that his style finally became one of the world's most widespread guitar sounds. It wasn't his own recordings that were so popular  but the recordings of people influenced by him, from Blind Boy Fuller to a whole generation of New York City folk singers; these continue to reach an audience that is worldwide.

This is clear not only from the testimony of older musicians who remember Davis's startling brilliance  but from the records themselves. Much of what he did is also there on the recordings that were made after he came onto the scene. Only Buddy Moss is also mentioned as one of the root sources of the style that finally developed, and he is never described as the guitarist Davis was. Instead he's talked about as an early influence, someone who got into it first, and who was a fine performer—while Davis was something unique. As Willie Trice, a younger Durham musician who knew and played with them all, told Bill Phillips: "While you were playing one chord, Gary  would play five."

Davis, a short, stocky, rumpled man when he was later part of the New York folk scene, has talked often about his early life, but some details are still vague, and he has always refused to discuss the circumstances of his blindness. It certainly isn't because he doesn't remember what happened to him. I drove him around New York in one period, when we were working on a recording together, and he would talk about his childhood  and things from the years when he was beginning as a musician. It was spring, and I often drove him up the East River Drive in New York  to his shabby apartment in the Bronx. He liked the window open in the car; we could feel the warmth in the air, and it brought back memories of his life on the small farm where he'd grown up in Laurens County, South Carolina. He was born there in 1896, April 30, so he was remembering back almost sixty years as he talked. He could remember how his grandmother made new bread from the ends of the old dried corn cakes, and he could remember that the hilly farm country was so lonely " . . . you couldn't hear nothing but owls after sundown."

Like most of the musicians who became bluesmen, he started playing when he was still a child.

> The first time I ever heard a guitar played I thought it was a brass band coming through. I was a small kid and I asked my mother what was it and she said that was a guitar. I said, "Ain't you going to get me one of those when I get large enough?" She said, "Yeah, I'll get you one." First thing I learned to play was an old banjo, you understand, I say old banjo because I learned how to play that. I was just going up and down, plunk a lunk, plunk a lunk, plunk a lunk. I thought I was doing something, playing that banjo.

The blues also came early for him. He remembers that it was in 1911.

> The first song that was a blues I heard was a man in a carnival singing "I'm on the road somewhere, if the train don't break down I'm on the road somewhere." . . . Then "Memphis Blues" and "Florida Blues" and some girl blues, kind of imitate to her feeling. This come to be very famous . . .

Much of Davis's early life is vague, but about this time he seems to have moved into Greenville, a busy market town in the northwest corner of South Carolina. It isn't far from Spartanburg, and between the two cities there was a large group of guitarists and singers. Josh White was to become the best known of the Greenville musicians, but he began traveling as a lead boy with blind singers when he was very young—he was born in Greenville on February 11, 1914—and he wasn't part of the musical scene, even though he came back from time to time to see his mother. Gary was married while he was living in Greenville, and he was playing in a large string band. He seems to have been in Greenville for many years—until the late 1920s—and he only left when his wife moved in with another musician, also blind, named Joe Walker. By this time Gary had been blind for many years and was pretty well able to get around by himself. He had been playing with musicians of considerable ability. Willie Walker was one of the members of the string band, and Joe Walker, the man Gary's wife left him for, was remembered as a strong guitarist.

Sometime after he left Greenville he went through his religious conversion, and in 1933 he was ordained as a minister in Washington, North Carolina, a small town about ninety miles outside of Durham. He seems to have come into Durham not long after, and he immediately became close to Fuller, who had come into the city a year or two earlier. In his article on Durham's musicians, Bill Phillips described a little of their life during this period.

> Through the Depression, both men depended on the Durham County Welfare Dpartment for periodic aid. And our few glimpses of their lives during this period come from the reports of their caseworkers. In order to be eligible for their $23 a month assistance, Fuller and Davis had to conceal the irregular income from their music, and the welfare records reveal a constant cat-and-mouse game with officials trying to determine their clients' eligibility. "Yes ma'am," Davis told an official who managed to find him in his rented room. "I know you been here several times, but you know I am inclined to preach the gospel, and I got to be gone a lot since God called me." The worker asked if he made any money on these trips. Davis wryly answered, "The only success I have is saving souls, which is pay enough." Before the caseworker could continue, Mary Hinton, Davis' kindly landlord, interrupted, complaining that the heat was about to kill her. That started Davis on a sermon about being prepared to die. Taking his text from "Be ye also ready," Davis launched into a detailed sermon on the necessity of preparation for the inevitable "flight to glory." He concluded by giving the worker a pamphlet he had written on the constancy of death, a theme which runs through many of Davis' songs. . . .
>
> On another occasion, Mary Hinton elaborated on Davis' religious convictions. "His mind runs backwards, you know, and I believe it's because he has just thought about the Bible and religion too much. A person can think too much, and I believe Gary has. He sometimes

159

*wakes me up at two or three o'clock in the morning going to bed, fall-*
*ing over a chair. He sits up and reads his Bible that late.*


At some point when he was younger Gary had attended the South Carolina Blind School and learned to read New York point, a kind of Braille, and his requests to the welfare workers over the years often mentioned a new Bible. It was also during these years that he was influencing the Durham musicians, his guitar playing so impressing them that years later the Trice brothers still shake their heads over his ability. Willie's final judgment was that Davis was " . . . the playingest man I ever saw." Certainly he left an indelible impression on the music of Blind Boy Fuller, and the style that grew in Durham's quiet streets was to make a strong mark on the blues of the thirties.


Although Fuller has been dead since 1940, he has never been an elusive figure in blues history. When I was gathering material for *The Country Blues* in the late 1950s, Sonny Terry and Brownie McGhee were often in the old offices of Folkways Records on West 46 Street in New York, and we'd talk about Fuller when we were in the office at the same time. His widow, Cora, is still living in Durham, and J.B. Long still has a store in Burlington, outside of Durham, where Bruce Bastin talked with him. Fuller was born in Wadesboro, North Carolina, a small town close to the border of South Carolina, about 1908 or 1909. His father was Calvin Allen, his mother's name Mary Jane. Fulton, as he was named at birth, was one of ten children. When he met the woman he was to marry, Cora Mae Martin, in 1927, the family had moved to Rockingham. She knew little about his earlier life, except that they hadn't been in Rockingham long before she met him. He was already partially blind, though she didn't know what had caused his sight problem. His eyesight was growing worse, and he became completely blind a year and a half after they were married. He had been playing a little music when they met, but when his sight failed he was just twenty—or maybe still in his teens—and there was no way for him to do any kind of work. He seems to have gotten help from local welfare agencies from the beginning, but at the same time he turned more and more to music as a way of making a living.

It's probable—as Bastin suggests—that Fuller came to music late enough so that he was primarily influenced by the phonograph record and by musicians that he met when he was playing. Also, by the late 1920s when he seems to have started playing fairly regularly, there was a great deal of recorded blues, and the forms and the styles were becoming rather clearly defined. If someone wanted to become a professional musician there were a number of sources of material for him and it wasn't necessary to synthesize a local style. Fuller listened to a lot of records, by Blind Blake certainly, among others, and he learned from the musicians around him. Some people remember him as easy to get along with, a small, neatly dressed man who enjoyed playing and worked at his music. Willie Trice, another Durham bluesman who knew Fuller well and went with him on the 1937 trip to New York, told Bill Phillips that although Fuller was easy to get along with, he also carried a pistol with him and had a "fiery" temper. "If

160

Fuller got mad at you, you better stand still and not say a word." He threatened to shoot J.B. Long during their disputes later in his career, and sometime in the thirties he did shoot his wife in the leg. Long was able to keep him out of jail, since Cora, as the only witness, wouldn't testify against him.

Fuller is usually remembered as wearing good clothes, always with a cap or hat on, difficult to get along with at times, but usually friendly. The group of musicians around him in Durham was close and mutually respectful in the way that the group around Bob Hicks was in Atlanta. He left Rockingham with Cora not long after they were married, and they first lived in Winston-Salem, another tobacco center west of Durham, in the low foothills of the Appalachians. They lived there on the streets close to the tobacco warehouses, also close to his brother Milton who was living in the city. They tried Danville, Virginia, for two months, another small city just over the North Carolina state line, then moved to Durham. He seems to have been in touch with the welfare authorities, since there was the letter from their office to the Durham police in 1933.

Fuller certainly wasn't the first of the Carolina musicians to record. Buddy Moss—from Georgia, but playing in a similar Blind Blake-derived style—had been recording since 1932, and Josh White—another Carolina bluesman who was to have a remarkable career as a folk and cabaret artist in New York later—had also started recording for the American Recording Corporation in 1932. It wasn't until three years later that Fuller got into a recording studio. J.B. Long finally heard him and took him to A.R.C. As Bastin described it:

> *In 1935, Long was promoted to manager of the United Dollar Stores at 2501 W. Club Boulevard in Durham, where Fuller had been living on Beaumont or Murphy Street, just off the negro [sic] "black bottom" on East Pettigrew. Parallel to Pettigrew are the railroad tracks and across these are the tobacco factories and warehouses upon which Durham's wealth depends. It was inevitable that Long and Fuller should meet. Long had been informed of a blind singer/guitarist who played behind the warehouses for dimes and nickels. By this time, Long had been selling blues records for some years, especially remembering Josh White's Blood Red River/Pickin' Low Cotton and Buddy Moss numbers. He appreciated the demand for blues and knew them very well, as buyers would quote a line, or only a few words, and expect Long to know on which record they appeared. Thus, when Fuller was led to Long's store, Long was not surprised and one of the longest relationships between manager and artist in the blues of the '30s began.*

Bastin didn't make clear that this was not only an extended relationship, it was almost a unique one. Usually the artists worked directly with the company, without any kind of business manager or agent to handle the business affairs for them. Long was not only a shrewd judge of talent; he had some idea of the kinds of money that could be made, and although he now says that it was more or less a hobby for him, the musicians who worked for him, such as Sonny Terry, felt that he treated them badly as far as the money was concerned. Sonny, talking about it in the Folkways office, was able to shrug it off.

*Long got us recording, you know, and at the beginning he got all the money. We didn't care, 'cause it got us our start.*

Fuller, however, seems to have resented the arrangement, threatened to shoot Long, and in 1937 made a strong effort to break loose and go his own way, but Long, who represented the very popular gospel quartet, Mitchell's Christian Singers, as well as Fuller, was too important for the companies to ignore, and the one session Fuller managed to do without Long was partly held off the market until after Fuller's death. Long was from a small North Carolina town, Hickory, and he'd been selling records in small general merchandise stores for several years when he began finding talent for the companies himself. He worked with both white and black artists, but he was considerably more successful with black music. The first sessions were done with the Mitchell Christian Singers in August 1934, and Fuller began recording in July 1935.

Long didn't go to New York with Fuller himself, but he sent him up as part of a Durham group. Another Durham singer, George Washington, who often led Fuller on the streets, seems to have taken care of getting Fuller there, and Gary Davis went along as well. Washington, who was often known as Bull City Red—the nickname coming from Durham's nickname of Bull City—usually played washboard with Fuller, but he also was an excellent guitarist in the Durham style, and he recorded at the same time. They were in the studio for four days, July 23, 24, 25 and 26, and the sessions were all productive. Fuller himself did twelve blues, Washington did eight, and Gary did his two blues as well as gospel material. For two of the numbers, "Rag, Mama, Rag" and "Baby You Gotta Change Your Mind," they played together as their old street trio, with Fuller and Davis on guitars and Washington playing washboard. The recording of "Rag, Mama, Rag," released on both A.R.C. and Vocalion labels with "I'm a Rattlesnakin' Daddy" on the other side, was rather successful, and Fuller's career was on its way.

Davis was the second guitarist on half of the songs Fuller did, and their accompaniment duets are often distinctively exciting. Davis's freer and more spontaneous playing seemed to give Fuller a sense of loose exuberance, and something like "Rag, Mama, Rag" moved with a carefree strut, like a boy laughing as he runs a stick along a picket fence. This kind of small blues group was to be very successful for Fuller over the five years he was to record. For the next session, however, in New York nine months later, April 28 and 29, 1936, he worked by himself. There were ten blues, two recorded the first day and eight the second. Probably at the request of Art Satherley, the A.R.C. recording director, when he came back to New York for his third group of sessions, in February 1937, he had Washington with him again, and another local guitarist, this time Floyd Council, usually known as Dipper Boy Council. They did fourteen blues, but Council played on only four of Fuller's titles. During the same session Council also did six blues of his own, finally released under the name "Blind Boy Fuller's Buddy" or "The Devil's Daddy-in-Law," as an answer to Peetie Wheatstraw, the St. Louis bluesman who had been recording since 1930 as "The Devil's Son-in-Law." The names were used as smaller titles under his own name on the record labels.

By this time, after less than two years of recording, Fuller had created an extensive body of blues, and he'd finally developed the style and the persona that carried him through the rest of his career. He found an image of himself that he could project on records, and it was in many ways a masculine counterpart of the themes that Memphis Minnie was developing in her recordings. There was a continuation of the old abject unhappiness at women's unfaithfulness or their demands, but, unlike singers of the twenties such as Blind Blake or Peg Leg Howell, Fuller often included verses of this type in blues that had much more assertive emotional attitudes. He could sing a verse like

> A working man ain't nothin' but a woman's slave,
> A working man nothin' but a woman's slave.
> When she start to lovin', Great God! it just won't 'have

which seems to be the more familiar twenties abject plea, but then in the same blues he went on:

> Have my dinner ready, don't let my coffee be cold,
> I said have my dinner ready, woman, don't let my coffee be cold.
> And don't forget, baby, save my sweet jelly roll

with a near swagger in his voice, telling his woman what he expected from her.

Also, like Memphis Minnie, Fuller used a self-projection that didn't really reflect the realities of his domestic situation. Minnie, who was married and living with a husband during most of her career, sang blues after blues about men leaving her and her response to the situation. Fuller, who is also remembered as living a generally quiet home life, sang blues after blues where at some point he emphasized his sexual proficiency.

> Said I got a new way of lovin' think it must be bad,
> I got a new way of lovin' think it must be bad.
> Said these here North Carolina women won't let Blind Boy Fuller rest.

In another blues he could say:

> I never loved, but a thousand women in my life,
> Oh no, a thousand women in my life.

In another:

> Hey mama, hey girl, don't you hear Blind Boy Fuller calling you.
> She's so sweet, so sweet,
> My little woman, so sweet.

This was all bound into a blues context of more or less familiar verses and attitudes, and the dominant mood was less assertive, more resigned, and there were many verses like:

But I'm goin' find my little woman, don't think she can't be found.
I say, hey hey, don't think she can't be found.
I'm goin' walk this hard hard road 'till my moustache drag the ground.

But there was the other side, the sexual boaster, the strong, assertive male figure that became the persona of his blues, although the texture, the structure of his material stayed close to the conventional patterns of the late thirties blues song.

At the same time that he was developing and defining his style Fuller was also becoming very successful, so successful that he tried to break off his arrangement with Long. Long's name was on most of the compositions Fuller had done as "composer," and this, as well as his practice of keeping most of the recording fees his artists got, meant that he was making the money. Long told Bastin that he did write the pieces and used verses he'd heard on other blues or made up, so perhaps he did compose some of the songs Fuller performed but Long was certainly working in a black idiom, and there was nothing in his texts that differed significantly from what other musicians in the Durham area were doing; so it would seem Fuller should have gotten the copyrights for the songs. Certainly when Fuller did break away and record on his own, the song material was almost identical with the kind of thing he'd been recording before; the only difference was that this time it was his name on the label as composer.

It was Mayo Williams, working as recording director for Decca's 7000 race series, who got Fuller briefly away from Long's heavy paternalism. Willie Trice, another Durham musician who was close to Fuller, told Bastin that it was Fuller who contacted Mayo Williams and that Williams came down to Durham to talk with him. When Williams met him Fuller was with the Trice brothers, Willie and his brother Richard, and Fuller insisted that they go along as well. It was on this trip to New York in 1937 that Willie had to take Fuller down to the street so he could do a little playing before they went to the studio. Fuller did twelve blues, ten on July 12 and two more on July 14. The Trices got their chance on July 13, doing six sides, two as a duet, and one solo record each. Willie remembers it as a strained and difficult time. Fuller was to do twelve sides, but an electrical storm came up the first day before he could finish, and he had to postpone the last two songs. The Trices were nervous and unsure of themselves, and the studio was hot and confining. Neither they nor Mayo Williams was happy with the result. He didn't bring them into the studio again, and of the six sides they did, two of them—the duet—were never released, and Richard's record wasn't released until two years later.

Long was taken by surprise by the first release from the Decca sessions—"If You See My Pigmeat" and "Why Don't My Baby Write to Me?" on Decca 7877—and according to Bastin was able to stop the release of the rest of the session. However, subsequent releases follow in close numerical sequence—"You Never Can Tell" and "Bulldog Blues" were the next number, Decca 7878—and it seems that Decca simply spaced out what they had, since Williams realized he wasn't going to get Fuller into the studio again. Long, in fact, had Fuller in New York again less than two months later, on September 7, 8, and 9, and some of the material was done again. "Bulldog Blues" became "Bull Dog Blues" and "Put You Back in Jail" became "Throw Your Yas Yas Back in Jail."

Perhaps because he'd hurried Fuller back into the studio to protect his A.R.C. contract Long sent him by himself, but only three months later he sent him back to New York again, this time with still another Durham musician—one of the greatest Carolinas bluesmen, and one of the greatest blues harmonica players, Sonny Terry. It was such a successful partnership that they were to stay together until Fuller's death and some of the sides they made together—often with Bull City Red or Oh Red, as he was later called—were among the most exciting blues done in the late thirties. It is difficult to believe that Long could have found another fine musician in Durham, but Terry was drawn to the city because of Fuller, and the Durham area was becoming better and better known as a blues center.

To see Sonny Terry play now—to listen to his sudden rhythmic sweeps and intensely lyric melodic lines—makes it almost impossible to believe that he's been recording for nearly forty years. His playing still has all the fire and the intensity of someone making his first record, and he seems to hunch over the harmonica as though he still expects to find something new in it every time he plays. Like the other musicians he came from outside of Durham, and in 1959, when we talked about his career for *The Country Blues*, he said that it was Fuller who brought him in. In the mid-thirties, perhaps 1937, when Fuller was visiting his sister in Watha, North Carolina:

> . . . *A harmonica player heard Fuller was in town, and went up to the house and asked if he could play some blues with him. They played together for three or four hours, and Fuller told him to look for him in Durham and they'd try to get a job together. The harmonica player was the young Sonny Terry.*

> *Sonny, like Fuller, was from North Carolina. He was born outside of Durham, October 24, 1911. He was born Sanford Terrell, the son of a farmer named Reuben Terrell. There were three brothers, Willie, Ronald, and Ashbury. He grew up on his father's twenty-acre farm learning to play the harmonica when he was still a little boy. His father was a good harmonica player and started Sonny on his favorite little songs, "Lost John" and "Fox Chase." A well-known harmonica player named DeFord Bailey came through town and Sonny learned a little from him, but mostly he picked it up from his father. When he was just learning, he'd sit for hours imitating the sounds of the trains that passed in the distance.*

*When Sonny met Fuller he was nearly blind himself. When he was eleven, he was beating a stick against a chair and a piece of it broke off and flew into his eye. The sight in that eye was impaired. Five years later a boy threw a small piece of iron at Sonny and put out his other eye. He realized that he'd have to start playing on the streets to make a living; so he started going into Durham and Raleigh, playing all afternoon; then walking home alone in the darkness. When he met Fuller he was twenty-three, playing in a distinctive wailing style that was a fine contrast to Fuller's dark voice.*

When Sonny moved to Durham he stayed with Fuller and his wife Cora and their adopted daughter at 805 Colfax. They soon were playing together on Durham's streets and J.B. Long got them into the recording studio.

With Sonny and Oh Red accompanying him, Fuller soon was to become more and more important as a recording artist. The country was beginning to shake off some of the effects of the Depression; sales generally were increasing, and Fuller was one of the artists who was part of the general swell. Also he had become even more productive with Terry. They did ten sides on their first sessions—December 15 and 16, 1937—then in 1938, in April and October, they did twenty-two songs together. In 1938 there were fourteen Blind Boy Fuller records released, more than any other blues artist. He was still getting very little of the money he was earning, and he made another futile effort to get free of Long, this time with the help of a caseworker from the State Blind Commission, William Lewis. Bill Phillips was able to reconstruct some of what happened from welfare reports and from Willie Trice's recollection.

> *. . . Fuller resented Long's middle-man profits and on at least one recording trip became so enraged he threatened to shoot him. "After a lot of talking," Willie Trice recalled, "he finally cooled down." In 1939, Fuller hoped to get out from under Long's management altogether and, since the State Blind Commission encouraged self-sufficency, caseworker William Lewis began seeking an independent contract with a record company for Fuller.*

> *Lewis learned that Fuller was under contract to Long to receive $200 each time he recorded twelve songs, although that amount varied depending on whose word is relied upon. Fuller and Lewis came to the agreement that Fuller would not renew his current contract with Long, which would expire on April 21, 1939,.and Lewis wrote both Long and the American Recording Corporation explaining this intent. Neither answered. Upon the expiration of the contract, Long wrote Lewis saying that while Fuller was no longer under contract to him, he was still bound to the American Recording Company. When Lewis wrote A.R.C. they simply referred him back to Long. In the wake of the confusion, Fuller agreed to go record for Long in Memphis with Sonny Terry in July, 1939. So ended Fuller's efforts at gaining an independent contract.*

The sessions in the summer of 1939 were particularly productive. On July 12 Fuller, Sonny Terry, and Oh Red did twelve blues. Some of them were covering successes by other artists, like Big Bill, and they did a "Jivin' Big Bill Blues," but others were continuing the persona of the hard swaggerer that Fuller had shaped in his earlier work. There were specific sexual cries like "I Crave My Pig Meat" and "I Want Some of Your Pie," and there was the strain of good-natured boasting that he'd begun in earlier blues like "I'm a Good Stem Winder" from the April 1938 session.

On the same day that they did their twelve blues, July 12, they stayed on and did three religious songs, the first that Fuller had recorded. They sang as a vocal trio and recorded "Have You Decided (Which Way to Go)?," "I See the Sign of Judgement," and "Everybody Wants to Know How I Die." The next day they did three more religious songs, "I Feel Like Shoutin'," "Jesus Touched Me," and "Talkin' with Jesus." There doesn't seem to have been any significance to this. Like most bluesmen Fuller also knew a lot of gospel songs, and religious material was selling well again. Art Satherley released the records under the name "Brother George and His Sanctified Singers," though they were clearly recognizable to anyone who was a regular buyer of Fuller's blues releases. It was still another instance of the old prejudice against bluesmen singing sacred songs. Josh White, also recording for Satherley, was "Pinewood Tom" on his blues releases and "Joshua White (The Singing Christian)" on his religious recordings.

Fuller's popularity continued to grow, and 1940 began as one of his biggest years. There were three sessions—again with Sonny Terry and Oh Red—in March, then another twelve-blues sessions on June 19. They were mixing sacred and blues material rather freely, and the songs ranged from the great hymn "Twelve Gates to the City" that Davis was to record several times later in New York, to a number of brilliant blues performances on songs like "I Don't Want No Skinny Woman" or "Thousand Woman Blues."

Sonny Terry had also started recording under his own name, and the three of them did a stunning "Harmonica Stomp" that's a classic example of country dance music on March 6; it was released on OKeh 05538. The day before there had been an unaccompanied harmonica solo and a startling harmonica and washboard duet—a loose, raggy stomp that had the headlong feel of a farm tractor wheeling down a dirt road. It was released on OKeh 05453 as "Harmonica and Washboard Breakdown."

Most of the material from the June session was released on the OKeh label, and it seems to have been aggressively distributed. Copies of the records were to be found in large quantities in junk shops and salvage stores everywhere in the South in the 1950s. These were some of Fuller's finest recordings—exciting and colorful and inventive, with an almost virtuoso brilliance in his rhythmic extensions and vocal lines. He seemed to have a new assurance and was using a characteristic chorus form for nearly all of his songs.

Said I walked last night, ba-by, feet got soak-ing wet.

Said I walked all night ma-ma

feet got soak-ing wet.____ Said I did-n't

find my wo-man. Ain't stopped walk-in' yet.____

Everything seemed set for them to go on to even more and wider-ranging success. What happened instead was that Fuller was suddenly taken sick.

Fuller had been suffering for some time with a kidney ailment, but it suddenly got worse, and even though he lived for eight more months he didn't record again. According to the death certificate, located by Bastin, Fuller was under a doctor's care from December 12, 1940, but the infection of both the kidneys and bladder had become too advanced. He died on the morning of February 12, 1941, and was buried three days later at Durham's Grove Hill Cemetery. As another young musician who had come into Durham sang:

> They called me to his bedside one morning, and the clock was striking four,
> They called me to his bedside one morning, and the clock was striking four.
> Gonna take my guitar and carry my baby home, I won't stay here no more.

The young singer who got Fuller's guitar was Brownie McGhee and for a time Long tried to have him take Fuller's place.

In the growing and popular blues scene of the late 1930s Fuller's death was not widely noticed. It was a time when a number of singers were very popular, and many younger men were starting to record. Fuller had been very successful, but it seemed that there were a number of artists ready to take his place. For some months it even looked as though Long would be able to replace him with McGhee. Brownie, who had come into Durham from Bristol, Tennessee, where he'd been working with a small instrumental group, had begun recording in the summer of 1940 with Jordan Webb and Robert Young. He did twelve blues for OKeh on August 6 and 7. There was a short session—only two blues—on May 22, 1941, then the next day he did ten more blues, including "Death of Blind Boy Fuller," on OKeh 06265. Many of these releases were labeled "Blind Boy Fuller No. 2," and for a group of religious songs the next day OKeh used the old "Brother George and His Sanctified Singers" name that they'd used for Blind Boy Fuller.

It was a strong effort on Long's part—he even sent Buddy Moss up to New York with McGhee in the fall of 1941, and Moss did his first recordings since 1935. At the same time, however, he sent Sonny Terry, and Brownie and Sonny began playing as a duet in New York, and they never returned to Durham. It had been a young man's scene—Fuller was only thirty-two when he died, and Brownie was twenty-five when he started recording. In December 1941, World War II broke out, and the lives of Durham's younger men became entangled with the war and its disruptions. Within a few months, first the shellac shortage, then the union recording ban, stifled the recording industry, and J.B. Long dropped out of the music business. With Fuller dead, and the most promising of the younger artists, Brownie McGhee, already on his way by himself, the blues scene in Durham suddenly died. The Trice brothers, who had gone with Fuller for his Decca date in 1937, still kept playing, and Richard even recorded again after the war, but they weren't strong enough as musicians or singers to keep the style going by themselves. The last of the important musicians left in the city was Gary Davis.

Davis dropped out of sight toward the end of the thirties; then the welfare agency got in contact with him in 1943. In 1944 he married and was living in Raleigh—then went to New York to visit his wife's children. He was spending more and more time in the North, but in 1948 the welfare agency received a call from the old Durham landlady of Gary's, Mary Hinton. Gary had turned up injured, with ugly leg infections, and in need of help. They arranged medical care for him, and when he was able to travel he went back to New York, to his singing and preaching on the streets, and to the fame and success that was ultimately waiting for him there. With his final departure, except for an occasional itinerant beggar or a little playing by one of the people still left, the streets of Durham fell silent.

# 19.
# To the End
# of the Thirties

The sudden expansion of the blues industry, and then the equally sudden dislo-cation of every aspect of American life during the war years, can be used as a dividing line between the blues of the earlier folk period and the blues styles that developed in the postwar period. But it can only be useful to consider this as a transition period in the blues if it's also kept in mind that it's a blurred and shaky point of division and that many things that may be thought of as charac-teristic of one period or another were either beginning, or fading, before the end of the Depression and the beginning of the war in Korea.

One of the dominant aspects of the country blues between the mid-twenties and 1940 was the richness and strength of the local rural styles. It's startling to consider the range in a musical form that could include both the gentle, wiry style of Luke Jordan in Virginia and the hard, harsh insistence of Charley Pat-ton in Mississippi. There were the broad regional styles of areas like Texas, the Mississippi Delta, and the Carolinas, and there were styles that were limited to a city and the area around it—such as Memphis and its jug bands and Atlanta with its group centering around its twelve-string guitar players.

The different regional styles of the blues were not only interesting from a musi-cal point of view; they were also interesting for what they suggested of blues origins and of the earlier song forms that became part of the blues. In the rhythms of the blues that Son House recorded in 1930 it was still possible to hear the rhythm of the axe strokes that had marked the work songs his blues had developed from. The dancelike finger-picking rhythms of Blind Blake's Southeast style reflect, just as clearly, a background of house servants and country entertainments. The early field recording units left behind a trove of cultural and musical materials that's so rich we've only begun to sift through its treasures.

But at the same time there were already performers who weren't particularly centered in any area's style. Blind Lemon Jefferson, one of the most successful country bluesmen of the mid-twenties, was clearly in a Texas tradition, and Blind Blake, almost as successful, was just as definitely from a Southeast tradition. But Lonnie Johnson, who was more successful than either of them, could have come from anywhere. He was living in St. Louis when he started recording in 1925, but his style was drawn from so many sources that it would be difficult to point to anything specifically Missourian about it. In the thirties there was an increasing number of artists—especially pianists—who had no clear stylistic home. Many of the most popular artists of the immediate prewar period had this more general identity as commercial blues singers, instead of Mississippi or Tennessee bluesmen. Artists like Peetie Wheatstraw, Roosevelt Sykes, Bumble Bee Slim, Big Bill, Sonny Boy Williamson, and Washboard Sam had absorbed so many influences that they were more like each other than like anything else. The blues, in their terms, was becoming another aspect of the professional music world, and it was that that drew them to the music.

So it isn't entirely useful to think of the prewar period as one dominated completely by regional artists and the instrumental techniques and vocal styles that they shared. There were many artists who were already part of a more general expression of the blues. Also, the war didn't end the regional styles. When small companies began recording in most of the cities of the South in the late forties and early fifties much of what they recorded clearly reflected the continuing local tradition. The music and artists that Trumpet recorded in Jackson, Mississippi, from Willie Love to the second Sonny Boy Williamson, were certainly different from the Texas blues that Bill Quinn recorded in Houston when he put Lightnin' Hopkins in the studio for his Gold Star label.

The war years, then, should probably be thought of as hastening and strengthening tendencies that were already present in the blues, but not as a decisive factor in themselves. The strongest effect the war had on the blues was to change the nature of the blues audience. The demand for labor, and the shifting of thousands of young men from the South, created a large urban black community. Again the shift of black families out of the South that had begun many years before took on the nature of an exodus, both for jobs and for social reasons. The bluesmen lost their country audience, and the blues that developed a few years after the war was a city style, more suited to a nightclub than to a cabin porch or a country juke joint.

At the same time there was a technical innovation—the electric guitar. Suddenly effects were possible that hadn't been before—like the slide technique of Elmore James. With an electric guitar he could sustain tones and emphasize the dramatic elements of what he was doing in a way he couldn't do with an acoustic instrument. The electric guitar also made it possible for a musician to play for a large audience without essentially changing the individualistic or personally expressive aspects of the blues style. It was loud enough to fill a noisy club and, since most of the early amplifiers could also be used with a small microphone to amplify singing or a harmonica, the bluesmen was not a small band.

Five or six years, too, is a long time in popular music, which the blues had certainly become. Between 1940 and 1946 or 1947 there would have been changes in the blues even without the war. The number of artists without clear regional identity had been growing, the people who wanted to hear the blues had been moving more and more to urban areas, and the blues had been moving from a music that was primarily a song form to a dance form for some time. It was the pressures of the war that hurried all these processes, but they were happening by themselves, and the blues was already beginning to reflect the changes.

The story of the blues, then, to the end of the thirties was primarily the story of the country bluesmen developing in their own areas and clarifying and defining their local styles. At the same time the growth of a commercial blues industry centered in Chicago was beginning, and through the thirties the artists active in Chicago, from Big Bill to Memphis Slim, were putting together the commercial elements that were to be utilized by men like Muddy Waters and Howling Wolf when the new generation of bluesmen entered the Chicago scene. The careers of all these artists seem to belong more to a detailed study of Chicago and of the blues that emerged from the postwar years than they do to a study of the local styles that the recording directors found in their wanderings in the twenties.

But all this wealth of music was the background of the postwar blues—then the early rock and roll styles—and finally the pop music of two generations of Americans. The bluesmen from this period probably didn't think of what they were doing in these terms, and even Chicago musicians who watched it happen in the fifties still aren't sure what it was that took place. For most bluesmen the music they play is something that was moving and shaping their society before they were born, and it has gone on taking its place in the larger American society while other styles of music have come and gone around it. It's no wonder that they say "The blues won't never die" or "The blues was here before I came and the blues will be here after I go."

Whatever the future of the blues will be it certainly is part of society's life today, and the roots of the blues that flourished in hundreds of small towns and back-country farms grew so deeply that it's hard to think they could easily be pulled up. The story of the bluesmen is a chronicle of the lives and music of men who were complex and fascinating human beings—and at the same time it's the story of a society and its life and its culture. It's not often in history that a small song has become so deeply entwined with the life of a people. It's this that gives the story of the blues its drama and its excitement.

# Notes to Part I

THE AFRICAN BACKGROUND

1. J. David Sapir, notes to The Music of
   the Diola-Fogny of the Casamance,
   Senegal, Folkways Record FE 4323
   (New York, 1965)

2. John Wesley Work, Folk Song Of The
   American Negro, (Nashville, Tenn.,
   1915)

3. Howard Odum and Guy Johnson, Negro Workaday Songs, (Chapel Hill,
   North Carolina, 1926)

4. Luis Felipe Ramon Y Rivera,
   "Rhythmic And Melodic Elements In
   Negro Music Of Venezuela," Journal
   of the International Folk Music Council, XIV (1962), 56-60.

5. Hugh Tracey, "Towards An Assessment Of African Scales," African
   Music Society Journal, II (1958), 15-
   20

6. A. M. Jones, "African Music in
   Northern Rhodesia and some other
   Places," The Occasional Papers of
   the Rhodes-Livingstone Museum, IV
   (1949), 11

7. Le Vaillant, 1781, quoted in Percival
   Kirby, The Musical Instruments Of
   The Native Races Of South Africa,
   (London, 1934)

8. John Wesley Work, American Negro
   Songs, (New York, 1940)

CHAPTER 2 - CHARLEY PATTON

1. Booker White, interviewed by John
   Fahey and Ed Denson, Bukka White,
   Mississippi Blues, Volume 1, Ta-
   koma Records B1001, (Berkeley,
   California, 1964)

2. Bernard Klatzko, notes to The Immortal Charlie Patton, Origin Jazz
   Library record OJL-7, (New York,
   1964)

3. J. D. Short, interviewed by Samuel
   Charters, Son House and J.D.Short,
   Folkways Record FA 2467, (New
   York, 1963)

4. Klatzko, op. cit.

5. Son House, interviewed by Julius
   Lester, Sing Out, XV, 3. (1965)
   38-45

6. Ibid.

7. Ibid.

CHAPTER 3 - SON HOUSE

1. Son House, op. cit.

2. Ibid.

3. Ibid.

4. Ibid.

CHAPTER 5 - ROBERT JOHNSON

1. Henry Townsend, interviewed by Samuel Charters, unpublished recording, 1962.

2. Son House, op. cit.

3. Ibid.

CHAPTER 7 - MISSISSIPPI/THE COUNTRY SINGERS

1. Son House, interviewed by Dick Waterman, quoted by Al Wilson, "Son House, A Biography and Analysis of his music," Boston Broadside (1965)

2. Son House, Lester, op. cit.

3. Klatzko, op. cit.

CHAPTER 8 - CENTRAL MISSISSIPPI AND JACKSON INTO THE' THIRTIES

1. Arthur Rosenbaum, notes to Shirley Griffith, Saturday Blues, Prestige Bluesville Record 1087, (Bergenfield, New Jersey, 1963)

CHAPTER 12 - BLIND LEMON JEFFERSON

1. Samuel Charters, The Country Blues, (New York, 1959), 57

2. Ibid., 60

3. Lightning Hopkins, interviewed by Samuel Charters, Lightnin' Hopkins, My Life In The Blues, Prestige Record 7370, (Bergenfield, N.J., 1965)

CHAPTER 14 - "TEXAS" ALEXANDER

1. Lightning Hopkins, op. cit.

# Index to Part I

# Index to Part II

# Other titles of interest

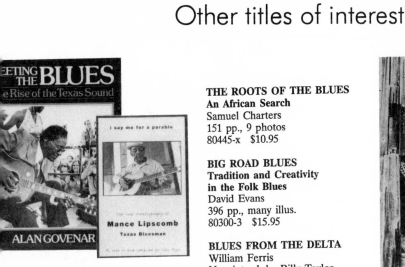

**THE ROOTS OF THE BLUES**
**An African Search**
Samuel Charters
151 pp., 9 photos
80445-x  $10.95

**BIG ROAD BLUES**
**Tradition and Creativity**
**in the Folk Blues**
David Evans
396 pp., many illus.
80300-3  $15.95

**BLUES FROM THE DELTA**
William Ferris
New introd. by Billy Taylor
226 pp., 30 photos
80327-5  $11.95

**BLUES OFF THE RECORD**
**Thirty Years of Blues Commentary**
Paul Oliver
132 pp., 17 photos
80321-6  $13.95

**BLUES WHO'S WHO**
Sheldon Harris
775 pp., 450 photos
80155-8  $35.00

**BOSSMEN**
**Bill Monroe & Muddy Waters**
James Rooney
163 pp., 42 photos
80427-1  $11.95

**CHICAGO BLUES**
**The City and the Music**
Mike Rowe
226 pp., 147 photos
80145-0  $11.95

**THE COUNTRY BLUES**
Samuel B. Charters
288 pp., 45 illus.
80014-4  $12.95

**THE FOLK MUSIC**
**SOURCEBOOK**
**Updated edition**
Larry Sandberg and Dick Weissman
288 pp., 97 photos
80360-7  $18.95

**MEETING THE BLUES**
Alan Govenar
48 pp., over 250 illus.
0641-X  $17.95

**LISTEN TO THE BLUES**
Bruce Cook
New introd. by the author
04 pp., 12 photos
0648-7  $13.95

**BIG BILL BLUES**
**William Broonzy's Story**
As told to Yannick Bruynoghe
76 pp., 4 drawings, 15 photos
0490-5  $10.95

**I'D RATHER BE THE DEVIL**
**Skip James and the Blues**
Stephen Calt
00 pp., 13 pp. of illus.
0579-0  $14.95

**I SAY ME FOR A PARABLE**
**The Oral Autobiography of Mance**
**Lipscomb, Texas Bluesman**
As told to and compiled by
Glen Alyn
Foreword by Taj Mahal
08 pp., 45 illus.
0610-X  $16.95

**LOVE IN VAIN**
**A Vision of Robert Johnson**
Alan Greenberg
New foreword by Martin Scorsese
272 pp., 9 photos
0557-X  $13.95

**I AM THE BLUES**
**The Willie Dixon Story**
Willie Dixon with Don Snowden
288 pp., 44 photos
80415-8  $12.95

**JAZZ: A History of the**
**New York Scene**
Samuel B. Charters and
Leonard Kunstadt
390 pp., 80 photos
80225-2  $13.95

**THE LEGACY OF THE BLUES**
**Art and Lives of Twelve**
**Great Bluesmen**
Samuel B. Charters
192 pp., 15 photos
80054-3  $9.95

**SCREENING THE BLUES**
Paul Oliver
302 pp., 8 photos
80344-5  $13.95

**STOMPING THE BLUES**
Albert Murray
272 pp., 127 illus.
80362-3  $13.95

**STORMY MONDAY**
**The T-Bone Walker Story**
Helen Oakley Dance
302 pp., 56 illus.
80413-1  $13.95

## Available at your bookstore

### OR ORDER DIRECTLY FROM

# DA CAPO PRESS, INC.

### 1-800-321-0050